Additions and Corrections to the W.P.A. Inventory of Seneca County, Ohio: TIFFIN

Jana Sloan Broglin

HERITAGE BOOKS
2025

HERITAGE BOOKS
AN IMPRINT OF HERITAGE BOOKS, INC.

Books, CDs, and more—Worldwide

For our listing of thousands of titles see our website
at
www.HeritageBooks.com

Published 2025 by
HERITAGE BOOKS, INC.
Publishing Division
5810 Ruatan Street
Berwyn Heights, MD 20740

(Originally Titled)
INVENTORY OF THE COUNTY ARCHIVES OF OHIO
Prepared by
The Ohio Historical Records Survey Project
Service Division
Work Projects Administration
No. 74. SENECA COUNTY (TIFFIN)
Columbus, Ohio
The Ohio Historical Records Survey Project
1942

International Standard Book Number
Paperbound: 978-0-7884-5076-1

TABLE OF CONTENTS

Foreword . . . . . . vii-viii
Preface
    Preface 2nd edition ix
    Preface 1st edition . . . . . . x-xi
List of Abbreviations, Symbols, and Explanatory Note . . . . . . xii-xv
Historical Sketch . . . . . . xvi-xxxii
Governmental Organization and Records System . . . . . . xxxiii-lxv
Housing, Care, and Accessibility of the Records . . . . . . lxvi-lxxiii
Courthouse Floor Plans . . . . . . lxxiv-lxxvii

Records of County Governmental Agencies

County Commissioners 1-31
    Minutes, Reports. Improvements: Roads; ditches; bridges; contracts and bids. Financial records. Miscellaneous. Relief administration. Aid for the blind.
Recorder 32-53
    Real property transfers: Deeds and registers; leases; mortgages; liens; maps, plats, and surveys; partitions. Personal property transfers. Corporations and Partnerships. Grants of authority. Financial records. Miscellaneous.
Clerk of Courts 54-72
    Dockets. General court records. Jury and witness records. Motor vehicles. Commissions and licenses. Elections. Partnerships. Reports. Financial records. Miscellaneous.
Court of Common Pleas 73-89
    Dockets, Court proceedings. Naturalization. Reports.
Supreme Court 90-93
Court of Appeals 94-103
    District court. Circuit court. Court of Appeals.
Probate Court 104-129
    Calendars and dockets. Court proceedings. Wills and determination of heirship. Estates and guardianships: Appointments, bonds, and letters; inventories, appraisements, and claims; sales; accounts and settlements; case records. Inheritance taxes. Records of incompetence. Naturalization.

Vital statistics: Births and deaths; marriages. Licenses and permits. Financial records. Miscellaneous.
Juvenile Court 130-140
Court proceedings. Dependents. Financial records. Aid to dependent children.
Jury Commissioners 141-142
Grand Jury 143-144
Petit Jury 144-145
Prosecuting Attorney 146-149
Coroner 150-152
Sheriff 153-165
Court orders and sales. Record of prisoners and futurities. Financial records. Miscellaneous.
Dog Warden 166
Auditor 167-200
Property transfers. Plats and maps. Tax records: Text levies and rates; tax appraisements and assessments; tax returns; tax lists, duplicates, and abstracts; additions, deductions, and refunds; delinquent taxes; inheritance taxes. Settlements, Financial records; Appropriations; bills and claims; general accounts; special accounts; pay-ins; vouchers and warrants. Licenses and permits. Reports and statements. Bonds. Miscellaneous. Weights and measures.
Treasurer 201-214
Tax records: Tax lists and duplicates; delinquent taxes; inheritance taxes; excise tax stamps; tax collections. Financial records. Bonds.
Budget Commissioners 215-216
Board of Revision 217-220
Board of Trustees of the Sinking Fund 221-222
Board of Elections 223-230
Minutes. Electors' records: Registers; poll books; absent voters. Candidates' records. Appointments. Financial records.
Board of Education 231-237
Minutes and reports. Teachers' records. Pupils' records. Financial records. Transfers.
Board of Health 238-242
Minutes and reports. Vital statistics. Financial records. Miscellaneous.

Tuberculosis Hospital 243-245
Superintendent of the County Home. 246-252
Minutes and reports. Case records. Financial records. Inventories.
Board of County Visitors 253-254
Soldiers' Relief Commission 255-257
Soldiers' Burial Committees. 258-259
Blind Relief Commission 260-261
Board of Aid for the Aged 262-267
County Engineer 268-280
Surveys, plats, and maps. Improvements: Roads; ditches, bridges, and culverts. Financial records. Miscellaneous.
Board of Park Commissioners 281-283
Board of Directors of the Conservancy District 284-285
Agricultural Society 286-289
Agricultural Extension Agents 290-294
Extension and Conservation records. 4-H Club records. Financial records. Correspondence.

Bibliography 295-300
Roster of County Officials 301-312
Addresses and Websites 313-315
Index to Inventory Entries. 316-331

The Historical Records Survey Program

Sargent B. Child, National Director
Willard N. Hogan, Regional Supervisor
Francis M. Foott, State Supervisor
Blair Hagerty, District Supervisor

Service Division

Florence Kerr, Assistant Commissioner
Mary Gillette Moon, Chief Regional Supervisor
Ruth Neighbors, State Director
Kelen W. Clifford, District Director

WORK PROJECTS ADMINISTRATION

F. H. Dryden, Acting Commissioner
George Field, Regional Director
Carl Watson, State Administrator
William B. Schmuhl, District Manager

Sponsors

The Ohio State University

The Board of County Commissioners of Seneca County
Bloom L. Myers
Harry L. Stultz
Clarence B. Baker

The *Inventory of the County Archives of Ohio* is one of a number of bibliographies of historical materials prepared throughout the United States by workers on the Historical Records Survey Program of the Work Projects Administration. The publication herewith presented, an inventory of the archives of Seneca County, is number 74 of the Ohio series.

The Historical Records Survey Program was undertaken in the winter of 1935-1936 for the purpose of providing useful employment to needy unemployed historians, lawyers, teachers, and research and clerical workers. In carrying out this objective, the project was organized to compile inventories of historical materials, particularly the unpublished government documents and records which are basic in the administration of local government, and which provide invaluable data for students of political, economic, and social history. Up to the present time more than 1,700 guides, inventories, and indexes have been issued by the Survey throughout the Nation. The archival guide herewith presented is intended to meet the requirements of the day-to-day administration by the officials of the county, and also the needs of lawyers, businessman, and other citizens who require facts from the public records for the proper conduct of their affairs. The volume is so designed that it can be used by the historian in his research in unprinted sources in the same way he uses the library card catalog for printed sources.

The inventories produced by the Historical Records Survey Program attempt to do more than give merely a list of records– they attempt further to sketch in the historical background of the county or other unit of government, and to describe precisely and in full detail the organization and functions of the government agencies whose records they list. The county, town, and other local inventories for the entire county will, when completed, constitute an encyclopedia of local government as well as a bibliography of local archives.

The successful conclusion of the work of the Historical Records Survey Program, even in a single county, would not be possible without the support of public officials, historical and legal specialists, and many other groups in the community. Their cooperation is greatly acknowledged.

The survey program was organized by Luther H. Evans, who served as director until March 1, 1940, when he was succeeded by Sargent B. Child, who had been Field Supervisor since the inauguration of the Survey. The Survey Program operates as a nation-wide series of locally sponsored projects in the service division of which Mrs. Florence Kerr, Assistant Commissioner, is in charge.

F. H. Dryden
Acting Commissioner

PREFACE
2nd Edition

In 1929 after the stock market crash along with the Great Depression which followed, President Herbert Hoover and his successor Franklin D. Roosevelt formulated relief projects, the most successful was the establishment of the Works Progress Administration (WPA).

Established as the Works Projects Administration in 1935, the WPA was the largest of the many programs developed during Roosevelt's "New Deal." In 1939, the agency's name was changed to Works Progress Administration, and continued as such until its demise in 1943.

The Federal Writers' Project, a division of the WPA (known as Federal Project Number One), created jobs for many unemployed librarians, clerks, researchers, editors, and historians. The workers went to courthouses, town halls, offices in large cities, vital statistics offices and inventoried records. Besides indexing works, many records were transcribed. One of these many projects was the *Inventory of the County Archives* which has benefitted genealogists and historians. The inventories listed the records, either by volumes or file boxes and years per record type, within the office. Although the WPA oversaw this project, the information for each volume of records may differ significantly by the information submitted.

The information herein is verbatim except for obvious spelling errors. Records listed may have met the requirement for retention and have been destroyed as per the records retention act, while other records are considered permanent records. (*See:* **https://codes.ohio.gov/ohio-revised-code** Ohio Revised Code, sections 149.31 and 149.34). Records once considered "open" to the public, such as lunacy, idiotic, and juvenile cases, may be "closed" due to a revision of state laws. However, the records may be opened to family members with adequate proof of lineage.

The addresses and website section of this edition list an up-to-date location guide to each office mentioned, if located.

This project was to encompass all of Ohio's 88 counties although approximately 30 of these inventories have been located while others may be missing or never done.

Jana Sloan Broglin
Fellow, Ohio Genealogical Society
Swanton, Ohio
2025

PREFACE
1st Edition

The Historical Records Survey of the Work Projects Administration began operation in Ohio in February 1936. The Project was organized and operated by the district supervisors of the Writers' Project until November 1936 when it became an independent part of the Federal Project No. 1. With the termination of the Federal Projects in September 1939, the Ohio unit became the Ohio Historical Records Survey Project, sponsored by the Ohio State Archaeological and Historical Society. On August 3, 1941, the Ohio Historical Records Survey Project became a unit of the Consolidated Records Assistance Project in Ohio, sponsored by the Ohio State University.

One of the purposes of the survey in Ohio has been the preparation of complete inventories of the records of the state and of each county, city, and municipal office. The *Inventory of the County Archives of Ohio* will, when completed, consist of a set of 88 volumes numbered according to the position of the county name in an alphabetical list of Ohio counties. Thus, the inventory herewith presented for Seneca County is number 74. Inventories of state archives and of municipal and other local records constitute separate publications.

The principle followed in the inventory of the county records has been to place a record in the office of origin rather than in the office of deposit. The records are arranged with those of the executive branch of government first, followed by law-enforcement, fiscal, welfare, and miscellaneous agencies. Minor agencies are placed in the general arrangement according to function rather than according to constitutional or statutory responsibility to a major subdivision. The legal development of each office or agency has been treated and a prefatory section precedes the inventory of the records of the office. Although a condensed form of entry is used, information is given as to the limiting dates of all extent records, the contents of individual series, and the location of records in courthouse, statehouse, or other depository.

The work of the Historical Records Survey in Seneca County was begun early in 1936. Since September 1939, the project has been under the administrative supervision of Mr. Blair Hagerty, and the final recheck of the records and compilation of the work was accomplished under the technical supervision of Mr. George Reichert. The Board of County Commissioners of Seneca County, serving as contributing co-sponsor, has provided the materials for the publication of this volume. The work in Seneca County was directed by Mrs. Alice Cook who is responsible for the thoroughness and completeness of the final product. The editorial work was done in Lucas County under the direction of Mrs. Marie Conroy, and was checked by the State Office staff, under the immediate supervision of Miss Winifred Smith, Assistant State Supervisor. We wish also to acknowledge the cooperation and assistance given by Mr. Ray A. Richley, Chief of Research and Records Projects, and Mr. Edward W. Jackson, District Supervisor of the Consolidated Records Assistance Project.

The volumes comprising the *Inventory of the County Archives of Ohio* are issued in mimeographed or printed form for free distribution to state and other public officials and to libraries in Ohio, and to a limited number of libraries outside the states. Request for information concerning particular units of the *Inventory* should be addressed to the Ohio Historical Records Survey Project, Room 216, Clinton Building, Columbus, Ohio.

Frances M. Foott
State Supervisor
Consolidated Records Assistance Project

Columbus, Ohio
April 1942

adm. . . . . . administration
am.. . . . . . amended
Arch. . . . . . Archaeological
Art. . . . . . Article
c. . . . . . . copyright
capias . . . . . . a warrant or order for arrest of a person, typically issued by the judge or magistrate in a case.
CCC. . . . . . Civilian Conservation Corps
certiorari . . . . . . to be more fully informed
chap(s). . . . . . chapter(s)
comp. . . . . . compiler
Const. . . . . . Constitution
ed(s). . . . . . editor(s)
et al. . . . . . . (et alii), and others
(et) passim . . . . . . and here and there
ex officio . . . . . . as a result of one's status or position
et seq. . . . . . . and following
fee simple . . . . . . full and irrevocable ownership
G. C. . . . . . . General Code
habeas corpus . . . . . . protection against illegal imprisonment
ibid. . . . . . . the same reference
loc. cit. . . . . . . (*loco citato)* in the place cited
N.P. . . . . . . The Ohio NISI PRIUS REPORTS
n.p. . . . . . . no place of publication shown
n. s. . . . . . . new series
nolle prosequi . . . . . . notice of abandonment by a plaintiff or prosecutor of all or part of a suit or action
O.L. . . . . . . *Laws of Ohio*
op. cit. . . . . . . (*opere citato*) In the work cited
posse comitatus . . . . . . a group of citizens called upon to assist the sheriff
praecipes . . . . . . a written request for action
prima facie . . . . . . on the first impression

pro rata . . . . in proportion
procedendo . . . . sends case from appellate court to a lower court
pt. . . . . part
quo warranto. . . . . by what authority or warrant
replevins . . . . return of personal property wrongfully taken or held by a defendant
R.S. . . . . Revised Statutes
sec(s). . . . . section(s)
sic . . . . thus, following copy
supersedeas. . . . . a stay of enforcement of a judgment pending appeal
v. . . . . versus
venires. . . . . a group of people summoned for jury duty
vol(s). . . . . volume(s)
WPA . . . . Works Progress/Projects Administration
writ . . . . a formal, legal document, a decree
x . . . . by
— . . . . current, to date
4-H . . . . (Four - H)

ABBREVIATIONS, SYMBOLS, AND EXPLANATORY NOTES

Each chapter or section of "County Offices and Their Records" consists of an essay describing the legal status and functions of one department of county government and an inventory of the records of that department.

Each record constitutes a separate entry. Entries are arranged under topical headings and subheadings.

Each entry sets forth, insofar as applicable, the following:

1. Entry number. Entries are numbered consecutively throughout the inventory.
2. The exact title as it appears on the record, or if the record has no title a supplied title in brackets. If the title of the record is non-descriptive, misleading, or incorrect an additional title (in capitals and lowercase letters), also enclosed in brackets, has been supplied.
3. Dates show inclusive years or parts of years covered by the record. Breaks in dates indicate that the record is missing or was not kept between dates shown. A dash in place of the final date indicates an open record. If no current entries have been made the date of the last entry is noted. Where no statement is made that the record was discontinued at the last date shown, it could not be definitely established that such was the case. Where no comment is made on the absence of prior and subsequent records, no definite information could be obtained.
4. Quantity, given in chronological order wherever possible.
5. Labeling. Numbers and letters within parentheses indicate labeling on volumes, file boxes, or other containers.
6. Variations in title. The current or most recent title is used but significant variations are shown with dates for which each was used.
7. Change of agency. Occasionally a record is discontinued as a county record and kept by some other agency.
8. Description. A statement of the nature and purpose of the record and of what the record shows. As the contents of a record may vary, over time the description may differ somewhat from the record at any one period. Wherever feasible, changes in content are shown with dates. In map and plat entries the names of author and publisher and the scale are omitted only when not available.

9. Arrangement. Records said to be alphabetically arranged are frequently alphabetized only as to initial letter of the surname. This is true especially where there is a secondary arrangement.
10. Indexing. Self-contained indexes are described in the entry. Separate indexes constitute separate entries with cross references to and from the record entry.
11. Nature of recording. Changes are indicated with dates.
12. Condition. No statement is made if good or excellent.
13. Number of pages. Averaged for the series.
14. Dimensions show size of volumes, maps, file boxes, or other containers and are expressed in inches in every instance. The dimensions of volumes are given in order of height, width, and thickness; of file boxes in order of height, width, and depth.
15. Location. Rooms referred to are in the county courthouse unless some other building is specified.

Title line cross references are used to complete series where a record is kept separately for a period of time or in other records for different periods of time. They are also used in all artificial entries which are made to show, under their proper office, records kept in the same volume or file with records of another office. In both instances, the description of the master entry shows the title and entry number of the record from which the cross reference is made. Dates shown in the description of the master entry are for the part or parts of the record contained therein, and are shown only when they vary from those of the master entry. Artificial entries show only title, dates, and description.

Separate third paragraph cross references from entry to entry, are used to show prior, subsequent, or related records which are not a part of the same series. If, however, both entries are under the same subject headings, no third paragraph references are made. "See also" references from subject headings refer to entries in the same department which contain records logically belonging under that heading but which have been classified under an equally appropriate heading.

Seneca County lies in the north-central part of Ohio. It contains 15 townships which are all regular in shape, and have an average size of 36.3 square miles. It is bounded on the north by Sandusky County, on the east by Huron, on the south by Crawford and Wyandot and on the west by Hancock and Wood Counties. It is 30 miles long, 18 miles wide, and has a total area of 545 square miles.

The surface of Seneca County is generally level to rolling, but the eastern sections are considerably more elevated than the middle and western areas. Erosion by streams has further made the inequalities of the drift surface. In southern Venice Township the elevation reaches 978 feet, and on the Sandusky River in northern Pleasant Township, is the lowest elevation of 674 feet. The topography west of the Sandusky has the flat characteristics of the black swamp region. East of the river the terrain is more broken, but the general relief is that of a plain. Bellevue, Tiffin, and Fostoria are approximately on the shoreline of the ancient glacial lake, and north of this line the surface is covered with a layer of silt and muck which give a characteristic quality to the soils. The entire area of the county is covered with glacial deposits, the region being one-fifth Lake Plains and four-fifths Till Plains, This glacial soil is a rich loam well suited for cultivation. Soils are estimated to be 70 percent limestone and 30 percent shale.

The Sandusky River, which crosses the central part of the county, is the principal stream and runs from south to north. Tributaries join it from the east and west. The county slopes to the north and drains into Lake Erie, nearly the entire area through the Sandusky River system. However, on the east side some areas drain into source streams of the Huron River, and on the west side there is some drainage into a branch of the Portage River.

The rock formations are those of the Niagara limestone in the west, Monroe Waterline in the central areas, and Columbus and Delaware limestones in the east. Some Olentangy and Ohio shales are found in the southeast corner. The average annual production of commercial limestone in Seneca County for the years 1920 to 1930 was 738,552 tons and was 5.5 percent of the total average annual production for the state. There is oil-producing territory in Jackson, Clinton, and Pleasant Townships, and several plants for burning lime have been operated in the vicinity of Tiffin.

Clay of suitable quality for brick and red pottery is found in all parts of the county. Bog-iron ore occurs in a number of places, but it is usually not in quantities sufficient to invite expenditure of capital.[1]

The earliest known inhabitants of Seneca County were the so-called Mound Builders. This race of prehistoric aborigines has left evidence of its presence in this region, the county having 23 recorded prehistoric sites consisting of two enclosures, three mounds, seven village sites, one cemetery, and 10 burials. Both the enclosures are located on Honey Creek, one in Bloom and the other in Eden Township. Thompson Township, in the extreme northeastern part of the county, presents many evidences of prehistoric occupation. The ancient Scioto Trail from the Ohio River to Sandusky Bay follows generally the course of the Sandusky River through Seneca.[2]

Few Ohio counties have rivaled Seneca in its rich tradition of Indian occupation. This region was once inhabited by a powerful warlike tribe known as the Wyandots or Hurons. They eventually came into contact with the Senecas who originally were the fifth nation of the Iroquois Confederacy. The Dutch along the Hudson called the latter tribe "Sinnekaas" which the English later spelled "Senecas." There was fierce intertribal warfare between the Senecas and Wyandots, and the latter afterwards settled along the Sandusky River. During the American Revolution they became extremely troublesome to the western counties of Virginia and Pennsylvania, and remained a menace until Wayne's decisive victory at Fallen Timbers in 1794. Seneca County was north of the Greenville Treaty line of 1795, but the Indians of this region remained at peace until influence by the machinations of Tecumseh preceding and during the War of 1812. In 1811 the power of the Indian confederacy was partially broken by the victory of William Henry Harrison at Tippecanoe, and after the War of 1812 had been terminated, the Indians sued for peace.

---

1. *Report of the Geological Survey of Ohio* (Columbus, 1873), series ii, I, pt. i, 611-624; Simon D. Fess *Ohio Reference Library* (Chicago and New York, 1930), III, 427; Ohio Study of Local School Units, *A Study of the Public Schools of Seneca County With Recommendations for Their Future Organization* (mimeographed, Columbus, 1937), 4-5. Hereafter cited, *Seneca Schools Survey*.
2. William C. Mills, *Archaeological Atlas of Ohio* (Columbus, 1914), 74.

On September 29, 1817, a treaty was made at the fort of Maumee Rapids with the Wyandots, Senecas, and other northern tribes. Cession was made of nearly all Indian claims in Ohio with the exception of those of certain individuals. At that time there was not a white settler within the present limits of Seneca County.[3]

By the Maumee treaty arrangement the United States assigned the chiefs of the Senecas a 30,000-acre tract upon the east side of the Sandusky River, mostly within the present limits of Seneca County. There was an addition of 10,000 acres, lying south of this tract but contiguous to it, granted to the Senecas by the treaty of St. Mary's on September 17, 1818. However, there were few pure-blooded Senecas in these reservations; the so-called Senecas were a number of remnants of past wars grouped under one name and included Cayugas, Mohawks, Oneidas, Onondagas, Tuscarawas, Wyandots, and a few Mingoes. To the south of the Seneca territory was a Wyandot reservation consisting of 25 square miles which included part of Big Spring Township in southwestern Seneca County. In 1831 the Senecas ceded their lands to the United States in return for territory in the west. The following year the Wyandots also abandoned their reservation and moved to western lands. Thus, by 1832 the 500 to 600 Indians of Seneca County had moved to areas less desired by the whites, and in a short time their reservations had been surveyed and sold to land hungry pioneers.[4]

Among the leaders of the tribes on these reservations were Hard Hickory, Good Hunter, Seneca John, Seneca Steel, Tall Chief, and Pumpkin. Chief Hard Hickory, however, violated the code of the tribe regarding strict veracity and was put to death. One savage named Peter Pork terrorized the reservation, and it is said that he killed at least eight Indians during his lifetime. In 1829 he killed a white man at Fort Seneca, and served three years in a penitentiary for his crime. In 1819 the government sent James Montgomery, a Methodist preacher, to the Seneca Reservation to act as Indian agent. He was well received and religious services were frequently held by the Indians, the Mohawks and the Oneidas being especially tractable and willing to adopt at least the outward vestiges of white man's civilization.

---

3. Consul W. Bitterfeld, *History of Seneca County* (Sandusky, 1848), 53-59; Charles S. Van Tassel, ed., *Story of the Maumee Valley, Toledo, and Sandusky Region* (Chicago, 1929), II, 1801.
4. A.J. Baughman, *History of Seneca County Ohio* (Chicago and New York, 1911). I, 20-23; Van Tassel, *op. cit.*, II, 1801-1806.

However, as late as 1825 superstition was still rampant, and a chief name Seneca John, on being convicted of witchcraft, was put to death at the hands of his fellow tribesmen. Several whites who had been taken prisoners by savages during the Indian wars continued to live with their former captors on the reservations, and numerous renegades also remained loyal to their Indian "brothers." Upon the decision of the tribes to move to the West, great preparations were made for the departure. Elaborate ceremonies were conducted, and solemn religious gatherings were held. Every effort was made to conceal burial mounds as the Indians feared the white man might disturb their dead. However, while the Indians had departed by 1832, signs and relics of their sojourn in Seneca County remained for many decades.[5]

The identity of the first white man to view the region of Seneca County is uncertain. LaSalle, the French explorer, may have passed down the Sandusky River as early as 1680,[6] and Father Hasles a Missionary who came to America in 1689, traveled widely in the northwest, possibly through Seneca County. James Smith, a captive of the Indians from 1755 to 1759, likely traversed this region on hunting trips with his captors.[8] The Moravians, who were taken by the British to Upper Sandusky in 1781, passed through or near Seneca. However, the first authentic reference to the territory now embraced in Seneca County is contained in a report of Captain Butler to the British commandant at Detroit. In 1782 Butler, as Irish Tory in the English Army, was sent to the Sandusky country, to aid in repelling Crawford's advance. On the night of June 3, 1782, Butler's and Elliott's commands camped in Pleasant Township, and then proceeded to the southern line of the county where a second camp was made. These troops took part in the defeat of Crawford on June 5, 1782.[9]

The Treaty of Greenville in 1795 left Seneca in the possession of Indians[10] and in 1808 they granted to the United States a tract of land 120 feet wide for a roadway from Fremont southward to the Greenville treaty line; however, failed to

---

5. Butterfield, *op. cit.*, 53-59, 122, 170; William Lane, *History of Seneca County* (Springfield, 1880), 70-76.
6. Frank Dildine, *From Wilderness to City* (n.p., n.d.), 15.
7. Warner, Beers and Company, comps, *History of Seneca County Ohio* (Chicago, 1886), 218.
8. William M. Darlington, ed., *An Account of the Remarkable Occurrence in the Life and Travels of Colonel James Smith* (Cincinnati, 1870), 43, 84, *passim.*
9. Warner, Beers, and Company, *op, cit.*, 218, 219, 329.
10. Eugene Holloway Roseboom and Francis Phelps Weisenburger, *A History of Ohio* (New York, 1934), 93.

provide for its establishment.[11] Early in the War of 1812 one of the routes chosen by General Harrison and his advance toward Detroit was along the Sandusky, and two stockade forts were set up in Seneca County. In 1812 an army road was marked off on the west bank of the Sandusky between Upper and Lower Sandusky.[12] In 1813 men under Colonel James V. Ball built a fort near the army road on the left bank of the Sandusky River in what is now Tiffin. This station, known as Fort Ball, was a small stockade enclosing about one-third of an acre, and was used during the war as a supply depot.[13] Fort Seneca, on the west bank of the Sandusky close to northern lines of the county in Pleasant Township, was erected by General Harrison in 1813 as a part of his line of communication between Lower Sandusky and Columbus. Harrison and an army of about 800 men had their headquarters at this port while Captain Croghan was making his inspired defense at Fort Stevenson (Fremont),[14] and it is said that news of Perry's victory on Lake Erie was received by Harrison while stationed at Fort Seneca.[15] An attempt by a treacherous Indian to assassinate Harrison while he bivouacked at this post was narrowly thwarted.[16]

Not until 1817 did the Indians cede this region to the Americans, but in the interim there were many whites in this region who lived among the Indians, usually by inclination, but sometimes as captives. Among these were William Spicer, Jacob Knisely, Sarah Williams, Sally Frost, Mrs. Castleman, Eliza Whittaker, John Van Meter, Benjamin F. Warner, Robert Armstrong, and William McCulloch.[17] The treaty of the Maumee in 1817 granted considerable land to the white prisoners of the Indians, to half-breeds, and to Indians who had given military or other special service to the United States. For example, John Van Meter, a white prisoner of the Indians, together with his wife's three brothers, was given 1000 acres in southern Seneca County.[18]

---

11. William E. Peters and Company, *Ohio Lands and their Subdivision* (Athens, 1918), 312.
12. Warner, Beers and Company, *op. cit.,* 329.
13. Butterfield, *op. cit.,* 79-80; A.A. Graham, "The Military Post, Ports and Battlefields Within the State of Ohio," *Ohio State Archaeological and Historical Quarterly,* III (1895), 310.
14. Nevin O. Winter, ed., *A History of Northwest Ohio* (Chicago and New York, 1917), I, 578; Butterfield, *op. cit.,* I, 416.
15. Baughman, *op. cit.,* I, 416.
16. Butterfield, *op. cit.,* 118-121; Henry Howe, comp., *Historical Collections of Ohio* (Norwalk, 1896), II, 573-574.
17. Baughan, *op. cit.,* I, 30-33.
18. Peters, *op. cit.,* 226-231.

In 1819 a Mohawk village of some 20 huts was located on this tract.[19] Robert Armstrong, who had been taken prisoner by the Indians and married a Wyandot woman, was granted 640 acres on the west side of the Sandusky in the vicinity of Fort Ball.[20]

Despite the fact that no land was sold in what is now Seneca County until 1821, many squatters had pushed into the region before that date.[21] On November 18, 1817, Erastus Bowe, of Vermont, came to Fort Ball where some hired men had erected a log cabin for him. Bowe had to been through this region as early as 1812 as a soldier under General Hull, and had been one of the frontier scouts who had kept watch upon Indian activities. Shortly after his arrival, this thrifty New Englander opened a tavern and general store.[22] William Harris a gunsmith, settled near Fort Seneca in 1820, and found employment in keeping the guns of the Indians in repair.[23] By 1821 there was at least 12 squatters in Eden Township alone.[24] Part of the Armstrong section, including the site of Bowe's tavern and Fort Ball, was surveyed by Joseph Vance as the town of Oakley in 1819. It was the first town and post office and the county. In the year 1823 Armstrong sold 400 acres to Jesse Spencer at whose direction David Risdon surveyed a new town named Fort Ball which included the old plat of Oakley.[25]

On the east side of the river almost opposite Fort Ball, Joshua Hedges of Mansfield entered land in 1821. It was surveyed by his brother, General James Hedges, and four men were given town lots on condition they build cabins and bring their families to this village which was named Tiffin in honor of Edward Tiffin, first Governor of Ohio. The town was faced by several severe handicaps, not the least of which were the prevalence of disease due to the proximity of the river, and the fact that the main thoroughfare from Columbus to Lake Erie passed through Fort Ball. In 1834, 63 inhabitants of Tiffin died of cholera, a terrible blow to the tiny village.

---

19. Butterfield , *op. cit.,* 97-99
20. Peters, *op. cit.,* 228.
21. Butterfield, *op. cit.,* 100.
22. *Ibid.,* 80-81.
23. Fess, *op. cit.,* III, 428.
24. Butterfield, *op. cit.,* 100.
25. Butterfield, *op. cit.,* 73, 83.

In 1829 a land office was temporarily located at Tiffin, the population growth remained slow and as late as 1840 the village had only 728 inhabitants.[26] However, in 1829 the post office was moved from Fort Ball to Tiffin, and in 1833 Hedges built a wooden toll bridge to connect the two towns. Prior to that time a ferry had been in operation. In later years three bridges were built, the first being constructed in 1837.[27]

Meanwhile, steps had been taken for the organization of the county. From 1795 to 1803 the area which is now Seneca County was part of Wayne County with the county seat at Detroit. In 1803 it became a part of Franklin County with Franklinton (Columbus) as the county seat, and in 1808 the Seneca district was included in Delaware County.[28] On February 12, 1820, the legislature divided into 14 counties the land attained by treaties from the Indians–the so-called "New Purchase." The ninth of the counties so created was Seneca which received its name from its Indian inhabitants. In 1820-1821 the townships in the county were surveyed with the exception of the Indian reservations which were surveyed in 1832. The land was offered for sale in August 1821, and the average price was a little higher than that established by law. One writer has pointed out that this was indicative of the fact that little land was entered by speculators and as a result the population of the county from the beginning has been of a permanent and industrious nature.[29]

Seneca was erected in 1820 and temporarily attached to Sandusky County,[30] and 1824 it was organized as an independent county.[31] Only one change has been made and the county's boundaries, and that was lost of territory by the organization by Crawford County which had previously been attached to Seneca.[32] Over the vigorous opposition of the citizens of Fort Ball, Tiffin was made the county seat despite the fact that there were but six cabins in the village.[33]

---

26. Daughters of the American Revolutions, Ohio - Dolly Madison Chapter, comp., *Ohio Early State and Local History* (Tiffin, 1919), 85; Butterfield, *op. cit.,* 84-87.
27. Van Tassel, *op. cit.,* II, 1817; Fess, *op. cit.,* III, 429.
28. *Seneca School Survey,* 1.
29. Butterfield, *op. cit.,* 70-71.
30. *Laws of Ohio,* XVIII, 92.
31. *Ibid.,* XXII, 40.
32. *Ibid.,* XXII, 88; XXIV, 46. See Randolph Chandler Downes, "Evolution of Ohio County Boundaries," *Ohio State Archaeological and Historical Quarterly,* XXXVI (1927), 472.
33. Baughman, *op. cit.,* I, 54.

Most of the early business and professional men had settled on the Fort Ball side of the river. Eli Dresback, the first doctor, and Rodolphus Dickinson, the first lawyer, were both inhabitants of Fort Ball. There was considerable acrimony between Joshua Hedges and Jesse Spencer regarding the matter of the county seat, dams on the Sandusky, and personal matters. After some troublesome litigation Spencer in 1825 sold his holdings to Hedges who had the village resurveyed and named New Fort Ball. In 1850 the two settlements were united under the name of Tiffin.[34] In 1822 Hedges erected a sawmill on Rock Creek, one-fourth mile east of the first plat of Tiffin, and a grist mill one-half mile north of Tiffin. He also built a two-story frame building on Virgin Alley now Court Street. This frame building was used for a store and after Seneca County was organized, sessions of court were held there. On some occasions the Methodist Church was used for holding court until a courthouse costing $9,500 was erected in 1836.[35]

A large portion of the early settlers were from New York,[36] but there were many from Maryland, Virginia, Pennsylvania, and older sections of Ohio. In later decades certain townships received numerous German immigrants as additions to their population.[37] The village of New Riegel, for example, was settled primarily by German Catholics, and a monastery, convent, and parochial school were erected there.[38] Many German and French families became permanent settlers in Big Spring Township between 1833 and 1842.[39] The population of the county reflected steady growth. In 1830 there were 5,159 persons in Seneca; in 1840, 18,128; in 1860, 30,868; in 1880, 36,947; and in 1900, 41,163.[40] In 1930 the population was 47,941, of whom 96.2 percent were native-born whites, 2.8 percent foreign-born whites, and 0.7 percent Negroes.[41] The 1940 census gives Seneca County a population of 48,499 and Tiffin 16,102.

---

34. Winter, *op. cit.,* I, 590-593; Butterfield, *op. cit.,* 82-83.
35. Baughman, *op. cit.,* I, 60; Winter, *op. cit.,* I, 584; Van Tassel, *op. cit.,* II, 1810.
36. Baughman, *op. cit.,* I, 310.
37. Butterfield, *op. cit.,* 131-132; H.S. Knapp, *History of the Maumee Valley* (Toledo, 1872), 439.
38. Winter, *op. cit.,* I, 598.
39. Van Tassel, *op. cit.,* II, 1828.
40. *Twelfth Census of the United States, 1900, Population,* I, pt. i, 35.
41. *Fifteenth Census of the United States, 1930, Population,* III, pt. ii, 484.

In the years following the establishment of Oakley, Fort Ball, Tiffin and many other villages were platted; among these being Belmore in 1824; Caroline in 1828; Rome, Risdon, and Middleburg in 1832; Attica and Sulfur Springs in 1833; Springville and Republic in 1834; Fort Seneca and Hopewell in 1836; New Fort Ball, Bloomville and Bascom in 1837; Bettsville, Elizabethtown, and West Lodi in 1838; Green Springs in 1839; Thompsonville in 1840; Lewisville in 1841; Rehoboth and Oregon (Adrian), in 1844; Berwick in 1845; Adamsville in 1846; and New Riegel in 1850.[42] Fostoria, next to Tiffin the most populous city in the county, has an interesting history. The village of Rome and Risdon in London Township are platted so close together that intense rivalry developed to the detriment of both communities. In 1853 the inhabitants of Risdon asked to be annexed to Rome and this was done in 1854. The name of the town was changed to Fostoria in honor of one of its most influential citizens, Charles W. Foster, father of Ohio's Governor Foster.[43] The elder Foster was a native of the state of Massachusetts and came to Seneca County in 1827. In 1832 he entered with two others a tract of 2,000 acres in what is now Fostoria.[44]

Seneca has two cities within her boundaries: Tiffin, which in 1930 had a population of 16,428; and Fostoria, which had 12,790 inhabitants in that year. The incorporated villages, with populations in 1930 were: Attica, 783; Green Springs, 750; Bloomville, 700; Bettsville, 656; Republic, 512; and New Riegel, 239.[45]

The economic progress of the county was closely related to the transportation facilities that were developed. "Bell's Road" was surveyed (or blazed) by General Bell of Wooster in 1812. It connected Upper and Lower Sandusky and was opened by a Mr. Meeker. It was a principal thoroughfare for troops and supplies in the War of 1812. After the war huge quantities of flour and other provisions from Lower Sandusky [renamed Fremont in 1849] were transported over this road, and many immigrants who came to the United States by way of Canada took this road to central and southern Ohio.

---

42. Butterfield, *op. cit.,* 241-242.
43. Winter, *op. cit.,* I, 596.
44. H.S. Knapp, *op. cit.,* 503.
45. Ohio Secretary of State, *Ohio Fifteenth Federal Census, 1930* (Columbus, 1931), 24.

In 1821 it was again surveyed and constituted a state road. Israel Harrington in 1820 surveyed a state road leading from Fremont to Delaware and passing through Seneca County to the east of the Sandusky River. In 1822 Colonel James Kilbourne opened a road from Sandusky to Upper Sandusky.[46] As early as 1830 an important stage route extended from Pittsburgh to Tiffin by way of New Lisbon, Canton, and Wooster.[47] Thus, at a comparatively early date, the produce of Seneca had access to lake and river shipping at Sandusky and Fremont, as well as a route overland to central and southern Ohio.

In 1849 private road companies were charted to construct toll roads to Lower Sandusky, to Fort Ball, and from Tiffin to Osceola.[48] Despite the special transportation advantages enjoyed by Seneca, the early businessman had their difficulties. Merchandise going to Baltimore took three weeks on the stagecoach, but if consigned to New York costs were lower as it was shipped by stage or wagon to Sandusky, sent by lake boat to Buffalo, and then by the Erie Canal and the Hudson River to New York. Nevertheless, transportation costs were heavy, and according to one account, this caused the selling price of certain goods to be marked double their original cost.[49] During the pre-civil war era another "road" was opened through Seneca County. The home of Doctor Jeremiah Chamberlain of Tiffin was an important station on the "Underground Railroad" in the route toward the lake ports. It is related that a United States marshal lived just across the street from the doctor, but never suspected the use to which his neighbor's house was being put.[50]

During the second decade of its existence the county had access to the second railroad built on Ohio soil. Ground for the Mad River and Lake Erie Railroad was broken at Sandusky in 1835 by General William Henry Harrison. In 1839 the railroad reached Bellevue, and in 1841 passed through Republic and Tiffin. A more direct route from Sandusky to Tiffin was constructed by way of Clyde and was leased to the Mad River and Lake Erie Railroad, the road through Bellevue being abandoned in 1853. From Tiffin the Mad River Railroad (now the Big Four) was extended south in 1845. Fostoria's first railroad was the Fremont and Indiana (now part of the Nickel Plate system), opened in April 1861, from Fremont to Findlay. The Chicago division of the Baltimore and Ohio system was completed

---

46. Butterfield, *op. cit.,* I, 57.
47. John Kilbourne, comp., *The Ohio Gazetteer . . .* (Columbus, 1831), 310.
48. Baughman, *op. cit.,* I, 57.
49. Daughters of the American Revolution, *op. cit.,* 59.
50. *Ibid.,* 91.

through Republic, Tiffin, and Fostoria in 1874. In 1873, the Mansfield and Coldwater (later part of the Pennsylvania), was completed through Tiffin, and in the 1890s the old Mad River roadbed from Sandusky to Bellevue was used in the construction of a road which also became part of the Pennsylvania system. The Hocking Valley from Toledo through Fostoria was in operation by 1877, and the Toledo and Ohio Central (now New York Central) was completed through this city by 1881.[51] At present seven railroads pass through the county.[52] These roads have more than 344 miles of track, and penetrate all but one township. There are also 1,165 miles of highway in Seneca including eight state routes and one United States route.[53]

Seneca County has always been an important agricultural region. Originally much of the land was poorly drained and the marshy area was called the "Black Swamp." However, farmers soon found means of overcoming this difficulty.[54] One writer in 1847 stated that wheat was a staple crop of the region, the average yield being 20 bushels to the acre. Indian corn was also grown in abundance, especially along the margin of the numerous streams, and orchards devoted to growing of apples, peaches, pears, and other fruits were numerous.[55] The first orchard in the county was planted near Tiffin by John Keller in 1824,[56] and Johnny Appleseed (John Chapman) made frequent trips to pioneer Seneca County, disposing of his nursery stock to the early settlers. In 1833 an agricultural society was organized, and after 1841 this took on considerable local importance.[57] In 1870 the county ranked fourth among Ohio counties in wheat production, and fifth in Ohio in oat production.[58]

In 1930 there were 2,893 farms in Seneca, [59] occupying 92.1 percent of the county's area, [60] and producing crops valued at $5,944,215.[61]

---

51. Fess, *op. cit.,* III, 430; Baughman, *op. cit.,* I, 55-57.
52. Ohio Tax Commission, *Annual Report, 1935,* 110.
53. *Seneca Schools Survey,* 9-10.
54. Abel Rawson, *Address Before the Seneca County Pioneer Association* (Tiffin, 1869), 2.
55. Butterfield, *op. cit.,* 188-189.
56. Daughters of the American Revolution, *op. cit.,* 99.
57. Baughman, *op. cit.,* I, 172-173.
58. Ohio Secretary of State, *Ohio Statistics, 1871,* II, 21.
59. *Fifteenth Census of the United States, 1930, Agriculture,* III, pt. i, 285.
60. *Ibid.,* II, pt. i, 104.
61. *Ibid.,* III, pt. i, 304.

These farms and buildings were appraised at $28,032,330,[62] or about 40 percent of the grand tax duplicate of the county for 1934.[63] Of the area in farm lands, 66 percent was in tilled crops, 24 percent was in woodlands, and 5 percent was in pasture.[64] In 1935 the county ranked fourteenth in the state in gross agricultural income, the average per farm being $1,667 in contrast to the state average of $1,122. The average income per acre was $14.89 or $2.36 more than the state average.[65]

Of Seneca's farms, about 51 percent in 1930 produced general crops; 15.1 percent were classified as animal-specialty farms; 13.2 percent were cash-grain farms, and 3.5 percent were dairy farms. All other groups were much smaller.[66] Twenty of the county's products equaled or exceeded the state average in amount of production; these included corn, wheat, oats, barley, rye, hay, potatoes, lumber firewood, horses, mules, cattle, milk, swine, sheep and wool, chickens, eggs, ducks, geese, bees and honey. All of these products were equal to or exceeded the state average in value. The most valuable products ranked as follows: grains, cattle, horses, milk, swine, hay, eggs, and chickens.[67]

Of the 47,941 persons in the county in 1930, 27,069 were classified as urban residents and 20,872 as rural residents.[68] Of those gainfully employed in the county about 23 percent were engaged in agriculture.[69] More than 34 percent of the farms were mortgaged in 1930, and 38.7 percent were operated by tenants.[70] These latter figures are rather high considering the agricultural wealth of the county.

The industrial development of Seneca County was originally based upon the primary products of timber and grain. Paul D. Butler erected a saw mill near Tiffin as early as 1819, and both Joshua Hedges and Jesse Spencer utilized the water power of the Sandusky River or its tributaries to operate saw mills and grist mills for their communities.

---

62. *Ibid.*, 292.
63. Ohio Auditor of State, *Annual Report, 1935,* 556.
64. *Fifteenth Census of the United States, 1930, Agriculture,* II, pt. i, 407.
65. *Seneca Schools Survey,* 5.
66. *Fifteenth Census of the United States, 1930, Agriculture,* III, pt. i, 285.
67. *Fifteenth Census of the United States, 1930, Agriculture,* II, pt. i, 421-467; *Seneca Schools Survey,* 6-7.
68. *Fifteenth Census of the United States, 1930, Population,* III, pt. ii, 484.
69. *Ibid.,* 510.
70. *Ibid., Agriculture,* II, pt. i, 471, 478.

At Melmore, Beaver Creek, and many other settlements mills were erected almost contemporaneously with settlement. Other early industries at Tiffin included a tannery in 1827; a lime kiln in 1828; a cabinet and chair factory in 1832; a pottery in 1834; a flour mill in 1835; a foundry about 1847; and a brewery in 1848. In later decades this city possessed brickyards, woolen mills, stove works, agricultural implement works, carriage factories, a churn manufacturer, and an emery wheel company; as well as manufacturers of commercial limestone, elevating and conveying machinery, lanterns, magnetos, flour, pottery, and glass. Fostoria's early industries were a grist mill in 1834, a carding mill in 1850, a foundry in 1860, a stave and barrel factory in 1871, an agricultural implement works in 1873, a spoke works in 1882, and a brass works in 1885.[71]

In 1937 Tiffin was the center for the production of glass, pottery, forging machines, well-drilling machinery, conveyors, and quarry products. Fostoria manufactured auto ignition systems, crankshafts, carbon, machinery, women's clothing, wire, pressed steel, glass products, railway signals, screws, flour, serum, piston rings, rubber goods, and electrical appliances. Attica manufactured rubber products, flour textiles, and cement; and Bettsville produced refractory material, fluxing stone, lime, and quarry products.[72] The various mineral springs of the county, notably at Green Springs, have attracted many visitors to the county, and in one sense the accommodation of these visitors maybe considered one of the older industries of Seneca.[73]

In 1930 there were 101 manufacturing establishments in the county, employing approximately 4,500 workers, and producing products valued at $24,572,447. Of this number Fostoria had 35 establishments and Tiffin had 54.[74] More than 30 percent of those gainfully employed in the county were engaged in manufacturing, and the clay, glass, and stone industry group employed 1,296 persons. Next in importance was the iron and steel industry which employed 1,149 persons.[75]

---

71. Butterfield, *op. cit.,* 75-76, 85, 157; Baughman, *op. cit.,* I, 126-127, 373-380, 417-424; Warner, Beers and Company, *op. cit.,* 525-531, 622-624.
72. N.W. Ayer and Sons, *Directory of Newspapers and Periodicals* (Philadelphia, 1937), 700, 701, 715, 730.
73. Warner, Beers and Company, *op. cit.,* 416.
74. *Fifteenth Census of the United States, 1929, Manufacturers,* III, 398-399.
75. *Ibid., Population,* III, pt. ii, 512.

In 1930 of the 17,764 normally employed workers, 825 were out of work and 318 were laid off.[76] Despite the fact that Seneca is in part an industrial county, its per capita relief cost for 1934 were only $5.26 in comparison with the state average of $9.22 per capita.[77] The diversity of its industries, and the fact that it has a large agricultural element enabled this county to combat successfully industrial depression.

The earliest financial institution to be established in the county was founded by Benjamin Tomb and R.G. Pennington at Tiffin in 1847. This was known as the Seneca County Bank. In 1852 a private bank opened at Tiffin, the Arnold and Tomb Bank, which was chartered in 1865 as the First National Bank. Other early Tiffin banks were the Bank of Tiffin organized in 1858, the National Exchange Bank in 1865, the Tiffin Saving Bank in 1873, and the Commercial Bank in 1876. Still others were founded in succeeding decades.[78]

The Methodists were the first to hold religious meetings in Seneca County. James Montgomery, agent to the Indians on the Seneca Reservation, was also a Methodist preacher, and he held services in Pleasant Township as early as 1819. Other early Methodist meetings were held in Eden Township and Tiffin in 1821 or 1822; in 1828 at Melmore; in 1829 in Reed Township; and in 1831 at Bascom. James Wilson, W. Brock, a Mr. Chase, and James Anderson were pioneer ministers of this faith. The Presbyterians were also early in this field, meetings being held at Fort Ball in 1823, Melmore in 1830, and Tiffin, Republic, and Venice Townships in 1830-1831. Reverends Messrs. Robinson, McCutcheon, and Thompson were early Presbyterian divines. Catholic gatherings were held at Tiffin as early as 1826, and St. Mary's Church of Tiffin, established about 1831, is the fourth oldest Catholic Church in Ohio. Father Quinn and Moynahan and Bishop Fenwick were the early spiritual leaders of this faith. The United Brethren Church had its first Seneca County organization at Melmore in about 1834; a Reformed Church was established in Thompson Township in 1830 under Reverend Stauch, and at tiffin in 1833 under Reverend Sanders; the Methodist Protestants trace their pioneer churches to meetings held at Fort Seneca in 1829, and at Tiffin in 1837; the Baptist met in 1827 at Bloomville under Reverend Seitz, and in 1837 organized at Republic; and the Evangelical Lutherans held their first meeting in Venice

---

76. *Ibid., Unemployment,* I, 800.
77. *Seneca Schools Survey,* 9.
78. Butterfields, *op. cit.,* 95-96; Baughman, *op. cit.,* I, 372-373.

Township in Tiffin in 1835 under Reverend Conrad.[79]

In 1926 there were 23,539 church members in the county. Of this number 10,125 were Catholics; 2,710 Methodist Episcopal; 2,477 members of the Reformed Church; 1,450 United Brethren; 1,175 Methodist Protestant; 920 Lutherans; 845 members of the Evangelical Church; 825 Presbyterians; and 780 Disciples of Christ. Other groups were much smaller in number.[80]

In 1826 the first cabin intended for school use was created in Seneca County. This was located near Melmore and James Lathan was the teacher. About the same time a school was opened in Pleasant Township with George Van Dorn as the master. Until 1832 school in Tiffin was held in the town hall which was leased for that purpose, and Daniel Dildine was probably the first Tiffin schoolmaster. He received a salary of $50 for a term of three months. In 1828 ground was secured from Joshua Hedges, but a school building was not erected thereon until 1831. Benjamin Crockett and Samuel Nolan were the first teachers in this school. This building could accommodate only 60 pupils, and in 1844 a new four-room structure was erected. In 1850 the Tiffin school board was organized, and the old tuition system abolished in favor of free, tax-supported schools. In 1854 a high school was organized, and a Union school building was finished in 1856, the first high school class graduating in 1859.[81]

The public schools consistently improved and expanded, and in 1935-1936 the 65 schools of the county enrolled 3,841 pupils.[82] Since 1890 the Junior Order United American Mechanics Orphan's Home has been located at Tiffin, and maintains its own primary and secondary school system of high caliber.[83] In 1930 only 1 percent of the county's population was illiterate, a figure far below the state and national averages.[84]

---

79. Baughman, *op. cit.*, I, 279-284, 401-409, 430-432; Lang *op. cit.*, 274-294; Winter, *op. cit.*, I, 588-590; D.J. Stewart, comp. *New Historical Atlas of Seneca County, Ohio* (Philadelphia, 1872), II, III; I.F. King, "Introduction of Methodism in Ohio," *Ohio State Archaeological and Historical Quarterly*, X (1902), 188.
80. Bureau of the Census, *Religious Bodies;* 1926, I, 657-660.
81. Daughters of the American Revolution, *op. cit.*, 115; Warner, Beers and Company, *op. cit.*, 625; Baughman, *op. cit.*, I, 128, 381, *Seneca Schools Survey,* 2-3.
82. *Ibid.*, 36.
83. Baughman, *op. cit.*, I, 410.
84. *Fifteenth Census of the United States, 1930, population,* III, pt. ii, 484.

At least two products of Seneca's schools have won national recognition. Tiffin was the home of William H. Gibson, a brigadier-general during the Civil War, and one of Ohio's most distinguished orators. A bronze figure of General Gibson has been erected on the courthouse lawn in Tiffin. Anson Burlingame, the diplomat, once taught school in Eden Township.[85]

To supplement the elementary educational system several academies were established in the county. The first was the Seneca County Academy at Republic which was incorporated in 1836 and opened in 1844-1845 with S.W. Shepard and Dr. Aaron Schuyler as its masters. The school closed in 1862 because 180 students had enrolled in the Union Army. A private school was maintained there until 1870 when the Northwestern Normal School was started by J.F. Richard. In 1874 this school failed as did the Republic Normal School also started in the old academy building. Other academics were also established. In 1844 the West Lodi Academy was chartered, and in 1850 the Tiffin Academy received a like grant. Local histories failed to mention these two schools, and so it is probably that they were never actually in operation. In 1858-1859, the Fostoria Academy was opened under the Reverend William C. Turner. This later became known as Fostoria Normal School, but in 1879 the United Brethren Church took over the institution and operated it under the name of Fostoria Academy. The enterprise was not a financial success, and when a fire damaged the property it was abandoned. In 1881 the Synod of Toledo established an academy at Green Springs, which school was for a time affiliated with Western Reserve University.[86]

Higher education was not neglected in the county. The Ohio Synod of the Reformed Church started a school known as Tarleton College near Lancaster, Ohio. However, through the efforts of Reverend Hiram Shaull, pastor of the First Reformed Church of Tiffin, the citizens of Tiffin pledged over $11,000 to locate that college in their city. Heidelberg College, as this new institution was called, was open in 1850, but it was 1853 before buildings were erected on the five-acre campus donated by Joshua Hedges. Jeremiah Good was professor of mathematics, and his brother Ruben was rector of the preparatory department.

---

85. Howe, *op. cit.,* II, 579-580.

86. *Seneca Schools Survey,* 3; Baughman, *op. cit.,* I, 424-426, 442: Warner, Beers and Company, *op. cit.,* 412-616, 662; *op. cit.,* Van Tassel, *op. cit.,* II, 1831; Edward A. Miller, "The History of Educational Legislation in Ohio," *Ohio State Archaeological and Historical Quarterly,* XXVII (1919), 167, 171.

A theological course was maintained along with the regular academic courses. Reverend E. V. Gerhart was the first president of the school. Heidelberg has been co-educational since its beginning, and was the second or third college in the United States to admit women. It also claims to have been the first nonsectarian college in this county.[87] In 1936 there were 373 students enrolled in this college, and there were 33 persons on the faculty.[83] In 1863 the Ursuline Sisters opened Ursuline College, a girl's school at Tiffin, and in 1878 this institution was incorporated.[89]

A surprisingly large number of newspapers have been initiated in Seneca County during the past decade, but only a few have managed to continue in operation for any length of time. The first paper to be established was the *Seneca Patriot* which was printed at Tiffin in 1832 by J.H. Brown and Eliza Brown. Other early Tiffin papers were the *Independent Chronicle and Seneca Advertiser,* established in 1834; the *Gazette and Seneca Advertiser,* in 1835; the *Gazette* in 1838; the *Van Burenite* in 1840; the *Seneca Advertiser* in 1842; the *Whig Standard* in 1845; the *Seneca Adler,* (German) in 1848; the *Western Whig Standard* in 1849. Many others were founded in following years including several German papers. The earliest Fostoria newspapers were the *News,* founded in 1860; the *Review,* 1866; and the *Democrat,* 1875. Other journals printed in the villages of the county were the *Attica Journal,* founded in 1876; the *Green Springs Sentinel* in 1874, and the *Times* in 1876; the *Bloomville Enterprise* in 1874, the *Banner* in 1875, the *Seneca County Record* in 1878, and the *Daily Record* in 1879; and the *Bettsville Optic* in 1882, and the *Enterprise* in 1883.[90]

At present the principal newspapers of the county are the Attica *Hub,* an independent weekly, founded in 1896; the Bettsville *Taxpayer,* an independent weekly, established in 1921; the Bloomville *Gazette,* an independent weekly, printed since 1900; the Fostoria *Democrat,* an independent-Democratic paper, founded in 1875; the Republic *Reporter,* a neutral weekly initiated in 1910; and the Tiffin *Advertiser-Tribune*, an independent daily, tracing its origin back to 1832.[91]

---

87. *Seneca Schools Survey,* 3; Baughman, op. cit., 384-395; Lang, *op. cit.,* 267-273.
88. *The World Almanac, 1937,* 387.
89. Baughman, *op. cit.,* I, 395.
90. Warner, Beers and Company, *op. cit.,* 320-328; Baughan, *op. cit.,* I, 396-398.
91. Ayer, *op. cit.,* 700-730, *passim.*

The county as a political institution and as a subdivision of the state for purposes of political and judicial administration is of ancient origin.[1] In a form substantially similar in all general features and functions it has existed in England since early times, and in America since its settlement. As the tide of migration moved westward, following the American Revolution, the institutions of the seaboard states were transferred to the newer west, undergoing such alterations as best suited frontier conditions.[2]

The earliest provision for the organization of counties in what is now the state of Ohio was contained in the Ordinance of 1787, by which the governor of the Northwest Territory was directed to "lay out the parts of the district in which the indian [sic] titles shall have been extinguished into counties and townships subject however to such alterations as may therefore be made by the legislature".[3] The organization of county government, therefore, began before the organization of the state and before the adoption of a state constitution. Prior to statehood nine counties were organized. The first county lines were drawn in 1788.[4] The last county lines were altered in 1888, exactly one hundred years later.[5]

The establishment of local government in the Northwest Territory was one of the first concerns of Governor St. Clair. The Ordinance of 1787 furnished the framework, but details of institutions had to be constructed. All county officials, under the provisions of the ordinance, were made appointive by the governor.

---

1. Edward Channing, *A History of the United States* (New York, 1905), I, 512-519.
2. Beverly W. Bond, Jr., *The Civilization of the Old Northwest: A Study of Political, Social, and Economic Development, 1788-1812* (New York, 1934), 58-59.
3. Clarence Edwin Carter, ed. and comp., *The Territorial Papers of the United States* (Washington, 1934), II, 44.
4. *Ibid.*, III, 279.
5. *Laws of Ohio,* LXXXV, 418; Randolph Chandler Downes, "Evolution of Ohio County Boundaries," *Ohio State Archaeological and Historical Quarterly,* XXXVI, (1927), 449.

St. Clair, a former resident of Pennsylvania, in providing for local administration, depended in a large part upon the Pennsylvania Code, which in some instances, was altered to meet the needs of pioneer communities.[6]

The provisions for local administration were, for the most part, simple and effective. In each county the court of general quarter sessions of the peace, composed of three or more justices of the peace, served as a fiscal and administrative board of the county, estimating county expenditures, appointing tax commissioners, and providing for highway and bridge construction.[7] By the end of the decade the court was authorized to enter into contracts for building and repairing the county jail and the courthouse.[8] Other county officials appointed during the territorial period included a sheriff, coroner, recorder, treasurer, a license commission, and justices and clerks of the various courts.[9]

Officers having been appointed, the next step in the organization of government was the establishment of a system of local courts. Evidence seems to indicate that the judicial system for the county had been carefully planned. The court of common pleas, composed of not less than three nor more than five appointed judges, was an inferior court having limited civil jurisdiction.[10] The court of general quarter sessions, besides serving as a fiscal and administrative board of the county, had jurisdiction in lesser criminal cases.[11] A probate court, composed of a single judge, was given jurisdiction in probate and testamentary matters.[12]

---

6. The governor and judges were given power to "adopt and publish in the district such laws of the original states" as they thought necessary and these laws were to remain in force unless disapproved by Congress. In many cases the governor and judges had not adopted laws of the original states, as the Ordinance stipulated, but had passed measures that conformed in spirit. Since there was some question of the legality of these laws St. Clair, in 1795, after the lower house the Congress disapproved of the laws passed at the legislative session by 1792, called a legislative session to revise the territorial Code. The commission, after sitting for three months, completed Maxwell's Code, named in honor of the printer, W. Maxwell. Few changes were made in the Maxwell Code by the territorial assembly which was elected in 1798. Carter, II, 43. The minutes of the legislative assembly are reproduced in *The Ohio State Archaeological and Historical Quarterly,* XXX (1921), 13-53.

7. Theodore Calvin Pease, comp., *The Laws of the Northwest Territory, 1788-1800,* 4, 36, 337; 69-70; 467-468; 74, 77, 453, 456, 485

8. *Ibid.,* 485.

9. *Ibid.,* 8, 24-25, 61, 68-69, 197.

10. *Ibid.,* 7.

11. *Ibid.,* 4-7.

12. *Ibid.,* 9.

In 1795, following St. Clair's revision of the territorial code, circuit courts were established and orphans' courts were instituted.[13]

In the meantime the local government was further developed by the organization of civil townships. The governor and judges adopted a law from the Pennsylvania Code requiring the justices of the court of quarter sessions to divide each county into townships and appoint in each a constable to act in townships and the county, a clerk, and one or more overseers of the poor.[14]

The territory entered a second stage of administration when, in 1798, the population having reached the requisite five thousand, the governor ordered the election of a representative assembly.[15] The system of local government continued as established by the governor and judges, and the transition was achieved without a disturbance of local administration.

The admission of Ohio as a state did not, in the main, materially affect county organization and administration. The system of local government having been organized by the governor and judges and the legislature of the Northwest Territory, the basic offices were continued. Except for the provision for the election of a county sheriff and a county coroner in each county, two officials of utmost importance in pioneer communities, the constitution was silent on such matters as titles, numbers, and duties of officials.[16]

It devolved, therefore, upon the legislature to confirm powers upon the county. In 1804 the legislature made provision for a board of county commissioners, composed of three members elected for a three-year term.[17] The board of county commissioners, supplanting the court of quarter sessions, became the administrative and fiscal board of the county. In 1803 the legislature, recognizing the need for a more adequate system of land records, provided for a recorder to be appointed by the court of common pleas for a seven-year term and for a surveyor to be appointed by the court of common pleas.[18]

---

13. *Ibid.,* 157, 181-188.
14. *Ibid.,* 37-41, 338. The system of local governmental administration was the result of sectional compromise, since it combined the county system of the southern and middle states with the elements of the New England town. Dwight G. McCarty, *The Territorial Governors of the Old Northwest: A Study in Territorial Administration,* 53-54.
15. Carter, *op. cit.,* III, 514-515.
16. *Ohio Const., 1802,* Art. VI, sec. 1.
17. *Laws of Ohio,* II, 150.
18. *Ibid.,* I, 136, 90-93.

Another act authorized the appointment of a county treasurer by the associate judges; a later one provided for his appointment by the county commissioners.[19]

The legislature also provided during its first session for a prosecuting attorney to be appointed by the supreme court to prosecute cases on behalf of the state.[20] In 1805 the appointing power was transferred to the court of common pleas.[21]

A new office was created in 1820, that of county auditor. The auditor, first appointed by the legislature, had as his duty the preparation of the tax duplicate.[22] The county board of revision, the purpose of which was to correct some of the inequities of assessments, was established in 1825. The first board of revision or equalization as it was sometimes called, was composed of the county commissioners, the auditor, and the assessors.[23]

The judicial power of the state in matters of law and equity was vested in the supreme court, the court of common pleas, and the justices' courts. The articles of the constitution provided for a court of common pleas to be composed of a president and associate justice. The members of the court, appointed by a joint ballot of both houses of the general assembly, were to hold court in three judicial circuits into which the state was to be divided by the legislature.[24] The court was assigned common law and chancery jurisdiction in all cases as provided by law.[25] To the court was assigned jurisdiction in probate and testamentary matters and in the appointment of guardians, functions performed during the territorial period by the probate court.[26] Finally, the court was authorized to appoint a clerk.[27]

The county offices created by the legislature were designed to transact the business of a state as yet unaffected by transformations wrought by industrialism and the problems presented by large urban areas. Aside from the maintenance of county poorhouses, the county had no functions in the administration of public welfare.

---

19. *Ibid.,* I, 97-98; II, 154; XX, 264.
20. *Ibid.,* I, 50.
21. *Ibid.,* III, 47.
22. *Ibid.,* XVIII, 70.
23. *Ibid.,* XXIII, 68-69.
24. *Ohio Const., 1802,* Art. III, secs., 3, 8.
25. *Ibid.,* Art. III, sec. 3.
26. *Ibid.,* Art. III, sec. 5; Pease, *op. cit.,* 9.
27. *Ohio Const., 1802,* Art. III, sec. 9.

As the wave of democratic philosophy swept across the country in the eighteen twenties and thirties there arose a demand not only for an extension for the franchise but also for the election of public officials. Accordingly the auditor became an elective official in 1821, the treasurer in 1827, the recorder in 1829, and the prosecuting attorney in 1833.[28]

While the legislature responded to the general demand for the election of county officials, there arose a further demand for a revision of the constitution which failed to meet the needs of an expanding state. This movement came as a result of dissatisfaction with the judicial system which placed the burden of judicial administration upon four judges who had the task of holding court each year in all the counties.[29] Then, too, there arose a demand for the election of all public officials, for the prohibition of charters that granted special privileges, and for a limitation on the power of the legislature to create a state debt. In February 1850 the legislature, following a favorable popular vote on the proposition, called for the election of delegates to meet in convention in May. The constitution drafted by the delegates, was approved by special election on June 17, 1851. The constitution of 1851, like the constitution of 1802, failed to provide a definite form of government and administration. Aside from the constitutional provision for the election of a county treasurer, sheriff, and clerk of courts and recreating the probate court which had existed during the territorial period, the organic instrument was silent on the administrative duties of the county.[30] Again all matters pertaining to county government were entrusted to the legislature. While the legislature conferred certain powers upon the county, it was limited by constitutional provision which required all laws of a general nature to be uniform throughout the state.[31]

---

28. *Laws of Ohio,* XIX, 116; XXV, 25-32; XXVII, 65; XXXI, 13-14.
29. J.V. Smith, rep., *Official Reports of the Debates and Proceedings of the Ohio State Convention . . . held at Columbus Commencing May 6, 1850, and at Cincinnati Commencing December 2, 1850,* 597 *et seq.* [Jacob] Burnet, *Notes on the Early Settlement of the North-Western Territory,* 356. See also the *Ohio State Journal,* December 11, 1840.
30. *Ohio Const. 1851,* Art. X, sec. 3; Art. IV, sec. 16; Art. IV, sec. 7.
31. *Ibid.,* Art. II, sec. 26.

The present administrative organization of Ohio county government presents a picture of extraordinary complexity. Each county quadrennially elects, besides the board of county commissioners, nine administrative officials: the recorder, the clerk of courts, the probate judge, the prosecuting attorney, the coroner, the sheriff, the treasurer, the auditor, and the county engineer. While these officials conduct a major portion of the country's business, there are a variety of appointive officers and boards, as well as ex-officio commissioners. For convenience the work the county government may be classified under the following general heads: administration, judicial system, law enforcement, finance and taxation, elections, health, public welfare, and public works.

Administration

The board of county commissioners is the central feature of the present structure of county government. The functions of this board touch either directly or indirectly every other branch and department. The board is the agency in whose name actions for and against the county are brought. This board is empowered to determine certain matters of policy for the conduct of county affairs such as adoption of the budget, establishment of services left optional by law, and the authorization of improvements.[32] Thus, in a limited sense it constitutes the legislative branch of the county. The commissioners however, have no ordinance-making powers. The board also functions as the central administrative body although much of the administration, centered in other elective offices, is beyond its immediate control. The county auditor was originally made secretary of the board and still functions as such in a majority of the counties.[33] Later provisions of the law permitted the board to appoint its own clerk, thus removing the duty from the auditor.

32. G. C. sec. 2421.
33. G. C. sec. 2566.

Judicial System

The constitution of 1851 made significant changes in the composition of the court of common pleas. The judges, heretofore appointed by the legislature, were made elective for a five-year term. For the purpose of electing judges the state was divided into nine districts. Each district was divided into three parts, in each of which one common pleas judge was to be elected. Court was to be held in every district or county with such jurisdiction as should be provided by law.[34] The legislature provided for the districts but left the jurisdiction of the court much as it had been in the earlier years of its existence.[35] The constitutional amendment of 1912 abolished the divisions and subdivisions provided by the constitution of 1851, and authorized the election of one or more common pleas judges in each county.[36]

The judicial system was extended in 1851 by the creation of district courts composed of one supreme court justice and several common pleas judges in each district.[37] For administrative purposes the nine common pleas districts were apportioned into five judicial circuits.[38] The courts were assigned original jurisdiction in the same matters as the supreme court and such appellate jurisdiction as might be provided by law.[39] The district courts, abolished by the constitutional amendment of 1883, were superseded by the circuit courts which were given the same jurisdiction as their predecessors. The state was divided into seven circuits. In each circuit three judges were to be elected.[40] The judicial system was again altered in 1912 when, by constitutional amendment, the circuits were renamed courts of appeals.[41] The state is divided into nine appellate districts. There are three judges in each district selected by the people of the district for a six-year term.[42]

---

34. *Ohio Const. 1851,* Art. IV, secs. 3, 4.
35. *Laws of Ohio,* LI, 145.
36. *Ohio Const. 1851,* (Amendment), Art. IV, sec. 3.
37. *Ohio Const. 1851,* Art. IV, sec. 5.
38. *Laws of Ohio,* L, 69.
39. *Ohio Const. 1851,* Art. IV, sec. 6.
40. *Ibid.,* Art. IV, sec. 6.
41. *Ibid.,* Art. IV. Sec. 6.
42. G. C. sec. 1514.

The constitution of 1851 re-created the probate court, which, existing during the territorial period, was abolished by the first constitution, its authority and jurisdiction being then vested in the courts of common pleas. Each county has one probate judge elected by the people for a four-year term.[43] By constitutional provision, the probate judge has original jurisdiction in probate and testamentary matters, the appointment of guardians, the settlement of the accounts of the executors, administrators, and guardians,[44] and the issuance of marriage licenses. An amendment to the constitution of 1912 authorized the common pleas judge, when petitioned by ten percent of the voters in counties having a population of less than sixty thousand, to submit to the voters at any general election the question of combining the probate and common pleas courts.[45] This combination exists in Adams, Henry, and Wyandot Counties.

Due to the increased amount of juvenile delinquency, the legislature, in 1904, authorized the judges of the court of common pleas, the probate court, and the superior and insolvency courts, where established, to appoint one of their members as juvenile judges to hear cases involving neglected, dependent, and delinquent children.[46] In Seneca County as in most Ohio counties the probate judge serves as judge of the juvenile court. In counties which have a court of domestic relations the judge of that court serves in this capacity.

Law enforcement

Closely related to the courts are the agencies of law enforcement in the county. Law enforcement is conducted by four officials: sheriff, prosecuting attorney, coroner, and dog warden. These officials are concerned primarily with the enforcement of state laws, and leave the enforcement of municipal ordinances, and, in some instances, of state statutes in urban centers to municipal law-enforcement agencies.

---

43. *Laws of Ohio,* CXIV, 32.
44. *Ohio Const. 1851,* Art. IV, sec. 8.
45. *Ibid.,* Art. IV, sec. 7.
46. *Laws of Ohio,* XCVII, 561-562.

The county sheriff, whose duties have been materially curbed by municipal law enforcement agencies and the state highway patrol, has as his duty the enforcement of state laws.[47] He serves as custodian of the county jail,[8] and as an executive agent of the court.[49] It has been estimated that approximately one-half of the sheriff's time is devoted to duties connected with the courts. The sheriff is restricted by lack of scientific equipment which has become essential to law enforcement.[50]

The county prosecuting attorney, the most important agent in the enforcement of criminal law, is directed by law to "inquire into the commission" of crime within his county, and to prosecute on behalf of the state all complaints, suits, and controversies to which the state is a party.[51] In conjunction with the state attorney general, he prosecutes in the supreme court cases arising in his county.[52] He acts also as legal counsel for the commissioners and other county officials.[53] The prosecuting attorney may institute proceedings against an individual, but as a rule charges must first be filed against the offender before action is taken. The prosecuting attorney has certain administrative duties such as serving as a member of the county budget commission and of the board of sinking fund trustees.[54]

---

47. G. C. sec. 2833. The sheriff's authority extends to all parts of the county, although for obvious practical purposes he rarely makes an arrest in incorporated areas.
48. G. C. sec. 3157.
49. G. C. sec. 2834.
50. *The Reorganization of County Government in Ohio*: *Report of the Governor's Commission on County Government,* 104. The sheriff system worked admirably in rural communities. From the standpoint of police administration, it is unsatisfactory in areas of dense population. In such areas there is need for a force of officers whose duty it is not merely to apprehend law violators but to prevent the infraction of the law by patrolling the territory. For an interesting discussion of some of the newer problems confronting law-enforcement agencies see Donald C. Stone, "The Police Attack Crime," *Nat. Mun. Review,* XXIV, (1935), 39-41.
51. G. C. sec. 2916.
52. G. C. sec. 2913.
53. G. C. sec. 2917.
54. *Laws of Ohio,* CXII, 399-400; CXV, pt. ii, 412; CXVI, 585; CVIII, pt. i, 700-702.

The county coroner has the ancient duty of determining the cause of death where death occurs under suspicious circumstances or by unlawful means,[55] the proper distribution of property found on or about the deceased,[56] and the management of the county morgue.[57] It has been suggested by authorities on county administration that the office be abolished and the duties transferred to a medical examiner appointed by the prosecuting attorney.[58]

Another law-enforcement agent existing within the county is the dog warden. This official is appointed by and is responsible to the county commissioners. No special qualifications are required for the office. The dog warden has as his duty the enforcement of sections of the General Code relative to the licensing of dogs, impounding and destruction of unlicensed dogs, and the payment of compensation for damages to livestock inflicted by dogs. The dog warden and his deputies, and in performance of their legal duties, have the same "police powers" as those conferred by statute upon sheriffs and police.[59] Prior to 1927 the duties now performed by the dog warden were performed by the county sheriff.[60]

Law enforcement in the county is defective in two respects: first, there is little or no co-ordination between the four agencies of law enforcement, and second, there is little or no responsibility for neglect of duty. Evidence seems to indicate that the present inefficient and antiquated system could be corrected by consolidating all law enforcement agencies into a county department of law enforcement under the immediate supervision of the county prosecuting attorney.[61]

The administration of criminal justice in the county has grown up in more or less hit-or-miss fashion and is for the most part unsatisfactory and extremely cumbersome.

---

55. G. C. sec. 2856.
56. G. C. secs. 2863, 2864.
57. G. C. sec. 2851-1.
58. W.F. Willoughby, *Principles of Judicial Administration,* 165-173. According to a recent act, effective June 8, 1937, only a licensed physician or a person who shall have previously served as coroner is eligible to fill the office. G. C. sec. 2856-3.
59. *Laws of Ohio,* CVIII, pt. I, 535; CXII, 348; G. C. sec. 5652-7.
60. *Laws of Ohio,* CVII, 535.
61. *Report of the Governor's Commission,* 117-122.

Arrests are made by the sheriff, or other police officers, who is theoretically an officer of the state, but who is under little or no supervision. The accused person is brought before a local magistrate for a preliminary hearing. In the event the accused is committed, it is necessary, in most cases, to receive an indictment before a grand jury.[62]

Finance and Taxation

There are three types of financial functions performed by county officers: tax administration, handling of the fiscal affairs of the county, and the trusteeship of funds held for individuals in court procedure. The principal financial authorities are the board of commissioners, the auditor, and the treasurer. The commissioners levy taxes, appropriate funds, and authorize payments.[63] The auditor's primary duties are keeping of accounts, issuance of warrants, valuation of real estate, and preparation of the tax list.[64] The treasurer collects taxes, receives and has custody of county money, and disburses it upon warrant from the auditor.[65] Other functions relating to county finance are performed by the board of revision, budget commissioners, and board of sinking fund trustees.

During the early years of Ohio history, the principal sources of state and county revenue were the general property tax, the poll tax, and the fees received from licenses and permits to engage in certain kinds of business.[66]

A tax law enacted by the first territorial legislature (1799) designated certain types of property as taxable for county purposes. All houses in towns, town lots, out-lots, all water and wind mills, ferries, cattle and horses, were put on the county duplicate.

---

62. For a criticism of the administration of criminal justice, see Edwin H. Sutherland, *Principles of Criminology,* chap., comp., xiv; Willoughby, *op. cit.,* chaps. xi, xiv, xxxvi.
63. G. C. secs. 5630, 5637, 7419.
64. G. C. secs. 2570, 2573, 2583-2589.
65. G. C. secs. 2649, 2649-1, 2656, 2674.
66. An act of 1825 levied a tax on the income of attorneys, physicians, and surgeons for state purposes. Amount of tax was determined by the court of common pleas. Salmon P. Chase, comp., *The Statutes of Ohio and of the Northwest Territory, 1788-1883,* 1471. This act was repealed in 1852, Maskell E. Curwen, comp., *Public Statutes at Large of the State of Ohio,* 1755. The poll tax was perpetually abolished by constitutional authority in 1802. *Ohio Const. 1802,* Art. VIII, sec. 23.

A tax on land subsequently used also for county purposes, was originally devoted exclusively to the needs of the territorial government. County officials were to assist in the administration of this tax as well as that of the county levy.[67]

In the course of time many additions were made to the original list of taxables. Taxable property came to include capital employed in merchandising (1826), exchange brokers (1825), pleasure carriages (1825), money loaned at interest (1831), and stock in steamboats.[68] In the latter year dividends of bank, insurance, and bridge companies were also made taxable.[69] The first act of a general nature directing the taxation of railroads was passed in 1851.[70] In 1862 a tax on the gross receipts of express and telegraph companies was enacted.[71] A levy on capital stock of freight lines was authorized in 1896.[72] Subsequent enactments brought into the category of "general property" the possessions of public utilities in general. By such accumulations "property," by the end of the nineteenth century, had become a much more inclusive term than it had been one hundred years earlier.

County agencies became even more useful with the discovery of new tax sources. When, at the turn into the twentieth century, the general property tax lost its importance as a revenue source for the state, taxes on inheritance and cigarettes, then, later, on gasoline, liquid fuel, liquor, retail sales, malt and the like, took its place.[73] County officials continued to administer the general property tax, which was devoted henceforth to the uses of local governments, but they assisted in the administration of a number of those newer taxes as well.

The assistance rendered by county officials has been equally extensive in the system of issuing licenses and permits. The issuance of marriage licenses began during the territorial period (1788).[74] An act to license merchants, traders, and tavern keepers was passed in 1792.[75] Ferry licenses were authorized in 1799.[76]

---

67. Chase, *op. cit.*, 267-279. Previous acts of 1792 and 1795 were temporary in nature.
68. Chase, *op. cit.*, III, 1517, 1476; *Laws of Ohio,* XXIX, 272-280.
69. *Laws of Ohio,* XXIX, 302-303.
70. Curwen, *op. cit.*, 1647.
71. J.R. Sayler, comp. *The Statutes of the State of Ohio,* 301.
72. *Laws of Ohio,* XCII, 89-93.
73. Ohio Tax Commission, *Financing State and Local Government in Ohio, 1900-1932,* 2.
74. Chase, *op. cit.*, I, 101.
75. Chase, *op. cit.*, I, 114-115.
76. Chase, *op. cit.*, I, 219.

With the passage of time one license after another has been required until unlicensed businesses have become something of an exception rather than the rule. Even with the increasing assumption of licensing authority by the state, county officials had continued to issue certain licenses assigned to the jurisdiction long ago.[77]

Under the territorial law of 1792 tax commissioners, appointed to annual terms by the courts of common pleas, were to list the male inhabitants above the age of eighteen, stocks of cattle, yearly value of improved land, and other property. Valuation of this property was made by township and village assessors, appointed annually by the court of common pleas.[78] These local assessors, who became elective in 1795, were again appointed in 1799.[79] In 1825 property valuation was assigned to a new official, the county assessor, also appointed by the court of common pleas.[80] This official, became elective in 1827, was succeeded in turn, in 1841, by township assessors to be elected annually.[81]

In conjunction with these administrators a system of real estate reappraisal was initiated. In 1846 county commissioners were directed to divide their counties into suitable districts and to appoint an assessor for each whose chief function should be to revise the valuation of real property.[82] An act of 1863 made these officers elective and provided for reappraisal every tenth year.[83] This was subsequently changed (1868) to every fifth year and in 1878 returned to the ten-year interval.[84]

In 1913 the assistance of county officers in tax administration was temporarily dispensed with and their duties were given to state officials. The county was again made an entire assessment district but district (or county) assessors were now to be appointed by the governor. The tax commission (established in 1910) was directed to supervise and direct the assessment of real and personal property.[85]

---

77. See pp. 34-35, 110, 129, 154, 207-208.
78. *Laws of the Territory of the United States Northwest of the Ohio River,* II, 17-18.
79. Chase, *op. cit.,* I, 169, 273.
80. Chase, *op. cit.,* II, 1477.
81. Curwen, *op. cit.,* 775-779.
82. Curwen, *op. cit.,* 1269.
83. Sayler, *op. cit.,* 413.
84. Sayler, *op. cit.,* 1641; *Laws of Ohio,* LXXV, 459.
85. *Laws of Ohio,* CIII, 786-787.

This attempt at unification of authority in the state was partially abandoned, however, in 1915, when assessment was returned to the county auditor and to elected township, village, and ward assessors.[86] In 1925 the latter officers were discontinued and the duties of assessment devolved upon the county auditor alone.[87]

The advent of the state tax commission brought no great alteration in the process of assessment. The county remains the basic unit and the county auditor continues to serve as an agent of the state. Though the state commission now assesses certain forms of property, certification is made to the county auditor. For example, public utilities are now assessed by the commission and proportional shares of the revenue are apportioned to the counties which contains such property.[88] Financial institutions report directly to the commission which certifies to each county auditor the assessment of each taxable deposit.[89] Intangible property (defined in 1931) owned by individuals and corporations, not otherwise accepted, is listed and valued by the county auditor. Returns showing more than $500 of taxable income are forwarded to the commission for appraisal and certified by it back to the county auditor.[90] From these certifications of the commission, the personal property list returned to him by individuals, and the real estate assessment for which he is personally responsible, the auditor makes up the grand duplicate of real and personal property taxes.

The county continues to be the basic unit also in the matter of budgeting and the levying of taxes on property. In 1792 the courts of general quarter sessions were directed to estimate the sums needed to defray the cost of county government, specifying as nearly as possible the purpose for which such sums were necessary. This earliest of budgets was to be laid before the governor and judges and approved by the legislature. Special commissioners were to apportion or levy the tax.[91]

---

86. *Ibid.*, CVI, 246 *et seq.*
87. *Ibid.*, CXI, 486-487. Revaluation of real estate was required in 1925 and every sixth year thereafter.
88. G. C. sec. 5430.
89. G. C. secs. 5412, 5412-1.
90. *Report of the Governor's Commission,* 75.
91. Chase, *op. cit.*, I, 118-119.

In 1799 it became the duty of these commissioners to ascertain the probable expense of the county as well as levy the tax–a duty which continued until refinements in administration were made necessary because of the increasing number of taxing authorities.[92]

In order to achieve some systematic arrangement in the county fiscal system, the function of estimating expenses, or budgeting, was consolidated in recent years in the hands of a county budget commission. Since the Ohio legislature, in 1911, established a tax rate limitation, it was necessary to establish a commission vested with authority to reduce the amounts set up in the annual tax budgets when the overlapping districts required more than the aggregate maximum tax rate permits.[93] Organized in 1911 the county budget commission was composed, for a time, of the auditor, the mayor of the largest municipality, and the prosecuting attorney. Taxing authorities in the county were directed to submit their budgets to this body through the agency of the auditor.[94] The board was authorized to make adjustments in the budgets, alterations which the taxing authority might appeal to the tax commission. The budget commission, directed in 1911 to certify its action to the auditor, was subsequently instructed to make such certification to the various taxing units which should themselves authorize the necessary tax levies and certify them to the auditor.[95] In 1927 the composition of this board was altered when the county treasurer replaced the mayor.[98]

Early appeals against unjust assessments (1792) were heard by judges of the general territorial court, judges of the common pleas court, or justices of the general quarter sessions court.[97] After 1795 petitions for redress were directed to the tax commissioners.[98] This appeal agency was superseded in 1825 by the board of equalization, composed of the commissioners, the assessors, and the auditor.[99]

---

92. Chase, *op. cit.,* I, 276-277.
93. G. C. sec. 5625-3. Search 1934 there has been a limitation of ten mills on the dollar. G. C. sec. 5625-2.
94. *Laws of Ohio,* CII, 270-272.
95. G. C. sec. 5625-25.
96. *Laws of Ohio,* CXII, 399.
97. *Laws of the Territory . . . Northwest of the River Ohio,* II, 20-21.
98. Chase, *op. cit.,* I, 171.
99. Chase, *op. cit.,* II, 1476-92.

This agency continued to function through the following years with occasional changes in ex-officio members.[100]

With the reorganization of property tax administration in 1913 the function of tax revision was taken away from the county officers. In each district (county) the tax commission was directed to appoint three persons for the term of three years to form a district board of complaints.[101] An act of 1915 abolished this plan, however, and returned the function of revision to the care of county officials. A board composed of the treasurer, the prosecuting attorney, the probate judge, and the president of the board of county commissioners, was directed to appoint a county board of equalization.[102] This plan, too, was soon dispensed with. An act of 1917 constituted the treasurer, auditor, and president of the board of commissioners as the county board of revision.[103]

The history of tax collection is equally intricate. The fiscal duties of the county treasurer, who now collects the property tax, comprised, in the very early period, only the receipt and custody of revenue funds. The actual collection was performed by other agencies. Due to the fact that in earlier years there were two district tax levies–one on land for territory and later the state, and one on other property for county purposes–tax collections involved a double operation and duplicate officials.

The collectors accounting levy assessed in 1792 were appointed by the judges of the court of common pleas who were empowered to designate the sheriff, constable, or any other suitable person to perform this function.[104] By provisions of an act of 1795 township collectors were appointed by tax commissioners and assessors.[105]

---

100. The county surveyor became a member at times, in 1868, for example Sayler, *op. cit.,* 1642.
101. *Laws of Ohio,* CIII, 790-791.
102. *Ibid.,* CVI, 254-255.
103. *Ibid.,* CVII, 40; G. C. secs. 5580, 5596. See also pp. 242-244. Highest appellate jurisdiction, held originally by the general court and later (1805) by the associate judges of common pleas, was given, in 1825, to a state board of equalization composed of the state auditor and one member from each congressional district. With the establishment of the state tax commission that agency was made the final appeal. *Laws of Ohio,* III, 111; Chase, *op. cit.,* 1481; Curwen, *op. cit.,* 1784; G. C. sec. 5625-28.
104. Chase, *op. cit.,* I, 119.
105. Chase, *op. cit.,* I, 171.

From 1799 to 1805 taxes for county purposes were collected by county collectors.[106] An act of 1805 designated the township listers as collectors of the county levy but, in 1806, the commissioners were permitted to appoint a county collector instead if they believed such a course to be expedient.[107]

The first statute of a general nature providing for a tax on land for territorial purposes was enacted in 1799. From 1799 to 1803 the collectors of county tax were to collect the territorial tax also.[108] In 1804, however, the county sheriff was specifically designated as the collector of the state tax.[109] From 1806 to 1816 the county commissioners were again permitted to use their own discretion as to whether a county or township collector should be appointed.[110] The county collector of the land tax mentioned in the statutes from 1816 to 1825 was, in all probability, the same official who collected the county tax, though due to a lack of definite terminology it is impossible to be certain.[111]

In 1825 the arrangement for a separate tax duplicate for state and county purposes was abolished and levies for both were made on the same property. In 1827 the office of county collector, who has performed that function in the intervening two years, was abolished and the treasurer, henceforth to be an elective officer, was given the duty of tax collection.[112]

The collection of certain taxes other than that on general property is performed by county agency. Thus, for example, the inheritance taxes, authorized by the legislature in 1894, are computed by the county auditor, adjusted by the probate court, collected by the county treasurer, and distributed to the proper agency by the county auditor.[113] County auditors certify to the tax commission lists of persons licensed to engage in the business of selling cigarettes. County treasurers are the agents of the state treasurer for the sale of cigarette tax stamps.[114]

---

106. Chase, *op. cit.,* I, 277.
107. Chase, *op. cit.,* I, 471, 527; II, 771, 1384-85.
108. Chase, *op. cit.,* I, 270.
109. Chase, *op. cit.,* I, 415.
110. Chase, *op. cit.,* I, 537, 727; II, 973.
111. Chase, op. cit., II, 973, 1370-71.
112. *Laws of Ohio,* XXV, 25.
113. G. C. secs. 5338, 5341, 5348-11.
114. G. C. sec. 5894-1 *et seq.*

The tax on wines, cordials, and beer is collected by means of the sale of stamps by county treasurers in a manner similar to that employed in collecting the cigarette tax.[115] The tax on brewers' wort and malt is collected in an identical manner.[116]

The dispersal of administrative functions among county agencies is demonstrated more effectively, perhaps, in the issuance of licenses and permits which furnish a source of revenue for both the state and the county. The county auditor has issued, collected, and accounted for dog licenses from 1917 to the present;[117] he has issued and the treasurer has collected the fees from cigarettes (1893—),[118] malt (1933—),[119] peddlers' (1862—),[120] and show licenses (1827—).[121] Hunting and fishing licenses have been issued by the clerk of courts since 1904 and 1919 respectively.[122] In addition, the clerk has issued for the court of common pleas ferry licenses (1805—),[123] auctioneers' licenses (1818—),[124] and peddler's licenses (1810-1862).[125] Marriage licenses, issued from 1803 to 1851 by the clerk of courts, since the latter date, have been in the jurisdiction of the probate court.[126]

The establishment of a board of trustees of the sinking fund (1919) was a logical development in the county fiscal administration. This board, composed of the auditor, treasurer, and prosecuting attorney, has as its principal function the payment of bonds issued by the county and the investment in bonds of moneys credited to the sinking fund.

---

115. G. C. sec. 6064-42.
116. G. C. sec. 5545 *et seq.*
117. *Laws of Ohio,* CVII, 534.
118. Jay F. Laning, comp., *Revised Statutes of the State of Ohio,* 1513.
119. G. C. sec. 5545-5 *et seq.*
120. Sayler, *op. cit.,* 273; G. C. sec. 6349.
121. Chase, *op. cit.,* III, 1582; G. C. secs. 6374, 6375.
122. *Laws of Ohio,* XCVII, 474; G. C. (Page and Adams) sec. 1430.
123. *Laws of Ohio,* III, 96; VIII, 107; XXIX, 447. Ferry licenses were issued by associate judges, 1803-1805. *Ibid.,* I, 94.
124. Chase, *op. cit.,* II, 1040; G. C. secs. 5864, 5869.
125. Chase, *op. cit.,* I, 670.
126. Chase, *op. cit.,* I, 354; *Ohio Const., 1851,* Art. IV, sec. 8.

Bonds issued in the process of county borrowing must be recorded in the office of the sinking fund trustees and signed by the auditor, as secretary of the board. The trustees certified to the board of commissioners the rate of tax necessary to provide a sinking fund for the payment of the principal and interest of the bonded indebtedness. The trustees are required to keep a full and complete record of transactions and a complete record of the funded debt of the county.[127]

Elections

During the first nine decades of Ohio history the county sheriff was charged with the duty of announcing the time and place of holding elections, providing ballot boxes, ballots, and other supplies, and the township trustees were directed by law to serve as judges of the elections.[128] This system continued, with slight alterations designed to facilitate the conduct of elections in municipal centers until 1892. At that time there were created the offices of the state supervisor of elections and deputy state supervisors of elections with duties prescribed for the conduct and supervision of all elections in the state.[129] The secretary of state, designated as the state supervisor of elections, was authorized and instructed to appoint four deputy supervisors for each county, who, in turn, appointed in all precincts four judges and two clerks of elections.[130]

Under the present election laws, provision is made for a chief election officer, a board of elections in each county, and judges and clerks in each precinct. The board of elections in each county consists of four qualified electors in the county, the members of which are appointed by the secretary of state, two of such members being appointed on the first day of March in the even-numbered years to serve a four-year term.[131]

---

127. G. C. sec. 2976-18 *et seq.*
128. *Laws of Ohio,* I, 76-77; III, 331-332; VII, 113; XXIX, 44; L, 312; LXVIII, 68. See also pp. 198, 248.
129. *Ibid.,* LXXXIX, 455. This act, however, did not apply to the election of school directors.
130. In 1870 each township, exclusive of the territory embraced within the limits of a municipal corporation which was divided into wards, composed an election precinct. See *Laws of Ohio,* LXVII, 47. An act of 1891 provided for the division of precincts in which 500 or more voters had been polled. *Ibid.,* LXXXVIII, 464.
131. G. C. secs. 4785-6, 4785-8. See also p. 248 *et seq.*

In making appointments to the membership of the board, equal representation is given to the political party polling the highest and next highest number of votes for the office of governor in the last preceding state election. In this connection provision is made for party recommendations of persons for such appointments.[132]

Under the early election law the canvassing board was composed of the clerk of the court of common pleas and two justices of the peace called by him to his assistance.[133] The practice continued until 1892 when the board of state supervisors of elections succeeded to the duties formally performed by both the clerk of the court of common pleas and the county sheriff. The sheriff, however, continued to announce the time and place of holding elections in the county until January 1, 1930 when the board of elections assumed this historic duty.[134] The duty of canvassing the returns, under the present statutes, is performed by the board of elections. The board in each county is required, within five days after each general or special election, to canvas the returns, and to prepare abstracts of the votes cast.[135] A certified copy of the abstract is to be transmitted to the secretary of state, and another copy filed in the office of the board.[136] The board is required also to prepare and transmit to the president of the senate a separate abstract of the returns of election of governor, lieutenant governor, secretary of state, auditor of state, and attorney general.[137]

---

132. G. C. sec. 4785-9. Under the Ohio election law, it is the duty of the secretary of state to appoint persons so recommended, unless he has reason to believe that such a person would not be a competent member of the board.

133. *Laws of Ohio,* I, 83; III, 336-337; VII, 119-120; XXIX, 49; L, 316; LXI, 68; LXXXII, 30.

134. G. C. sec. 4785-5; *Laws of Ohio,* LXXXIX, 455; CXIII, 307. The election laws of Ohio were revised and recodified by an act of the general assembly, passed April 5, 1929. *Laws of Ohio,* CXIII, 307-413.

135. G. C. secs. 4785-152, 4785-153.

136. G. C. sec. 4785-153.3

137. *Ohio Const. 1851,* Art. III, sec. 3; G. C. sec. 4785-154.

Health

Prior to 1919 the county had few responsibilities regarding health administration. With the development of urban centers with congested areas the problem of health administration was brought to the attention of the legislature. Prior to the enactment of the present health code in 1919, jurisdiction in matters of health was vested in the city's villages and townships. Under the act of 1919 all villages and townships in the county were combined into a general health district under the supervision of a board appointed by the advisory council composed of the mayors of villages, and chairman of township trustees. Each city in the district is organized as a separate health district. Two general health districts or a general health district and the city health district located within such a district may combine.[138] All physicians are required to report communicable diseases to the district health commissioners who impose quarantines.[139]

The legislature has placed on the county the burden of responsibility in the treatment of tuberculosis. Any county, regardless of its size, may employ nurses, operate clinics, and care for patients in private, municipal, or county sanatoriums. Any county having a population of 50,000 or more inhabitants may with the consent of the state department of health, erect and operate sanatoriums, and two or more counties may form districts for the same purpose. The sanatoriums are operated by special boards appointed by the county commissioners.[140]

Besides establishing sanatoriums for the treatment of tubercular patients counties are authorized to operate general hospitals. The county hospital is operated by a board appointed by the county commissioners.[141] Evidence seems to indicate that the county is a proper unit for hospital administration.

---

138. *Laws of Ohio,* CVIII, pt. I, 238; CVIII, pt. ii, 1085-86.
139. *Ibid.,* CVIII, pt. ii, 1088-89.
140. G. C. secs. 3148-1, 3148-3. See p. 221.
141. G. C. secs. 3127-3138-4.

Public Welfare

The administration of public welfare is one of the most complex and one of the most expensive functions of county government. The administration of institutional and outdoor relief is delegated to eight boards and commissions operating independently and with little regard for efficiency.

The administration of the county home is vested in the county commissioners and a superintendent appointed from a list of names of persons eligible under civil service regulations. Employees are appointed by the superintendent.[142]

Although provision was made for the institutional care of the county's indigent as early as 1816, it was not until after the conclusion of the War between the States when hundreds of Ohio children were left homeless, that the legislature enacted measures for the care of dependent children.[143] Prior to the act of 1865, the trustees of the poorhouses were authorized to apprentice dependent children. The administration of the children's home is vested in a board of trustees, appointed by the commissioners, and a superintendent appointed by the board of trustees.[144]

The board of county visitors, an agency for the examination of county institutions, was created by the general assembly in 1882. Until 1906 the board was appointed by the court of common pleas and after that date by the probate judge.[145] The board consists of six persons appointed for a term of three years.

In 1886 counties were required by law to provide relief for indigent soldiers and sailors and their indigent wives, children, and parents.[146] Soldiers' relief is administered by a commission consisting of three persons appointed by the court of common pleas for terms of three years. This commission, in turn, selects township and ward committees.[147]

In 1884 the legislature made provision for soldiers' burial committees in each county.[148]

---

142. G. C. secs. 2522, 2523.
143. *Laws of Ohio,* III, 276; VIII, 223-224.
144. G. C. secs. 3081, 3084.
145. *Laws of Ohio,* LXXIX, 107; G. C. secs. 3082-1, 3085; XCVIII, 28.
146. *Laws of Ohio,* LXXXIII, 232-234.
147. G. C. secs. 2930, 2933.
148. *Laws of Ohio,* LXXXI, 146-147.

The administration of soldiers' burials is vested in committees consisting of two persons in each township and ward appointed by the county commissioners.[149]

Counties maintain a system of pensions for the needy blind. Prior to 1936 blind relief was administered in the county by the probate judge (1904-1908), by a blind relief commission appointed by the probate judge (1908-1913), and by the county commissioners (1913-1936).[150] The present system originated in 1936 when the legislature accepted the provisions of the Federal Social Security Act. Blind relief is financed by federal, state, and local funds and is administered in the state by the Ohio commission for blind and in the county by the county commissioners, whose decisions are subject to review by the Ohio commission for the blind.[151]

Prior to 1932 the county confined its relief activities to the institutional care of the indigent. Outdoor relief, except for those persons lacking a legal settlement, was provided and administered by the townships and cities. With the coming of the economic depression the resources of the municipalities and township proved inadequate for financing relief activities. Accordingly, in 1932, the legislature conferred on all counties the authority to care for the poor in their own homes. Funds for such purposes were provided by the issuance of bonds and by a diversion of gasoline taxes for financing such services. While the state relief commission, created for administering state relief, is required to pass upon local relief budgets, the county relief offices, administered by the county commissioners, provide relief services in the county.

Today old age pensions are relieving the counties of the increased burdens of institutional relief. This system, originating in 1933, provides for persons sixty-five or more years of age. No person may be granted a pension if the net value of his property is in excess of $3,000 or his annual income is in excess of $480.[152] The old age pension system is financed by state and federal funds and is administered by a division of the department of public welfare through county boards of aid for the aged.[153]

---

149. G. C. sec. 2950.
150. *Laws of Ohio,* XCVII, 392-394; XCIV, 56-58; CIII, 60.
151. *Ibid.,* XVIV, pt. ii, 195-200. See also pp. 3-4, 106, 260.
152. *Laws of Ohio,* CXV, pt. ii, 431-439; CXVI, pt. ii, 86-88, 216-221; G. C. sec. 1359-2.
153. *Laws of Ohio,* CXV, pt. ii, 431-439.

Under the provision of the initial act the county commissioners served as ex-officio members of the board of aid for the aged in the county. Since May 1, 1937, the chief of the division has been required by law to appoint an advisory board in each county consisting of five members. This board, appointed for a two-year term, succeeded to the duties formerly performed by the county commissioners.[154]

Aid to dependent children, although provided by the legislature in 1913 in the form of mothers' pensions, assumed a new significance, when, in 1936, the legislature accepted the provisions of the Federal Social Security Act. Aid to dependent children is financed by federal, state, and local funds. The administration of the act in the state is delegated to the department of public welfare and in Seneca County to the probate judge serving as juvenile judge.[155]

Public Works

The responsibility for the administration of public works in the county rests with the board of county commissioners, the county engineer, and the sanitary engineer. The county commissioners, since the inauguration of county government, have had the responsibility with authorization and financing of public works. With the immense development of highway improvements, occasioned by the introduction of automobiles and trucks as means of transportation, public works became one of the most important functions of the county commissioners and consequently the county engineer, who, during the first one hundred and twenty years of his office, had as his principal duty the surveying of lands, received new duties and responsibilities with respect to the construction of roads, culverts, ditches, and in most cases bridges.[156] Within the last two decades the township roads, under the joint authority of the county and the township trustees, have been gradually absorbed by the county state system of highways.[157]

---

154. G. C. sec. 1359-12. See also pp. 7, 262-263
155. *Laws of Ohio,* CXVI, pt. ii, 188-196.
156. *Laws of Ohio,* XCVIII, 245-247; CVIII, pt. I, 497.
157. The centralization of highway construction was guaranteed under the road law of 1915. The township trustees, at one time one of the most important agencies in local highway construction, have become a local improvement board with powers to authorize but not to supervise road construction. *Laws of Ohio,* CV, 589-594.

The Ohio counties were formed to meet the needs of rural pioneer communities with a population spread relatively uniformly over the entire state. Recent decades have brought remarkable changes. Many sections of the state have become thoroughly industrialized, and, as a result of the change, have been forced to treat of such problems as housing, health, sanitation, police administration, scientific transportation, and sewage disposal. These problems with which the county organization has been unable to cope are rapidly taking the forms of city problems.

The census of 1940 shows that of the 1,217,250 persons in Cuyahoga County 878,336 were in Cleveland, of the 388,712 people in Franklin County 306,087 were in Columbus, of the 621,978 people in Hamilton County 45,610 were in Cincinnati, and that of the 344,333 people in Lucas County 282,349 were in Toledo. It is not strange therefore that demands were made for a reorganization of county government to eliminate the waste and confusion occasioned by overlapping jurisdiction of county and municipal function.[158]

In view of the growth of large cities and the confusion occasioned by the conflict of county and municipal powers, there has been an attempt to work out a more satisfactory relationship between the two organs of local government. This took the form of a constitutional amendment, which, defeated in 1919, was placed on the ballot in 1933 by initiative petition and adopted by the electorate. The amendment provides:

> "The general assembly shall provide by general law for the organization and government of counties, and may provide by general law–alternative form of county government. No alternative form shall become operative in any county until submitted to the electors therefore and approved by a majority of those voting thereon under regulations provided by law. Municipalities and townships shall have authority, with the consent of the county, to transfer to the county any of their powers or to revoke the transfer of any such power, under regulations provided by general law, but the rights of initiative and referendum shall be secured to . . . every measure . . . giving or withdrawing such consent."[159]

---

158. *Sixteenth Census of the United States, Population of the State of Ohio Final Figures: 1940,* Series P-2, No. 41, P-1. C.A. Dykstra "Cleveland's Effort for City-County consolidation," *Nat. Mun. Review,* VIII (1919), 551-556.

159. *Ohio Const. 1851,* (Amendment, adopted November 7, 1933), Art. X, sec. 1.

The constitutional amendment of 1933 altered the status of the county. Where the status of the county was formerly fixed by statute, it is now subject to local determination in the same manner as municipalities.

The arguments advanced in favor of the system fall under three heads;

1. It makes possible a different form of government for urban centers where political, social, and economic conditions differ from those of rural counties.
2. It promotes efficiency and economy by the elimination of duplicate officers and employees.
3. It promotes efficiency by the centralization of power and responsibility.[160]

A commission on county government was appointed by Governor White in 1933 to formulate optional plans by county government for submission to the legislature.[161] Accordingly, in 1935, the commission submitted to the legislature ten bills embodying its recommendation as to matters of county reorganization. The major bills authorized three optional forms of county government, subject to adoption by local electorate: (1) a county manager plan, (2) the elective plan, (3) the appointed executive plan.[162] Of the ten bills presented, two became laws. One of these authorized the transfer to the county of any local governmental activity by voluntary agreement between the county and a local subdivision within the county. This measure, of course, opened the way for the consolidation of such activities as welfare, police, and sewer construction which need unification in counties having a large urban population.[163] The other act authorized the charter county to take over health administration, noninstitutional relief, and park construction.[164]

---

160. *The Ohio State Journal,* (Amendment, adopted November 7, 1933), Art. X, sec. 1.
161. R.C. Atkinson, "County Home Rule Developments in Ohio," *Nat. Mun. Review,* XXIII (1934), 235.
162. R.C. Atkinson, "Ohio– Optional County Legislation, *Nat. Mun. Review,* XXIV (1935), 288.
163. *Laws of Ohio,* CXVI, 102-104.
164. *Ibid.,* CXVI, 132-135.

While the amendment offers an opportunity for the improvement of local government in counties in which large municipalities have developed, no use has been made of the provision.[165] At present Franklin County with a population of 361,055 has essentially the same type of county government as Vinton County with the population of 10,287.[166]

While unsuccessful attempts have been made to correct some of the defects of county administration in areas containing large urban populations, little consideration has been given to rural counties where, due to a constant decline in population, the old governmental organization has become unduly expensive and ill-suited to the needs of the population. This is particularly true in the counties located in the southeastern and northwestern portions of the state where the population has steadily declined since 1880. There is a question as to whether the services of modern government in such counties can continue to be maintained without the consolidation of continuous territory for purposes of administration. The Ohio Constitution, from its beginning in 1802, has contained a restriction upon the legislature regarding the minimum area of counties. None could be formed with less than 400 square miles–or reduced below that size.[167] With the development of modern means of transportation and communication this area is ridiculously small. The combination of administrative purposes by sparsely populated counties, having common social and economic interests would eliminate waste, overhead, and duplication of personnel.

Governmental service is constantly requiring the employment of better trained officials. Evidence seems to indicate that only by enlarging the size of the administrative area to make possible the specialization in work can the requisite degree of training and skill be secured in the performance of public service.[168]

---

165. Home rule charters were submitted to the voters in Hamilton, Cuyahoga, Lucas, and Mahoning Counties. Advocates of home rule attributed the defeat of these measures to politicians who saw in the scheme the destruction of the spoils system. See R.C. Atkinson, "Ohio– County Charter Elections," *Nat. Mun. Review,* XXIV (1935), 702-703.

166. *Fifteenth Census of the United States, 1930, Population,* III, pt. ii, 520, 531.

167. *Ohio Const. 1802,* Art. VII, sec. 3; *Ohio Const. 1851,* Art. II, sec. 30.

168. Cf. H. Eliot Kaplan, "A Personal Program for County Service," *Nat. Mun. Review,* XXV (1936), 596-600

The relation of the county to the state is also a matter of importance. As a result of radical changes in economic life, matters which were at one time a purely local interest and concern have become of state-wide importance. During recent years the old type of county organization has proven inadequate to meet the needs of modern civilization. Recognition of this fact is found in a steady growth of state control of such matters as public accounting, health and welfare administration, and law enforcement.

At the same time the county has definitely supplanted the township as the administrative unit. This is particularly noticeable in the substitution of the general health district for the township district, and the transfer of tax assessment from the township assessors to the county auditor. The county-state administration of highway maintenance and public welfare has been affected. Although many deplore the passing of the little red schoolhouse, the substitution of the county school district for the township area has resulted in better educational advantages for children residing in rural areas.

It is significant that modern invention has removed the necessity for the role of administrative units of such small proportions. The transfer of power from the smaller to the larger unit has arisen out of the desire for better service and economy.

Records System

It has been the duty of most officials since the beginning of county government to keep a record of the business of their offices. Differences in population between counties however, forced a wide variance and the recording as evidenced by the fact that several types of records were kept in the same book in some counties, and in others were kept in separate books. As indicated in detail in the office essays, preceding the records of each office, the legislature eventually prescribed not only what records were to be kept but also the content. In this field there was a remarkable advance following the adoption of the constitution of 1851. Such legislation assured some uniformity in the county records' system.

There are three county officials whose work is clerical, consisting mainly in the preparation and custody of records: the recorder, the clerk of courts, and the judge of probate court. They each have some part in the recording of instruments affecting the title of property and of other documents presented for records.

The clerk of courts serves as clerk of both the court of common pleas and the court of appeals, and the probate judge cares for the records of his court.

It is the duty of the county recorder to copy, index, and file documents authorized to be recorded in his office. The system of recording is prescribed in detail by law. In most counties recording is done by typewriter with considerable use of printed forms. The photographic method of copying is in use in Clark, Hamilton, Lucas, Montgomery, and Summit Counties. Deeds, mortgages, plats, and leases must be copied into separate books, and indexed by direct and reverse indexes.[169] The recorder is required, also, to prepare daily an alphabetical index to such instruments.[170]

The principal records of the clerk of courts are prescribed by statute. They include an appearance docket, trial docket, execution docket, journal, and a complete record of proceedings, a system of indexes, and a file of original papers.[171] The clerk is responsible for a variety of non-judicial records work of which the filing and indexing of automobiles bills of sale was a major item. The bill of sale law was repealed by an act effective January 1, 1938, requiring the clerk to issue certificates of title to motor vehicles in triplicate and to file a duplicate of the certificate.[172]

At present the clerk of courts may act as the agent of the state for the sale of hunting, and fishing licenses.[173] He also issues auctioneers' and ferry licenses.[174]

The clerical office of the probate court performs the following services: the recording of miscellaneous instruments, including marriage licenses[175] and certificates of physicians, surgeons, and nurses which authorize them to practice their professions in the state.[176] The court record system of the office, originating in 1853 and continued by the probate code of 1931, is prescribed by statute and involves the proper keeping of papers in each case and copying materials in appropriate record books.[177]

---

169. G. C. secs. 2757, 2764.
170. G. C. secs. 2764, 2766.
171. G. C. secs. 2878, 2884, 2885.
172. G. C. sec. 6290-6.
173. G. C. sec. 1432.
174. G. C. secs. 5868-5869, 5947-5950.
175. *Ohio Const. 1851,* Art. IV, sec. 8.
176. *Laws of Ohio,* XCII, 45-47; XCIX, 499; CVI, 193.
177. *Ibid.,* CXIV, 321-322.

Few records are prescribed for the law-enforcement agencies. The county sheriff is required by law to keep at least three books: foreign execution docket,[178] cashbook,[179] and jail register.[180] Indexes, direct and reverse, to the foreign execution docket were prescribed in 1925.[181] The system of recording is prescribed by statute. The county coroner's records consist of two: reports of findings in cases of unlawful death,[182] and an inventory of articles found on or about the body of the deceased.[183] Such records are required by law and the contents of the records minutely prescribed.

The number and type of records kept by county prosecuting attorneys vary widely. In some counties the records of the prosecuting attorney are kept on standard forms and include such records as a grand jury docket, a grand jury testimony record, and a criminal court docket. In Seneca County the prosecuting attorney keeps files of criminal case papers dating from 1916 and a file of current correspondence. However in many counties of the state no records or files are kept and individual memoranda are disposed of by the retiring official. Since the prosecuting attorney is vested with large discretionary powers, there is need of special records and files. Such records according to authorities on judicial administration should include, among others, a permanent record of the names and addresses of witnesses, the deputy or division handling the case, and the reason for failure to prosecute, and the reason for which a *nolle prosequi* was asked and granted.

The records of the financial agencies of county government are prescribed by statute. Although records were kept in the earlier years, it was not until 1902 that the matter of keeping and the content of such records attracted the attention of the legislature. It was evident that accounts had not only been poorly kept but there had been little uniformity among the counties of the state. Accordingly, in 1902, the legislature enacted the most important and far-reaching laws on the subject.

---

178. G. C. sec. 2837.
179. G. C. sec, 2839.
180. *Laws of Ohio,* XLI, 74; G. C. sec. 3158.
181. *Laws of Ohio,* CXI, 31; See also p. 199.
182. G. C. sec. 2857.
183. G. C. sec. 2859.

This act provided for a uniform system of accounting, auditing, and reporting, under the supervision of a newly created bureau of inspection located in the office of the auditor of state. The act further provided for the annual examination of finances of all public offices.[184]

The governor's commission on the reorganization of county government, after studying the county records' system and noting the illogical combination of administrative, judicial, and financing functions, made the following recommendations:[185]

1. County charters and optional forms of government should provide for a department of records and court service to take over the functions of the recorder and clerk of courts, the non judicial record work of the probate court, and the functions of the sheriff as a court officer.
2. The issuance of licenses should be transferred from the clerk of courts to the department of finance.
3. Wider use should be made of the photographic process of recording in large counties.
4. Legislation should be adopted permitting the destruction of chattel mortgages and automobile bills of sale after they have ceased to have effect.
5. The requirement of three systems of indexes of cases in the clerk's office should be eliminated from the code and only the index of pending suits and living judgments should be required.
6. Provisions should be made in the rules of the common pleas court for service of process by mail and that method should be brought into general use.

---

184. *Laws of Ohio,* XCV, 511-515.
185. *Report of Governor's Commission,* 186-187. See also R.E. Heiges, *The Office of Sheriff in the Rural Counties of Ohio,* 55-56, 60-61.

Concurrently with the development of a record system, steps were taken to assure the proper restoration of damaged or dilapidated records treating of lands and surveys. The county engineer, when directed by the county commissioners, is required by law to transcribe any and all dilapidated maps and the records of plats and field notes of surveys from the records of the court of common pleas, auditor, recorder, or other officer in the state where they may be procured.[186] Similarly, the county recorder, when authorized by the county commissioners, is required to transcribe from the records of the counties all deeds, mortgages, powers of attorney, and other instruments of writing, for the sale, conveyance, or encumbrance of lands, tenements, or hereditaments, situated within his county.[187]

The large accumulation of county records, occasioned by increasing governmental services, presents a serious problem. It is important, on the one hand, the valuable space in county courthouses and other county depositories be not cluttered up with vast quantities of useless materials. On the other hand, it is important that every precaution be taken to prevent public officials from destroying valuable public records in order to make space for current business.

Within recent years photography has become an increasingly important aid in archival administration. The Ohio legislature, following the modern trends in recording, has enacted measures looking forward to the conservation of space in the county courthouses by permitting county officials to destroy records which have been reproduced photographically. Under this act, passed in 1937, any county official charged with keeping public records may, when the space requires it, have such records copied or reproduced by any photographic process and destroy the original papers. The original records, however, must be preserved until the time for filing legal proceedings based upon the documents shall have elapsed.[188]

While the legislature has attempted to enact legislation looking forward to the conservation of much needed space in county courthouses, a significant trend is to be observed in the increasing interest which is being displayed for a department of county archives where all noncurrent records may be properly housed, classified, listed, and made more readily accessible to those interested in consulting them.

---

186. G. C. sec. 2804.
187. G. C. sec. 2763.
188. G. C. sec. 32-1.

The arguments advanced in favor of such a system are: (1) that the preservation of county records should be viewed as a distinct function of county government, (2) that the administration of county archives should be under the direction of those qualified to serve efficiently and effectively both the needs of the administration and historians, (3) that the construction of county archives buildings for noncurrent records would make available more space for current business, which, at present, is seriously curtailed.

In the field of archival administration the state, rather than the county, has been the experimental laboratory and the results have been eminently successful.[189]

---

189. For an interesting and informative article on the administration of state archives, see Charles M. Gates, "The Administration of State Archives," *The Pacific Northwest Quarterly,* XXIX (January 1938), No. 1; also in *The American Archivist,* I (July 1938), 130-141.

HOUSING, CARE, AND ACCESSIBILITY OF THE RECORDS

Seneca County waited twelve years, after organizing in 1824, to build its first courthouse. A fire of uncertain origin destroyed this building in 1841, but the only records lost were those of the treasurer. Of these only official bonds were saved. This is the only serious gap in the county's records of 116 years of history. Yet in spite of this early misfortune and the transfers from one courthouse to another, the Seneca County archives have been preserved, and their condition reflects credit upon those entrusted with their care.

From the beginning, Tiffin has been the seat of government. When the county was formed, Tiffin consisted merely of five cabins and one frame house. This house, and oblong weather-boarded structure with plain gable ends was the first frame built in Tiffin, and it was here that the first session of common pleas court was held.[1] Joshua Hedges, the owner of the house, had a relative who was a close friend of Edward Tiffin; it is said that this factor influenced the placing as well as the naming of the county seat.

County officials supplied their own quarters and billed the commissioners for rent, which average about $10 a year.[2] Among the early citizens to furnish office space in the county seat were: John Miman, Neal McGuffey, Horton Howard, John Goodin, George Donaldson, and Able Rawson.[3] When the Hedges building became too small for a courtroom, the commissioners arranged for the use of the Methodist Episcopal Church on Market Street, at a rental charge ranging from $9 to $12 a session. This arrangement lasted until a courthouse was built in 1836.[4] On March 4, 1828, the board met to consider "the property" for building a courthouse, Calvin Bradley, architect, was commissioned to draw plans, after first visiting and studying the courthouses of Lorain, Portage, and Richland Counties.[5] On Friday, January 17, 1834, the board decided on a brick courthouse[6] and on February 14, contracted with John Baugher to build it, at his bid of $9,500. It was not until August 19, 1836, however, that the completed structure was formally accepted by the county commissioners.[7]

---

1. Daughters of American Revolution, *op. cit.,* 75.
2. Lang, *op. cit.,* 175.
3. Commissioners' Journal, I, 27, 38, 67, 70, 99.
4. Commissioners' Journal, I, 7; Daughters of the American Revolution, *op. cit.,* 75.
5. Commissioners' Journal, I, 50, 141, 153.
6. Lang *op. cit.,* 59.
7. Commissioners' Journal, II, 59.

The building contained the offices of the recorder, treasurer, auditor, clerk of the courts, and grand jury; those of both the grand jury and the treasurer were used as private law offices.[8]

The citizens of Seneca County believed the first courthouse to be fireproof. Oak logs, hewed one foot square, were laid close together over the entire lower story and were covered with sand 18 inches deep. The builder had believed that should the upper story ever burn, the sand would arrest the progress of the flames, saving the records and the other contents of the lower story. When the fire occurred on May 22, 1841, most of the records and furniture were preserved, but nothing remained of the courthouse except the brick walls.[9]

On June 10th after the fire, the commissioners met to arrange for the rebuilding of the courthouse. Plans were made to use the brick walls of the old building. On July 23, 1841, contracts were awarded for the new structure as follows:[10]

Carpenter and joiner work and painting, John Baugher,	$2,990.00
Brick work and masonry, Jacob Emick and Jacob Rock,	800.00
Plastering, Allison Phillips	450.00
Painting, John Andrews	150.00
One bell, G.W. Cofflin Co.	152.00
Lightning rods, Ruben Williams	28.00
Total	$4,570.25

The final payment of $1,080 was made in the summer of 1843 when the completed work was accepted.[11]

The new courthouse was a colonial style brick structure with a portico, its classic frieze and pediment supported by six fluted columns. A balcony above the entrance was partly visible from the front, the view broken by the columns. Twelve shuttered windows in each sidewall were arranged in vertical decorative units, each of which embraced one lower and one upper story window. Four chimneys were set on each side of the sloped roof.

---

8. Lang, *op. cit.,* 179.
9. Lang, *op. cit.,* 180.
10. Commissioners' Journal, II, 192; Lang, *op. cit.,* 181.
11. Commissioners' Journal, II, 192, 196, 197, 200, 244; III, 11.

The building was surmounted by an octagonal bell tower, with domed top. The tower rested on a broad square base.[12] In 1847 and again in 1866 the courthouse was remodeled. It continued in useful service as a seat of justice until 1884, when it was razed and replaced by the present structure.

Present Courthouse. This building is located on Washington Street and extends to Market Street. It has three stories and is built of light gray sandstone. The general square shape is relieved by numerous curves and angles. It has four entrances, each with loftily arched opening, flanked by massive piers supporting the pediment at the roof level. The Washington Street entrance is deeply recessed. The level is surrounded by an artistic parapet. Above it rises a square, pedimented, open tower, surmounted by cupola and clock, covered by a pyramidal roof with curved sides, at the apex of which is a figure representing Justice. All floors have transverse corridors which quarter the building. It was erected at a cost of $214,821.[13]

Hanging in the corridors of the main floor are oil paintings depicting memorable events: "Flood of the Sandusky River, 1883"; "Execution of Seneca John"; "First Courthouse in Seneca County"; "First House in Tiffin and the County, Erected November, 1817, by Erastus Bowe, Sr."; "Fort Ball"; "Fort Seneca"; "Colonel William Crawford's Cruel Fate." In the county commissioners' office is another painting called "Battle of Manila." These paintings are the work of Colonel Edward Lepper and were done sometime between 1906 and 1909.

In the following description of county offices, the locations, with exceptions noted, are in the courthouse, the floor plans of which follow this chapter.

County Commissioners. This department occupies two rooms and a vault in the southeast corner of the first floor. The main office is 18.25 by 26.5 feet, private office is 12 by16.5 feet, and the vault is 4.5 by 11 feet. The current records are filed in the main office. Most of the commissioners' records are in the auditor's vault, a few scattered records are in the auditor's main office, the store room on the fourth floor, and in the office of the state examiner. The records are well kept and in good condition. Space is ample, light and ventilation are good, and the records are easily accessible for use.

---

12. Henry Howe, comp., *Historical Collections of Ohio* (Cincinnati, 1900), illustrated on page 580.
13. Baughman, *op. cit.,* 62; part of the description is from observation.

The relief administration and the aid for the blind share an office located at 35 Court Street, Tiffin, Ohio. Approximately 55 percent of the bound and 70 percent of the unbound records are housed in fire-resistant cabinets at the administration headquarters, which consists of a suite of three rooms. The remaining 45 percent of the bound records are in the store room on the fourth floor of the courthouse and the other 30 percent of unbound papers are in the state examiner's room. The records are in good condition and order. All records required by statute have been kept. Facilities for work and consultation are satisfactory, space is ample, and lighting and ventilation are excellent.

Recorder. The recorder occupies two rooms and a vault in the northeast corner of the second floor. The main office is 25.5 by 28 feet and contains about 27 percent of the recorder's maps, 12 percent of his unbound records and a few bound records. The private office is 16.5 by 17 feet, and houses 73 percent of the maps, 37 percent of the bound, and 13 percent of the unbound records. The vault is 10.5 by 17.5 feet and contains 63 percent of the volumes, and 75 percent of the unbound records. The records are well kept and in good condition. The offices are crowded; there is little room for expansion, which is very much needed. Lighting and ventilation are good, and facilities for consultation of the records are adequate.

Clerk of Courts. This department occupies three rooms and a vault in the southwest corner of the third floor. The clerk's main office is 24 by 31.5 feet and contains only current records. The private office is 10 by 10.5 feet and contains no records; the file room is 6 feet and 8 inches by 25 feet and contains files of original court papers and bills of exceptions. Approximately 97 percent of the bound and 98 percent of the unbound records are in the vault, which is 10.5 by 20 feet. Records are kept in an orderly manner and are well preserved. Shelving and file boxes are of steel. Space is ample and there seems to be little need at present for expansion. Lighting and ventilation in the office are satisfactory, but the lighting of the vault is poor. The facilities generally are adequate for present needs. The records of each of the courts are segregated.

Court of Common Pleas. The records of the court are kept by the clerk of courts.

Supreme Court. The records of the court are kept by the clerk of courts.

Court of Appeals. The records of this court and those of its predecessors, the district and circuit courts are kept by the clerk of courts.

Probate Court. The probate court exclusive of the juvenile division occupies four rooms and a vault in the northwest corner of the second floor of the courthouse. The main office is 19 by 24 feet, probate room is 12.5 by 24 feet, the probate judge's private office is 10.5 by 13 feet. These rooms contain few permanent records. The probate deputy's office is 10.5 by 12 feet. The probate court vault is 8.5 by 18.5 feet, and is the main depository for records. The equipment for care of the records consists of steel shelving and metal file boxes. Twenty percent of the volumes and 9 percent of the unbound records are in the juvenile court vault. Approximately 1 percent of the records are in the store room on the fourth floor. The office space is ample, new shelving has been added recently and there will be no need for expansion for a number of years. The records are kept in an orderly manner. Some of the original records were destroyed by fire on February 14, 1894, but they had all been recorded in volumes prior to the fire. The juvenile division of the probate court occupies one room and a vault on the north side of the first floor. The room is 18.5 by 23.5 feet, and is shared by the board of elections. The vault is 8.5 by 22 feet and contains all the juvenile records. The records are in good condition, but facilities for consultation are poor. The office of aid to dependent children is located at 76½ South Washington Street, Tiffin, Ohio. It occupies two rooms. The records are unbound and are filed in an orderly manner in metal file cases. They are not open to public inspection.

Jury Commissioners. This agency has no office, and its one volume and one file box of records are kept by the clerk of courts.

Grand Jury. No records are kept by the grand jury.

Petit Jury. No records are kept by the petit jury.

Prosecuting Attorney. The prosecuting attorney keeps the records in his own private office, consequently, the location varies with the incumbent. At this time they are in the custody of Robert C. Carpenter, 90½ South Washington Street, Tiffin, Ohio. They are filed systematically and are in good condition, and facilities for their care are excellent.

Coroner. Like that of the prosecuting attorney the office of the coroner varies with the incumbent. At present it is the office of Dr. Perry T. Perin, at Green Springs, Ohio. The records are kept in the coroner's office, where housing facilities are excellent.

Sheriff. The sheriff's office is in the northwest corner of the third floor with the entrance from the north corridor. It consists of one room, 17.5 by 24 feet. Adequate facilities are available to house the records of the department. Jail registers and prisoners case records are housed in the county jail office. All records required by statute were located except that the cashbook is extant only for 1868 to date. Lighting, ventilation, and accommodations for the use of the public are good.

Dog Warden. This official keeps no permanent records.

Auditor. This department occupies four rooms and a vault in the southwest corner of the second floor with an entrance from the south corridor. The main office is 27.5 by 28 feet. All of the maps, 9 percent of the volumes, and 30 percent of the unbound records are in this room. The auditor's private office is 10 feet by 16 feet 8 inches and contains 3 percent of the bound, and 2 percent of the unbound records. The auditor's vault is 10 by 16 feet and contains 60 percent of the bound, and 68 percent of the unbound records. Other rooms housing records for this office are: The state examiner's office and closet containing 12 percent of the volumes; the sealer's office, housing 6 percent of the volumes; and the fourth floor storeroom which contains 10 percent of the volumes. There is ample space for work and the facilities for examination are adequate. Lighting and ventilation are excellent.

Treasurer. The treasurer occupies three rooms and two vaults, which are in the southeast corner of the second floor. The treasurer's main office is 18 by 28 feet and contains all of the maps, 6 percent of the bound, and 30 percent of the unbounded records. The treasurer's office 2 is 14 by 17 and treasurer's office 3 is 10 by 17 feet. These rooms contain no records. Treasurer's vault 1 is 8.5 by 10.5 feet. It is the principal depository, containing 81 percent of the bound and 70 percent of the unbound records. Vault 2 houses 5 percent of the bound records. In addition to the above, 7 percent of the treasurer's volumes are in the fourth floor room, and 1 percent in the state examiner's office. Equipment provided for filing of records consists of steel shelving for bound and metal files for unbound records. The fire of 1841 destroyed all the records up to that date. Indiscriminate "house-cleaning" about 20 years ago destroyed many other records. This accounts for the lack of early dates of the inventory entries for the treasurer's records. Office space is ample and accommodations for the use of the records are good. Lighting and ventilation are also good.

Budget Commissioners. This agency has no office. The records are in the custody of the auditor.

Board of Revision. The records are kept in the county sealer's office and the auditor's vault.

Trustees of the Sinking Fund. These records are in the auditor's vault.

Board of Elections. This board shares one room with the juvenile court in addition has two vaults on the north side of the first floor with an entrance from the west corridor. This office is 18.5 by 23.5 feet. All records are located in the vaults. Metal filing equipment is provided.

Board of Education. This office is located at 70 East Market Street, Tiffin, Ohio. The records are well cared for and in good condition. Space is ample, facilities adequate, lighting and ventilation good.

Board of Health. This agency occupies two rooms on the northeast corner of the first floor, consisting of a public and a private office. The public office is 16 feet 2 inches by 17 feet and is provided with metal filing equipment. The private office is 10 by 11 feet. Space is ample and facilities for care of the records are good.

Tuberculosis Hospital. The hospital is located two and a half miles south of Tiffin on State Route 100. The records are kept in the superintendent's office. They consist of less than one cubic foot of unbound material.

County Home. The institution is situated on State Route 100, two and a half miles south of Tiffin, Ohio. A few of the older records are located in the auditor's vault. The other records are located in the superintendent's office at the county home.

Soldiers' Relief Commission. This office is located at 112½ South Washington Street. The records are in good condition. There is less than one linear foot of the bound and less than one cubic foot of the unbound records.

Soldiers' Burial Committees. No permanent records are kept by these committees.

Board of Aid for the Aged. The office for this board is in a large room at 112½ East Market Street, Tiffin, Ohio. The records are housed in a section of the room partitioned off for the purpose, where steel, fireproof cabinets have been provided. This is up-to-date and space and equipment are adequate for present needs.

County Engineer. This department occupies four rooms and a vault in the southwest corner of the first floor of the courthouse. The engineer's main office is 20 by 27 feet. It contains all of the maps, 4 percent of the bound and 20 percent of the unbounded records. The engineer's private office is 10 by 11 feet and contains 2 percent of the bound, 19 percent of the unbound records.

The drafting room is 23 by 27 feet and contains 58 percent of the bound records. The blueprint room is 5 by 8 feet; it contains no records. Both vaults are 10.5 by 13.5 feet; they contained 35 percent of the bound and 61 percent of the unbound records. Metal filing equipment is provided. The records are in good condition; the two rooms are not crowded and facilities for examination of the records are very good. Lighting and ventilation are satisfactory.

County Park Board. One volume of records is at the residence of the secretary, R.H. Molineaux, 65 Washington Avenue, Tiffin, Ohio.

Agricultural Society. The records for this agency are at the residence of C.B. Baker, secretary of the society, Rural Route 4, Tiffin, Ohio.

Agricultural Extension Agents. This department occupies one room on the second floor of the Federal Building, Tiffin, Ohio. The entrance is from the north corridor. Metal filing equipment is provided and the records are filed and kept in an orderly manner. Ample space and facilities for care of the records are provided.

Fourth Floor Storeroom. This room is in the southwest end of the attic, directly above the office of the clerk of courts. It is divided into four smaller rooms. One of these, the northeast room referred to in the entries as attic storeroom, contains records of probate court, auditor, treasurer, and relief administration. The room is 16 by 20 and has volume space 6.25 by 32 feet.

The Seneca County records are generally well preserved, having been recorded on good paper with high grade ink. They also show careful handling. Some of the papers that were faded and time-worn or otherwise damaged have been renewed or repaired, a practice that should be followed with a number of others. The less frequently consulted records and those in the storerooms were occasionally found to be dusty, but have suffered no apparent damage from this cause. Records in most offices could be more readily accessible if proper equipment for handling them were installed, and the unbound records sorted and properly labeled. All records of each series should be brought together in a single location.

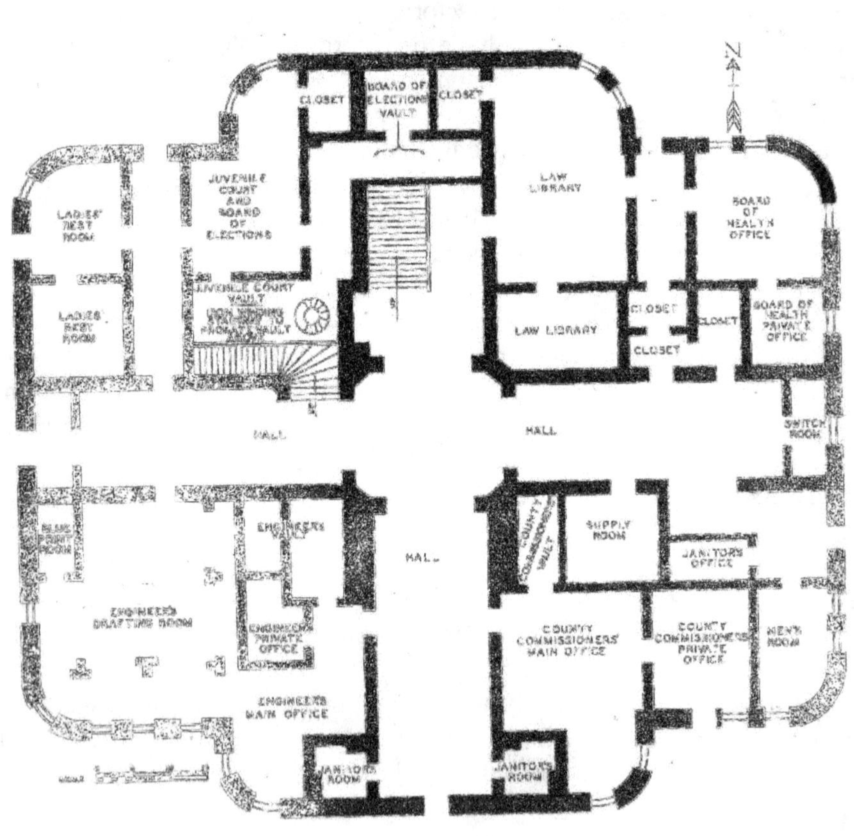

FIRST FLOOR PLAN
SENECA COUNTY COURTHOUSE
TIFFIN, OHIO

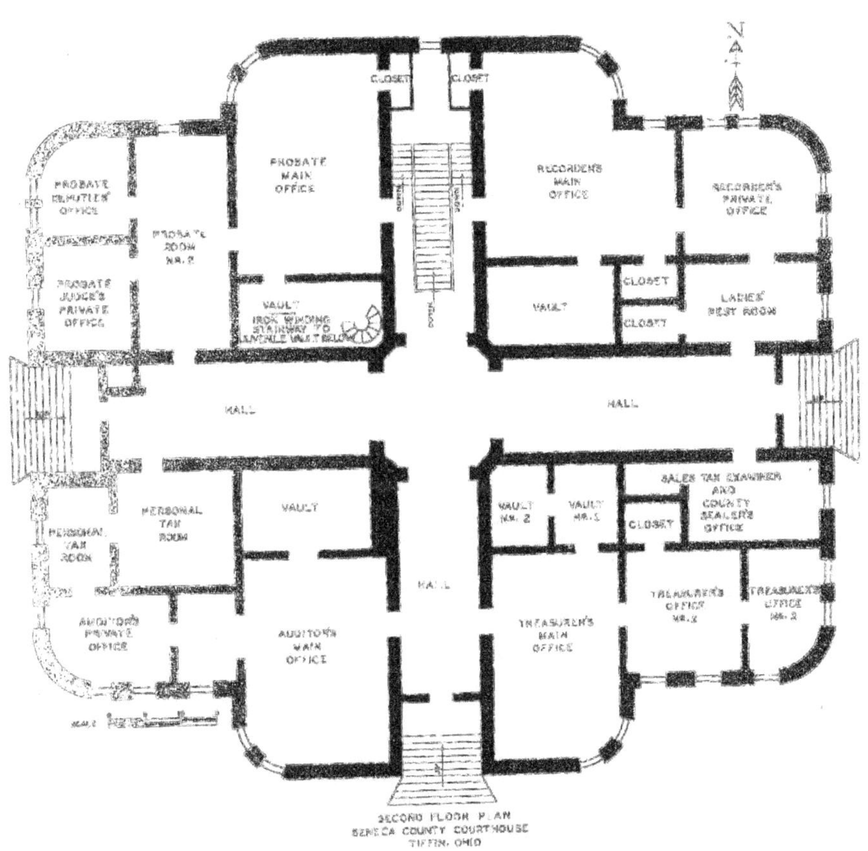

SECOND FLOOR PLAN
SENECA COUNTY COURTHOUSE
TIFFIN, OHIO

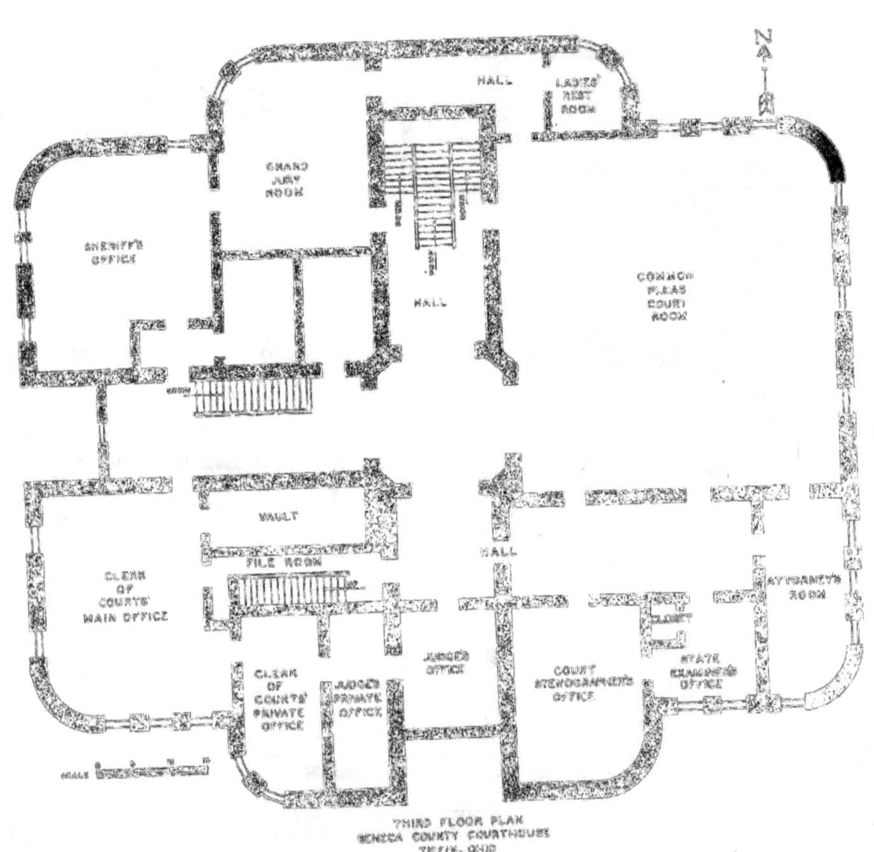

THIRD FLOOR PLAN
SENECA COUNTY COURTHOUSE
TIFFIN, OHIO

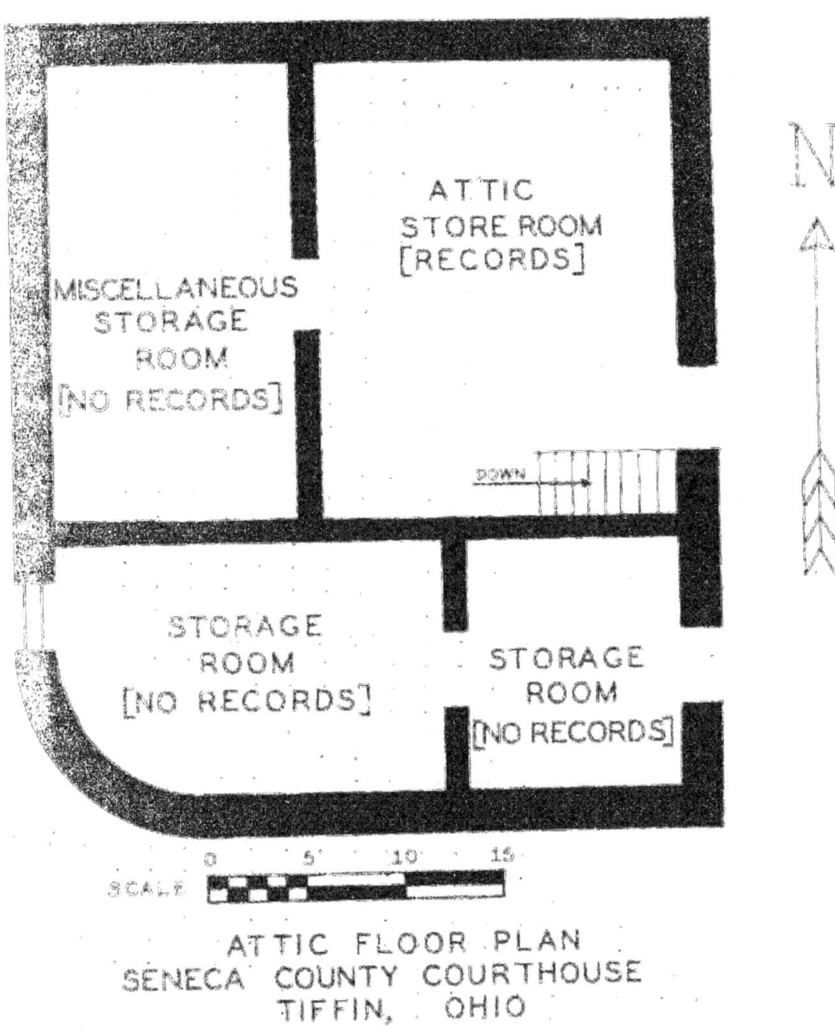

ATTIC FLOOR PLAN
SENECA COUNTY COURTHOUSE
TIFFIN, OHIO

The governmental system established in 1802, under the first constitution of Ohio, made no provision for the office of county commissioners and its existence is due entirely to statutory enactment. The board, created in 1804, was the successor of the courts of general quarter sessions, which, during the territorial period, served as a representative agent of the county. The board of county commissioners consisted of three members elected for a three-year term.[1] In 1807 the commissioners were made a corporate body vested with the power to sue and be sued.[2] They were required to keep a record of their proceedings, to levy taxes for support of the county, appoint a county treasurer, and to supervise the construction of bridges.[3] They were paid on a per diem basis. Moreover, during the same period (1804) they were given the task of constructing courthouses, jails, and offices for the clerk of courts, court of common pleas, sheriff, auditor, and treasurer.[4] From 1805 to 1820 the commissioners were required to fix the amounts of tavern and ferry licenses and the rates for transportation by ferry.[5] Of these earlier duties the commissioners retain all but those of fixing the amounts of tavern and ferry licenses, and ferriage rates and that of appointing a county treasurer. However, since 1831 they have been authorized to examine and inspect the accounts of the county treasurer and to examine the condition of county finances.[6]

Besides the duties regarding county building construction and finance, the commissioners were given the task of constructing local highways when so authorized by the legislature. During the first 30 years of Ohio history the duties of the commissioners in this respect were local in nature. But as the system of road construction expanded they were given the additional duty of converting free turnpikes into state roads.[7] Although numerous plank roads had been constructed by private companies doing the eighteen forties, it was not until 1850 that the general assembly authorized incorporation for this purpose.[8] When those companies were caught in the stringency of a financial depression in1857, the commissioners were authorized to purchase their holdings.

---

1. *Laws of Ohio,* II, 150.
2. *Ibid.,* V, 97.
3. *Ibid.,* VIII, 45.
4. *Ibid.,* II, 154-157; XXIX, 315.
5. *Ibid.,* III, 96; VIII, 107; XVIII, 170.
6. *Ibid.,* XXIX, 291. See also G. C. sec. 2644.
7. *Laws of Ohio,* XLVI, 74.
8. *Ibid.,* XIVIII, 49; L, 282.

If such transaction were made, the transfer sign by the president of the company was to be deposited with the county auditor.[9] In 1871 the commissioners, although earlier subjected to regulatory measures by the legislature, were prohibited from levying taxes for roads to exceed three and a half mills on the dollar on the taxable property in the county.[10] Later, in 1885, they were authorized to levy taxes not to exceed five mills on the dollar on all taxable property in the county for the maintenance of roads which had been damaged by excessive wear or were damaged by other causes.[11]

With the development of modern means of transportation, scientific principles were applied to road construction and maintenance. Although the county surveyor, now the county engineer, had in earlier years furnished the commissioners with the estimates for bridge construction, it was not until the latter part of the nineteenth century that they were authorized to utilize his scientific knowledge in road construction.[13]

Although the county commissioners have never been closely associated with the administration of criminal justice, their earlier duties regarding the construction of county jails qualified them, in the earlier period, for additional duties in this respect. During the middle of the nineteenth century the commissioners of Cuyahoga County were authorized to employ persons on construction work who were confined in the county jails.[14] While this provision was repealed by the criminal code adopted in 1853, other earlier functions applicable to all counties were continued. Since 1843 the commissioners have provided equipment and fixtures for places of incarceration, food and clothing for prisoners, and have appointed a jail physician.[15] Since 1869 they have been authorized to offer a reward for the detection or apprehension of any person charged with a felony in the county.[16] Since 1892 the commissioners in any county where there is no workhouse may, under certain conditions, release or parole an indigent person confined in the jail.[17]

---

9. *Ibid.,* LIV 198.
10. *Ibid.,* LXVIII, 117.
11. G. C. sec. 7419.
12. *Laws of Ohio,* LXXXIX, 172; XCVIII, 245-247.
13. *Laws of Ohio,* CVIII, pt. i, 497.
14. *Ibid.,* XXXVII, 54.
15. *Ibid.,* XLI, 74; LXXVII, 186.
16. *Ibid.,* LXVI, 321.
17. *Ibid.,* LXXXIX, 408; CXIII, 203.

With the extension of modern crime into the rural areas in the form of small-town bank robbing, the commissioners were given the duty of furnishing motorcycles to the sheriff and his deputies in an attempt to compete with the high-powered equipment used by modern gangs. One of the latest functions in this respect is the contracting with radio stations for the broadcasting of descriptions of fleeing criminals.[18]

Besides providing for those who have violated the laws, the commissioners were given the duty of caring for persons who, because of poverty or physical or mental defects, became public charges. Thus, county relief for the indigent, one of the most pressing problems of the twentieth century, was met in frontier Ohio. As early as 1805 and act, modeled from the territorial law was passed which was similar in all respects to the poor laws of seventeenth century England.[19] Under the early enactments the township trustees were authorized to appoint overseers of the poor. In 1816 the county commissioners were authorized to construct "poor houses" for the care of the county's indigent. As the system developed in succeeding decades the county was made responsible for those who had become permanently disabled, and for paupers who could not be satisfactory cared for except at the county infirmary, now called the county home. Since 1913 they have been authorized, in any county containing a city which has an infirmary, to contract with the director of public safety for the care of the county's indigent.[20]

The township trustees and officials of municipal corporations were made responsible for providing temporary relief to needy residents of the state, of the county, township, or city. In the event any person became chargeable to a township in which he had not gained legal residence, it was the duty of the overseers, later the township trustees, to remove him to the township where he has legally settled. With slight alterations, the principles of this system continued until the twentieth century.[21]

Since 1908 the commissioners have been authorized to issue warrants for the relief of the blind in sums varying from $100 to $400 per year.[22]

---

18. G. C. sec. 2414-1.
19. *Laws of Ohio,* III, 272.
20. G. C. sec. 2419-1.
21. For an excellent study, but biting criticism, of the administration of relief in Ohio prior to 1934 see Aileen Elizabeth Kennedy, *The Ohio Poor Law and Its Administration.*
22. See P. 262.

When the blind relief commission was abolished in 1913 its powers and duties were transferred to the county commissioners who were authorized, on evidence furnished by a registered physician or surgeon that the applicant for blind relief might have such disability benefited or removed by medical or surgical treatment, and with the written consent of the patient, to expend all or part of a year's relief allowance for this purpose.[23]

Six years later, in 1919, this allowance for blind relief was raised to $200 per person per annum, and the county commissioners were authorized to appoint such clerks as they might deem necessary to investigate applications and to serve at the pleasure of the county commissioners.[24]

In 1927 the maximum benefit for blind relief was increased to $400 per person per annum, but in the event of both a husband and wife being blind and both receiving relief, the total maximum benefit for the two was fixed at $600 per annum.[25]

In April 1936 the state accepted the provisions of the Federal Social Security Act approved August 14, 1935, providing federal grants for state aid to the blind, and the legislature designated the Ohio commission for the blind the administration agency in the state, and the county commissioners were made the administration agency in the county. The county commissioners were directed to appropriate from the general fund of the county a sum sufficient when supplemented by federal and state grants to provide for the blind a substance "compatible with decency and health," and if they failed to make such appropriations the attorney general was directed to bring *mandamus* proceedings against them.

The act of 1936 provides that those entitled to blind relief or persons not less than 18 or more than 65 years old, who have lost their sight while residents of the state, and who have resided in the state for a period of five years in the nine years immediately proceeding application, the last year of which period residence shall have been continuous. Applications for blind relief are filed with the county commissioners who are required by statute to list such claims in their order of application in books kept for that purpose. At least ten days prior to action on a claim the applicant files a duly certified statement, including a certificate from a registered physician "skilled in the diseases of the eye"

---

23. *Laws of Ohio,* CIII, 60.
24. *Ibid.,* CVIII, pt. i, 421-422.
25. *Ibid.,* CXII, 109.

Stating to what extent the applicant's vision is impaired, and written evidence from two reputable citizens that they know the applicant to be blind and that "he has the qualifications to entitle him to the relief asked." The county commissioners may allow the examining physician a fee not to exceed five dollars, and may employ an additional physician to examine the applicant. If after such inquiry the county commissioners are satisfied that the applicant is entitled to relief, they are directed by statute to issue an order for such sum as the board finds necessary, not to exceed the maximum fixed in 1927, such sum to be paid monthly from the fund created for that purpose. The ruling of 1913 concerning medical and surgical treatment for applicants remains in effect. Persons whose applications are denied by the county commissioners may appeal to the state commission for the blind which on its own motion may revise any decision of the county commissioners. Both the Ohio commission for the blind and the county commissioners have power to issue subpoenas, compel presentation of papers, and examined witnesses.

At least once a year, oftener if directed by the Ohio commission for the blind, the county commissioners must examine the qualifications, disabilities, and needs of all persons on the list of the blind, and may increase or decrease the amount of relief according to the budgetary requirements within the limits fixed by law. If the county commissioners remove a name from the list of the blind they are required to notify the county auditor and the Ohio commission for the blind as to their action.[26]

In addition to furnishing financial aid to the civilian population the commissioners were authorized, in 1886, to levy a tax for the relief of indigent Union soldiers, sailors, or marines of the Civil War, or if such veterans were deceased, for their dependents.[27] In 1919 the provisions of the original act were amended to include all indigent veterans of the World War.[28] The commissioners were authorized also, in 1884, to defray the funeral expenses of any honorably discharged soldier, sailor, or marine who died indigent. Ten years later the provisions of the act were extended to include the mother, wife, or widow of any soldier, sailor, or marine; and the war nurses.[29]

---

26. *Laws of Ohio,* CXVI, pt. ii, 195-200.
27. *Laws of Ohio,* LXXXIII, 232. See also p. 255.
28. *Laws of Ohio,* CVIII, pt.i, 633.
29. *Ibid.,* XC, 177.

The humanitarian duty of caring for the county's dependent and neglected children was delegated to the county commissioners. Since 1866 they have been authorized to establish and maintain a children's home. At the beginning of the present century, when the treatment of children was undergoing a remarkable change, they were authorized to place dependent and neglected children in private homes or institutions where they would receive food, clothing, and medical and dental treatment.[30] The development of the juvenile court system added new responsibilities. In order to completely segregate juvenile offenders from adults being tried in the regular criminal courts, the commissioners were authorized to provide a separate building, to be known as the "juvenile court."[31]

The unprecedented depression in the third decade of the twentieth century provided the antiquated, uncentralized system of relief administration entirely inadequate. As a result of the abnormal employment conditions and the crop failures following the drought of 1930, many local subdivisions of the county charged by law to administer support and medical relief to the indigent were unable to discharge their obligations. Accordingly, in 1931, the legislature passed an emergency act authorizing the county, township, and municipal taxing authorities to borrow money and issue bonds for poor relief, providing the state tax commission found that no other funds were available.[32]

During the early months of 1932 the governor, aware of the widespread suffering in the state, called the legislature into special session.[33] At this session the legislature authorized him to appoint a state relief commission composed of five members to study the relief situation. This commission was permitted to co-operate with the national, state, or local relief commission, which, in many counties, had been established and was already functioning. Since the county and township treasuries were depleted, on account of the excessive drain caused by the mounting relief load and the steady decline of tax collections, the legislature authorized an excise tax on utilities, for the year 1932-1937, to be used for relief purposes. This state tax was to be allocated to the counties on the basis of population, the tax duplicate, and the value of the utilities property in the county as of 1930.

---

30. *Laws of Ohio,* CIX, 533.
31. *Ibid.,* CXIII, 470.
32. *Ibid.,* CXIV, 11-12.
33. See message of the governor to the eighty-ninth general assembly in *Laws of Ohio,* CXIV, pt. ii, 6-8.

The funds allocated to each county under this act were to be credited to the "county poor relief excise fund."[34]

The county commissioners were authorized to borrow money for emergency relief and evidence such indebtedness by the issuance of negotiable bonds and notes. Upon submission of such resolution to the state tax commission, the commission was directed to estimate the amount which would probably be allocated to the county from the public utility excise taxes and was directed to calculate the total amounts of bonds, the principal and interest on which might be paid out of such estimated allocation. The date of maximum maturity of such bonds was to be on or before March 15, 1938. If, in the year 1932, additional funds were needed for poor relief, the county commissioners were authorized, after the state tax commission found that no other funds were available, to issue additional bonds in the amount not exceeding one tenth of one percent of the general tax list and duplicate of the county. The maturity date of such additional bonds was to be on or before September 15, 1940.[35]

The proceeds of the sale of such bonds were to be placed in a special fund, denominated the "emergency relief fund." No expenditures were to be made from this fund except in accordance with the method and under the uniform regulations prescribed by the state relief commission, and in no case after December 31, 1933. The county commissioners were authorized to distribute, prior to the first of March 1933, portions of the fund to the political subdivisions of the county, according to the needs for poor relief determined by the county and set forth in such an approved budget. The money distributed to the subdivisions was to be expended in them for poor relief, including the renting of lands and the purchase of seeds for gardening by the unemployed.[36] County poor relief included mothers' pensions, soldiers' relief, temporary assistance to nonresidents, maintenance of a county and a children's home, and work and direct relief. In the townships in municipalities relief was interpreted to be the support of the poor and the burial of persons who died indigent. Each subdivision administering funds under the act was expected to require labor in exchange for relief given to any family in which resided an able-bodied wage earner.[37]

---

34. *Laws of Ohio,* CXIV, pt. ii, 19-20.
35. *Ibid.,* CXIV, pt. ii, 18-21.
36. *Ibid.,* CXIV, pt. ii, 21-22.
37. *Ibid.,* CXIV, pt. ii, 17.

In the same year the county commissioners were designated as a board to administer the state law providing aid for the aged.[38] In February 1933 the tenure of the state relief commission was extended to March 1, 1935.[39] In the same year the legislature levied an additional stamp tax on the sale of bottled and bulk beer, malt, cosmetics, and toilet preparations to furnish additional funds for emergency relief.[40] The state treasurer was authorized to appoint the county treasurer as his deputy for the purpose of selling tax stamps to be affixed to such articles.[41]

The commissioners' duties regarding poor relief were further extended in 1935. They were authorized to provide noninstitutional support, care, assistance, or relief for the indigent in the county. In 1935 the state relief commission ceased to exist by reason of the terms of the act creating it. The legislature however, passed a measure design to co-ordinate and correlate all emergency poor relief work, activities, and administration with the Federal Emergency Relief Administration which was authorized to administer and direct the distribution and expenditure of federal funds for relief in the state. Accordingly, all powers previously vested in the state relief commission were transferred to the county commissioners. Whenever in their opinion such action was necessary in order to continue the co-ordination of state, local, and federal funds they were authorized to appoint, with the approval of the director of finance of the state of Ohio, a representative or representatives of such emergency relief.[42] If such officer was appointed, he succeeded to all powers and functions, which, under the act, were delegated to the county commissioners. This representative, however, was subject to such terms and conditions in respect to auditing, examinations, and reports as were directed by the county commissioners and such federal agency. The county commissioners were directed to conduct relief activities outside the limits of municipal corporations through township trustees, insofar as practicable, and were to be guided by the recommendations of the trustees with respect to relief needs in the township.

---

38. *Ibid.,* CXV, pt. ii, 431-439.
39. *Laws of Ohio,* CXV, 22.
40. *Laws of Ohio,* CXV, 642, 647; CXV, pt. ii, 5, 33, 83, 177, 200, 247, 256.
41. *Ibid.,* CXV, 642.
42. *Ibid.,* CXVI, 571. On January 26, 1933, the Seneca County relief administration was set up by the county commissioners. Commissioners' Journal, XXXV, 586. A relief commission was appointed on September 30, 1933, *Ibid.,* 653. On October 1, 1935, a second agency was organized. The two agencies functioned simultaneously but independently; the former administering relief to employable clients and the latter to unemployables. On December 1, 1935, the first commission was abolished and the second, which is still operating, assumed both functions.

Again, as in 1932, the commissioners were authorized, if the state tax commission found that no other means existed to provide funds to borrow money and issue bonds in the year 1935-1936. The maximum maturity date of such bonds was to be on or before March 1, 1944.[43] Other bonds, in addition to those secured by the county's share of the excise tax, might be issued not to exceed one fifth of one percent of the general tax duplicate of the county.[44] If the county was unable to issue bonds by reason of the limitations imposed by the constitution,[45] the taxing authority of each subdivision was authorized to submit the question of issuing bonds to the electorate either at a general or special election.[46]

The year 1936 saw the re-creation of the state relief commission. Consisting of four members appointed by the governor, this body was authorized to serve until January 31, 1937. Again, as in 1932, the commission was directed to study problems of relief, to receive advice from federal, state, and local governmental departments, to co-operate with agencies of the national and local governments and private agencies engaged in the administration or financial support of direct or indirect relief, to administer moneys appropriated to the commission for poor relief, to examine the conduct of local governmental agencies in administering relief, and to order the distribution and payment of moneys for state treasury.

The county commissioners were authorized to administer all advances by the state to the relief commission, were directed to operate through duly authorized agencies of townships, municipalities, and school district. Within the appropriations made by the commissioners and subject to the rules and regulations of the state relief commission, the commissioners were instructed to appoint assistants and such other employees as were necessary.[47]

The county commissioners, like the state relief commission, were directed to co-operate with all agencies of the federal, state, county governments, and with private agencies which were engaged in administering relief or financial support to the needy.

---

43. *Laws of Ohio,* CXVI, 571.
44. *Ibid.,* CXVI, 575.
45. *Ohio Const. 1851.* Art. XII, sec. 2.
46. *Laws of Ohio,* CXVI, 578.
47. *Laws of Ohio,* CXVI, pt. ii, 133-148.

It was made the duty of all county, township, and municipal governments administering relief or assistance to dependents to report to the county commissioners, at their request, the names and addresses of all persons to whom they were providing aid and the amount and character of aid given.[48]

The principle of issuing bonds and securing them by the county's share of the utility taxes was continued. Moreover there was appropriated to the state relief commission from the general revenue fund the sum of $3,000,000 which was designated as the "state relief rotary fund." The various counties of the state which had not issued bonds that were not authorized to do so without the consent of the people, were empowered to obtain an advance from the state relief rotary fund in an amount equal to that of the bonds which were permitted to be issued under the provisions of this act. If the county failed to repay the total of all advances and interest at two percent before June 1936, the state relief commission was directed to refuse to make further allocations or distributions to the county.[49]

In the early months of 1937 the legislature authorized the state relief commission to serve until April 1937. Under this act the county commissioners are authorized to give temporary support and medical relief to nonresidents and to all needy persons possessing legal residence in the county. Funds may be expended for both direct and work relief. However, all persons on relief able and competent to perform labor who refuse to accept private employment under prevailing conditions and prevailing wages, maybe dropped from the relief rolls. This ruling does not apply, however, to areas where strikes are prevalent. On the other hand, any person receiving relief in the county is permitted to engage in any business without losing his relief status. During the period of such employment, he is required to forfeit the *pro rata* amount of relief received by him, and is eligible to his former relief status upon the conclusion of such employment.

The county commissioners are required to file with the state relief commission a budget and a detailed statement and plan showing how the funds to be received are to be expended, the purpose for which they are to be used, the nature and kind of work to be carried on, and the number of persons to be aided by such relief.

---

48. *Ibid.,* CXVI, pt. ii, 133-148, 240.
49. *Ibid.,* CXVI, 133-148.

Besides this, the county commissioners must file a complete analysis of their proposed expenditures, together with an estimate of all available resources, including the unencumbered proceeds of any bonds heretofore issued and the amount of bonds which the county commissioners have a right to issue without a vote of the people on the approval of the state tax commission of Ohio as authorized in 1935.[50]

Of the funds allocated to the county by the state relief commission for direct relief, the commissioners may, when they believe that the cost of administration may be reduced, reallocate the funds on a percentage basis of relief requirements of the various subdivisions.[51]

The emergency relief measures passed during the period 1932-1937 gave the counties for the first time a centralized relief administration. All records on this work are located in a relief administration office.

In addition to other forms of relief the county commissioners provide funds for aid to dependent children.[52] They are required to include in the annual tax budget an amount not less than that computer to yield a levy of fifteen one-hundreds of one mill on each dollar of the general tax list of the county. Funds are also provided by the federal and state governments. If the commissioners fail to comply with the provisions of the act relative to appropriations, the state department of public welfare is directed to institute *mandamus* proceedings against them.[53]

While control over relief work has become one of the most important phases of the commissioners' work, particularly in recent years, many other responsibilities have been assigned to them. The commissioners, by the authority conferred upon them to construct public buildings, were given duties regarding educational advancement. Since 1871 they have been authorized to accept bequests for the construction of county libraries, and since 1923 to issue bonds, after receiving the approval of the voters, for the construction of libraries, or to contract with existing libraries for the use of people in the county.[54] Moreover, during the same period, they were authorized to provide and maintain civic centers in the county and to employ an expert director to supervise and administer them.[55]

---

50. *Laws of Ohio,* XVI, pt. ii, 133-148.
51. *Ibid.,* CXVII, 13.
52. See p. 132.
53. G. C. secs. 1359-31, 1359-45; *Laws of Ohio,* CXVI, pt. ii, 188-195.
54. G. C. secs. 2454, 2455; *Laws of Ohio,* CX, 242.
55. G. C. sec. 2457-3.

Other duties not closely related to the original ones have been added from decade to decade. For example, in 1850 the commissioners were authorized to subscribe to one leading newspaper of each political party in the county and cause them to be bound and deposited with the county auditor as public archives.[56] The newspapers on file in the auditor's office have not been listed in this inventory as they are to be subject of a separate publication. Amendment to the original act, passed in 1923, provided for the preservation of such newspapers for a period of ten years, after which they may be removed to the Ohio State Archaeological and Historical Society library.[57] They have been authorized also to promote historical research by appropriating annually a sum not to exceed $100 to defray the expenses of compiling and publishing historical data for historical societies not incorporated for profit.[58]

During the early years of the twentieth century the commissioners were given the duty of providing facilities for county sanitation, which, in previous years had been sadly neglected. In 1917 they were authorized to lay out, establish, and maintain one or more sewer districts within the county. Since 1917 no sewer or sewage treatment works may be constructed outside of any incorporated municipality by any person, persons, firms, or corporations until the plans have been approved by the commissioners.[59]

Then, too, during the same period the commissioners were authorized to provide facilities for the treatment of tuberculosis. In 1908 they were authorized to establish a county tuberculosis hospital and in 1909 to co-operate with the commissioners of other counties for the establishment of a district tuberculosis hospital.[60] Seneca County maintains a tuberculosis hospital under the general supervision of the superintendent of the county home.[61] Since 1917 the commissioners have been authorized to establish tuberculosis dispensaries and provide by tax levies the necessary funds for their establishment and maintenance.[62]

---

56. *Laws of Ohio,* XLVIII, 65.
57. *Ibid.,* CX, 4.
58. G. C. sec. 2457-1.
59. G. C. sec. 6302-1; *Laws of Ohio,* CVII, 440.
60. *Laws of Ohio,* XCIX, 62; C, 87.
61. See p. 243.
62. G. C. sec. 3148-1, 3153-4, 3153-5.

Finally, the county commissioners have acted in a supervisory capacity over other county officials. Since 1850 they have been authorized to compare the annual reports and statements made to them by the prosecuting attorney, clerk of courts, sheriff, and treasurer; take measures to rectify errors, correct discrepancies, and record in their journal the results of such examination. Prior to the transfer of the duties of secretary to the board of county commissioners to a full-time commissioners' clerk, appointed in 1937[63] under provisions of the act of 1904,[64] these reports were required to be filed with the county auditor, who had custody of the commissioners official acts and proceedings.[65] In 1896 the commissioners were given their present duty of visiting hospitals, detention homes, private asylums, and any other institution exercising a reformatory or correctional influence over individuals, and reporting on sanitary conditions and the treatment of inmates.[66] Although these reports are required to be filed with the prosecuting attorney and kept open to the inspection and examination of the public, they were not located in the inventory of Seneca County records.

The board of county commissioners offers a typical example of an office, which, design primarily for an agricultural society, has expanded to meet the needs and requirements of modern society. At present the commissioners are elected for a four-year term.[67]

---

63. Commissioners Journal, XXXIX, 469.
64. *Laws of Ohio,* XCVII, 304.
65. G. C. sec. 2504; *Laws of Ohio,* XLVIII, 66.
66. *Ibid.,* XCII, 212.
67. *Ibid.,* CVIII, pt. ii, 1300.

Minutes

1. COMMISSIONERS' JOURNAL
1824—. 37 volumes. (1-37).

Minutes and records of proceedings of board of county commissioners, consisting of resolutions, motions, and other legislation proposed and acted upon, showing date and place of meeting, names of members present, record of action taken, and date of filing or approval of reports, petitions, and claims. Includes records of construction and maintenance of county buildings; approval of surety bonds filed by principal petitioners, contractors, and county officials, showing amount of bond, names of sureties, and for what purpose; appropriations of funds for operation and maintenance of county offices and departments; authorization of issue of debenture bonds to finance public improvements, 1941—, showing date and amount of debenture bonds authorized; approval of annual reports filed by county officials, 1850-1870; and copies of annual reports filed by county officials, 1871—; appropriations to agricultural society, 1842—; approval for payment of bills and claims filed; examination of county treasurer's account annually, 1825-1858, semiannually, 1859-1870; record of adjustment of property values for taxation and tax assessments (board of equalization), 1827-1850; approval of tax assessments, 1825-1850; establishing tax levy for all county purposes, 1824-1911; approval of income tax levies on physicians and lawyers, 1831-1850; provision for payment of bounty on wolf scalps, 1827-1854; approval of sheriff's accounts for maintenance of prisoners confined in county jail, 1827—; approval of release or parole of indigent prisoners sentenced to county jail, 1836—; appointment of county treasurer, 1824, tax lister, 1824-1843, tax collector, 1824-1827, keeper of the standard measure, 1826, members of soldiers' burial committees, 1884—, dog warden, 1927—, commissioners' clerk, 1937—; copies of claims for compensation by owners of domestic animals killed or injured by dogs, 1878—; approval of magistrates' cost bills in criminal cases, 1869—; copies of rules and regulations governing relief of dependents of volunteers, 1862-1872, with schedule of relief to be allowed by township committees, and names of committee members; authorization of issue of debenture bonds to finance payment of volunteers' bounties, 1862-1868; appropriation of funds and authorization of issue of debenture bonds to finance emergency relief, 1933; approval of bills and claims, showing name of creditor, for what, and amount, 1824—, also shows voucher number, 1902—. Also contains: Commissioners' journal Roads, 1827-1931, entry 1A; Commissioners' Journal Ditches, 1860-1930, entry 1B; Commissioners' Journal Bridges, 1832-1932, entry 1C; Commissioners 'Infirmary Journal, 1934-1936, entry 3. Arranged chronologically by dates of meetings. 1824-1874, no index; for index 1875-1930, see entry 2; 1931—, indexed alphabetically by names of roads, ditches, bridges, creditors, contractors, or other subject matter; also separate index to roads, 1824-1929, entry 11. 1824-1902, handwritten; 1902—, typed. Average 600 pages. 18 x 12 x 3. 28 volumes, 1824-1921, auditor's vault; 9 volumes, 1921—, Commissioners' main office.

1A. COMMISSIONERS' JOURNAL ROADS

1932—. 2 volumes. (1, 2). 1827-1931 in Commissioners' Journal, entry 1. Records of proceedings of board of county commissioners relative to roads, consisting a journal entries of petitions filed by freeholders for establishment, change of route, extension, improvement or vacation of public roads, notices of hearings on petitions, petitioners' bonds, order to view, reports of viewers, orders to survey, surveyor's specifications, notices of hearing claim for compensation for damages (compensation for lands appropriated), notices to bidders of proposals for construction or improvement, record of bids received, contracts let, contractors and principal petitioners' bonds, showing name and number of road, description and location of road, names of principal petitioners, dates of hearings, date viewed, names of viewers, surveyor's sketch of route, showing distance between angles, fills, elevation, names of owners of abutting lands, total length of road, specifications as to method and type of construction and surfacing, detailed estimate of cost, amount of compensation awarded and names of landowners, names of bidders and amount of bids, name of contractor, amount and terms of contract, amount of petitioners and contractors bonds and names of sureties, date and place of meeting, and names of members present. Arranged chronologically by dates of meetings. Indexed alphabetically by names of roads. Typed. 600 pages. 17x12 x 3. Commissioners' office.

1B. COMMISSIONERS' JOURNAL DITCHES

1931—. 1 volume. (1). 1860-1930 in Commissioners' Journal, entry 1. Record of proceedings of board of county commissioners relative to county drainage ditches, consisting of copies of petitions filed by property owners, notices of hearings on petition and proposal to establish, orders to view, viewer's reports, order to survey, surveyor's reports and specification for construction and estimate of cost, notice to bidders of letting contract, contractors, petitioners' and contractor's bonds, and schedule of assessment, showing name of ditch, location of township and sections, names of principal petitioners, date viewed, names of viewers, surveyor's sketch of route, boundary lines of farm tracts and lots in drainage basin, number of acres in each, names of owners, points of beginning and ending, length of ditch, specifications as to depth, width, and size of tile, detailed estimate of cost, names of bidders, amount of bids, name of contractor, amount and terms of contract, and amount assessed each property owner, date and place of meeting, and names of members present. Arranged chronologically by dates of meetings. Indexed alphabetically by names of ditches. Typed. 600 pages. 17 x 12 x 3. Commissioners' office.

1C. COMMISSIONERS' JOURNAL BRIDGES

1933—. 1 volume. (1). 1832-1932 in Commissioners' Journal, entry 1.

Record of proceedings of board of county commissioners relative to construction and repair of county bridges, consisting of journal entries of proposals, notices to bidders of proposals, bids received, contracts, bonds, and commissioners' resolutions approving construction or repair, showing name of bridge, highway or stream, name of township, date of resolution approving proposed repair, surveyor's date on survey of approaches, detailed specifications as to type of construction and materials, estimate of cost of labor, total cost, names of bidders, amount of bids, name of contractor, amount and term of contract, amount of contractor's bonds and names of sureties, date and place of meeting, and names of members present. Arranged chronologically by dates of meetings. Indexed alphabetically by names of bridges. Typed. 600 pages. 17 x 12 x 3. Commissioners' office.

2. INDEX TO COMMISSIONERS' JOURNAL

1875-1930. 10 volumes. (1-10).

Index to Commissioners' Journal, entry 1, in 3 divisions: bills, roads and ditches, and miscellaneous, showing date of entry, name of creditor, road, ditch, contractor, appointee, or other principal or subject, and volume and page number of journal. Arranged alphabetically by names of creditors, roads, ditches, contractors, appointees, or other principles. Handwritten on forms. Average 575 pages. 18 x 12 x 3. Auditor's vault.

3. COMMISSIONERS' INFIRMARY JOURNAL

1913—1933. 1 volume. (1). 1934-1936, Commissioners' Journal, entry 1; in Journal County Home and Tubercular Hospital, entry 4.

Minutes and record of proceedings by county commissioners organized as board of infirmary directors, consisting of copies of resolutions and motions proposed and acted on, record of bills and claims approved for payment, showing date and place of meeting, names of members present, record of yea and nay votes, names of creditors, amount of bill, for what, and voucher number. Arranged chronologically by dates of meetings. Indexed alphabetically by names of creditors, principles, or subjects. Typed. 600 pages. 18 x 12 x 3. State examiner's office.

For prior county home and record, see entry 514.

4. JOURNAL COUNTY HOME AND TUBERCULAR HOSPITAL
1937—. 1 volume. (1).

Minutes and record of proceedings of county commissioners relative to administration of tuberculosis hospital, consisting of copies of resolutions and motions proposed and acted on, appointment of superintendent of hospital, rules and regulations governing operation of hospital, approval of bills and claims filed, showing date and place of meeting, names of members present, record of yea and nay votes, names of appointees, names of creditors, amount of bill, for what, and voucher number. Also contains Commissioners' Infirmary Journal, entry 3. Arranged chronologically by dates of meetings. No index. Typed. 600 pages. 16 x 11 x 3. Commissioners' main office.

Reports

(See also entries 399-411)

5. BURIAL RECORD INDIGENT SOLDIERS
1884-1913, 1919—. 4 volumes. (1-3, 3).

Copies of reports filed by township and city ward soldiers' burial committees recommending payment of burial expense of indigent soldiers and sailors, and 1896—, war nurses and dependents of soldiers and sailors, showing date of report, name of township or city and ward number, name of deceased veteran, nurse or dependent, what war, rank, company, regiment, occupation, place of burial, itemized statement of burial expense, total bill, names of committee, and date filed; 1905—, includes copy of commissioners' voucher for payment of burial expenses, showing date approved, voucher number, name of payee, amount each item, and total amount of voucher; 1884-1904, contains list of appointees to soldiers' burial committees in the various townships and city wards, showing name of township, city and ward number, names of appointees, and date of appointment. Reports arranged chronologically by dates filed; appointments, alphabetical by names of townships, numbered thereunder by city wards, and chronologically thereunder by dates of appointments. Reports, alphabetically indexed by names of decedents; otherwise no index. Handwritten on printed forms. Average 200 pages. 18 x 12 x 1.25. 2 volumes, 1884-1904, 1909-1913, state examiner's office; 2 volumes, 1904-1909, 1919—, Auditor's vault.

6. REPORTS

1910-1921, 1924—. 5 file boxes.

Original annual financial and statistical reports from county officials, showing period covered by report, what office or department, itemized account of receipts and expenditures, detailed statement of volume of official business, signature and title of official, and date filed. Also includes sheriff's report on cost of maintenance of prisoners in county jail. Arranged chronologically by dates filed. No index. Handwritten and typed on printed forms. 10.5 x 4.5 x 14. Auditor's vault.

7. AUDITOR'S FINANCIAL STATEMENTS

1916—. 1 file drawer, 6 sheets.

Original monthly statements filed by auditor of cash receipts and expenditures: receipts, showing month, year, credits each fund, source, amount, total credits all funds; itemized statement of expenditures each fund, showing name of payee, warrant number, amount, for what, total expenditures all funds, and date filed. Arranged chronologically by dates filed. No index. Typed on printed forms. File drawer, 12 x 16 x 22; sheets, 15 x 10. 1 file drawer, 1916-1939, Auditor's vault; 6 sheets, 1940—, posted on door to auditor's private office.

8. [REPORTS, DOG WARDEN]

1933—. In Miscellaneous, entry 29.

Dog wardens original weekly reports of unlicensed dogs seized and impounded, showing period of report, date of report, number of dogs impounded, number unclaimed and destroyed, number claimed, amount of license fees and penalties collected, and signature of dog warden; also includes original reports filed by dog warden on investigation of claims for compensation by owners of domestic animals killed or injured by dogs, showing date of investigation, name and address of claimant, number, kind and grade of animal killed, number injured, amount of compensation claimed, findings and recommendations of dog warden, and date filed.

9. [REPORTS, COUNTY HOME]

1913—. In County Home, entry 25.

Copies of superintendent's annual reports to division of charities, department of public welfare, and to county commissioners, showing year, itemized list of expenditures for salaries, medical services, medicines, groceries, fuel, light, dry goods, livestock, burial expense, new equipment, and structure; itemized receipts for sale of farm produce, or contributions towards inmates' expenses by relatives; roster of inmates showing name, age, sex, color, physical and mental condition, and nativity; signature of superintendent and date filed.

For superintendent's copies, see entry 516.

Improvements
(See also entries 552, 554, 555, 557, 558, 560-562)

Roads

10. ROAD RECORD

1824-1929. 5 volumes. (1-5).

Record of establishment, extension, change of route, or vacation of public roads, consisting of copies of petitions filed by freeholders, notices of hearings on petitions, petitioners' bonds, orders to view, reports of viewers, order to county surveyor to survey route and submit specifications and estimates, surveyor's reports, notices of hearings on claims for compensation for damages (compensation or lands apportioned), notices to bidders of proposal for construction, record of bids received, contracts, contractor's bonds, showing name of principal petitioners, township, name of road, description and location of route, names of viewers, date viewed, dates of hearings, surveyors' sketch of route showing distance between angles, fills, elevation, names of owners of abutting lands, total length of road, specification as to method and type of construction and surfacing, detailed estimate of cost of construction, amount of compensation awarded and names of landowners, names of bidders and amount bid, name of contractor, amount of contract, terms of contract, amount of petitioner's bond, of contractor's bond, names of sureties, dates of filing various papers; 1868—, includes improvements of surfacing to established roads, and assessments to abutting or benefited property owners. Arranged chronologically by dates of filing petitions. For index, see entry 11. Plats hand drawn; 1824-1911, handwritten; 1912—, typed. Average 525 pages. 18 x 12 x 3. Commissioners' main office.

11. INDEX TO ROADS

1824-1929. 1 volume.

Index to Road Record, entry 10, and to journal entries for roads in Commissioners Journal', entry 1, showing name of road, date established or improved, name of principal petitioner, range, township, and section numbers of points of beginning and ending, and volume and page numbers of records. Arranged alphabetically by names of roads. Handwritten on forms. 200 pages. 16 x 11 x 1.25. Commissioners' main office.

12. [ROAD PAPERS]
1872—. 27 file boxes, 7 file drawers.

Original papers filed relative to establishment, extension, change of route, or improvement of public roads, consisting of petitions, notices of hearings, orders to view and to survey, reports of viewers and surveyor, notices to bidders, bids, contracts, bonds, and assessment orders, showing name of petitioner, description and location of route, and name of road; 1917—, shows road number, names of viewers, and surveyor's report, showing sketch of route, distance between angles, streams, names of abutting landowners, bills, cuts, elevations and specifications as to type of construction and of material to be used, detailed estimate of cost of construction, name of bidders and amount bid, name of contractor, amount of term of contract, amount of petitioner's and contractor's bonds, names of sureties, amount assessed abutting or benefited landowners for share of cost of construction, date of issue, and date filed. 1872-1924, all papers of each road banded together; 1925—, filed together in a folder, showing name of road and road number. 1872-1924, arranged chronologically by dates of filing petitions; 1925—, arranged alphabetically by names of roads. No index. 1872-1914, Handwritten and handwritten on printed forms; 1915—, typed and typed on printed forms. File boxes, 10.5 x 4.5 x 14; file drawers, 12 x 14 x 24. 27 file boxes, 1872-1924, Auditor's main office; 7 file drawers, 1925—, Commissioners' main office.

13. [STATE ROAD PAPERS]
1914-1923. 2 file boxes.

Original papers filed relative to construction and improvement of state highways, consisting of engineers' surveys, specifications and estimates, journal entries, county commissioners' resolutions to cooperate with state highway department, assessment schedules, auditor's certifications that funds are in treasury, and property owners' protest of assessments, showing title of paper, highway number, section symbol, points of beginning and ending, engineer's sketches of route distance between angles, total distance, named of abutting lands, elevation, grades, curves, fills, cuts, blueprint cross sections of construction, detailed specifications as to construction and material to be used and estimate on cost of construction, amount assessed each property owner for his share of construction cost, and date issued and filed. No index. Handwritten and typed on printed forms. 10.5 x 4.5 x 14. Auditor's vault.

14. [INTER-COUNTY HIGHWAY PAPERS]
1914-1930. 1 file box.
Original papers filed relative to construction and improvement of inter-county highways, consisting of petitions by property owners, engineer's specifications and estimates, legal notices, bids, and statements of pro-rated cost, showing points of beginning and ending, total length of road, names of townships and towns, name and number of highway, names of petitioners, detailed specifications as to type of construction and material to be used and estimate of cost of construction, itemized statement of cost to state, county, township or town, and abutting property owners, and dates issued and filed. Arranged chronologically by dates filed. No index. Handwritten and typed on printed forms. 10.5 x 4.5 x 14. Auditor's vault.

Ditches

15. DITCH RECORD
1859—. 24 volumes. (A-X). Last entry 1930.
Record of the estimate and construction of county and township drainage ditches, consisting of copies of petitions filed by property owners, notices of hearings on petitions and proposal to establish, orders to view route, viewer's reports, orders to survey, surveyor's report and specifications for construction and estimate of cost, notices to bidders of letting contract, contracts, petitioners' and contractors' bonds, and schedule of assessments, showing name of ditch, location by township and sections, names of principal petitioners, date route viewed, names of viewers, surveyor's sketch of route, boundary lines of farm tracts and lots and drainage basin, number of acres in each, names of owners, points of beginning and ending, length of ditch, specifications as to depth, width, or size of tile, detailed estimate of cost, names of bidders, amount of bids, name of contractor, contract price, terms of contract, amount of principal petitioners' and contractors' bonds, names of sureties, amount assessed each benefited property owner, date contract completed, total cost, and dates of filing various papers. Arranged chronologically by dates of filing petitions. Indexed alphabetically by names of ditches. Sketches, hand drawn; 1859-1902, handwritten; 1903—, typed. Average 475 pages. 18 x 12 x 2.5. Engineer's main office.

16. [DITCH PAPERS]

1889—. 120 file boxes, 2 file drawers. (labeled by contained letters of alphabet).

Original papers filed relative to establishment and construction of county and township drainage ditches, consisting of petitions for establishment from property owners, notices of hearings on petitions and proposal to establish and to bidders of proposal to construct, viewers' and surveyor's reports, surveyor's specifications and estimates, bids received, contracts, bonds, and assessment schedules, showing title of paper, name of ditch, location by township and sections, names of petitioners, dates viewed, names of viewers, date surveyed, surveyor's sketch of proposed route, fall and all survey data, boundary lines of farm tracts and lots in drainage basin, names of owners and area of each tract, surveyors detailed specification for construction and estimate of cost, names of bidders, amount of bid, name of contractor, contract price, terms of contract, amount of principal petitioners' and contractors' bonds, names of sureties, assessment for property owners share of cost, showing name of owner, township, section number, number of acres, number of acres assessed, amount assessed, and dates issued and filed. 1889-1924, all papers for each ditch in a jacket, and 1924—, in folders showing name of ditch, location and date established. Arranged alphabetically by names of ditches. No index. Sketches, hand drawn; 1889-1919, handwritten on printed forms; 1920—, typed on printed forms. File boxes, 10.5 x 4.5 x 14; file drawers, 12 x 14 x 24. 120 file boxes, 1889-1924, Engineer's main office; 2 file drawers, 1924—, Commissioners' main office.

17. INDEX TO DITCHES

1874-1924. 1 volume. Obsolete. [Ditch Papers], entry 16, have been rearranged in file boxes.

Index to original ditch papers, showing name of ditch, location by township and section numbers, date established, name of principal petitioner, and file box number. Arranged alphabetically by the names of ditches. Handwritten on printed forms. 60 pages. 15 x 9.5 x .5. Auditor's vault.

18. DITCH CASH RECORD

1890—. 5 volumes. (2-6).

Record of expenditures and assessments on benefited lands, showing name of ditch, ditch number, date established, names of townships, length of ditch, date contract awarded, cost of construction, total assessments, property owners share of cost, name of property owners, and amount assessed. Arranged chronologically by dates established. Indexed alphabetically by names of ditches. Handwritten on printed forms. Average 300 pages. 12 x 12 x 1.5. 4 volumes, 1890-1930, Auditor's vault; 1 volume, 1931—, Commissioners' main office.

Bridges

19. [BRIDGE PAPERS]
1913—. 5 file boxes, 1 file drawer.

Original papers relative to construction and repair of bridges and culverts, consisting of journal entries, commissioners' resolutions approving construction or repair, engineer's surveys, sketches, blueprints, specifications and estimates, notice to bidders of proposals, bids received, contracts, and bonds, showing bridge number, name of bridge, highway, stream, and township, date of resolution approving construction, surveyor's data on survey of approaches, sketch and blueprint of proposed construction, measurements (no scale), detailed specifications as to type of construction and materials, estimate of cost of material and labor, total cost, names of bidder, amount of bid, name of contractor, contract price, amount of contractor's bond, names of sureties, and dates filed. 1913-1929, arranged chronologically by dates of resolutions; 1930—, arranged numerically by bridge numbers, all papers of each proposal file together and a jacket or folder. No index. Sketches, hand drawn; handwritten and typed on printed forms. File boxes, 10.5 x 4.5 x 14; file drawer, 12 x 14 x 24. 5 file boxes, 1913-1929, Auditor's main office; 1 file drawer, 1930—. Commissioners' main office.

20. BRIDGE CONTRACTS
1870-1914. 18 file boxes. (dated).

Copies of contracts with firms and individuals for construction or repair of bridges and culverts, showing contract number, proposal number, name, number, location, and type of structure, name of contractor, contract price, terms of agreement, date of contract, and date filed. Arranged chronologically by dates filed. No index. Handwritten on printed forms. 10.5 x 4.5 x 14. Auditor's vault.

Contracts and bids

21. CONTRACT RECORD
1923—. 1 volume. (1).
Record of contracts let for construction or repair of roads, bridges, and culverts, showing proposal number, name and number of project, date contract approved, name of contractor, amount of contract, amount of contractor's bond, names of sureties, record of payments to contractor on account, date contract completed and accepted, balance due contractor, and date paid. Arranged chronologically by dates contracts approved. Indexed alphabetically by names of roads, bridges, or culverts. Handwritten on printed forms. 530 pages. 18 x 12 x 2.5. Commissioners' main office.

22. BIDS AND CONTRACTS
1892-1926. 3 file boxes.
Original bids and contracts for construction and repair of county buildings, showing proposal number, what building, location, date filed, name of bidder, amount of bid, name of contractor, contract price, terms of contract; includes architect's sketches, plans, specifications, and estimates of cost of construction; also includes copies of franchises granted various public utility companies, 1908-1922, to erect communication lines or lay pipe lines showing date granted, name of utility company, amount of compensation, terms of agreement, and date filed. No index. Sketches hand drawn; Handwritten and typed on printed forms. 10.5 x 4.5 x 14. Auditor's vault.

23. BRIDGE WORK [Proposal and Bids County Projects]
1916—. 2 file boxes. (1, no title).
Original papers pertaining to construction work in county consisting of proposals, legal notices to bidders, and bids submitted on various county construction and repair projects, showing proposal number, name and location of project, dates of proposals and notices, specifications for construction and materials, names of bidders, amount of bid, and date filed. Arranged chronologically by dates filed. No index. Proposals and notices, typed; bids, handwritten and typed on printed forms. 10.5 x 4.5 x 14. Auditor's vault.

24. SURVEYOR'S FORCE ACCOUNT RECORD

1930-1934. 1 volume. Discontinued.

Record of expenditures for road construction and repair by direction of county surveyor, showing what project, location, date of entry, name of payee, amount, for what, and total for project. Arranged chronologically by dates of entries. No index. Handwritten on forms. 200 pages. 20 x 15 x 1.25. Commissioners' main office.

25. COUNTY HOME

1904—. 1 file box.

Contract for remodeling of the county home building, showing date, name of contractor, contract price, specifications and remodeling including specifications for lighting equipment and power plant, dates of completion, and dates filed. Also contains [Reports, County Home], 1913—, entry 9. Arranged chronologically by dates filed. No index. Typed on printed forms. 10.5 x 4.5 x 14. Commissioners' main office.

Financial Records

26. SHEEP CLAIMS

1934—. 2 file boxes.

Original claims for compensation for sheep or other domestic animals killed or injured by dogs, showing claim number, date of claim, name of claimant, township, date of damage, number, kind and grade of animals killed, number injured, appraised value less amount received for pelts and carcasses, amount of claim, names of appraisers, date file, date approved, amount approved and volume and page numbers of Commissioners' Journal, entry 1. Arranged numerically by claim numbers. No index. Handwritten on printed forms. 10.5 x 4.5 x 14. Commissioners' main office.

27. CLAIMS REJECTED

1891-1923. 1 file box.

Original bills and claims filed on which payment was refused, showing bill number, date of bill, name of claimant, amount of bill, for what, reason for rejection, and date filed. No index. Handwritten and types, mostly on statement forms. 10.5 x 4.5 x 14. Commissioners' main office.

28. RECEIPTS AND EXPENDITURES, CLASSIFIED
1908—. 3 volumes. (1-3).
Record of cash receipts and expenditures for county home; receipts, showing date received, item sold, name of payer, amount; expenditures, showing date paid, amount paid out for food, clothing, drugs and medical services, tobacco, burials, furnishings, farm equipment, hay and grain, seed and fertilizer, livestock, and repairs; total annual receipts and expenditures. Arranged chronologically by dates of receipts and expenditures. No index. Handwritten on forms. Average 200 pages. 17 x 15 x 1.25. 1 volume, 1908-1922, State examiner's office; 2 volumes, 1908—, Commissioners' main office.

Miscellaneous

29. MISCELLANEOUS
1880—. 9 file boxes. 7, no title.
Original or copies of documents relative to commissioners department covering a great many subjects of minor importance consisting in part of: Petitions by property owners and city council for annexation of territory to city of Tiffin, 1893-1907; report by clerk of courts of fines and costs assessed and collected in common pleas court cases, 1881; resolutions authorizing transfer of funds from one county fund to another, 1905, 1911, 1924; surveyor's sketch of courthouse and jail grounds; petitions from freeholders for erection of public scales at Old Fort, 1904; petitions from property owners for erection of a water tank in third ward city of Tiffin, 1880; record of special canvass of votes cast for land appraisers, 1889; copies of commissioners' resolutions covering a large number of subjects, 1898—; copies of certificates of award and of revision of grant, blind pensions, 1913-1936; all showing date of document, title, names of principles, text of document, and date filed; also, 1928—, original bids filed by dealers on coal proposals, showing proposal number, name and address of bidder, number of tons, grade, amount of bid per ton, and date filed; original bids filed by dealers on proposal to furnish crushed stone for road construction and repair, showing proposal number, name and address of bidder, number cubic yards, grade, amount of bid per cubic yard, and date filed; county budgets set up by budget commission, showing year, amount allocated to each office, department, or fund, total for county, and date filed; original bills filed by sheriff for expense of transporting prisoners, showing date of bill, name of prisoner, places transported from and to, total bill, date filed and signature of sheriff; copies of commissioners resolutions approving sheriff's and coroner's

expense accounts and authorizing payment; copies of pay rolls of county employees under civil service, showing date of pay roll, name of employee, position, classification, wage rate, amount, total amount of pay roll, and date filed; Also contains [Reports, Dog Warden], 1937—, entry 8. Arranged chronologically by dates filed. No index. Handwritten and typed mostly on printed forms. 10.5 x 4.5 x 14. 7 file boxes, 1880—, Auditor's vault; 2 file boxes, 1928—, Commissioners' main office.

Relief Administration

30. CASE RECORDS

1935—. 4 file boxes. 2 subtitled Active Cases; 2 Inactive Cases.

Original papers filed relative to emergency relief consisting of applications for relief, showing application (case) number, name and address of applicant, date of application, age, sex, color, nationality, nativity, marital status, names, ages and relationship of dependents, education, occupation, property and income statement, and signature of applicant; investigator's reports, showing case number, name and address of applicant, home conditions, findings and recommendations as to need of relief; record of relief granted, showing date application approved, amount and kind of relief provided and dates distributed. Inactive files are case records of clients removed from roles by reason of private employment, removal from county, death or other sufficient cause and include same type of records as active files with the addition of a certificate of cancellation, showing date, case number, name of client, and reason for cancellation. All papers of each case filed together in a folder, showing case number. Arranged numerically by case numbers. For index, see entry 31. Handwritten and typed on printed forms. 11 x 12.5 x 26. Relief administration office, 35 Court Street, Tiffin.

31. MASTER FILE

1935—. 2 file boxes. 1 subtitled Active Cases; 1 Inactive Cases.

Index to case records, entry 30, showing name and address of client, case number, date of application, date relief granted, age of applicant, number of dependents, marital status, physical defects, occupation, and if inactive shows date closed. Arranged alphabetically by names of clients. Handwritten on printed forms. 4 x 5.5 x 11. Relief administration office, 35 Court Street, Tiffin.

32. POSTING LEDGER

1935—. 2 volumes.

Record of relief provided, showing name and address of client, case number, date distributed, item, quantity, value, and total each month. Arranged alphabetically by names of clients and chronologically thereunder by dates distributed. No index. Handwritten on forms. Average 340 pages. 9 x 14 x 2. Relief administration office, 35 Court Street, Tiffin.

33. ENCUMBRANCE AND VOUCHER REGISTER

1935—. 1 volume.

Ledger record, showing date of entry, amount appropriated and available for relief expenditures each twelve-month period, amount allocated to cash relief, groceries, clothing, shelter, fuel, medical care, administrative, and sundries; record of vouchers issued on each fund, showing dates, voucher number, amount, and name of payee. Arranged chronologically by dates of entries. No index. Handwritten on forms. 180 pages. 10 x 12 x 1. Relief administration office, 35 Court Street, Tiffin.

34. ENCUMBRANCE REGISTER, RURAL RECOVERY

1934-1935. 1 volume.

Ledger record of funds appropriated to rural recovery program, showing date of entry, amount of federal funds, amount of state funds, amount of county funds, and total appropriation for year; amount allocated to purchase of livestock, of hay and grain, of tools and equipment, of seeds and fertilizer, repairs, rentals, administration cost, and sundries; record of vouchers issued on each fund, showing date, voucher number, amount, and name of payee. Arranged chronologically by dates of entries. No index. Handwritten on forms. 100 pages. 11 x 17 x .75. Attic store room. County courthouse.

35. VOUCHERS

1935—. 12 bundles.

Duplicate vouchers issued authorizing payment of relief bills and claims, showing voucher number, date issued, name of payee, amount, for what, name of relief client, and signature of issuing official. Arranged numerically by voucher numbers. No index. Handwritten on printed forms. 8.5 x 6 x 4. Relief administration office, 35 Court Street, Tiffin.

36. VOUCHER INDEX

1935. 1 file box. Discontinued.

Index record of vouchers issued authorizing payment of relief bills and claims showing name of payee, voucher number, date issued, amount, and for what. Arranged alphabetically by names of payers. Handwritten on forms. 5 x 7 x 11. Relief administration office, 35 Court Street, Tiffin.

37. VOUCHER REGISTER

1934-1935. 1 volume.

Register of vouchers issued authorizing payment of relief bills and claims, showing voucher number, date issued; name of payee, amount, and for what. Arranged numerically by voucher numbers. No index. Handwritten on forms. 275 pages. 11 x 17 x 1.5. Attic store room. County courthouse.

38. WPA CERTIFICATIONS

1935—. 9 file boxes. 2, subtitled active; 1, Waiting List; 2, Inactive; 4, Cancelled.

Copies of certification to work projects for eligibility for employment, showing case number, name and address of client, identification number, sex, age, color, marital status, education, occupation, trade or profession, physical defects, and date certified; inactive cases also shows date transferred to inactive file and reason for transfer; cancellations also shows date cancelled and reason for cancellation. Arranged alphabetically by names of clients. No index. Typed on printed forms. 6 x 9 x 11. Relief administration office, 35 Court Street, Tiffin.

39. CORRESPONDENCE

1935—. 4 file drawers.

Original incoming correspondence and carbon copies of outgoing correspondence relative to emergency relief administration between the local agency and other county and state relief agencies, Work Projects Administration, and social agencies, showing date of correspondence, from whom or to whom, subject, signatures, and official titles. Arranged alphabetically by subject correspondence and chronologically thereunder by dates of correspondence. No index. Typed. 11 x 12.5 x 26. Relief administration office, 35 Court Street, Tiffin.

Aid for the Blind
(See also entries 372, 373, 529)

40. BLIND RELIEF RECORD

1913-1936. 1 volume. Discontinued; superseded by Aid for the Blind.
Record of applications for blind relief, showing case number, name and address of applicant, date filed, age, sex, color, date application approved, amount of grant, and date effective. Arranged alphabetically by names of applicants. No index. Handwritten on forms. 200 pages. 17 x 14 x 1. Commissioners' main office, County courthouse,

For prior records, see entry 528.

41. REGISTER OF CASES

July 1936—. 1 volume.
Register of applications for blind relief and of grants and revisions, showing name and address of applicant, case number, date of application, age, sex, color, marital status, number of dependents, date application approved, amount of grant, and date grant effective, date of revision, amount of revised grant, and reason for revision. Arranged numerically by case numbers. No index. Typed or printed forms. 10 pages (loose-leaf binder) 11.5 x 17.5 x .25. Relief administration office, 35 Court Street, Tiffin.

42. CASE RECORDS

July 1936—. 1 file drawer.
Complete case histories of applicants and clients for aid to blind consisting of:

a. Applications, showing application number, date of application, name and address of applicant, age, date of birth, birthplace, sex, color, marital status, number of dependents, how long blind, degree of blindness, cause of blindness, and former occupation.

b, Social security board physician's report to county board for blind relief, on eye examination of applicant, showing address, sex, color, date of birth, age at onset of blindness, right or left eye, and physician's diagnosis; also showing date of examination, date of report, signature and address of physician.

c. Social date card or condensed history of person granted relief, showing date of application, name, address, personal history, other social assistance, status of case, case number, date of action, amount of age, and warrant number; also rejections.

d. Certificates to auditor toward, revise, or terminate blind relief, consisting of certificate of award, nonresident; certificate of award for medical care; certificate of revision; certificate of termination; all showing date, name or recipient, amount of award per annum, date approved and date effective.

e. Vouchers to county auditor for monthly payments to recipients, showing date, name of recipient, total monthly payments, warrant number, and approval of board of county commissioners. These records are on form BR-31.

f. Copies of monthly statistical reports to Ohio commissioners for the blind on applications filed, showing month and year of report, number of applications for blind relief, number pending from last five months, number disposed of during month, number of individuals granted relief, amount of obligation incurred for relief during the month, totals, and signature of authorized official; September 1937—, record of hospitalization included.

Arranged by subject; papers of each subject filed together in a folder. No index. Typed in front of forms. Folders, 8.5 x 11; file drawer, 9 x 12 x 20. Relief administration office, 35 Court Street, Tiffin.

The office of county recorder, modeled on the public land registers of the colonial period, was established in the territory of which the present state of Ohio is a part, by an act of the Northwest Territory, effective August 1, 1795. This act provided for the appointment by the governor of a recorder in each county, whose principal duty was the recording of deeds.[1] When Ohio entered the union in 1803 no constitutional provision was made for the continuation of the office, but the legislature during its first session passed an act providing for a recorder in each county to be appointed by the judges of the court of common pleas for a seven-year term.[2] The recorder continued to be an appointive office until 1829, when, by legislative act, he became elective for a three-year term.[3] The tenure year of the office remained at three years until the constitutional amendment of November 7, 1905 which provided for the election of all county officers in the even-numbered years.[4] The term of office was fixed at two years, and so continued until the amendment of 1933 which extended the term of the incumbent until January 1937, at which time the recorder elected at the regular election in November 193? began to serve a four-year term.[5]

The first county recorder was directed by statute to record "all deeds, mortgages and conveyances of lands and tenements," lying within his county, and also all instruments and writing required by law to be recorded.[6] In 1805 he was directed to record all plats and maps of newly laid-out villages. In 1835 he was permitted, when authorized by the county commissioners, to transcribe from the records of other counties all deeds, mortgages, and other instruments of writing for the sale or conveyance of land, tenements, or hereditaments affecting land titles in his county.[8]

Since the establishment of the office many duties besides those of recording land titles have been added. The present practice of recording powers of attorney had its beginning in 1818.[9]

---

1. Pease, *op. cit.,* 197-199.
2. *Laws of Ohio,* I, 136.
3. *Ibid.,* XXVII, 65.
4. *Ohio Const. 1851,* (Amendment, 1905), Art. XVII, secs. 1, 2; *Laws of Ohio,* XCVIII, 271.
5. *Laws of Ohio,* CXV, 191.
6. *Ibid.,* I, 137.
7. *Ibid.,* III, 213-215.
8. *Ibid.,* XXXIII, 8; XXXV, 10-11.
9. *Ibid.,* XVI, 155-156.

Although the mechanics of Cincinnati were authorized to file mechanics' liens with the recorder as early as 1823, it was not until 1843 that the privilege was extended to the laborers of Seneca County.[10] Successive acts in 1865, 1872, 1881, 1884, 1888, 1904, and 1923 added new duties to the office in the recording of soldier' discharges,[11] copies of certificates of compliance authorizing insurance company not incorporated under the law of Ohio to transact business in the state, and certified copies of renewals as granted by such companies to their agents,[12] limited partnership agreements,[13] stallion keepers' liens,[14] oil and gas leases,[15] partition fence records,[16] and federal tax liens.[17] The recording of chattel mortgages and conditional sales began in 1846. Such instruments were to be deposited with the township clerk where the mortgagor was a resident. In all townships, however, in which the recorder maintained his office such instruments were to be deposited with him.[18] Since 1906 chattel mortgages have been filed with the county recorder exclusively.[19] It is provided that in order to be valid against subsequent mortgages, the chattel mortgage must be deposited with the county recorder of the county where the mortgagor resides at the time of its execution, and to retain its validity the mortgage must be renewed every three years.[20] In 1936 the legislature passed an act authorizing the recorder to destroy such instruments six years after the time of refiling has expired.[21]

An important extension of the method of recording land titles known as the "Torrens System," was provided by an act of the general assembly in 1896.[22] In 1897 this act was declared unconstitutional by the supreme court of Ohio as being contrary to section 16 of the bill of rights of the state constitution.[23]

---

10. *Ibid.,* XXI, 8-10; XLI, 66.
11. *Ibid.,* LXII, 59.
12. *Laws of Ohio,* LXIX, 32, 148; XCVII, 405.
13. *Ibid.,* LXXVIII, 248.
14. *Ibid.,* LXXXI, 43.
15. *Ibid.,* LXXXV, 179.
16. *Ibid.,* XCVII, 140.
17. *Ibid.,* CX, 252.
18. *Ibid.,* XLIV, 61.
19. G. C. sec. 8561.
20. G. C. sec. 8565.
21. *Laws of Ohio,* CXVI, 324.
22. *Ibid.,* XCII, 220.
23. *Ohio State Reports,* LVI, 575.

The act of 1913, amended later in 1913 and again in 1915, provides for the examination of land titles by the recorder in the issuance, if the title to be held in fee simple, of a certificate of title by the court of common pleas or probate court. The official certificate becomes the title of ownership and is indefeasible. However, in the event an interest is found in the land, after the issuance of the certificate, a claim is allowed to be the legal claimant from a fund created for that purpose at the time of registration.[24] This system, although adopted by a few counties, excluding Seneca, is not used as widely as it might be because of the difficulty of replacing the traditional complicated system.

The recorder, like other county officials, had been required in earlier years to keep records of the business of his office, but it was not until the middle of the nineteenth century that the legislature, looking forward to some uniformity in land registration, enacted measures prescribing the form and contents of such records. Since 1850 the recorder has been required to keep a record of deeds in which is recorded all deeds, powers of attorney, and other instruments of writing for the unconditional sale of land, tenements, or hereditaments. The same year saw the beginning of a record of mortgages in which were recorded all mortgages, powers of attorney, and other instruments of writing by which land, tenements, or hereditaments "shall or maybe mortgages" or otherwise conditionally sold; and a record of plats in which was to be recorded all plats and maps of town lots and of the subdivisions thereof, and of other divisions or surveyed lands, in like regular succession according to the priority of their presentation.[25] Since 1851 the recorder has been required to keep a separate record of deeds and mortgages denominated respectively as "Record of Deeds" and "Record of Mortgages."[26] Since 1865 the recorder has been required by statute to keep a separate record of leases.[27] The present practice of keeping a daily register of deeds and a daily register of mortgages has been required by statute since 1896.[28] In Seneca County a separate record of mortgages has been maintained since 1836, a separate record of leases since 1850, and a daily register since 1867.

---

24. G. C. secs. 8572-34—8572-56; *Laws of Ohio,* CIII, 914-960; CVI, 443.
25. *Laws of Ohio,* XLVIII, 64.
26. *Ibid.,* XLIX, 103.
27. *Ibid.,* LXII, 170.
28. *Ibid.,* XCII, 268.

Although indexes had been prepared in earlier years, the present system of indexing had its beginning in 1851 and took practically its present form in 1896.[29] At present the recorder, at the beginning of each day's business, is required to take and maintain a general alphabetical index, direct and reverse, of all names of both parties of all instruments recorded by him. The indexes show the kind of instruments, the date, the range, the township and section, the survey number and the number of acres or the lot and sublot numbers and the part thereof, of each tract or lot of land described in any such instrument of writing; the name of each grantor is entered in the direct index under the appropriate letter and followed on the same line by the name of the grantee; the name of each grantee is entered in the reverse index under the appropriate letter and followed on the same line by the name of the grantor.[30]

From 1859 to 1867 the recorder in every county with more than 200,000 population was required to maintain sectional indexes to the recorders of all real estate in the county. Since 1867 recorders have been required to maintain such indexes in all counties in which the commissioners have instituted them.[31]

Present duties of the recorder do not differ, in the main, from those prescribed in the middle of the nineteenth century. His records, bound in large bulky volumes, are open to the inspection of the public and are transferred to his successor.

---

29. *Ibid.,* XLIX, 103; XCII, 268; CII, 288.
30. G. C. sec. 2764.
31. *Laws of Ohio,* LVI, 20; LXIV, 256; LXXVI, 49, CII, 289; G. C. sec. 2766.

Real Property Transfers
(See also entries 316-319)

Deeds and Registers

43. DEED RECORD
1821—. 234 volumes. (1, 1, 2, 1-231).

Copies of instruments transferring title to real estate, showing instrument number, names of grantor and grantee, kind of instrument, description and location of tract or lot, amount of consideration, or if miscellaneous instrument text of agreement or power delegated, notarization, names of witnesses, date of instrument, and date filed and recorded; One volume (1), 1821-1824, is transcribed from Sandusky County deed records. Also contains: Lease Record, 1821-1849, entry 50; Mortgage Record, 1823-1835, entry 54; Record of Mechanics' Liens, 1844-1845, entry 61; Power of Attorney Record, 1827-1892, entry 94; Miscellaneous Record, 1822-1919, entry 100. Mortgage cancellations recorded on page margins, 1827-1835. Arranged chronologically by dates recorded. For indexes, see entries 44, 45. 1821-1912 handwritten; 1913—, typed. Average 600 pages. 18 x 12 x 3. Recorder's vault.

44. GENERAL INDEX TO DEEDS, GRANTORS
1821—. 18 volumes. (1-18).

Direct index to Deed Record, entry 43, showing names of grantor and grantee, volume and page numbers of record, amount of consideration, lot number, description of tract or lot, number of acres, kind of instrument, and date of instrument. Arranged alphabetically by names of grantors. Handwritten on forms. Average 630 pages. 20 x 13 x 3.25. Recorder's main office.

45. GENERAL INDEX TO DEEDS, GRANTEES
1821—. 18 volumes. (1-18).

Reverse index to Deed Record, entry 43, showing names of grantee and grantor, volume and page numbers of record, amount of consideration, lot number, description of tract or lot, number of acres, kind of instrument and date of instrument. Arranged alphabetically by names the grantees. Handwritten on forms. Average 630 pages. 20 x 13 x 3.25. Recorder's main office.

46. CEMETERY DEED RECORD
1875—. 1 volume. (1).

Copies of instruments conveying title to cemetery lots, showing names of grantor (cemetery association) and grantee, instrument number, description and location of lot, names and titles of association officials attesting instrument, date of instrument, and dates filed and recorded. Arranged chronologically by dates recorded. Indexed alphabetically by names the grantees. Handwritten on printed forms. 428 pages. 18 x 12 x 2.5. Recorder's vault.

47. INDEX TO ORIGINAL ENTRIES
1821-1861. 1 volume. (1).

Index record of original entries and subsequent transfers of tracts and lots, showing name of township, section, township and range numbers, names are grantor and grantee, volume and page numbers of Deed Record, entry 43, description and location of entry, tracts or lot, number of acres, and date of entry or transfer. Arranged by townships, numerically thereunder by section numbers, and chronologically thereunder by dates of transfers. Handwritten on forms. 580 pages. 18 x 12 x 3. Recorder's main office.

48. CERTIFICATE OF TRANSFER OF REAL ESTATE
1904—. 6 volumes. (1-6). Title varies: Certificate– Real Estate Devised by Will, 4 volumes, 1904-1932.

Copies of certificates of transfer of title to real estate devised by will issued by probate court, showing certificate number, date issued, name of testator, date will probated, copy of that part of will designating distribution of real estate, names of devisees, description and location of tract or lot, volume and page numbers of Will Record, entry 228, and dates filed and recorded. Arranged chronologically by dates recorded. Indexed alphabetically by names of testators showing name of devisees. 1904-1915, handwritten on printed forms. 1915—, typed on printed forms. Average 300 pages. 18 x 12 x 1.5. Recorder's vault.

49. FILE REGISTER
1867-1875, 1889—. 10 volumes. (2-9; two unlabeled). Title varies: Register of Deeds and Mortgages, 1867-1875, 1 volume; Deed Register, 1889-1900, 1 volume.

Daily register of instruments, except chattel mortgages, showing date filed, names of grantor and grantee, kind of instrument, instrument number, to whom delivered, number of acres, amount of consideration. Also contains: File Register of Leases, 1895-1900, 1916—, entry 53; File Register–Mechanics' Liens, 1916—, entry 64. Arranged numerically by instrument numbers. No index. Handwritten on forms. Average 500 pages. 22 x 13 x 2.5. Recorder's vault.

Leases

50. LEASE RECORD
1850—. 30 volumes. (1 unlabeled; 2-30). Volume 20, subtitled Sun Oil Company Leases. 1821-1849 in Deed Record, entry 43.

Copies of instruments conveying right to use of lands, tenements, and equipment, also right to prospect premises for oil and natural gas, showing instrument number, names of lessor and lessee, description and location of tract, lot or equipment, terms of agreement, date of instrument, notarization, names of witnesses, dates filed and recorded. Volume 20 includes Sun Oil Company and other leases. Arranged chronologically by dates recorded. For indexes, see entries 51, 52. 1850-1910, handwritten; 1910—, typed on printed forms. Average 450 pages. 18 x 12 x 2.5. Recorder's vault.

51. GENERAL INDEX TO LEASES, LESSORS

1850—. 3 volumes. (1-3).

Direct index to Lease Record, entry 50, showing names of lessor and lessee, volume and page numbers of record, amount of consideration, lot number, description and location of tract, lot or equipment, and date of instrument. Arranged alphabetically by names of lessors. Handwritten on forms. Average 350 pages. 18 x 12 x 2. Recorder's main office.

52. GENERAL INDEX TO LEASES, LESSEES

1850—. 3 volumes. (1-3).

Reverse index to Lease Record, entry 50, showing names of lessee and lessor, volume and page numbers of record, amount of consideration, lot number, description and location of tract, lot or equipment, and date of instrument. Arranged alphabetically by names of lessees. Handwritten on forms. Average 350 pages. 18 x 12 x 2. Recorder's main office.

53. FILE REGISTER OF LEASES

1906-1915. 1 volume. (1). 1895-1900, 1916—, in File Register, entry 49.

Register of instruments conveying right to use of land, tenements, and equipment, showing date filed, names of lessor and lessee, instrument number, to whom delivered, and date delivered. Arranged numerically by instrument numbers. No index. Handwritten on forms. 250 pages. 14 x 15 x 1.5. Recorder's vault.

Mortgages

54. MORTGAGE RECORD

1836—. 138 volumes. (1-138). 1823-1835 in Deed Record, entry 43.

Copies of instruments conveying conditional title to real estate for value received, showing instrument number, names of mortgagor mortgagee, date of instrument, description and location of tract or lot, amount of encumbrance, terms of obligation, notarization, names of witnesses, and dates filed and recorded. Cancellations recorded on page margins, showing date cancelled, amount cancelled, by whom authorized, date recorded, and signature of recorder or deputy. Arranged chronologically by dates recorded. For indexes, see entries 55, 56. 1836-1919, handwritten; 1920—, typed on printed forms. Average 600 pages. 18 x 12 x 3. Recorder's vault.

55. GENERAL INDEX TO MORTGAGES–GRANTORS
1836—. 12 volumes. (1-12).

Direct index to Mortgage Record, entry 54, showing names of grantor and grantee, volume and page numbers of record, amount of encumbrance, lot number, description and location of tract or lot, name of town, number acres, notation of release of mortgage, and date instrument recorded. Arranged alphabetically by names of grantors. Handwritten on forms. Average 630 pages. 20 x 13 x 3.25. Recorder's main office.

56. GENERAL INDEX TO MORTGAGES–GRANTEES
1836—. 12 volumes. (1-12).

Reverse index to Mortgage Record, entry 54, showing name of grantee and grantor, volume and page number of record, amount of encumbrance, lot number, description and location of tract or lot, name of town, number acres, notation of release of mortgage, and date instrument recorded. Arranged alphabetically by names of grantees. Handwritten on forms. Average 630 pages. 20 x 13 x 3.25. Recorder's main office.

57. MORTGAGES—TIFFIN SAVINGS AND LOAN ASSOCIATION
1868-1880. 2 volumes. (1, 2).

Copies of instruments conveying conditional title to real estate to the Tiffin Savings and Loan Association for value received, showing instrument number, name of mortgagor, date of instrument, description and location of tract or lot, amount of encumbrance, terms of obligation, names of witnesses, notarization, and dates filed and recorded. Cancellations recorded on page margins, showing date cancelled, amount cancelled, by whom authorized, date recorded, and signature of recorder or deputy. Arranged chronologically by dates recorded. Indexed alphabetically by names of mortgagors. Handwritten on printed forms. Average 650 pages. 18 x 12 x 3. Recorder's vault.

58. MORTGAGES—CITIZENS BUILDING ASSOCIATION
1885-1891. 1 volume. (1).

Copies of instruments conveying conditional title to real estate to the Citizens Building Association for value received, showing instrument number, name of mortgagor, date of instrument, description and location of tract or lot, amount of encumbrance, terms of obligation, names of witnesses, notarization, and date filed and recorded. Cancellations recorded on page margins, showing dates cancelled, amount cancelled, and by whom authorized, date recorded. Arranged chronologically by dates recorded. Indexed alphabetically by names of mortgagors. Handwritten on printed forms. 320 pages. 18 x 12 x 1.5. Recorder's vault.

59. REGISTER OF MORTGAGES AND CANCELLATIONS
1889-1893. 1 volume.

Register of instruments filed for recording conveying conditional title to real estate, showing instrument number, name of mortgagor mortgagee, date file, description of tract or lot, number of acres, amount of encumbrance, date delivered, to whom delivered, and date cancelled. Arranged numerically by instrument numbers. No index. Handwritten on forms. 240 pages. 16 x 11 x 1.5. Recorder's vault.

60. SPECIAL RELEASE RECORD
1891—. 5 volumes. (1-5). Title varies: Certificates of Discharge of Mortgages, 1891-1928. 3 volumes.

Copies of certificates of release or discharge of mortgages on real estate issued by county courts, showing certificate number, date of issue, court of issue, names of mortgagor and mortgagee, date of mortgage, description and location of tract or lot encumbered, amount cancelled, and date filed and recorded. Indexed alphabetically by names of mortgagors showing names of mortgagees. 1891-1910, handwritten on printed forms; 1910—, typed on printed forms. Average 300 pages. 18 x 12 x 1.5. Recorder's vault.

Liens

61. RECORD OF MECHANICS' LIENS
1855—. 9 volumes. (1, 3-10). 1844-1855 in Deed Record, entry 43.

Copies of instruments filed by laborers or merchants to protect and secure claim for wages due and/or for materials furnished, showing instrument number, name of creditor and debtor, itemized statement of claim (item, quantity, amount), total amount of claim, description and location of real estate or other property attached as security, date of instrument, notarization, dates filed and recorded. Two volumes, originally number 1 and 2, 1855-1871, transcribed and combined in one volume, number 1. Also contains Sub-contractors' liens, 1855-1928, entry 62. Arranged chronologically by dates recorded. Indexed alphabetically by names of creditors showing names of debtors. 1855-1915, handwritten; 1915—, typed. Average 450 pages. 18 x 12 x 2.5. 7 volumes, 1855-1913, recorder's vault; 2 volumes, 1913—, Recorder's main office.

62. SUB-CONTRACTORS' LIENS

1929—. 1 volume. (1). 1855-1928 in Record of Mechanics' Liens, entry 61.
Register of liens by subcontractors as security for claims for labor performed and materials furnished, showing name of payer (property owner), name of creditor (subcontractor), name of debtor (contractor), itemized statement of claim, instrument number, date of lien, date filed, and date cancelled. Original liens, 1936—, in folder attached inside front cover. Arranged alphabetically by names of payers. No index. Handwritten on forms. 300 pages. 16 x 11 x 1.5. Recorder's vault.

63. LIENS–SUBCONTRACTORS

1888-1903, 1929-1935. 4 bundles.
Original liens filed by subcontractors as security for labor and materials furnished, showing instrument number, affidavit supporting claim, name of payer (property owner), name of creditor (subcontractor), name of debtor (contractor), itemized statement of labor perform and materials furnished, amount claimed, description and location of construction project, notarization, signatures of payment and witnesses, title of official attesting affidavit, date of affidavit (lien), date file, and signature of recorder. Arranged chronologically by dates filed. No index. Handwritten and typed on printed forms. 9 x 3.5 x 2. Recorder's vault.

64. FILE REGISTER–MECHANICS' LIENS

1910-1915. 1 volume. 1916— in File Register, entry 49.
Register of liens filed for recordings, showing date filed, name of creditor and debtor, instrument number, kind of instrument, date delivered, and to whom delivered. Arranged numerically by instrument numbers. No index. Handwritten on printed forms. 250 pages. 24 x 15 x 1.5. Recorder's vault.

65. STALLION KEEPERS' LIENS

1840-1892. 1 volume.

Copies of liens filed as security for stallion service fees, showing instrument number, date of instrument, name of owner of stallion, name of owner of mare, description of mare, amount of lien, and dates filed and recorded; cancellation of lien recorded on page margin. Arranged chronologically by dates recorded. Indexed alphabetically by names of owners of stallions showing names of owners of mares. Handwritten. 300 pages. 14 x 9 x 1.5. Recorder's vault.

66. TAX LIEN RECORD

1894-1933. 1 volume. (1).

Copies of authority to pay delinquent real estate taxes and lien on property as security, showing recorders file number, date of authority, name of property owner, amount of taxes, description and location of tract or lot, amount of lien, and dates filed and recorded. Arranged chronologically by dates filed. Indexed alphabetically by names of property owners. 1894-1914, handwritten; 1915-1933, typed. 590 pages. 18 x 12 x 3. Recorder's vault.

67. EXCISE AND FRANCHISE TAX LIEN INDEX, AND INDEX TO CORPORATION RECORD

1931—. 1 volume. (1).

In front half of volume, index record of liens by state tax commission for delinquent excise and franchise taxes of public utilities, showing recorder's file number, name of public utility, date file, amount of tax, penalty, and total due; index to corporate record, showing recorder's file number, notice of payment of tax, date filed, amount of tax and penalty assessed, date paid, amount paid, and page number of corporation record in back of volume. Arranged alphabetically by names of public utilities. Handwritten on forms. Corporation record in back half of volume, consisting of notices filed by state tax commission for payments of delinquent excise and franchise taxes and cancellation of liens thereof, showing number of notice, date of notice, name of public utility, amount of tax and penalty, date paid, amount paid, date lien cancelled, and dates filed and recorded. Arranged chronologically by dates recorded. For index, see Excise and Franchise Tax Index and Index to Corporation Record in front of volume. Handwritten on printed forms. 315 pages. 12 x 17 x 2. Recorder's main office.

68. EXCISE AND FRANCHISE TAX LIENS

1931—. 1 bundle.

Original notices of liens filed by state tax commission against public utility companies for delinquent excise and franchise taxes, showing date of lien notice, name of public utility, amount of delinquent tax, penalty due, and dates filed and recorded. Arranged chronologically by dates filed. No index. Typed on printed forms. 9 x 3.5 x 1. Recorder's vault.

69. FEDERAL TAX LIEN INDEX

1923—. 1 volume (1).

Index record of liens filed against the delinquent taxpayers, showing recorder's file number, name of taxpayer, collector's number, notice of lien, date filed, amount of delinquent tax, penalty, total due, recorder's file number, notice of payment and cancellation of lien, date notice filed, collector's number, notice of payment and cancellation of lien, amount of tax and penalty assessed, date paid, amount paid, and date lien cancelled. Arranged alphabetically by names of taxpayers. Handwritten on forms. 250 pages. 17 x 16 x 1.5. Recorder's main office.

70. INDEX AND RECORD OF LIENS–MOTOR VEHICLE LIABILITY BONDS

1937—. 1 volume. (1).

Index record of liens filed against motor vehicle operators or owners on damage claims, showing recorder's file number, date filed, name of operator or owner, amount of lien, description of property attached, amount of liability bond, and names of sureties. Arranged alphabetically by names of operators or owners. Handwritten on printed forms. 28 pages. 17 x 13 x .25. Recorder's main office.

71. INDEX TO LIENS SURETY OF RECOGNIZANCE

1929—. 1 volume. (1).

Index record of liens filed against sureties of recognizance (bail bonds), showing recorder's file number, date filed, names of sureties, name of defendant, offense, amount of recognizance, description and location of real estate pledged as security, and date cancelled. Arranged alphabetically by names that sureties. Handwritten on printed forms. 400 pages. 17 x 14 x 2. Recorder's main office.

72. BOND LIENS

1929—. 1 bundle.

Original notices of liens filed against sureties of recognizance, showing date of notice, names of sureties, name of defendant, offense, amount of recognizance, description and location of real estate pledged as security, and dates filed and recorded. Arranged chronologically by dates filed. No index. Typed on printed forms. 9 x 3.5 x 2. Recorder's vault.

Maps, Plats, and Surveys (See also entries 320-322, 543-545, 547-551)

73. PLATS OF SENECA COUNTY

1821-1889. 2 volumes. (1, 2).

Copies of plats, original surveys, subsequent surveys of land tracts, and town plats and additions, showing name of plat or survey, survey number, range, township, and section lines, town plat or farm tract boundaries, lots lines, in-lot dimensions, farm tract and out-lot areas, names of owners, roads, trails, streams, fords, streets, alleys; also description of survey, showing line bearings, location and kind of landmarks, length of boundary line between angles, area, by whom survey ordered, date of survey, name of surveyor and chairmen, and dates filed and recorded. 1821-1824 are transcriptions from Sandusky plat and survey records transcribed in 1883 by Seneca County surveyor. These plats and surveys were transcribed in 1888, by county surveyor's department into Township Plats, entry 75, City of Tiffin Plats, entry 76, and City of Fostoria Plats, entry 77. Arranged chronologically by dates recorded. For index, see entry 74. Handwritten and hand drawn; plat drawings black and white. Scale vary. Average 210 pages. 21 x 24 x 2. Recorder's vault.

74. GUIDEBOOK TO RECORD OF PLATS

1821-1889. 1 volume. Discontinued.

Index to plats of Seneca County, entry 73, showing name of plat or survey, and volume and page numbers of record. Arranged alphabetically by names of plats or surveys. Handwritten on forms. 150 pages. 18 x 10.5 x 1. Recorder's vault.

75. TOWNSHIP PLATS

1837—. 3 volumes. (1-3).

Copies of plats and surveys of townships, showing survey number, name of plat or owner, date of survey, boundary lines of plat or tract, range and section numbers, area of tract or plat, roads, streams, and railroads; plats of towns, villages, and additions, showing boundary lines, lot lines, lot number, in-lot dimensions, out-lot area, and names of owners, streets, alleys, railroads, and streams; description of survey, showing bearing of boundary lines, landmarks, distance between angles, area of plat or survey, by whom survey ordered, dates filed and recorded, and names of surveyor and chainmen. 1837-1889 transcribed from Plats of Seneca County, entry 73. Prepared by county surveyors department. Arranged chronologically by dates recorded. For index, see entry 78. Handwritten and hand drawn, black on white on linen-back paper. Scales vary. Average 99 pages. 24 x 21 x 2. Recorder's vault.

76. CITY OF TIFFIN PLATS
1821—. 4 volumes. (1-4).

Copies of plats and surveys, city of Tiffin and additions, showing survey number, name of plat or owner, date of survey, boundary lines of tract or survey (1832-1841 township surveys, show range, township, and section lines), lot lines, lot numbers, in-lot dimensions, out-lot area and name of owner, ward boundaries, showing bearing of boundary lines, landmarks, distance between angles, area of plat or survey, by whom survey ordered, dates filed and recorded, and names of surveyor and chairmen. Prepared by county surveyor's department. Also includes plats of surveys other than of Tiffin, 1821-1836. 1821-1887 transcribed from plats of Seneca County, entry 73. Prepared by county surveyor's department. Arranged chronologically by dates recorded. For index, see entry 78. Handwritten and hand drawn, black on white on linen-back paper. Scales vary. Average 60 pages. 23 x 21.5 x 1.25. Recorder's vault.

77. CITY OF FOSTORIA PLATS
1832—. 2 volumes. (1, 2).

Copies of plats and surveys, city of Fostoria and additions, showing survey number, name of plat or owner, date of survey, boundary lines of tract or survey (1832-1841 township surveys, show range, township, and section lines), lot lines, lot numbers in-lot dimensions, out-lot area and name of owner, ward boundaries, ward numbers, streets, alleys, streams, and railroads; description of plat or survey shows, bearing of boundary lines, landmarks, distance between angles, area of plat or survey, by whom survey ordered, dates filed and recorded, and names of surveyor and chairmen. Also includes some surveyors other than Fostoria, 1832-1841. 1832-1887 transcribed from plats of Seneca County, entry 73. Prepared by county surveyor's department. Arranged chronologically by dates recorded. For index, see entry 78.

Handwritten and hand drawn, black and white on linen-back paper. Scales vary. Average 75 pages. 24 x 20 x 1.5. Recorder's vault.

78. INDEX TO PLATS (CHARTS)
[1821—]. 1 chart.

Index to township plats, entry 75, City of Tiffin Plats, entry 76, and City of Fostoria Plats, entry 77, showing name of plat (survey, town, village, addition) or survey (name of owner), title of plat record, volume and page numbers of record. Arranged alphabetically by names of plats or surveys. Handwritten on forms. 24 x 30. Recorder's main office, on north wall.

79. MAP–SENECA COUNTY
1864. 1 map.

Political map of Seneca County, showing boundaries, names of adjoining counties, township, town, village and farm tract boundaries, range, section, and section lines, range, township, and section numbers, names of townships, towns, villages and farm tract owners, roads, streams, and watercourses, and railroads. Also includes names of county officials, 1864. Survey by Cyrus Stone and Clarence Titus, Tiffin, Ohio. Published by Thomas Wagner, publisher, Philadelphia, Pennsylvania, 1864. Printed, colored; framed. Scale, 1.5 inches equals 1 mile. 56.5 x 56. Recorder's private office, on wall.

80. MAP–SENECA COUNTY
1917. 1 map.

Political map of Seneca County, showing county boundaries, names of adjoining counties, township, range, section and quarter section lines, names of townships, range, township, and section numbers, city, town, village, and farm tract boundaries, names the cities, towns, villages, and farm owners, number of acres of farm tracts, unapproved and improved roads, streams, and watercourses, railroads, and electric railroads. Prepared by J. J. Oberlander, Tiffin, Ohio, 1917. Blueprint. 53 x 35. Recorder's private office, on wall.

81. MAP–CITY OF TIFFIN
1919. 1 map.

Political map of city of Tiffin and suburbs, showing corporation boundary, boundaries of suburban plats, names of suburban plats, lot lines and numbers, out-lot areas, names of owners, streets, allies, streams, steam and electric railroads, ward boundaries, and ward numbers. Location of public buildings shown. Prepared by H. B. Puffenberger, Tiffin, Ohio. Blueprint. Scale 1 inch equals 300 feet. 33 x 28. Recorder's private office, on wall.

82. MAP–CITY OF FOSTORIA
1930. 1 map.

Political map, city of Fostoria and suburbs, showing corporation boundary, boundaries of suburban plats, names of suburban plats, lot lines and numbers, out-lot area and names of owners, streets, alleys, streams, railroads, highway route numbers entering city, ward boundaries, and ward numbers. Prepared by H.B. Bradner, C. E., Fremont, Ohio. Blueprint. Scale, 1 inch equals 300 feet. 51 x 62. Recorder's main office, on wall.

83. MAP OR SURVEY JOSHUA HEDGES LANDS
1859. 1 map.

Original map prepared as an exhibit in litigation relative to settlement of the Joshua Hedges estate, showing outline of Survey of city of Tiffin and surrounding territory with tracts and lots owned by Mr. Hedges designated by letters, streets, alleys, lot lines, lot numbers, railroads, and streams; a key chart shows lot numbers and area of each lot and total area of each designated group of lots and total area owned, 672 acres. Prepared by C. H. Heming, C. E., Tiffin, Ohio. Hand drawn, black and white; framed. 32.5 x 41; key chart, 22 x 28. Recorder's private office, on wall.

Partitions

84. PARTITION FENCE RECORD
1905—. 1 volume. (1).

Record of location and division of line fence between lands and lots consisting of copies of petitions of complaining landowners to township trustees for a view of the dividing line and a division established for each landowner to erect and maintain, trustees' orders to view, decisions of viewers and orders of trustees to each owner, showing date of petition, name of township, names of complainant and defendant, names of viewers, date viewed, part of fence each owner to erect and maintain, and dates filed and recorded. Arranged chronologically by dates recorded. Indexed alphabetically by names of complainants showing names of defendants. 1905-1917, handwritten; 1917—, typed. 440 pages. 18 x 12 x 2.5. Recorder's vault.

Personal Property Transfers

85. CHATTEL MORTGAGE RECORD

1877—. 1 volume. (1). Last entry 1904.

Copies of instruments conveying conditional title to chattel property for value received, showing instrument number, names of mortgagor and mortgagee, itemized list of chattel encumbered, amount of encumbrance, terms of obligation, notarization, date of instrument, and dates filed and recorded. Arranged chronologically by dates recorded. Indexed alphabetically by names of mortgagors showing names of mortgagees. Handwritten. 450 pages. 18 x 12 x 2.5. Recorder's vault.

86. CHATTEL MORTGAGES

1887-1915, 1921—. 113 bundles, 94 file boxes. (labeled by contained instrument numbers).

Estimates filed conveying conditional title to chattel property for value received, showing instrument number, names of mortgagor and mortgagee, itemized list of chattels encumbered, amount of encumbrance, terms of obligation, notarization, date of instrument, and date filed. Arranged numerically by instrument numbers. For indexes, see entries 87, 89. 1887-1912, handwritten, and handwritten on printed forms. 1921—, typed on printed forms. Bundles, 9 x 3.5 x 2.5; file boxes, 10.5 x 4.5 x 14. 19 file boxes, 1887-1915, 1921-1935, 113 bundles, recorder's vault; 75 file boxes, 1925—, Recorder's main office.

87. INDEX TO CHATTEL MORTGAGES

1877-1900, 1907-1926. 14 volumes. (2-4, 1-9; two unlabeled).

Record of instruments filed conveying conditional title to chattel property, showing name of township, date of instrument, names of mortgagor mortgagee, instrument number, date files, amount secured, date renewed, and date cancelled. Serves as an index to chattel mortgages by showing instrument number. 1907-1926, direct index in front of volume, reverse in back; 1877-1900, arranged alphabetically by names of grantees; 1907-1926, arranged alphabetically by names of mortgagors and mortgagees. Handwritten on forms. 5 volumes average 430 pages. 20 x 12 x 2.25. 9 volumes average 540 pages. 22 x 15 x 3. Recorder's vault.

88. CHATTEL INDEX, DIRECT

1927—. 7 volumes. (10-16).

Direct index to Chattel Mortgages, entry 86, showing instrument number, date of instrument, names of mortgagor mortgagee, amount secured, date filed, date refiled, and date cancelled. Arranged alphabetically by names of mortgagors. Handwritten on forms. Average 500 pages. 20 x 14 x 2.5. Recorder's main office.

89. CHATTEL INDEX, REVERSE

1927—. 7 volumes. (10-16).

Reverse index to Chattel Mortgages, entry 86, showing instrument number, date of instrument, names of mortgagee and mortgagor, amount secured, date filed, date refiled, and date cancelled. Arranged alphabetically by the names of mortgagees. Handwritten on forms. Average 500 pages. 20 x 14 x 2.5. Recorder's main office.

90. RECORD OF NOTICE OF INTENTION TO SELL GOODS

1908-1910. 1 volume. (1).

Copies of legal notices of sale a goods and stocks in bulk sale, showing date of notice, name of owner, name of trustee, names of creditors, kind of goods, estimated or appraised value, date and place of sale, and dates filed and recorded. Arranged chronologically by dates recorded. Indexed alphabetically by names of owners. Handwritten on printed forms. 340 pages. 16 x 11 x 2. Recorder's vault.

Corporations and Partnerships

(See also entries 145, 146)

91. CORPORATION RECORD

1873—. 1 volume.

Copies of incorporation and partnership agreements of companies and firms, showing name and business address of company or firm, date of agreement, names of stockholders, shares of stock owned by each, value for share, total capital stock, kind of business, text of agreement, names of officials, notarization and dates filed and recorded; also includes copies of petitions filed by property owners of towns and villages for incorporation, tally sheets of special elections on proposals to incorporate towns and villages, and counties surveyor's plats of proposed incorporation, showing date of petition, name of town or villages, name of petitioners, number votes cast for and against proposal, total votes cast, boundary lines of proposed incorporation, streets, alleys, streams, lot lines, lot numbers, out-lot areas, names of corporation officials elected, and dates filed and recorded. Arranged chronologically by dates recorded. Indexed alphabetically by names of companies, firms, or towns. Handwritten; plats, hand drawn. 275 pages. 16 x 11 x 1.5. Recorder's vault.

92. CORPORATION RECORD–SOCIETIES

1846—. 1 volume.

Copies of articles of incorporation of church organizations, fraternal and benevolent societies, civic and social societies, showing name of organization, names of officials, by-laws, and dates filed and recorded. Arranged chronologically by dates recorded. No index. 1846-1911, handwritten; 1912—, typed. 400 pages. 18 x 12 x 2. Recorder's vault.

93. PARTNERS AND TRADERS RECORD

1864-1886. 1 volume. (1). Discontinued; law repealed.

Register of firms and individuals engaged in business, showing date filed, firm name, business address, name and address of each individual member, and kind of business. Arranged chronologically by dates filed. Indexed alphabetically by firm names. Handwritten on forms. 588 pages. 18 x 12 x 3. Recorder's vault.

Grants of Authority

94. POWER OF ATTORNEY RECORD

1893—. 1 volume. (1). 1827-1892 in Deed Record, entry 43.

Copies of instruments granting authority to another to act as agent in specified matters, showing instrument number, names of principal and agent, date of instrument, duties and powers delegated, notarization, and date filed and recorded; also includes copies of revocation of power of attorney, showing instrument number, names of principal and agent, date of instrument, text of instrument, and dates filed and recorded. Arranged chronologically by dates recorded. Indexed alphabetically by names of principles showing names of agents. 1893-1910, handwritten; 1911—, typed. 430 pages. 18 x 12 x 2.5. Recorder's vault.

95. CERTIFICATES OF COMPLIANCE; INSURANCE AGENT'S LICENSE

1915—. 25 bundles.

Copies of certificates issued by state division of insurance certifying that named insurance company has complied with insurance regulations and granting permission to solicit and write insurance in the state, showing certificate number, date issued, name and home office address of company, statement of companies assets and liabilities, and date filed; copies of licenses issued by state department of insurance to firms and individuals to solicit and write insurance, showing license number, date issued, name and address of licensee, name of employer, and date filed. Arranged chronologically by dates filed. No index. Typed on printed forms. 10 x 4 x 3. Recorder's vault.

96. RECORD OF INSURANCE CERTIFICATES
1868-1869. 1 volume. (1).

Copies of certificates of authority issued by state division of insurance to insurance companies, showing date issued, name and home office address of company, statement that the company has met all the requirements of an act passed April 1867, governing insurance companies, kind of insurance written, names of authorized agents in Seneca County, and date filed. Arranged chronologically by dates filed. Indexed alphabetically by names of companies. Handwritten. 434 pages. 18 x 12 x 2.5. Recorder's vault.

Financial Records

97. RECORDERS CASH BOOK AND THE RECORD OF FILES
1907—. 23 volumes. (1-23).

Record of fees received for services rendered, showing date of entry, name of payer, total fees, amount for recording, filing, searching, cancellations, and sundries. Arranged chronologically by dates of entries. No index. Handwritten on forms. Average 240 pages. 18 x 12 x 1.5. 17 volumes, 1907-1931, recorder's vault; 6 volumes, 1931—, Recorder's main office.

98. EX-OFFICIO SERVICE
1921—. 1 volume. (1).

Record of services requested (making certified copies or searches), showing date of request, name of person making requests, service requested, amount of fee, and date delivered. Arranged chronologically by dates of request. No index. Handwritten on forms. 220 pages. 16 x 11 x 1. Recorder's main office.

99. RECEIPTS

1921—. 202 volumes. (labeled by contained receipt numbers).

Carbon copies of recorder's receipts for fees received, showing receipt number, date issued, name of payer, amount, for what service, and signature of recorder or deputy. Arranged numerically by receipt numbers. No index. Handwritten on printed forms. Average 125 pages. 14 x 6 x 1. Recorder's main office.

Miscellaneous

100. MISCELLANEOUS RECORD

1920—. 1 volume. (1). 1822-1919 in deed Record, entry 43.

Copies of miscellaneous instruments consisting in part of agreements of various nature, contracts, bills of sale, affidavits, court orders and decrees, limited partnership agreements, amendments to articles of incorporation, showing instrument number, title of instrument, names of principals, date of instrument, text of instrument, notarization, names of witnesses, and dates filed and recorded. Indexed alphabetically by names that grantors or other principals showing names of grantees or other principals. Typed. 600 pages. 18 x 12 x 3. Recorder's vault.

101. RECORD OF SOLDIERS' DISCHARGES

1866—. 5 volumes. (1, 2, 1, 1, 2). 2, 1866—, subtitled Civil War; 1, 1898—, Spanish-American War; 2, 1918—. World War.

Copies of certificates of discharges from the army, navy, and marine corps, showing certificate number, name of soldier, sailor or marine, date of enlistment, place of enlistment, branch of service, what war, age, birth date, birthplace, physical description, company, regiment, brigade or vessel, rank, service record, date of discharge, place of discharge, reason for discharge, amount of pay due, name and rank of commanding officer, and dates filed and recorded. Arranged chronologically by dates recorded. Indexed alphabetically by names of soldiers. 1866-1916, handwritten on printed forms; 1917—, typed on printed forms. Average 500 pages. 16 x 11 x 2.5. Recorder's vault.

102. COMPLETE RECORD JOSIAH HEDGES ESTATE

1860. 1 volume.

Record of settlement and distribution by Josiah Hedges estate, consisting of copies of will, inventory and appraisement, journal of entries district court proceedings, and sale bills, showing date of filing and various proceedings, names of principals, names of appraisers, itemized inventory and appraisement, total appraisement, title and text of journal entries, date of sale, itemized sale bill, total amount of sale, total cost and fees, amount for distribution, names and distributees, dates distributed, and dates filed and recorded. Arranged chronologically by dates filed. Indexed alphabetically by names of principals or subjects. Handwritten. 265 pages. 18 x 12 x 1.5. Recorder's vault.

103. RECORD OF PROTESTS

1905-1910. 2 volumes. (1, 2).

Record of checks, notes, and drafts on which payment is protested by banks and bankers, copies of instruments with endorsements, showing instrument number, date of instrument, name of drawee, amount, name of drawer, names of endorsers, name of bank protesting, date protested, and dates filed and recorded. No index. 1905-1908, handwritten; 1908-1910, typed. Average 100 pages. 11 x 8 x 1. Recorder's vault.

105. PROTESTS

1924-1934. 1 envelope.

Copies of protested checks, notes, and drafts and notarized statement of protest by banking institutions, showing instrument number, date of instrument, name of drawee, amount, name of drawer, names of endorsers, date protested, name of protesting bank, name of notary public, and date filed. Arranged chronologically by dates filed. No index. Handwritten and typed on printed forms. 12 x 8 x .75. Recorder's main office.

105. [MISCELLANEOUS FILES]

1842—. 77 file boxes. (labeled by contained letters of alphabet).

Original deeds, mortgages, leases, mechanics' liens, power of attorney, and other instruments filed for recording and uncalled for, showing recorder's file number (instrument number), title of instrument, names of grantor and grantee, date of instrument, text of instrument, notarization, signatures at grantor and witnesses, date filed, and if recorded volume and page numbers of record. Arranged alphabetically by names of grantees and chronological thereunder by dates filed. No index. Handwritten, handwritten on printed forms, typed, and typed on printed forms. 10 x 5 x 14. Recorder's private office.

The office of clerk of courts, an ancient English institution originating before the time of Edward I[1] was transplanted to America during the colonial period. The American Revolution made no radical change in the political heritage derived from England, and the office was continued by the states. The duties of the office were modified in the newer states, however, because of a separation of administrative and judicial functions, which under the English system had been combined.

The sections of the Ohio Constitution of 1802 creating the judicial system for the state provided for the appointment of a clerk of courts by the judges of the court of common pleas. He was to serve a seven-year term, but was subject to removal by the appointing power for a breach of good behavior.[2] The constitution of 1851 made the office of clerk elective with a three-year term.[3] A constitutional amendment in 1905 provided that the terms of all elective offices should be for an even number of years not exceeding four. In compliance with this amendment, the general assembly passed an act fixing the term of office of the clerk at two years.[4] The term remained at two years until 1936 when it was extended to four years.[5] The remuneration of the office was by fees until 1906 when the legislature prescribed a definite salary based on the population of the county.[6]

The duties of the clerk of courts, like those other county officers, are prescribed by statute. In 1853 a code of civil procedure was adopted summarizing the earlier duties and forming the basis for the present ones which are in most respects similar to those prescribed during the early years of the office. The clerk of courts was directed to issue all writs and orders for provisional remedies; endorse the date upon all papers filed in his office; keep the journal, record books, and papers appertaining to the court of common pleas and record its proceedings; and keep five books to be called the appearance docket, the trial docket and a printed duplicate of the trial docket, the journal, the record, and the execution docket.[7]

---

1. Sir Frederick Pollock and Frederic William Maitland, *The History of English Law Before the Time of Edward I,* I, 184.
2. *Ohio Const. 1802,* Art. III, sec. 9.
3. *Ohio Const. 1851,* Art. IV, sec. 10.
4. *Laws of Ohio,* CXVIII, 273.
5. *Ibid.,* CXVI, pt. ii, 184.
6. *Ibid.,* XCVIII, 94, 117. The salary in Seneca County for 1939 was $3,005. Ohio Auditor of State, *Annual Report, 1939,* 373.
7. *Laws of Ohio,* LI, 107, 158-159; LXXVIII, 108; LXXIX, 115; LXXXVI, 174.

The present practice of keeping an index, direct and reverse, to judgments began in 1866.[8] In 1871, the clerk was made official custodian of the law reports and books furnished by the state for the use of the court and bar, and was made liable in the event of their destruction.[9]

Some of the duties of the clerk as defined by civil code of 1853 are still effective, others have been added by subsequent legislation. Thus, for example, in 1858 the clerk was directed to receive notary commissions for record.[10] He was required, also, to receive for record special police commissions (1867), timber trademarks (1883), partnership agreements (1894), copies of judgments of federal courts (1898), marks of ownership [trade-marks] (1911), motor vehicles bills of sale (1921), and certificates of judgments to operate as a lien (1935).[11] Since January 1, 1938 he has issued certificates of title to motor vehicles.[12] On the other hand, many of the earlier duties of the clerk have been transferred to other departments of local government or have been abolished. The clerk issued marriage licenses and recorded ministers' licenses until 1852, after that date the former have been issued and the latter recorded by the probate court,[13] to which court the records have been transferred. Moreover the clerk issued peddlers' licenses until the decade of the sixties, since that time they have been issued by the auditor.[14] The clerk has been authorized to act as an agent of the state in the sale of hunting and trapping licenses to nonresidents of the state since 1904 and to residents since 1919.[15] He has been authorized also to serve as agent in the sale of fishing licenses to nonresidents since 1919 and to residents since 1925.[16] The practice of recording in the office of the clerk, the name of black or mulatto persons to be used as certificates of freedom was, of course, discontinued after the close of the War between the States in 1865.

---

8. *Ibid.,* LXIII, 10; LXXV, 103; LXXVIII, 88; LXXXII, 115; LXXXVI, 26.
9. *Ibid.,* LCVIII, 109.
10. *Laws of Ohio,* LV, 13; XCIII, 406.
11. *Ibid.,* LXIV, 60; LXXX, 195; XCI, 357; XCII, 25; XCIII, 285; CII, 513-514; CIX, 333; CXVI, 274.
12. G. C. sec. 6290-6.
13. *Laws of Ohio,* I, 31; XXIX, 429; L, 84; *Ohio Const. 1851,* Art. IV, sec. 8.
14. *Laws of Ohio,* LIX, 67.
15. *Ibid.,* XCVII, 474; CVIII, pt. i, 595.
16. *Laws of Ohio,* CVIII, 923; CXI, 276.

In 1856 the clerk was directed by the legislature to preserve a list of births, marriages, and deaths as returned to his office by the assessor, and to transmit annually, on or before the first day of June, a copy of such statistics to the secretary of state. These lists are no longer preserved. From these county lists, the secretary of state prepared tabular statements showing the vital statistics in each county. The clerk received 10 copies of the report, one of which he was required to preserve in his office.[17] The clerk was relieved of the task of collecting and preserving vital statistics, when, in 1867, such powers and duties were vested in the probate judge.[18]

The clerk of courts was given other duties in addition to those of serving the court of common pleas and receiving documents for record. Since 1850 he has been required to report each year to the county commissioners all finds assessed by the courts in criminal cases, together with the names of parties to each case, and the amount of money he has paid to the county treasurer.[19] Duplicate copies of these reports have not been preserved in the clerk's office. More over, since 1867 he has been required to report annually to the secretary of state the number of crimes committed in his county, the number of pending cases, and the amount of fines collected.[20] An act of 1927, amending the act of 1867, directed the clerk to report on any matters which the secretary of state might require, and to forward a duplicate copy of his report on crime in his county to the state board of clemency [board of pardons and paroles.][21] The state board of clemency was abolished in 1921 and its duties were assigned to a board of pardons and parole within the department of public welfare.[22]

The county clerk of courts, like the county prosecuting attorney, is one of the important persons in the judicial system. His significance and influence, however, was not recognized until recent years.

---

17. *Ibid.,* LIII, 73-75.
18. *Ibid.,* LXIV, 63-64.
19. *Ibid.,* XLVIII, 66; LVIII, 69; LXXXVI, 239.
20. *Ibid.,* LXIV, 17.
21. *Ibid.,* CXII, 203.
22. *Ibid.,* CIX, 111, 124.

Dockets

106. EXECUTION DOCKET

1838—. 22 volumes. (1-22).

Docket of executions ordered to satisfy judgments rendered by Seneca County courts, showing names of attorneys, names of judgment creditor and debtor, title of case, case number, nature of judgment, date of judgment, amount of judgment, date of execution order, date judgment satisfied, how satisfied, 1915—, volume and page numbers of Clerk's Cash Book, entry 150. Also contains Execution Record 1872—, entry 113. Arranged chronologically by dates of execution orders. 1838-1857, indexed alphabetically, on left-hand half of page by names of judgment creditor showing names of judgment debtors; on right-hand half of page by names of judgment debtors showing names of judgment creditors; also separate index, 1858—, entry 107. 1838-1914, handwritten on forms; Average 540 pages. 18 x 12 x 3. Clerk of courts' vault.

107. GENERAL INDEX TO EXECUTION DOCKET

1858—. 2 volumes. (1-2).

General index to Execution Docket, entry 106, direct on the left-hand page, showing name of judgment creditor and judgment debtor, case number, title of case, volume and page numbers of docket, and date execution issued; reverse on right-hand page, showing names of judgment debtor and judgment creditor, case number, title of case, volume and page number of docket, and date execution issued. Arranged alphabetically by the names of judgment creditors and judgment debtors. Handwritten on forms. Average 500 pages. 18 x 12 x 2.5. Clerk of courts' vault.

108. EXECUTION LIEN DOCKET

1877-1881. 1 volume. (1). Discontinued.

Copies of transcripts of executions appealed to common pleas court from magistrates' courts, showing name of litigants, title of case, date transcript filed, amount of judgment, nature of judgment, date execution order issued, itemized cost bill of magistrate's court, and volume and page numbers of magistrate's docket. Arranged chronologically by dates of filing transcripts. Indexed alphabetically by names of plaintiffs showing names of defendants. Handwritten on forms. 580 pages. 18 x 12 x 3. Clerk of courts' vault.

109. ORDER OF SALE DOCKET
1879—. 9 volumes. (1-9).

Records of orders of sale issued in foreclosure and partition proceedings consisting of copies of order of sale, sheriff's returns on writ, and legal notices of sheriff's sale, showing case number, names of attorneys, names of plaintiff and defendant, title of case, date order of sale issued, volume and page numbers of [Common Pleas] Journal, entry 174, amount of judgment and interest, description and location of tract or lot, date of sale, to whom sold, amount of sale, date sale confirmed and deed ordered, volume and page numbers of Law Records, entry 178, file box number in [Case Records], entry 182, itemized cost bill, date cost paid, and volume and page numbers of Clerk's Cash Book, entry 150. Arranged chronologically by dates orders of sale issued. Indexed alphabetically by names of plaintiffs showing names of defendants and case number. Handwritten and handwritten on printed forms. Average 500 pages. 18 x 12 x 2.5. Clerk of courts' vault.

110. JUDGMENT DOCKETS
1935—. 1 volume.

Copies of certificates of judgments filed to operate as a lien, showing by what court issued, case number, title of case, date of judgment, names of judgment creditor or debtor, amount of judgment, rate of interest, and date from which interest is computed, volume and page numbers of docket or journal of court where recorded, date filed, clerk's filing fee, and signature of clerk of courts. Arranged chronologically by dates filed. Indexed alphabetically by names of judgment creditors showing names of judgment debtors. Handwritten on printed forms. 500 pages. 18 x 12 x 2.5. Clerk of courts' main office.

General Court Records

111. TRANSCRIPTS
1857—. 14 file boxes. 1824-1856 in [Case Records]. Entry 182.

Original transcript from magistrates' courts in criminal cases, showing what court, name of magistrate, case number, name of defendant, offense, date of preliminary hearing, name of complaint, brief of evidence submitted, date bound over from magistrates court, date filed, itemized statement of magistrate's court cost, and volume and page numbers of magistrate's criminal docket where entered. Arranged chronologically by dates no index. Handwritten on printed forms. 9.5 x 5 x 12. Clerk of courts' file room.

112. EXECUTIONS

1836—. 56 file boxes. (1836-1907, dated; 1908—, labeled by contained letters of alphabet). 1824-1835 in [Case Records], entry 182.

Original execution orders issued to satisfy judgments rendered, showing case number, names of litigants, title of case, date issued, amount of judgment, date of judgment, description and location of property levied on, copy of sheriff's return, date of return, date filed, volume and page numbers of Execution Docket, entry 106. 1836-1907, chronological by dates filed; 1908—, alphabetical by names of plaintiffs. No index. 1836-1843 handwritten; 1844-1714, handwritten on printed forms; 1915—, typed on printed forms. 9.5 x 5 x 12. Clerk of courts' file room.

113. EXECUTION RECORD

1855-1871. 5 volumes. (1-5). 1872—, in Execution Docket, entry 106.

Record of executions to satisfy judgment decrees consisting of copies of execution orders, sheriff's returns, and clipped copies of legal notices of sale of property levied on, showing case number, volume and page numbers of Appearance Docket, entry 162, names of attorneys, names of judgment creditor and judgment debtor, title of case, date execution order issued, nature of judgment, amount of judgment, itemized cost bill, total amount due on judgment, description and location of property levied on, dates advertised, name of newspaper publishing legal notice of sale, date of sale, to whom sold, amount of sale, and dates of sheriff's returns. Arranged chronologically by dates of execution orders. Indexed alphabetically by names of judgment creditors showing names of judgment debtors. Handwritten. Average 700 pages. 18 x 12 x 3.5. Clerk of courts' vault.

114. SPECIAL JUDGMENTS-SALES TAX

1937—. 1 volume. (1).

Record of judgments rendered in favor of state against retail merchants on evasion of the sales tax provisions, showing name of merchant, vendors license number, business address, serial number of tax commission's certificate of violation and assessment, date final entry filed, amount of tax and penalty assessed, and interest rate with date from which interest is to be computed. Arranged chronologically by dates of filing final entries. Indexed alphabetically by names of merchants. Handwritten on printed forms. 100 pages. 15 x 10 x .5. Clerk of courts' office.

115. INDEX TO PENDING SUITS, LIVING JUDGMENTS AND EXECUTIONS

1870-1885. 2 volumes. (1, 2).

Index record of pending suits, living judgments, and living executions, showing names of litigants (not designated as plaintiff and defendant), case number, date filed, judgment number, date of decree, execution number, and date execution issued. Alphabetical by names of litigants. Handwritten on forms. 300 pages. 18 x 12 x 1.5. Clerk of courts' vault.

116. [PENDING CASES]

1936—. 12 file boxes. (labeled by contained letters of alphabet).

Original papers issued and filed in pending cases consisting in part of petitions, affidavits, pleas, motions, and writs, showing case number, title of paper, names of litigants, title of case, text of paper, date to file, and volume and page number of record where recorded. Alphabetical by names of plaintiffs. No index. Typed on printed forms. 9.5 x 5 x 12. Clerk of courts' main office.

117. BILLS OF EXCEPTIONS

1871—. 580 bills.

Original bills of exceptions to common pleas court decisions or jury verdicts filed as basis of appeal to higher courts or for new trial, showing names of litigants, title of case, case number, date filed with clerk of courts, text of exceptions, and name of attorney filing exceptions. Each bill bound separately. No obvious arrangement. No index. 1871-1892, handwritten; 1893—, typed. Average 150 pages. 14.5 x 9 x 1. Clerk of courts' file room.

Jury and Witness Records

118. JURY DOCKET

1869-1877. 1 volume.

Docket of grand jurors, showing court term, names of jurors, number of days in attendance, mileage, total fees due, number of cases investigated, number of indictments returned, number of cases ignored, and number continued; docket of petit jury panels, showing term of court, names of plaintiff and defendant, title of case, names of jurors, number of days in attendance, mileage, total fees due, and verdict returned. Arranged chronologically by court terms. Grand jury, no index;

petit juries, indexed alphabetically by names of plaintiffs showing names of defendants. Handwritten on forms. 300 pages. 15 x 10 x 1.5. Attic store room.

119. GRAND JURY DOCKET
1911—. 2 volumes.

Docket of grand jurors, showing court term, names of jurors, dates of sessions, number of days in attendance, mileage, and total fees due. Also contains Grand Jury Witness Book, entry 123. Arranged chronologically by court terms. No index. Handwritten on forms. Average 315 pages. 12 x 8.5 x 1.5. Clerk of courts' vault.

120. WITNESS AND JURY DOCKET
1911—. 4 volumes. (1-4).

Docket of witnesses subpoenaed and appearing before county courts and of jury panels: Petit jury panels, showing term of court, names of plaintiff and defendant, title of case, case number, names of jurors, date sworn in, number of days in attendance, mileage, and total fees due; witness docket showing names of plaintiff's witnesses, of defendant's witnesses, number of days in attendance, mileage, total fees due, and verdict. Arranged chronologically by court terms. Indexed alphabetically by names of plaintiffs showing names of defendants. Handwritten on forms. Average 300 pages. 16 x 11 x 1.5. Clerk of courts' vault.

121. JUROR'S RECORD BOOK
1881-1911. 2 volumes.

Record of petit jury panels, showing court term, names of plaintiff and defendant, title of case, names of jurors, date sworn in, number of days in attendance, mileage, total fees due, verdict, and date paid. Arranged chronologically by court terms. Indexed alphabetically by names of plaintiffs showing names of defendants. Handwritten on forms. Average 300 pages. 16 x 11 x 1.5. Clerk of courts' vault.

122. WITNESS DOCKET
1893-1911. 6 volumes.

Docket of witnesses subpoenaed and appearing before county courts, showing what court, court term, names of plaintiff and defendant, title of case, names of plaintiff's witnesses, names of defendant's witnesses, number of days in attendance, mileage, and total fees due. Arranged chronologically by court terms. Indexed alphabetically by names of plaintiffs showing names of defendants. Handwritten on forms. Average 80 pages. 14 x 9 x .5. Clerk of courts' vault.

123. GRAND JURY WITNESS BOOK

1889-1911. 1 volume. 1911—, in Grand Jury Docket, entry 119.

Record of witnesses subpoenaed and appearing before grand jury, showing term of court, name of witness, date subpoenaed, in what matter, number of days in attendance, mileage, and total fees due. Chronological by court terms. No index. Handwritten on forms. 320 pages. 14 x 9 x 1.5. Clerk of courts' vault.

124. JURY LISTS

1892-1910, 1918—. 1 volume, 3 file boxes.

Clerk of courts' copies of electors eligible for jury duty filed by board of elections, showing year, name of subdivision, precinct number, name and address of elector, and date filed. Chronological by dates filed. No index. Volume, handwritten on forms; file box records, typed on forms. Volumes, 320 pages. 12 x 8.5 x 1.5; file boxes, 10.5 x 4.5 x 14. Volumes, 2 file boxes, 1892-1910, 1918-1936, clerk of courts' vault; 1 file box, 1937—, Clerk of courts' file room.

For jury commissioners' record, see entry 292.

Motor Vehicles

125. BILLS OF SALE AND SWORN STATEMENTS OF OWNERSHIP

1921-1937. 99 file boxes. (labeled by container instrument numbers). Discontinued; law repealed.

Copies of bills of sale and sworn statements of ownership of motor vehicles, showing instrument number, date filed, names grantor and grantee, date of purchase, new or used, make of vehicle, model, type, horsepower, motor number, serial number, and name of manufacturer. Numerical by instrument numbers. For indexes, see entries 126, 127. Handwritten and typed on printed forms. 9 x 5 x 12. Clerk of courts' main office.

126. INDEX TO MOTOR VEHICLE SALES AND STATEMENT OF OWNERSHIP–GRANTORS

1921-1937. 4 volumes. (1-4).

Direct index to Bills of Sale and Sworn Statements of Ownership, entry 125, showing instrument number, names of grantor and grantee, date filed, kind of vehicle, make, type, model, horsepower, motor number, serial number, new or used vehicle, and date purchased. Alphabetically by name of grantors. Handwritten on forms. Average 500 pages. 17 x 15 x 2.5. Clerk of courts' main office.

127. INDEX TO MOTOR VEHICLE SALES AND STATEMENT OF OWNERSHIP–GRANTEE

1921-1937. 4 volumes. (1-4).

Reverse index to Bills of Sale and Sworn Statements of Ownership, entry 125, showing instrument number, names of grantee and grantor, date filed, kind of vehicle, make, type, model, horsepower, motor number, serial number, new or used vehicle, and date of purchase. Arranged alphabetically by names the grantees. Handwritten on forms. Average 500 pages. 17 x 15 x 2.5. Clerk of courts' main office.

128. CLERKS CERTIFICATE

1923-1930. 4 volumes.

Carbon copies of certification that a bill of sale or sworn statement of ownership has been filed, showing certificate number, name and address of owner, from whom purchased, date filed, make of vehicle, model, type, motor number, serial number, bill of sale number signature of clerk of courts, and date of certificate. Arranged numerically by certificate numbers. No index. Handwritten on printed forms. Average 150 pages. 11 x 7 x 1. Clerk of courts' vault.

129. CERTIFICATE OF TITLE

1938—. 6 file drawers. (labeled by contained certificate numbers).

Copies of certificates of title to motor vehicles, showing certificate number, name of purchaser, name of vendor, vendor's license number, make of vehicle, model, type, motor number, purchase price, notation of liens, name of lien holder, amount of lien, date issued, and amount of fee; notations of cancellation of liens are attached to certificate of title, showing certificate number, date cancelled, names of creditor and debtor, amount of lien cancelled, and fee. Arranged numerically by certificate numbers. For index, see entry 130. Typed on printed forms. 11 x 13 x 26. Clerk of courts' main office.

130. INDEX TO CERTIFICATE OF TITLE

1938—. 1 file drawer.

Index to certificate of title, entry 129, showing certificate number, name and address of owner, description of motor vehicle, and name and address of previous owner. Arranged alphabetically by names of owners. Typed on printed forms. 5.5 x 11.5 x 26. Clerk of courts' main office.

Commissions and Licenses

131. NOTARIES COMMISSIONS

1860—. 7 volumes. (1-5, 7-8).

Copies of commissions of authority issued by the governor to notaries public, showing name of notary, address, date issued, date effective, date of termination, names of governor, governor's secretary, and secretary of state, and dates filed and recorded. Arranged chronologically by dates recorded. Indexed alphabetically by names the notaries. Handwritten or printed forms. 400 pages. 14 x 9 x 2. 6 volumes, 1860-1934, clerk of courts' vault, 1934—, Clerk of courts' main office.

132. RECORD JUSTICES COMMISSIONS

1859—. 4 volumes, (one unlabeled; 1-3).

Copies of commissions of authority issued by the governor to elected or appointed justices of the peace, showing name of justice, name of township, date issued, date effective, term of office, names of governor, governor's secretary, and secretary of state, and dates filed and recorded; also includes copies of oath of office of justice of the peace, showing date of oath, name of justice, name of township, date elected or appointed, name and title of official administering oath, dates file and recorded. Arranged chronologically by dates recorded. Indexed alphabetically by names that justices. Handwritten on printed forms. Average 375 pages. 15 x 10 x 2. Clerk of courts' vault.

RECORD OF RAILROAD POLICE COMMISSIONS

1888—. 1 volume. (1).

Copies of commissions of authority issued by the governor to special police officers for railway duty, showing name of officer, address, date issued, name of railroad company, date effective, date of termination, names of governor, governor's secretary, and secretary of state, dates filed and recorded; also includes officers' oath of office, showing date oath, name of officer, name of railroad company, name and title of official administering oath, and dates filed and recorded. Arranged chronologically by dates recorded. Indexed alphabetically by names of officers. Handwritten on printed forms. 200 pages. 15 x 1.25. Clerk of courts' vault.

134. EMBALMERS' LICENSE RECORD

1903. 1 volume.

Copies of licenses issued by state board of embalming, showing license number, date of examination, name of licensee, date of graduation, school from which graduated, and names of chairman and secretary of the board of examiners. Only one entry. No index. Handwritten on printed forms. 316 pages. 10 x 8 x 1.5. Clerk of courts' and vault.

135. RECORD OF HUNTERS' LICENSE

1913-1933. 4 volumes.

Record of hunters' licenses issued, showing license number, name and address of licensee, date issued, age, color, height, weight, occupation, and license fee. Arranged alphabetically by names of licensees. No index. Handwritten on forms. Average 120 pages. 16 x 11 x 1. Clerk of courts' vault.

136. HUNTING LICENSE

1936—. 9 volumes. (dated).

Stubs of hunting licenses issued, showing license number, date issued, name and address of licensee, age, color, weight, height, color of eyes and occupation. Arranged numerically by license number. No index. Handwritten on printed forms. Average 50 pages. 4 x 8 x .5. Clerk of courts' main office.

137. RECORD OF FISHERS' LICENSE

1925-1933. 1 volume.

Record of fishers' licenses issued, showing license number, name and address of licensee, date issued, age, color, height, weight, occupation, and license fee. Arranged alphabetically by names of licensees. No index. Handwritten on forms. 150 pages. 17 x 14 x 1. Clerk of courts' vault.

138. FISHING LICENSE

1934—. 6 volumes. (dated).

Stubs of fishing licenses issued, showing license number, date issued, name and address of licensee, color, age, height, weight, color of eyes, and occupation. Arranged numerically by license number. No index. Handwritten on printed forms. Average 50 pages. 4 x 8 x .5. Clerk of courts' main office.

139. OPTOMETRY RECORDS
1920—. 1 volume. (1).

Copies of licenses issued by state board of optometry, showing name and address of licensee, date of examination, date license issued, names of president and secretary of board, and dates filed and recorded. Arranged chronologically by dates recorded. Indexed alphabetically by names of licensees. Handwritten on printed forms. Average 200 pages. 14 x 9 x 1. Clerk of courts' vault.

140. REGISTER OF REAL ESTATE LICENSES
1936—. 1 volume.

Register of real estate brokers and salesmen licensed, showing license number, date of license, name of licensee, address and name of employer. Arranged alphabetically by names of licensees. No index. Handwritten on forms. 200 pages. 14 x 16 x 1. Clerk of courts' main office.

Elections
(See also entries, 470-473)

141. RECORD OF MAYOR'S CERTIFICATES OF ELECTION
1877-1903. 1 volume.

Copies of certificates of election of mayors of municipalities, showing date certified, name of mayor, name of municipality, date of election, date term of office begins, date of termination, name of municipal clerk, and dates filed and recorded. Arranged chronologically by dates recorded. Indexed alphabetically by names of mayors. Handwritten on printed forms. 380 pages. 14 x 9 x 2. Clerk of courts' vault.

142. CERTIFICATE OF ELECTIONS, MAYOR
1917—. 2 file boxes.

Original certificates of election of mayors of municipalities, showing date certified, name of mayor, name of municipality, date of election, date term of office begins, date of termination, name of municipal clerk, and date filed. Arranged chronologically by dates filed. No index. Handwritten and typed on printed forms. 9 x 5 x 12. Clerk of courts' file room.

143. POLL BOOKS AND TALLY SHEETS, GENERAL ELECTIONS
1934—. 480 volumes. (dated). Subtitled by names of subdivisions and by precinct numbers.

Poll books and tally sheets for general elections filed with clerk of courts: Poll books, showing year, date of election, name of township, town or city (if city, ward number) precinct number or letter, consecutive voters number, name and address of voter; tally sheets, showing name of office, names of candidates, tally of votes received by each candidate, and total vote for each candidate; summary of ballots cast, showing total number of ballots cast, number of unmarked ballots, number of defaced ballots, and names of precinct judges and clerks. Poll books numerical by consecutive voters number; tally sheets arranged by offices in order of importance. No index. Handwritten on forms. Average 26 pages. 22 x 14 x .25. Attic store room.

144. POLL BOOKS AND TALLY SHEETS PRIMARY ELECTIONS
1934—, 372 volumes. (dated). Subtitled by names of subdivisions and by precinct numbers; also by names of political parties.

Poll books and tally sheets for primary elections filed with clerk of courts: Poll books, showing year, date of election, party affiliation, name of township, town or city (if city, ward number) precinct number or letter, consecutive voters number, and name and address of voter; tally sheets, showing name of office, names of candidates, tally of votes received by each candidate, and total votes for each candidate; summary of ballots cast, showing total number of ballots cast, number of unmarked ballots, number defaced ballots, and names of precinct judges and clerks. Poll books arranged numerically by consecutive voter numbers; tally sheets by offices in order of importance. No index. Handwritten on forms. Average 24 pages. 11 x 14 x .25. Attic store room.

Partnerships
(See also entry 91-93)

145. REGISTER OF PARTNERSHIPS
1894—. 1 volume. (1).

Register of Partnerships, showing firm name, certificate number, business address, name and address of each partner, kind of business, amount of capital, amount owed by each partner, and date filed. Arranged chronologically by dates filed. Indexed alphabetically by names of firms. Handwritten on forms. 250 pages. 16 x 11 x 1.25. Clerk of courts' main office.

146. CERTIFICATES OF PARTNERSHIPS

1884—. 1 file box.

Copies of certificates of partnerships, showing certificate number, date of certificate, name of firm, business address, name and address of each partner, kind of business, amount of capital, amount owed by each partner, and date filed. Arranged chronologically by dates filed. No index. Handwritten and typed on printed forms. 10.5 x 4.5 x 14. Clerk of courts' vault.

Reports

147. RECORD OF INQUESTS

1887-1909. 1 volume.

Copies of reports by coroner or justices of the peace of inquest held in cases of sudden, accidental, or homicidal death, showing date of inquest, place of inquest, name of decedent, color, age, physical description, nativity, date of death, place of death, cause the death, names of witnesses, names of jurors (if jury impaneled), inventory of effects found on body, itemized cost bill, name of coroner or justice, and date filed. Arranged chronologically by dates filed. Indexed alphabetically by names of decedents. Handwritten on printed forms. 300 pages. 18 x 12 x 1.5. Clerk of courts' vault.

For other records, see entries 276, 296, 297.

148. CORONER'S INQUESTS

1883—. 16 file boxes.

Original reports of inquest and investigations in cases of sudden, accidental, or homicidal death filed by coroners or justices of the peace, showing case number, name of decedent, date of inquest or investigation, place of inquest, age, color, nativity, and physical description of decedent, names and address of realities (if known), date, cause, and place a death, names of witnesses, names of jurors (if jury impaneled), inventory of effects found on body, itemized cost bill, name of coroner or justice, and date filed. No index. Handwritten on printed forms. 9 x 5 x 12. 14 file boxes 1883-1929, Attic store room; 2 file boxes, 1930—, Clerk of courts' file room.

For other records, see entries 276, 296, 297.

149. REPORTS

1935—. 1 file drawer.

Copies of clerk's annual reports to secretary of state on judicial statistics, showing year of report, number of divorce cases filed, number of divorce cases pending at beginning of year, number of divorce cases disposed of, and number of divorce cases each cause for action; total amount of fines assessed, and costs assessed, and total amount collected; amount of forfeited recognizance; number cases civil judgments, total amount of judgments rendered; total amount jury fees civil cases, criminal cases; number of prosecutions for crime against the person, number for each offense, for crimes against property, number for each offense, for crimes against public peace and health, number for each offense, for crimes against public justice and policy, number for each offense; for crimes against morals and chastity, number for each offense; number of convictions for crimes or offenses lower than charged in indictments; number of inquest and investigations held by coroner; number of cases pending at beginning of year, number filed during year, number pending at time of report; number of naturalization certificates issued with nativity of naturalized citizens, and date filed. Arranged chronologically by years. No index. Handwritten on printed forms. 4 x 15 x 12. Clerk of courts' office.

Financial Records

150. CLERK'S CASH BOOK

1907-1910, 1913—. 14 volumes. (1, 3-15).

Clerk's record of cash receipts and disbursements: Receipts, showing date received, volume and page numbers of Appearance Docket, entry 162, or Criminal Appearance Docket, entry 164, case number, name of payer, total amount received, amount credited to clerk's fees, county, sheriff, foreign sheriff, witnesses, judgments, deposits, and sundries; disbursements, showing date of disbursement, name of payee, check number, total amount, and amount debited clerk's fee, county, sheriff, foreign sheriff, witnesses, judgments, deposits, and sundries. Also contains Alimony Record, 1907-1910, 1914-1936, entry 156. Arranged chronologically by dates received or disbursed. Indexed alphabetically by names of payers. Handwritten on forms. Average 400 pages. 17 x 15.5 x 2. 13 volumes, 1907-1910, 1913-1939, clerk of courts' vault; 1 volume, 1939—, Clerk of courts' main office.

151. CLERK'S CASH

1897-1909. 2 volumes. (1, 2).

Record of fees paid to clerk of courts in common pleas court cases, showing name of litigants, case number, volume and page numbers of Execution Docket, entry 106, and Order of Sale Docket, entry 109, date of entry, amount of fees charged, amount paid, date paid, and by whom paid. Arranged alphabetically by names of plaintiffs. No index. Handwritten on forms. Average 480 pages. 17 x 12 x 2.5. Clerk of courts' vault.

152. RECORD OF ACCRUED FEES

1907-1917. 2 volumes. (1, 2).

Record of fees accrued in cases disposed of, showing date accrued, case number, to whom charged, amount of fees, and date paid. Arranged chronologically by dates accrued. No index. Handwritten on forms. Average 240 pages. 18 x 12 x 1.5. Clerk of courts' vault.

153. CERTIFICATE FOR FEES

1898-1900, 1928—. 7 volumes. (labeled by contained certificate numbers).

Stubs of certificates issued for witness and jury fees, showing certificate number, date issued, name of payee, amount, for what service, term of court, and in what matter. Arranged numerically by certificate numbers. No index. Handwritten on printed forms. 250 pages. 14 x 11 x 1.5. Clerk of courts' main office.

154. CLERK'S DAILY RECEIPTS

1898-1901. 1 volume.

Daily record of cash receipts paid to clerk of courts, showing day and date of entry, name of payer, for what, and amount. Arranged chronologically by dates of entries. No index. Handwritten on forms. 380 pages. 14 x 9 x 2. Clerk of courts' vault.

155. PAY INDEX

1876-1915. 5 volumes. (3-7).

Index record of payments to clerk of courts, showing date paid in, by whom paid, amount, for what, and to whom due. Arranged alphabetically by names of payers. No index. Handwritten on forms. Average 315 pages. 16 x 11 x 1.5. Clerk of courts' vault.

156. ALIMONY RECORD

1911-1913, 1937—. 2 volumes. (1, 1). 1907-1910, 1914-1936 in Clerk's Cash Book, entry 150.

Record of alimony and support payments received and disbursed, showing case number, name of defendant (payer), date received, amount, name of plaintiff (payee), date disbursed, amount, and check number. Arranged chronologically by dates received. Indexed alphabetically by names of defendants. Handwritten on forms. 240 pages. 16 x 13 x 1.5. Clerk of courts' main office.

Miscellaneous

157. OATHS OF OFFICE AND APPOINTMENTS

1885—. 2 file boxes.

Journal entries of appointments of court reporters and bailiffs, showing date of entry, name of appointee, position, term of appointment, salary, volume and page numbers of [Common Pleas] Journal, entry 174; oaths of office of reporters, bailiffs, deputy sheriff, and clerk of courts' deputies, showing date of oath, name of appointee, position, name and title of official administering oath, and date filed. Arranged chronologically by dates filed. No index. Handwritten on printed forms. 9 x 5 x 12. Clerk of courts' main office.

158. POWER OF ATTORNEY

1933—. 1 file box.

Original certificates authorizing named agent to act for principal as specified, showing date of issue, names of principal and agent, duties and limitations specified, notarization, and date filed; also includes revocation of power of attorney, showing date issued, name of principal and agent, date effective, and date filed. Arranged chronologically by dates filed. No index. Handwritten and typed. 9 x 5 x 12. Clerk of courts' main office.

159. NOTICES OF STRAYS

1841-1913. 1 volume, 2 file boxes. Title varies: Estray Records, 1841-1962. 1 volume.

Original notices and copies of notices filed of stray domestic animals, by person having possession of animals, showing date of notice, date animal penned, name and township of residence of person reporting, kind and description of animal, date animal will be sold at public auction if not claimed, and date filed. Arranged chronologically by dates filed. 1841-1862, indexed alphabetically by names of persons filing report; 1863-1913, no index. Handwritten. Volumes, 210 pages. 15 x 10 x 1.25; file boxes, 9 x 5 x 12. 1 volume, 1841-1962, clerk of courts' vault; 2 file boxes, 1841-1913, Clerk of courts' main office.

160. QUADRENNIAL ENUMERATION
1895, 1899, 1903. 783 volumes. (dated). Subtitled by names of townships, corporations or city wards.

Quadrennial enumeration reports filed by townships, corporations and city ward personal property assessors of inhabitants 18 to 45 years of age, showing name of township, town or city ward, year, name, address, age, name of assessor, and date filed. Arranged alphabetically by names of inhabitants. No index. Handwritten on forms. 30 pages. 11 x 8 x .25. Attic store room.

161. [MISCELLANEOUS]
1898-1908, 1934—. 1 file box.

Papers of clerk of courts including copies of muster roll, Ohio National Guard 1898-1908, showing company, regiment, name, rank and address of members, date of muster, and date filed; copies of certificates of registration of trade-marks (bottles and other containers), 1934—, showing certificate number, date issued, date registered, name of owner, facsimile trademark, and date filed. Trademarks, arranged chronologically by dates filed; otherwise no obvious arrangement. No index. Muster roll, handwritten; other papers typed on printed forms. 9 x 5 x 12. Clerk of courts' main office.

The court of common pleas, like many other county institutions, originated in England during the reign of Henry II.[1] Established in America during the colonial period, the office was continued by the states following the War of American Independence.

The Northwest Ordinance of 1787 established a government consisting of a governor, a secretary, and three judges all appointed by Congress. The judges were to form a court, known as the general court, which had common law jurisdictions and together with the governor were authorized to draw up a code of civil and criminal law. The territorial act of 1788, establishing the American colonial policy in the newer west in respect to the judiciary, contained sections authorizing the establishment in each county of a common pleas court to be composed of not less than three no more than five members. These members appointed and commissioned by the territorial governor were given jurisdiction in all civil matters.[2] The same act established in each county a primary court called the court of general quarter session of the peace to be composed of no more than five nor less than three justices of the peace, appointed and commissioned by the governor.[3] This court, which has limited jurisdiction in criminal matters, was not re-established by the constitution of 1802 and the jurisdiction which had been exercised by this court was conferred upon the justices of the peace and the court of common pleas.[4]

When a constitution was drafted for Ohio in 1802, preparatory to the entrance of the state into the union, provision was made for a continuation of the territorial court of common pleas.[5] The articles of the Ohio Constitution, regarding the judiciary, provided for a court of common pleas in each county to be composed of a president and associate judges. For each county[6] not more than three nor less than two associate judges were to be appointed, with one president for each of the three traditional districts into which the counties were grouped. The associate judges were not as a rule men who had a legal education.[7]

---

1. George Burton Adams, *Constitutional History of England,* 109, 134.
2. Pease, *op. cit.,* 7.
3. Pease, *op. cit.,* 4.
4. Pease, *op. cit.,* 5; *Laws of Ohio,* I, 40; II, 235.
5. *Ohio Const. 1802,* Art. III, sec. 1.
6. At this time there were eight counties in the state.
7. Francis J. Amer, *The Development of the Judicial System in Ohio from 1787 to 1932,* 17.

The members of the court, appointed by joint ballot of both houses of the general assembly, were to hold court in three judicial districts into which the state was to be divided by legislative action. Their term of office was seven years "if so long they behave well."[8]

It was almost half a century before any significant changes were made in the structure of the court. The constitution of 1851 provided that judges of the common pleas court were to be elected for a five-year term. For the purpose of their election the state was divided into nine districts composed of three or more counties. Each district, in turn, was to be subdivided into three parts, in each of which one, common pleas judge was to be elected. The court of common pleas was to be held by one or more of these judges in each county in the district.[9] Power was given to the general assembly to increase or diminish the number of districts of the court of common pleas, or the number of judges in any district, and to change the districts or the subdivisions thereof, whenever two-thirds of the legislature concurred therein.[10] Provision was also made for the removal of judges by a concurrent resolution of two-thirds of the members elected to each house of the legislature.[11] An appellate court known as the district court was created, which was to be composed of one supreme court judge and the several common pleas judges of the district. This court was to be held in each county of the district at least once each year or at least three annual sessions were to be held in not less than three places.[12] The district courts were not a success, and after many attempts at revision the circuit courts, staffed by a separate group of elected judges, were adopted by vote of the people in 1883, thus relieving the common pleas judges of this appellate work.[13]

The juvenile court was created in 1904 with the jurisdiction in special matters relating to minors. The court was to be held by a judge of the court of common pleas, the court of insolvency, or the probate court who should be designated by three judges to serve as judge of the juvenile court.[14]

---

8. *Ohio Const. 1802,* Art. III, sec. 8.
9. *Ohio Const. 1851,* Art. IV, secs. 3, 4.
10. *Ibid.,* Art. IV, sec. 15.
11. *Ibid.,* Art. IV, sec. 17.
12. *Ibid.,* Art. IV, sec. 5, 6.
13. Amer, *op. cit.,* 31-33; *Laws of Ohio,* LXXXI, 168.
14. *Laws of Ohio,* XCVII, 562.

At the opening of the twentieth century sweeping changes in the organization of the courts were made. Constitutional amendments adopted in 1912 abolished the divisions and subdivisions of the common pleas provided by the constitution of 1851, and authorized the election of one or more common pleas judges in each county.[15] The chief justice of the supreme court was given authority to determine the disability or disqualification of any judge of the court of common pleas and also to assign any judge to hold court in any county.[16] Eleven years later the selection of a chief justice of the court of common pleas was authorized. Under an act of March 13, 1923, in counties more populous than Seneca, having two or more common pleas judges, a chief justice might be designated by vote of the judges. The justice so designated by his colleagues was to serve in such capacity until the expiration of his term, after which time the office was to be an elective one.[17] The elective section of the act was nullified in effect in 1924 by the supreme court on the grounds that the creation of a new elective office was unconstitutional. Accordingly, in 1927 and amendment was passed eliminating the elective provision of the act.[18]

In recent years attempts have been made to improve the efficiency of the court by imposing stricter qualifications upon those who seek election to the bench. In 1917 an act was passed providing that a common pleas judge shall have been admitted to practice as an attorney at law for a period of six years preceding his election.[19] The salary of the office was also increased to $3,000 per year plus an amount based on the population of the county[20] – thus making the position financially attractive, especially as the term of office is six years.[21] In addition to the regular salaries, common pleas judges may be paid a per diem and expenses when assigned to special duty by the chief justice of the supreme court in a district not their own. When dockets became crowded or judges are incapacitated or disqualified, such assignments may be made.[22]

---

15. *Ohio Const. 1851,* Art. IV, sec. 3.
16. *Ibid.,* Art. IV, secs. 3, 6.
17. *Laws of Ohio,* CX, 52.
18. *State ex rel.,* v. *Powell, Ohio State Reports* CIX, 383; *Laws of Ohio,* CXII, 5.
19. *Laws of Ohio,* CVII, 164.
20. G. C. secs., 2251, 2252.
21. G. C. sec. 1532.
22. *Ohio Const. 1851,* (Amendment, 1912), Art. IV, sec. 3; G. C. secs. 1469, 1687, 2253.

In a few large counties certain common pleas judges have specialized duties such as that of hearing domestic relations cases and serving as judge of the juvenile court. This practice promotes traditional efficiency.

The jurisdiction of the court of common pleas has also been the product of a long period of historical development. The territorial law of 1788 which created the court provided that "the judges so appointed and commissioned . . . shall hold pleas of *assizes, scire facias, replevins,* and hear and determine all matter of pleas, actions, suits, and causes of a civil nature, real, personal, and mixed, according to the constitution and laws of the territory."[23] Individually, each judge of the common pleas was given jurisdiction over contract actions not exceeding five dollars.[24] The probate court was established by an act adopted August 30, 1788, and two other judges of the court of common pleas sat with this judge in ruling on contested points, definitive sentences, and final judgments. Under the laws of 1788 the common pleas had no criminal jurisdiction, and the quarter sessions of the peace had no civil jurisdiction. There was no provision for an appeal from one court to another except from the probate court to the general court of the territory.[25]

In 1795 the judicial system underwent the first general revision and this increase the duties of the court of common pleas. A single justice of the peace or judge of the common pleas was given jurisdiction to hear certain civil actions up to $12. Actions under $5 were exclusive with the judges or justices and there was no appeal from their judgment. Actions between $5 and $12 could be appealed to the court of common pleas. In 1799 this jurisdiction was raised to $20 and appeals could be taken to the common pleas if the judgment was over $2. If the judgment was for plaintiff, he could appeal only if the original demand was $4 more than the sum recovered.[26] Appeal from the common pleas to the general court was provided for in 1795, but could not be taken unless the title to land was in question or unless the amount in controversy exceeded $50.[27]

---

23. Salmon P. Chase, comp., *The Statutes of Ohio and of the Northwestern Territory, 1788-1833,* I, 94.
24. Pease, *op. cit.,* 8.
25. Chase, *op. cit.,* I, 96.
26. Chase, *op. cit.,* I, 143, 233, 307.
27. Chase, *op. cit.,* I, 306.

The constitution of 1802 gave the court of common pleas jurisdiction in each common law and chancery cases as should be directed by law. It was also given jurisdiction of all probate and testamentary matters, and the appointment and supervision of guardians.[28] Moreover, the court of common pleas and supreme court were assigned to such original cognizance of criminal cases as might be provided by law.[29] Appeals in civil cases might be made to the court of common pleas from the county commissioners, justices of the peace, and other inferior courts.[30]

An act of the first general assembly in 1803 provided for the organization of the courts and defined their jurisdiction. The court of common pleas was given original jurisdiction in all cases, both in law and in equity, when the matter in dispute exceeded the jurisdiction of the justice of peace; of all probate, testamentary, and guardianship matters; and of all criminal matters exceeding the jurisdiction of the justice of peace, except when the punishment of the crime was capital. It was allowed to review certain cases from the justices of peace and also to review the decisions of the county commissioners in highway matters. In addition, the court had the same power to issue remedial and other process, writs of error, and *mandamus* excepted, as had the supreme court.[31] In 1804 the courts jurisdiction in chancery cases was limited to cases involving less than $500,[32] and in 1805 it was given appellate jurisdiction from the justices of peace in all cases regardless of the amount involved.[33] In 1806 crimes wherein the punishment was capital could be tried in a common pleas court if the accused so elected.[34] In 1807 it was given jurisdiction in all chancery cases and concurrent jurisdiction with the supreme court in such cases involving over $500.[35] In 1810 all cases in which the common pleas had original jurisdiction were permitted to be appealed to the supreme court.[36] By this act the right to appeal was established in Ohio in all civil cases. However, the business of the supreme court increased so rapidly that in 1845 the right to appeal on a judgment of the common pleas court to the supreme court in actions at law was abolished.

---

28. *Ohio Const. 1802,* Art. III, secs. 3, 5.
29. *Ibid.,* Art. III, sec. 4.
30. Chase, *op. cit.,* I, 421, 425.
31. Chase, *op. cit.,* I, 425.
32. *Laws of Ohio,* II, 261.
33. *Ibid.,* III, 14.
34. *Ibid.,* IV, 57.
35. *Ibid.,* V, 117.
36. *Ibid.,* VIII, 259.

Instead, new trials were allowed "when law and justice required it."[37] Even earlier, appeals to the common pleas from inferior courts had been limited.[38] The chancery act, adopted in 1824, conferred general chancery powers on the court,[39] and in 1843 it was given concurrent jurisdiction with the supreme court in cases of divorce and alimony.[40]

The constitution of 1851 left jurisdiction of the common pleas court to be fixed by law.[41] The jurisdiction conferred on this court by subsequent legislation was essentially the same as that exercised since 1810, with the exception of the jurisdiction which was transferred to the supreme court,[42] and the addition, in 1853, of exclusive jurisdiction in divorce and alimony cases.[43] The court of common pleas was denied jurisdiction in cases of probate, testamentary, and guardianship matters, but final orders, judgments, and decrees of the probate court could be reviewed in common pleas on appeal or by writ or *certiorari.*[44] In 1853 the court of common pleas was given original jurisdiction of all crimes and offenses except minor criminal cases, the exclusive jurisdiction of which was vested in the justice of peace or other minor courts.[45]

The creation of criminal, mayors', and police courts also made certain changes in the powers and duties of common pleas courts.[46] The right to appeal from common pleas to the district court was restored in all civil actions in which the common pleas had original jurisdiction,[47] but by an act of 1858 appeals were allowed to the immediate court only and non-jury cases. However, the same act provided for a second jury trial in common pleas as a matter of right in jury cases. This was granted upon demand made by either party at the close of the first trial on condition of his giving bond.[48]

---

37. *Ibid.,* XLIII, 80.
38. *Ibid.,* XXXVIII, 27.
39. *Ibid.,* XXII, 75.
40. *Ibid.,* XLI, 94.
41. *Ohio Const. 1851,* Art. IV, secs. 3, 4.
42. *Laws of Ohio,* L, 87. Records pertaining to probate matters were to be transferred to the probate court wherever it was possible to separate them from common pleas records. *Ibid.,* L, 88.
43. *Laws of Ohio,* LI, 377.
44. *Laws of Ohio,* L, 84; LI, 145.
45. G. C. sec. 13422-5; *Laws of Ohio,* LI, 474; LII, 73.
46. *Ibid.,* L, 90, 240, 246, 251, 253.
47. *Ibid.,* L, 93.
48. *Ibid.,* LV, 81.

The abuse of this privilege led to its abolition in 1875.[49]

This period witnessed the re-establishment of superior courts in the state which were given the same jurisdiction as the courts of common pleas with certain exceptions.[50] At the same time as the superior court was established at Cincinnati, the legislature abolished the criminal court and transferred its jurisdiction to the common pleas court.[51] The criminal jurisdiction of the probate court was transferred to the common pleas court in 1857.[52] The probate court of Seneca County was subsequently granted limited criminal jurisdiction for certain periods.[53] A limitation was placed on the right to appeal from probate court to common pleas in 1854.[54] This limitation was repealed, however, in 1856.[55]

For many years there were few changes in the powers of the court of common pleas except in the forms of appeal to higher courts,[56] and such added powers as resulted from the decline in the number of superior courts.[57] In 1906 the probate court was given concurrent jurisdictions with common pleas in all counties in the trial of misdemeanors and all proceedings to prevent crimes.[58]

Since 1906 the court of common pleas has had jurisdiction in naturalization proceedings. In that year the federal statute was amended to limit jurisdiction in the granting of naturalization to the United States district courts and state courts having a clerk, a seal, and jurisdiction in matters of law and equality in which the amount of controversy is unlimited.[59]

Constitutional amendments adopted in 1912 had little effect upon the jurisdiction of the court of common pleas, this power being determined by law.[60] However, the establishment of municipal courts, beginning in 1910, relieved common pleas courts in many counties, exclusive of Seneca, of certain civil jurisdiction,[61]

---

49. *Ibid.,* LXXII, 34.
50. *Laws of Ohio,* LII, 34; LIII, 38; LIV, 37.
51. *Ibid.,* LII, 107.
52. *Ibid.,* LIV, 97.
53. See p. 106.
54. *Laws of Ohio,* LII, 104.
55. *Ibid.,* LIII, 8.
56. *Ibid.,* LXXIV, 359; LXXXII, 230.
57. *Ibid.,* LXII, 58; LXXII, 89, 105; LXXXII, 85.
58. *Ibid.,* XCVIII, 49.
59. *United States Statutes at Large,* XXXIV, pt. i, 596.
60. *Ohio Const. 1851,* Art. IV, sec. 6.
61. *Laws of Ohio,* CI, 364; CIII, 279.

but in 1911 in certain counties, also exclusive of Seneca, which had such jurisdiction, this was balanced by the abolition of the jurisdiction of the probate court in divorce, alimony, foreclosure, and partition cases.[62] The jurisdiction of the common pleas court of today is essentially the same as that of 1913. The few changes that have been made in the judicial system are found in the local, special courts, particularly in the rapidly developing municipal courts.

The common pleas court has never possessed extensive appointive powers. The constitution of 1802 authorized each court to appoint a clerk,[63] and in 1805 it was directed to appoint a county prosecuting attorney.[64] During the first three decades of Ohio history, the movement for the extension of the popular election of public officers deprived the court of common pleas of the privilege of appointing the county recorder (1829), the county surveyor (1831), and the county prosecuting attorney(1833).[65] The court continued to appoint a clerk of courts until 1851. In recent years, however, as new functions have been added to the county government, the court has again been given a limited appointive power. Successive acts in 1886, 1881, 1913, 1914, and 1925 authorized the court to appoint a soldiers' relief commission, jury commission, assignment commissioner, conservancy district board, and probation officer.[66] In 1882 the court was empowered to appoint a local board of visitors but this power was transferred to the probate court in 1906.[67] Other appointments authorized are those of court interpreter and criminal bailiff (1911),[68] inspectors of meetings of corporation stockholders, trustees for county memorial buildings, and boards of trustees for endowed libraries.[69]

The court may also appoint a court reporter (or reporters),[70] and may cooperate with the county commissioners for the establishment of a county department of probation, in which case the court appoints certain probation officers and supervisors their work.[71]

---

62. *Ibid.,* CII, 100.
63. *Ohio Const. 1802,* Art. III, sec. 9.
64. *Laws of Ohio,* III, 47.
65. *Ibid.,* XXVII, 56; XXIX, 399; Chase *op. cit.,* III, 1935.
66. *Laws of Ohio,* LXXXIII, 232; LXXXVIII, 200; CIII, 512; CIV, 423.
67. *Ibid.,* LXXI, 107; XCVIII, 28.
68. G. C. sec. 1541.
69. *Laws of Ohio,* LXXXIV, 115; XCV, 41; CVI, 485.
70. G. C. secs. 1546-1554.
71. G. C. secs. 1554-1 – 1554-6.

In case the sheriff is absent, disabled, or disqualified from serving the court's warrant, the judge may appoint, temporarily, an official for this service.[72] The court of common pleas has shared with other governmental agencies the function of issuing various licenses.[73] Since 1805 the court has been authorized to issue ferry licenses[74] and tavern keepers licenses.[75] Both ferry and tavern licenses may now be issued by municipal corporations also and the latter by the state fire marshal.[76] From 1803 to 1852 this court also issued licenses to ministers to solemnize marriage ceremonies; since the latter year this function has been exercised by the probate court.[77]

The keeping of the records of the common pleas court presented no particular difficulties for many decades. However, with the increased number of issues presented to the court in recent years the problem of judicial administration has become greater. This problem was solved in part by the creation of the office of chief justice of the court of common pleas who has been given the duties of superintending the business of the court, classifying it, and distributing it among the judges. Besides the duties enumerated, the chief justice annually makes a report to the clerk of courts showing the work performed by the court and by each judge in the preceding calendar year. Moreover, he reports such other data as the chief justice of the supreme court may require.[78]

Judges of the common pleas court are also required to issue an annual order as to the exact time of sessions. The clerk of courts is required to make this information public and also send a copy to the secretary of state. The law sets certain requirements as to the sessions of the court and the power of the judge to call special sessions.[79] The records of the court are deposited for safekeeping with the clerk of courts. The clerk is custodian also of all law reports and books furnished by the state for the use of the court and the bar and is made liable in the event of their destruction.[80]

---

72. G. C. sec. 2828.
73. See pp. XLV, 1-2, 55, 104, 168,169.
74. *Laws of Ohio,* III, 96; G. C. secs. 5947, 5949.
75. *Laws of Ohio,* III, 96; XXIX, 310.
76. G. C. secs. 3642, 3672, 843-3.
77. *Laws of Ohio,* I, 31; L, 84.
78. G. C. sec. 1558.
79. G. C. secs. 1533-1539.
80. *Laws of Ohio,* LXVIII, 109.

Dockets

162. APPEARANCE DOCKET

1834—. 76 volumes. (1-3, 3-8, 8-74 and 1875—, also by contained case numbers).

Dockets of civil cases filed in common pleas court, including divorce cases, July 1849—, showing term of court, names of attorneys, names of litigants, title of case, date petition or transcript filed, dates and titles of various writs filed and court orders issued, dates of sheriff's returns, itemized statement of clerk's and sheriff's fees; 1875—, also shows case number; 1879—, volume and page numbers of [Common Pleas] Journal, entry 174, Law Record, entry 178, Execution Docket, entry 106, and Order of Sale Docket, entry 109; 1898—, file box number of Case Records, entry 182. Also contains Criminal Appearance Docket, 1824-1869, entry 164. Arranged chronologically by dates cases filed. 1834-1841, no index; for index, 1842—, see entry 163. Handwritten on forms. Average 500 pages. 18 x 12 x 2.5. 75 volumes, 1834-1939, clerk of courts' vault; 1 volume, 1939—, Clerk of courts' main office.

163. INDEX TO APPEARANCE DOCKET

1842—. 8 volumes. (1842-1892 labeled by numbers of dockets indexed; 1893—, darted).

General index to Appearance Docket, entry 162: direct on left-hand page, showing term of court, names of plaintiff and defendant, date case filed, and volume and page number of docket; reverse, on right-hand page, showing term of court, names of defendant and plaintiff, date case filed, and volume and page numbers of docket. Arranged alphabetically by names of plaintiffs and defendants. Handwritten on forms. Average 460 pages. 18 x 12 x 2.5. Clerk of courts' vault.

164. CRIMINAL APPEARANCE DOCKET

1870-1921. 5 volumes. (1-5). 1834-1869 in Appearance Docket, entry 181, 1922— in Criminal Judgment Docket, entry 165.

Docket of criminal cases filed in common pleas court, showing term of court, names of attorneys, name of defendant, offense charged, case number, date transcript filed, date indictment returned, dates and titles of various writs filed and court orders issued, dates of sheriff's returns, amount of bond, names of sureties, itemized statement of magistrate's court costs and clerk's and sheriff's fees, volume and page number of Common Pleas Journal, entry 174, and Law Record, entry 178. Arranged chronologically by dates transcripts filed. Indexed alphabetically by names of defendants. Handwritten on forms. Average 300 pages. 18 x 12 x 1.5. Clerk of courts' vault.

165. CRIMINAL JUDGMENT DOCKET
1859—. 9 volumes. (1-9).
Docket of judgments in criminal cases showing term of court, name of defendant, offense, date indictment returned, verdict of jury, date of sentence, sentence, and itemized statement by clerk's and sheriff's fees. Also contains Criminal Appearance Docket, 1922—, entry 164. Arranged chronologically by dates indictments returned. Indexed alphabetically by names of defendants. Handwritten on forms. Average 400 pages. 16 x 11 x 2. Clerk of courts' vault.

166. COURT DOCKET
1860-1907. 100 volumes. (labeled by court terms).
Docket of civil cases assigned for trial, showing term of court, assignment number, names of attorneys, names of plaintiff and defendant, title of case, case number, date of trial, status of case, and court orders. Arranged chronologically by court terms and chronologically thereunder by trial dates. Indexed alphabetically by names of plaintiffs showing names of defendants. Handwritten on forms. Average 80 pages. 16 x 11 x .5. Clerk of courts' vault.

167. COMMON PLEAS CIVIL DOCKET
1908—. 11 volumes. (dated).
Docket of civil cases assigned for trial and disposed of in common pleas court, showing case number, date case filed, names of attorneys, names of litigants, title of case, dates of hearing, dates of final orders, volume and page numbers of, Common Pleas Journal, entry 174, and if execution ordered, volume and page numbers of Execution Docket, entry 106. Arranged chronologically by dates filed. No index. 1908-1914, handwritten on forms; 1915—, typed on forms. Average 600 pages. 10 x 15 x 3.5. 4 volumes, 1908-1921, Attic store room; 7 volumes, 1922—, Clerk of courts' main office.

168. CRIMINAL DOCKET
1870-1884, 1895-1911. 5 volumes. (1; 4 unlabeled).
Docket of criminal cases assigned for trial, showing term of court, assignment number, names of attorneys, name of defendant, offence, case number, date of trial,

status of case, and court orders. Arranged chronologically by court terms and chronologically thereunder by trial dates. Indexed alphabetically by names of defendants. Handwritten on forms. Average 200 pages. 16 x 11 x 1.25. Clerk of courts' vault.

169. TRANSFER CRIMINAL DOCKET
1912—. 2 volumes. (dated).

Docket of criminal cases assigned for trial and disposed of in common pleas court, showing case number, date transcript filed, date indictment returned, names of attorneys, name of defendant, offense, date of plea, plea, date of trial, verdict, sentence, date of final orders, volume and page numbers of [Common Pleas] Journal, entry 174, and file box numbers of Case Records, entry 182. Arranged chronologically by dates indictments returned. No index. 1912-1915, handwritten on forms; 1916—, typed on forms. Average 300 pages. 10 x 15 x 2. Clerk of courts' office.

170. BAR DOCKET AND WITNESS BOOK
1868-1908. 84 volumes. (labeled by court terms).

Docket of civil and criminal cases assigned for hearing, showing term of court names of attorneys, names of litigants, title of case, case number, date of trial, status of case, court orders, and names of witnesses subpoenaed by each litigant. Arranged chronologically by court terms and thereunder by trial dates. No index. Handwritten on forms. Average 160 pages. 16 x 11 x 1. Attic store room.

171. MOTION DOCKET
1894—. 7 volumes. (1-7).

Copies of motions *demurrers* filed in cases pending in common pleas court, showing date filed, names of litigants, title of case, name of attorney, in whose behalf filed, text of motion or *demurrers*, volume and page numbers of Appearance Docket, entry 162, or Criminal Appearance Docket, entry 164, Criminal Judgment Docket, entry 165. Arranged chronologically by dates filed. No index. 1894-1911, handwritten; 1918—, typed. Average 180 pages. 16 x 11 x 1. Clerk of courts' vault.

172. JUDGMENT DOCKET
1826-1927. 12 volumes. (1-12).

Record of judgments rendered in civil cases, showing term of court, names of litigants, title of case, date case filed, names of attorneys, nature of judgment, date judgment rendered, copy of judgment decree, and name of judge or judges. Arranged chronologically by dates of judgments. For index, see entry 173. Handwritten. Average 380 pages. 16 x 11 x 2. Clerk of courts' vault.

173. INDEX TO JUDGMENT DOCKET
1826-1867. 3 volumes. (1-3).

Index to Judgment Docket, entry 172, direct on left-hand page, showing names of plaintiff and defendant, title of case, nature of judgment, date of judgment, and volume and page numbers of docket; reverse on right-hand page, showing names of defendant and plaintiff, title of case, nature of judgment, date of judgment, and volume and page numbers of docket. Arranged alphabetically by names of plaintiffs and defendants. Handwritten on forms. Average 400 pages. 16 x 11 x 2. Clerk of courts' vault.

Court Proceedings

174. Common Pleas JOURNAL
1834—. 56 volumes. (1-56).

Copies of journal entries in civil and criminal actions consisting of affidavits, motions, pleas, writs, court orders, and sheriff's returns; also includes entries of probate matters, 1834-1852; tavern licenses, 1834-1865; ferry licenses, 1834-1863; ministers' licenses, 1834-1852; naturalization records, 1837-1859, 1906—; auctioneers' licenses, 1835—; appointment of members soldiers' relief commission, 1887—; appointment of members board of county visitors, 1891-1906; approval of annual reports of county commissioners, 1863—; grand jury reports; appointment of court attendants and approval of appointments of sheriff's deputies and sureties bonds filed by deputies and court attendants; all showing term of court, date of entry, names of litigant or principals, title of case, and title and text of entry. Arranged chronologically by court terms and chronologically thereunder by dates of entries For index, see entry 175. 1834-1916, handwritten; 1917—, typed. Average 640 pages. 18.5 x 12.5 x 3. 55 volumes, 1834-1939, clerk of courts' vault; 1 volume, 1939—, Clerk of courts' main office.

175. INDEX TO JOURNAL
1834—. 13 volumes. (1-13).

Index to Common Pleas Journal, entry 174, direct on left-hand page, showing date of entry, names of plaintiff and defendant or principal, title of case, title of entry, and volume and page numbers of journal; reverse on right-hand page, showing date of entry, names of defendant and plaintiff, title of case, title of entry, and volume and page numbers of journal. Arranged alphabetically by names of plaintiffs or principles and defendants. Handwritten on forms. Average 460 pages. 18 x 12 x 2.5. Clerk of courts' main office.

176. JUDGMENT INDEX, DIRECT
1835—. 11 volumes. (1-11).

Direct index record of judgments rendered, showing names of judgment creditor and debtor, date of judgment, case number, volume and page numbers of Appearance Docket, entry 162, Law Record, entry 178, nature of action, nature and amount of judgment, volume and page numbers of Execution Docket, entry 106, date of execution, and date judgment satisfied. Arranged alphabetically by names of judgment creditors. Handwritten on forms. Average 450 pages. 18 x 12 x 2.5. Clerk of courts' vault.

177. JUDGMENT INDEX, REVERSE
1835—. 11 volumes. (1-11)>

Reverse index record of judgments rendered, showing names of judgment debtor and creditor, date of judgment, case number, volume and page numbers of Appearance Docket, entry 162, and Law Record, entry 178, nature of action, nature and amount of judgment, volume and page numbers of Execution Docket, entry 106, date of execution, and date satisfied. Arranged alphabetically by names of judgment debtors. Handwritten on forms. Average 450 pages. 18 x 12 x 2.5. Clerk of courts' vault.

178. LAW RECORD
1825—. 139 volumes. (1-139). Title varies: Complete Record, 1825-1845, 5 volumes.

Complete record of proceedings in civil and criminal actions disposed of, consisting of copies of bills of particulars, affidavits, transcripts, indictments, petitions, pleas, motions, *demurrers*, briefs of evidence and trial proceedings, verdict of jury, and court orders, showing term of court, name of judge, date case filed, names of litigants, title of case, case number, date of trial, names of witnesses, names of petit jurors, verdict or judgment rendered, and sentence. Arranged chronologically by court terms and chronologically thereunder by trial dates. 1825-1853, indexed alphabetically, direct, on left-hand half of page by names of plaintiffs showing names of defendants; reverse, on right-hand half of page by names of defendants showing names of plaintiffs; also separate indexes, see entry 179, 1910—, entry 183. 1825-1913, handwritten; 1914—, typed. Average 600 pages. 18 x 12 x 3. Clerks of courts' vault.

179. LAW RECORD INDEX
1825—. 5 volumes. (1-5).

Index to Law Records, entry 178, direct on left-hand page, showing term of court, name of plaintiff and defendant, title of case, date case filed, and volume and page numbers of record; reverse on right-hand page, showing term of court, names of defendant and plaintiff, title of case, date case filed, and volume and page numbers of record. Arranged alphabetically by names of plaintiffs and defendants. Handwritten on forms. Average 600 pages. 18 x 12 x 2.5. Clerk of courts' vault.

180. CHANCERY RECORD
1825-1860. 11 volumes. (1-11).

Complete record of proceedings in chancery cases consisting of copies of petitions, affidavits, pleas, motions, briefs of testimony, court orders, and sheriff's returns, showing term of court, name of judge during case, date case filed, names of litigants, title of case, date of hearing, and date case disposed of. Arranged chronologically by court terms and chronologically thereunder by dates of hearings. For index, see entry 181. Handwritten. Average 500 pages. 18 x 12 x 2.5. Clerk of courts' vault.

181. INDEX TO CHANCERY RECORD
1825-1860 2 volumes. (1, 2).

Index to Chancery Record, entry 180, direct on left-hand page, showing date case filed, names of plaintiff and defendant, title of case, term of court, and volume and page numbers of record; reverse on right-hand page, showing date case filed, names of defendant and plaintiff, term of court, and volume and page numbers of record. Arranged alphabetically by names of plaintiffs and defendants. Handwritten on forms. Average 200 pages. 16 x 11 x 1.25. Clerk of courts' vault.

182. [CASE RECORDS]
1824—. 623 file boxes. (1-623).

Original papers filed in civil and criminal cases disposed of, consisting of bills of particulars, affidavits, indictments, petitions, motions, *demurrers*, writs, sheriff's returns, court orders, and cost bills, showing case number, title of paper, names of litigants, title of case, date issued, volume and page numbers of record where recorded, and date filed. Also contains: Transcripts, 1824-1856, entry 111; Executions, 1824-1835, entry 112. 1825-1858 all papers each case banded together; 1859—, all papers each case filed together in a jacket, showing case number, file box number, volume and page numbers of Order of Sale Docket, entry 109, and Execution Docket, entry 106, names of litigants, title of case, names of attorneys, date filed, date disposed of, and volume and page numbers of Law Record, entry 178. Arranged chronologically by dates disposed. For index, see entry 183. 1824-1845, handwritten; 1845-1910, handwritten on printed forms; 1911—, typed on printed forms. 10.5 x 4.5 x 14. Clerk of courts' vault.

183. GENERAL INDEX TO FILES
1824—. 2 volumes. (1, 2).

Index to [Case Records], entry 182, and 1910—, to Law Record, entry 178, direct on left-hand page, showing term of court, name of plaintiff and defendant, file box number, and volume and page numbers of record; reverse on right-hand page, showing term of court, names of defendant and plaintiff, file box number, and volume and page numbers of records. Arranged alphabetically by names of plaintiffs and defendants. Handwritten on forms. 500 pages. 18 x 12 x 2.5. Clerk of courts' vault.

Naturalization
(See also entries 258, 259)

184. DECLARATION OF INTENTION
1906—. 4 volumes. (1-4).

Copies of declarations of intention to become naturalized citizens as filed by aliens, showing case number, name and address of declarant, nativity, date of embarkation, date of entry, port of entry, age, sex, number of dependents, name and title of ruler of native land, and date filed; also copies of affidavits by two citizens as to residence and character of declarant. Arranged chronologically by dates filed. Indexed alphabetically by names of declarants. Handwritten on printed forms. Average 100 pages. 16 x 11 x .75. Clerk of courts' vault.

185. NATURALIZATION RECORD
1907—. 3 volumes. (1-3).

Copies of petitions for naturalization, affidavits, court orders granting citizenship, and oaths, showing case number, date of filing petition, petition number, name of petitioner, age, sex, birth date, birthplace, nativity, name and ages of dependents, affidavits of citizens as to length of residence and character of petitioner, date citizenship granted, and date of allegiance and renunciation of allegiance to ruler of native land. Arranged chronologically by dates petitions filed. Indexed alphabetically by names of petitioners. Handwritten on printed forms. Average 100 pages. 18 x 12 x .5. Clerk of courts' vault.

186. CERTIFICATE OF CITIZENSHIP
1907—. 5 volumes.

Stubs of certificates of citizenship granted aliens, showing certificate number, date issued, name of naturalized citizen, age, nativity, date citizenship granted, petition number, and place of residence of dependents. Arranged numerically by certificate numbers. No index. Handwritten on printed forms. Average 50 pages. 12 x 10 x .5. Clerk of courts' vault.

Reports

187. GRAND JURY REPORTS
1921—. 2 file boxes.

Original reports of grand jury sessions to common pleas court, showing term of court, date jury sworn in, names of jurors, name of foreman, number of cases investigated, number of indictments returned, number indictments each class of crime, number of cases ignored, number of cases continued, report of conditions of county jail, number of days in session, and date reports filed. No index. Typed on printed forms. 10.5 x 4.5 x 14. 1 file box, 1921-1936, Clerk of courts' vault; 1 file box, 1937—, Clerk of courts' file room.

The first constitution of Ohio provided for a supreme court consisting of three judges appointed by a joint ballot of the legislature for a seven-year term. This court was required to hold sessions at least once a year in each county.[1] The number of judges, according to constitutional provisions, might be increased to four after a period of five years, in which case the judges were permitted to divide the state into two circuits. Accordingly, in 1808, the membership of the court was increased to four and the state was divided into the requisite number of circuits.[2] Two years later, in 1810, the membership of the court was reduced to three;[3] in 1824 it was again increased to four.[4]

By constitutional provision, this court was given original and appellate jurisdiction "both in common law and chancery," in such cases as should be provided by law.[5] Accordingly, by statutory provision, the court was assigned exclusive cognizance of all cases of divorce and alimony and concurrent jurisdiction of all civil cases both of law and equity where the title to land was in question, or the matter and dispute exceeded $1,000; and appellate jurisdiction from the court of common pleas "in all cases respecting the title of lands or where the matter in controversy exceeds the value of one thousand dollars, and all cases where the proof or validity of wills or the right of administration shall be in question."[6] During the first half century of Ohio history the legislature granted decrees of divorce. Although the constitution of 1802 did not prohibit the legislature from exercising such jurisdiction, the supreme court prohibited the practice in 1848.[7] The constitution of 1851, Article II, section 32, contained a prohibiting clause. Moreover, the court was given original cognizance in the trial of capital offenses.[8] All cases in which the title of land or freehold was in question were to be tried in the county where the land was situated. Furthermore, the court was given appellate jurisdiction from the court of common pleas in all cases in which the court of common pleas had original jurisdiction.[9]

---

1. *Ohio Const. 1802,* Art. III secs. 2, 8, 10.
2. *Laws of Ohio,* VI, 32.
3. *Ibid.,* VIII, 259.
4. *Ibid.,* XXII, 50.
5. *Ohio Const. 1802,* Art. III, sec. 2.
6. *Laws of Ohio,* I, 36-37; XIV, 310.
7. *Bingham* v. *Miller, Ohio Reports,* XVII, 445.
8. *Laws of Ohio,* I, 36-37.
9. *Ibid.,* XIV, 310-354.

In 1831 the supreme court was directed to meet annually in the town of Columbus for the final adjudication of all such questions of law as may have been reserved in any county for decision. This session accord, known as the court in bank, was required to have its decision in each case reduced to writing, and transmitted to the clerk of the supreme court in each county in which such question was reserved. The clerk was directed to enter such decisions "on the journal of the said court" and such proceedings were to be taken as if such decisions had been made in the county.[10] Six years later, in 1837, an act was passed providing that the final judgments in the supreme court, held in any county within the state, could be reexamined and reversed or affirmed in the court in bank upon writ of error.[11]

This judicial arrangement continued until the adoption of the constitution of 1851, which provided a judicial system modeled upon the federal system existing at the time. The supreme court, as established in 1851, became for the first time in Ohio history, a reviewing court of last resort in the state. At the same time the jurisdiction of the supreme court was restricted. In 1853 the court of common pleas, rather than the supreme court, was given original cognizance of all crimes and offenses, except minor criminal cases, the exclusive jurisdiction of which was vested in the justice of the peace and other minor courts.[12] The supreme court, which, between the years 1803 and 1843, had exclusive original cognizance in divorce and alimony cases and from 1843 to 1853 had concurrent jurisdiction with the court of common pleas in such cases, was denied such jurisdiction in 1853 when the latter court was granted exclusive jurisdiction in these cases.[13]

The opinions of the supreme court on circuit and the decisions of the court in bank, as transmitted to the clerk of supreme court in each county, are in the offices of the respective clerk of courts.

---

10. *Ibid.,* XXIX, 93-94.
11. *Ibid.,* XXXV, 60-62.
12. G. C. sec. 13422-5; *Laws of Ohio,* LI, 474; LII, 72.
13. *Laws of Ohio,* XLI, 94; LI, 377.

188. COURT DOCKET

1847-1858. 1 volume.

Docket of cases assigned for trial in supreme court, showing term of court, names of attorneys, names of litigants, title of case, trial, status of case, and court orders. Also contains Court Docket [District Court], 1852-1858, entry 194. Arranged chronologically by court terms and chronologically thereunder by trial dates. No index. Handwritten on forms. 200 pages. 15 x 10 x 1.25. Attic store room.

189. [Supreme Court] JOURNAL

1825-1876. 3 volumes. (1-3).

Copies of journal entries in civil and criminal cases consisting of petitions, affidavits, pleas, motions, writs, sheriff's returns, and court orders, showing term of court, names the litigants, title of case, title of entry, text of entry, and date filed. Includes records of divorce cases, July 1826- September 1852. Also contains: Supreme Court Record, 1825-1937, entry 191; District Court Journal, 1852-1876, entry 197. Arranged chronologically by court terms and chronologically thereunder by dates of filing. For index, see entry 190. Handwritten. Average 450 pages. 18 x 12 x 2.5. Clerk of courts' vault.

190. INDEX JOURNAL, SUPREME COURT–DISTRICT COURT

1825-1884. 1 volume. (1).

Index to Supreme Court Journal, 1825-1876, entry 189, and District Court Journal, 1877-1884, entry 197, direct on left-hand page, showing term of court, names of plaintiff and defendant, and volume and page numbers of journal; reverse on right-hand page, showing term of court, names of defendant and plaintiff, and volume and page numbers of journal. Arranged alphabetically by names of plaintiffs and defendants. Handwritten on forms. 160 pages. 16 x 11 x 1. Clerk of courts' vault.

191. SUPREME COURT RECORD

1837-1860. 3 volumes. (1-3). 1825-1837 in [Supreme Court] Journal, entry 189.

Complete record of proceedings in cases of original jurisdiction and civil and criminal cases appealed from common pleas court, consisting of copies of bills of particulars, transcripts, petitions, affidavits, pleas, motions, *demurrers*, summons, briefs of trial proceedings, court orders, and sheriff's returns, showing term of court, names of judges, names the litigants, title of case, date case filed, date of trial, names of witnesses, names of jurors, verdict and sentence or judgment. Also contains District Court Record, 1852-1860, entry 198. Arranged chronologically by court terms and chronologically thereunder by trial dates. For index, see entry 192. Handwritten. Average 500 pages. 18 x 12 x 2.5. Clerk of courts' vault.

192. INDEX TO SUPREME COURT RECORD AND DISTRICT COURT RECORD
1825-1884. 1 volume.

Index to Supreme Court Record, 1837-1860, entry 191, and District Court Record, 1860-1884, entry 198, and to supreme court record, 1825-1837, as entered in [Supreme Court] Journal, entry 189, direct on left-hand page, showing term of court, names of plaintiff and defendant, and volume and page numbers of record; reverse or right-hand page, showing term of court, names of defendant and plaintiff, and volume and page numbers of record. Arranged alphabetically by names of plaintiffs and defendants. Handwritten on forms. 400 pages. 18 x 12 x 2.5. Clerk of courts' vault.

193. [ORIGINAL PAPERS]
1825-1952. 16 file boxes. (dated).

Original papers filed in supreme court cases consisting of bills of particulars, transcripts, petitions, exceptions, affidavits, pleas, motions, *demurrers*, writs, court orders, sheriff's returns, and cost bills, showing title of paper, names of litigants, title of case, case number, date issued, date filed, and volume and page numbers where recorded. All papers of each case banded together showing term of court, names of litigants, and title of case. Arranged chronologically by court terms. No index. Handwritten. 9.5 x 5 x 12. Attic store room.

Until 1851 the judicial power of the state of Ohio in matters of both law and equity was invested in the supreme court, the court of common pleas, and the justices' courts.[1] During the first 50 years of Ohio history the supreme court served as a court of appeals, holding court in each county annually.[2] When a new constitution was adopted in 1851 the judicial system was extended by the creation of district courts composed of one supreme court justice and several common pleas judges in the district. These courts were assigned original jurisdiction in the same matters as the supreme court, in such "appellate jurisdiction" as might be provided by law.[3] Thus, by constitutional provision the courts were assigned original cognizance in *quo warranto, mandamus, habeas corpus,* and *procedendo.* In addition to this, in 1852 the general assembly authorized the courts to issue writs of error, *certiorari, supersedeas, ne exeat,* and all other writs not specially provided by statute whenever such writs were necessary for the exercise of its jurisdiction. The same act assigned the courts appellate jurisdiction from the court of common pleas in civil cases wherein the latter court at original jurisdiction.[5]

For the purposes of the district courts the nine common pleas districts were apportioned into five judicial districts. A judge of the supreme court was designated to preside at the sessions of the district courts; in the event that no judge of the supreme court was present, as was often the case, the judge of the court of common pleas in whose subdivision court was being held was directed to preside.[6]

The district courts failed to function properly. Evidence seems to indicate that the increasing number of cases coming before the supreme court made it difficult for the judges to attend the meetings of the district courts. Indeed, six years before the creation of the district courts, the supreme court dockets were overcrowded. In 1845 the legislature found it necessary to afford temporary relief by prohibiting appeals from the courts of common pleas to the supreme court.[7] A similar condition of overcrowding existed in the sixties; so that, in 1865, the supreme court justices were relieved of the duty of attending the meetings of the district courts for that particular year.[8]

---

1. *Ohio Const. 1802,* Art. III, sec. 1.
2. See p. 90.
3. *Ohio Const. 1851,* Art. IV, secs. 5, 6.
4. *Ibid.,* Art. IV, sec. 2.
5. *Laws of Ohio,* L, 69.
6. *Ibid.,* L, 69.
7. *Ibid.,* XLIII, 80.
8. *Ibid.,* LXII, 72.

The judicial system had become slow and cumbersome. The courts declined rapidly after 1865 and were finally abolished.

Following the complete collapse of the district courts an amendment to the constitution, adopted in 1883, made provision for circuit courts. "The circuit courts," stated the amendment, "shall be the successor of the district courts, and all cases, judgments, records, and proceedings pending in said district court, in the several counties, of any district, shall be transferred to the circuit courts." The district courts, however, were to continue in existence until the election and qualification of the judges of the new circuit court.[9] The circuit courts were assigned the same "original jurisdiction with the supreme court, and such appellate jurisdiction as may be provided by law." The composition of the courts and the number of circuits were left to the discretion of the legislature. Accordingly, in 1884, an act was passed dividing the state into seven circuits, and providing for the election of three judges in each circuit.[10]

The circuit courts, in addition to the jurisdiction conferred upon them by the constitution,[11] were authorized by the legislature to issue writs of *supersedeas* in any case, and all other writs not specially provided by statute when they were necessary for the exercise of their jurisdiction.[12] Moreover, the courts were authorized to make and publish, as they deemed expedient, rules of procedure in their respective circuits not in conflict with the law or rules of the supreme court. The legislature directed that all cases taken to the circuit courts were to be entered on the docket in the order in which they were commenced, received, or file, and "to be taken up and disposed in the same order." However, cases in which persons seeking relief were imprisoned or were convicted of a felony; cases involving the validity of any tax levy or assessment; cases involving the constitutionality of a statute; and cases involving public right and proceedings in *quo warranto, mandamus, procedendo*, or *habeas corpus,* could be taken up in advance of their assignment or order of the docket.[13]

The judicial system of Ohio was again slightly changed in 1912 when, by constitutional amendment, the circuit courts were renamed courts of appeals.

---

9. *Ohio Const. 1851,* Art. IV, sec. 6.
10. *Laws of Ohio,* LXXXI, 168.
11. *Ohio Const. 1851,* Art. IV, sec. 6.
12. *Laws of Ohio,* LXXXI, 168.
13. *Ibid.,* LXXXI, 168.

"The court of appeals shall continue the work of the respective circuit courts and all pending cases and proceeding in the circuit courts shall proceed to judgment and be determined by the respective courts of appeals." The judges of the several circuit courts were designated as judges of the courts of appeals, and were directed to perform the duties thereof until the expiration of their term of office. Vacancies caused by the expiration of terms of office of the judges were to be filled by the electors of the respective appellate districts. The term of office was fixed at six years.[14]

The jurisdiction of the court of appeals remained much the same as that of the district court in 1851. However, the court was assigned original cognizance in writs of prohibition and appellate jurisdiction in the trial of chancery cases.[15] Certain restrictions were imposed upon the court: "No judgment of a court of common pleas, a superior court or other court of record" shall be reversed except by "the concurrence of all judges of the court of appeals."[16]

At present the court consists of three judges in each of the nine districts into which the state is divided, each of whom shall have been admitted to practice as an attorney at law in the state for a period of six years immediately preceding his election. One court of appeals judge is chosen every two years, and he holds office for six years beginning on the ninth day of February next after his election. The salary of the court of appeals judge, fixed at $6,000 per year in 1913, was increased to $8,000 in 1920 and so continues.[17] The judges hold at least one session of court annually in each county in the district.[18]

---

14. *Ohio Const. 1851,* (Amendment, 1912), Art. IV, sec. 6.
15. *Ohio Const. 1851,* Art, IV, sec. 6.
16. *Ibid.,* Art. IV, sec. 6.
17. *Laws of Ohio,* CIII, 418; CVIII, pt. II, 1301.
18. G. C. sec. 1517.

194. COURT DOCKET District Court

1859-1884. 3 volumes. (dated). 1852-1858 in Court Docket, entry 188.

Docket of cases assigned for hearing, showing term of court, year, names of attorneys, names of plaintiff and defendant, case number, title of case, date of hearing, status of case, and judges memoranda. Arranged chronologically by court terms and chronologically thereunder by dates of hearing. Indexed alphabetically by names the plaintiffs showing names of defendants. Handwritten on forms. Average 300 pages. 15 x 10 x 1.5. Attic store room.

195. JUDGMENT DOCKET

1852-1884. 2 volumes. (1, 2).

Docket of decisions handed down by district court, showing term of court, case number, names of attorneys, names of plaintiff and defendant, title of case, brief of decision or judgment rendered, and names of judges concurring. Arranged chronologically by court terms. Alphabetical by names of plaintiffs showing names of defendants. Handwritten on forms. Average 200 pages. 16 x 11 x 1.5. Clerk of courts' vault.

196. BAR DOCKET

1856-1884. 3 volumes. (dated).

Docket of cases filed on appeal from lower courts for hearing, showing term of court, year, names of attorneys, names of plaintiff and defendant, title of case, case number, nature of appeal, and date appeal motion filed. Arranged chronologically by court terms and chronologically thereunder by dates of appeals. Indexed alphabetically by names of plaintiffs showing names of defendants. Handwritten on forms. Average 300 pages. 15 x 10 x 1.5. Attic store room.

197. DISTRICT COURT JOURNAL

1877-1884. 1 volume. (4). 1852-1876 in [Supreme Court] Journal, entry 189.

Journal entries consisting of petitions, affidavits, pleas, motions, *demurrers*, writs, court orders, and sheriff's returns, showing term of court, title and date of entry, names of litigants, title of case, case number, and text of entry. Chronological by court terms and chronologically thereunder by dates of entries. For index, see entry 190. Handwritten. 630 pages. 18 x 12 x 3.5. Clerk of courts' vault.

198. DISTRICT COURT RECORD

1860-1884. 6 volumes. Title varies: 1860, 1 volume, Complete Record of Partition of the Estate of Josiah Hedges. 1852-1860 in Supreme Court Record, entry 191.

Complete record of proceedings in cases heard by district court on appeal from lower courts consisting of copies of exceptions, petitions, motions, pleas, affidavits, *demurrers*, summonses, sheriff's returns, court orders and judgments, showing term of court, names of judges, names of litigants, title of case, case number, date exceptions filed, date of hearing, brief of hearing, final decision and amount of judgment rendered, and date case disposed. Arranged chronologically by court terms and chronologically thereunder by dates of hearings. For index, see entry 192. Handwritten. 525 pages. 16 x 11 x 2.5. Clerk of courts' vault.

199. [ORIGINAL PAPERS]

1852-1884. 35 file boxes. (dated).

Original papers filed in cases appealed from lower courts consisting of motions to appeal, exceptions, petitions, pleas, motions, affidavits, writs, court orders, sheriff's returns, and cost bills, showing title of paper, case number, names of litigants, title of case, nature of appeal, text of paper, date filed, and volume and page numbers where recorded. All papers of each case filed together in a jacket, showing case number, names that litigants, names of attorneys, title of case, nature of appeal, date filed, date case disposed, and 1852-1876, volume and page numbers of Supreme Court Journal, entry 189, 1877-1884, District Court Journal, entry 197, Supreme Court Record, 1852-1860, entry 191, and District Court Cecord, 1860-1884, entry 198. Arranged chronologically by dates disposed. No index. Handwritten on printed forms. 9.5 x 5 x 12. Attic storage room.

Circuit Court

200. CIRCUIT COURT APPEARANCE DOCKET

1884-1913. 2 volumes. (1, 2).

Docket of cases filed in circuit court on appeal from lower courts, showing term of court, case number, names of attorneys, names of the litigants, title of case, date motion to appeal filed, dates and title of various papers filed, date final order filed, date of sheriff's returns, itemized statements of clerk's and sheriff's fees, volume and page numbers of Circuit Court Journal, entry 204, and Circuit Court Record, entry 206. Arranged numerically by case numbers. For index, see entry 201.

Handwritten on forms. Average 600 pages. 18 x 12 x 3. Clerk of courts' vault.

201. INDEX TO CIRCUIT COURT APPEARANCE DOCKET
1884-1913. 1 volume.

Index to Circuit Court Appearance Docket, entry 200, direct on left hand page, showing names of plaintiff and defendant, case number, date file, and volume and page numbers of docket; reverse on right hand page, showing names of defendant and plaintiff, case number, date file, and volume and page numbers of docket. Arranged alphabetically by names of plaintiffs, and defendants. Handwritten on forms. 350 pages. 18 x 12 x 2. Clerk of courts' vault.

202. CIRCUIT COURT DOCKET
1884-1912. 3 volumes. (1-3).

Docket of cases appealed from lower courts, showing year, term of court, names of attorneys, names that litigants, title of case, case number, status of case, and remarks. Arranged chronologically by court to terms. No index. Handwritten on forms. Average 260 pages. 16 x 11 x 1.5. Clerk of courts' vault.

203. CIRCUIT COURT BAR DOCKET AND WITNESS BOOK
1885-1935. 2 volumes.

Docket of cases assigned for hearing on appeals from lower courts, showing term of court, names of attorneys, plaintiff, and defendant, title of case, case number, date of hearing, date case disposed, how disposed, and names of witnesses subpoenaed and appearing for each litigate. Also contains [Bar Docket and Witness Book], 1911-1935, entry 211. Arranged chronologically by court terms and thereunder by dates of hearing. Indexed alphabetically by names of plaintiffs showing names of defendants. Handwritten on forms. 250 pages. 16 x 11 x 1.5. Clerk of courts' vault.

204. CIRCUIT COURT JOURNAL
1884-1913. 2 volumes. (1, 2).

Copies of entries consisting of petitions, pleas, affidavits, motions, *demurrers*, writs, court orders, and sheriff's returns, showing term of court, names of litigants, case number, title of case, title of entry, text of entry, and date of entry; includes schedule of sessions of circuit court for each county in district each term of court. Chronological by court terms and thereunder by dates of entries. For index, see entry 205. Handwritten. Average 340 pages. 18 x 12 x 2. Clerk of courts' vault.

205. INDEX TO CIRCUIT COURT JOURNAL
1884-1913. 1 volume. (1).

Index to Circuit Court Journal, entry 204, direct on left-hand page, showing names of plaintiff and defendant, title of case, volume and page number of journal, and date case filed; reverse on right-hand page, showing names of defendant and plaintiff, title of case, volume and page number of journal, and date filed. Arranged alphabetically by names of plaintiffs and defendants. Handwritten on forms. 400 pages. 18 x 12 x 2. Clerk of courts' vault.

206. CIRCUIT COURT RECORD
1884-1913. 6 volumes. (1-6).

Complete record of proceedings in cases heard in circuit court on appeal from lower courts consisting of copies of exceptions, petitions, pleas, motions, affidavits, *demurrers*, summonses, sheriff's returns, and court orders, showing term of court, names of judges, date of hearing, names of litigants, title of case, case number, from what court appealed, brief of evidence, names of witnesses, names of jurors (if jury impaneled), date case disposed, and how disposed. Arranged chronologically by court terms and chronologically thereunder by dates of hearing. For index, see entry 207. Handwritten. Average 600 pages. 18 x 12 x 3. Clerk of courts' vault.

207. INDEX TO CIRCUIT COURT RECORD
1883-1913. 1 volume. (1).

Index to Circuit Court Record, entry 206, direct on left-hand page, showing term of court, names of plaintiff and defendant, and volume and page numbers of record; reverse on right-hand page, showing term of court, names of defendant and plaintiff, volume and page numbers of record. Arranged alphabetically by names of plaintiffs and defendants. Handwritten on forms. 500 pages. 18 x 12 x 2.5. Clerk of courts' vault.

208. [ORIGINAL PAPERS]
1884-1913. 59 file boxes. (dated).

Original papers filed and cases appealed to circuit court from lower courts consisting of motions to appeal; petitions, affidavits, pleas, motions, writs, *demurrers*, sheriff's returns, court orders, and cost bills, showing title of paper, date filed, and volume and page numbers where recorded. All papers of each case filed together in a jacket, showing case number, names of litigants, title of case, names of attorneys, date appeal filed, date case disposed, volume and page numbers of

Circuit Court Journal, entry 204, and of Circuit Court Record, entry 206. Arranged chronologically by dates cases disposed. No index. Handwritten on printed forms. 9.5 x 5 x 12. Clerk of courts' file room.

Court of Appeals

209. APPEARANCE DOCKET, COURT OF APPEALS

1913—. 1 volume. (1).

Docket the cases filed on appeal from lower courts, showing term of court, case number, lower court case number, names of attorneys, names of litigants, title of case, date motion to appeal filed, dates and titles of various writs filed, dates of sheriff's returns, volume and page numbers of Journal, Court of Appeals, entry 212, and Court of Appeals Record, entry 214, itemized statement of courts' and sheriff's fees, and date case disposed. Arranged numerically by case numbers. For index, see entry 210. Handwritten on forms. 450 pages. 18 x 12 x 2.5. Clerk of courts' vault.

210. INDEX TO APPEARANCE DOCKET, COURT OF APPEALS

1913—. 1 volume. (1).

Index to Appearance Docket, Court of Appeals, entry 209, direct on left-hand page, showing term of court, names of plaintiff and defendant, case number, and volume and page numbers of docket; reverse on right-hand page, showing term of court, names of defendant and plaintiff, case number, and volume and page numbers of docket. Arranged alphabetically by names of plaintiffs and defendants. Handwritten on forms. 320 pages. 18 x 12 x 2. Clerk of courts' vault.

211. [BAR DOCKET AND WITNESS BOOK COURT OF APPEALS]

1913-1935, In Circuit Court Bar Docket and Witness Book, entry 203.

Docket of cases assigned for hearings in court of appeals, showing same information as entry 203.

212. JOURNAL, COURT OF APPEALS
1913—. 1 volume. (1).

Copies of journal entries in cases appealed from lower courts consisting of affidavits, motions, petitions, pleas, *demurrers*, writs, court orders, and sheriff's returns, showing term of court, names of litigants, title of case, case number, text of entry, and title of entry; also include schedule of court terms for each county of the judicial district. Arranged chronologically by court terms. For index, see entry 213. 1913-1915, handwritten; 1916—, typed. 640 pages. 18 x 12 x 3.5. Clerk of courts' vault.

213. INDEX TO JOURNAL, COURT OF APPEALS
1913—. 1 volume. (1).

Index to Journal, Court of Appeals, entry 212, direct on left-hand page, showing term of court, names of plaintiff and defendant, case number, and volume and page numbers of journal; reverse on right-hand page, showing term of court, names of defendants and plaintiffs, case number, and volume and page numbers of journal. Arranged alphabetically by names of plaintiffs and defendants. Handwritten on forms. 350 pages. 18 x 12 x 2. Clerk of courts' vault.

214. COURT OF APPEALS RECORD
1913—. 3 volumes. (1-3).

Complete record of proceedings in cases heard on appeal from lower courts consisting of copies of motions to appeal, briefs of exceptions, petitions, pleas, affidavits, motions, writs, *demurrers*, briefs of testimony, and court orders, showing term of court, names of judges, date of hearing, names of litigants, title of case, case number, from what court appealed, names of witnesses, names of jurors (if jury used), date case disposed of, and how disposed. Arranged chronologically by court terms and chronologically thereunder by dates of hearings. For index, see entry 215. Typed. Average 630 pages. 18 x 12 x 3.5. Clerk of courts' vault.

215. INDEX TO COURT OF APPEALS RECORD
1913—. 1 volume. (1).

Index to Court of Appeals Record, entry 214, direct on left-hand page, showing term of court, names of plaintiff and defendant, case number, volume and page numbers of record; reverse on right-hand page, showing term of court, names of defendant and plaintiff, case number, and volume and page numbers of record . Arranged alphabetically by names of plaintiffs and defendants. Handwritten on forms. 450 pages. 18 x 12 x 2.5. Clerk of courts' vault.

216. ORIGINAL PAPERS
1913—. 36 file boxes. (dated).

Original papers issued and filed in case appealed from lower courts consisting of motions, affidavits, pleas, petitions, writs, *demurrers*, court orders, sheriff's returns, and cost bills, showing title of paper, case number, names of litigants, title of case, text of paper, date filed, and volume and page numbers where recorded. All papers of each case filed together in a jacket, showing case number, names of litigants, title of case, names of attorneys, date appeal filed, date case disposed of, volume and page numbers of Journal Court of Appeals, entry 212, and Court of Appeals Record, entry 214. Arranged chronologically by dates cases disposed. No index. Handwritten and typed on printed forms. 9.5 x 5 x 12. Clerk of courts' file room.

The probate court, established by an act of the Northwest Territory on August 30, 1788, consisted of a probate judge with jurisdiction in probate, testamentary, and guardianship matters, and two judges of the court of common pleas, who sat with him and ruled on contested points, definitive sentences, and final judgments.[1]

The judicial system established under the first constitution of Ohio in 1802 did not provide for a probate court but vested the court of common pleas with such powers as had been exercised by the court in the territorial period. The constitution of 1851 re-created the probate court and gave it original jurisdiction in "probate and testamentary matters, the appointment of administrators and guardians, the settlement of the accounts of executors, administrators and guardians, and such jurisdiction in *habeas corpus,* . . . and for the sale of land by executors, administrators and guardians, and such other jurisdiction, . . . as maybe provided by law."[2] An amendment to the constitution, adopted in 1912, authorized the common pleas judge, when petitioned by 10 percent of the qualified voters in the counties having a population less than 60,000 to submit to the voters at any general election the question of combining the probate court and the court of common pleas.[3]

One of the primary functions of the court since its inception has been the settlement of estates. The civil code adopted in 1853 gave the court original jurisdiction in taking proof of wills, in granting letters testimony and in settling accounts of executors and administrators.[4] Until 1854 the court had jurisdiction in enforcing the payment of debts and legacies of deceased persons. While the court retains the original jurisdiction regarding estates, new duties have been added in recent years. With the development of inheritance tax laws in 1919 as a new means of taxation the probate court has been required to determine and assess the tax after the county auditor has appraised the decedent's estate.[5]

By constitutional provision the probate court has original jurisdiction in granting marriage licenses.[6] The court also issues licenses to ministers to solemnize marriages.[7]

---

1. Pease, *op. cit.,* 9.
2. *Ohio Const. 1851,* Art. IV, secs. 7, 8.
3. *Ibid.,* Art. IV, sec. 7 (as amended, 1912).
4. *Laws of Ohio,* LI, 167.
5. *Ibid.,* CVIII, pt. i, 561.
6. *Ohio Const. 1851,* Art. IV, sec. 8.
7. *Laws of Ohio,* L, 84.

The former provision was modified by an act adopted in 1931, which requires an elapse of at least five days between the time of application and that of the issuance of marriage licenses. However, power to suspend the operation of the act is vested in the probate judge.[8]

The jurisdiction of the court extends to the state's unfortunates. By the probate code of 1853, re-enacted in 1854, exclusive jurisdiction was granted to the court to make inquests respecting lunatics, insane persons, idiots, and deaf and dumb persons, subject by law to guardianship.[9] In 1856 the court was authorized to commit mentally incompetent persons to state institutions maintained for the care of such persons.[10] Two years later the court was given power to appoint and remove guardians over minors[11] The act of 1859 authorized the court to render adoption decrees.[12] Since 1904 the court has been given jurisdiction in trial cases involving neglected, dependent, and delinquent children.[13]

Since the middle of the nineteenth century the probate judge has been required to keep a record of vital statistics. In 1867 the duty of keeping a permanent record of births and deaths, which, in 1856, had been conferred upon the clerk of courts, was transferred to the probate judge.[14] When, in 1908, a bureau of vital statistics under the direction of the secretary of state was created the probate judge was relieved temporarily of this task.[15] In 1921 the act of 1908 was amended so as to require the local registrars to transmit to the district health commissioner, who was directed to serve as a state deputy registrar of vital statistics, all certificates of birth and deaths received during the preceding month, and a copy of all such certificates to the probate court. Although the General Code still requires the probate judge to keep a permanent record of birth and deaths and an index to such records[16] neither has been kept in Seneca County since 1908.

---

8. *Ibid.,* CXIV, 93.
9. *Ibid.,* LI, 167; LII, 103.
10. *Ibid.,* LIII, 81-86.
11. *Ibid.,* LV, 54.
12. *Ibid.,* LVI, 82; LXVII, 14.
13. See P. 282.
14. *Laws of Ohio,* LXIV, 63-64.
15. *Ibid.,* XCIX, 296-307.
16. G. C. sec. 10501-15.

Jurisdiction in naturalization proceedings was exercised by the probate court until 1906 when an amendment to the federal statute vested exclusive jurisdiction in naturalization matters and the United States district courts and all state courts of record having a seal, a clerk, and jurisdiction in actions at law and equity in which the amount in controversy was unlimited.[17] The General Code still requires the probate judge to keep naturalization records and an index to the records,[18] but jurisdiction was transferred to the court of common pleas. No naturalization records have been kept since 1906.

During the early years of its existence the court was given limited criminal jurisdiction in cases in which the sentence did not impose capital punishment or punishment by imprisonment. By the code of civil procedure adopted in 1853 the judgments and final decrees of the probate court could be reviewed by the court of common pleas on error.[19] In 1857 the criminal jurisdiction of the probate court was transferred to the court of common pleas,[20] but later acts retained it in certain counties only. Thus, in 1858 the probate courts of certain counties, exclusive of Seneca, were granted jurisdiction in all crimes in which the sentence did not impose capital punishment or imprisonment in a penitentiary.[21] This act was repealed in 1878 and the probate courts of certain counties, excluding Seneca, were granted concurrent jurisdiction with the court of common pleas in all misdemeanors and proceedings to prevent crime.[22] In 1885 the provisions of this act were extended to Seneca.[23] Except for a brief period during 1886-1887 the probate court retained such jurisdiction until 1931 when the last vestige of criminal jurisdiction disappeared with the adoption of the probate code.[24]

Miscellaneous duties, remotely related to probate and testimony matters, have been added by legislative action. Since 1888 the court has been required to file a certified list of all unknown depositors as furnished by institutions or persons engaged in lending money for profit.[25]

---

17. *United States Statutes at Large,* XXXIV, pt. i, 596; See also *State of Ohio* v. *George G. Metzger and Albert L. Irish,* 10 N. P., n. s., 97 *et seq.*
18. G. C. secs. 10501-15, 10501-16.
19. *Laws of Ohio,* LI, 145.
20. *Ibid.,* LIV, 97.
21. *Ibid.,* LV, 186.
22. *Ibid.,* LXXVII, 48.
23. *Ibid.,* LXXXII, 42.
24. *Ibid.,* LXXXIII, 135; LXXXIV, 227; CXIV, 475.
25. *Ibid.,* LXXXV, 65; G. C. sec. 9864.

In 1896 the probate court was given concurrent jurisdiction with the court of common pleas in the matter of changing the names of persons who desired it,[26] a matter in which the court of common pleas had exclusive cognizance from 1842 to 1896.[27] Since 1896 the probate court has been required to record certificates of doctors and surgeons, and since 1916 the certificates of registered nurses and practitioners of medicine and surgery which authorized them to practice their profession in the state.[28] Since 1913 the court has been vested with the power to grant injunctions,[29] and since 1915 has had concurrent jurisdiction with the court of common pleas in condemnation proceedings for roads.[30]

In like manor the appointive powers of the probate judge have been expanded. In addition to the authority to appoint administrators and guardians he has been authorized by the act of 1891 to appoint members for the county board of elections; however this appointee power was abrogated by the act of 1892.[31] Then, too, from 1908 to 1913 the probate judge was authorized to appoint a county blind relief commission[32] comprised of three members each of who served a three-year term.[33] Since 1906 he has had authority to appoint members of the board of county visitors.[34]

The probate judge, like other county officials, has been required by statute to keep a record of the business of his office. The present system of records, originating for the most part in 1853 and continued by the probate code of 1931, includes a criminal record, an administrative docket, a guardians' docket, a marriage record, a record of bonds, a naturalization record, and a permanent record of birth and deaths.[35]

The probate judge has the care and custody of files, papers, books, and records belonging to the probate office and is ex-officio clerk of the court.

---

26. *Laws of Ohio,* XCII, 28.
27. *Ibid.,* XL, 28-29.
28. *Ibid.,* XCII, 46; XCIX, 499; CVI, 193, 202.
29. *Ibid.,* CIII, 427.
30. *Ibid.,* CVI, 583.
31. *Ibid.,* LXXXVIII, 449; LXXXIX, 455.
32. See p. 260.
33. *Laws of Ohio,* XCIX, 56; CIII, 60.
34. *Ibid.,* XCVIII, 28; CIII, 173-174.
35. *Ibid.,* LI, 167; LII, 103; LXXV, 9; CXIV, 324.

The probate code, adopted in 1931, directed the probate judge to preserve for future reference and examination of all pleadings, accounts, vouchers, and other papers in each estate, trust, assignment, guardianship, or other proceedings, such papers to be properly jacketed and tied together; he is required also to make proper entries and indexes omitted by his predecessors. Certificates of marriages, reports of birth, and similar papers not a part of a case or proceeding are to be arranged and preserved separately in the order of dates in which they are filed.[36]

At present the probate judge is elected for a four-year term.[37] In recent years there has been an attempt to raise the qualification of those seeking election to the office. Accordingly, an amendment to the probate code in 1935 restricted eligibility to the office to a practicing attorney or to a person who "*shall have previously served as probate judge immediately prior to his election.*"[38]

---

36. *Ibid.,* CXIV, 321-322.
37. *Ibid.,* CXIV, 320.
38. *Ibid.,* CXIV, 481.

Calendars and Dockets

217. COURT CALENDAR

1933—. 8 volumes. (dated).

Daily calendar of assignments of probate matters, showing year, day and date, case number, name of decedent, ward, or other principal, in what matter, and volume and page numbers of Journal, entry 223. Arranged chronologically by daily entries. No index. Handwritten on forms. 240 pages. 18 x 12 x 1.5. Probate court main office.

218. CIVIL DOCKET

1852—. 10 volumes. (1-10).

Docket of all civil and administrative matters filed in probate court, showing term of court, name of judge, case number, names of plaintiff and defendant or principals, title of action, date case filed, dates and titles various writs and entries filed, dates of sheriff's returns, and date case disposed of. Arrange numerically by case numbers. Indexed alphabetically by names of plaintiffs, decedents, wards, assignors, or incompetents; also separate index, see entry 226. Handwritten on forms. Average 550 pages. 18 x 12 x 3. 9 volumes, 1852-1938, Probate court vault; 1 volume, 1938—, Probate court's main office.

219. CRIMINAL DOCKET

1853-1857, 1885-1931. 4 volumes. (1-4).

Docket of criminal actions filed and record of proceedings, showing term of court, case number, names of attorneys, name of defendant, offense, date affidavit of complaint or transcript the magistrate's court filed, dates and titles of writs and court orders filed, dates of sheriff's returns, copies of affidavits of complaint or transcripts from magistrate's court, petitions, pleas, motions, writs, brief of trial proceedings, court orders, and sentence, showing date of trial, name of complainant, names of witnesses, names of jurors (if jury impaneled), itemized cost bill, date case disposed of, and name of judge. Arranged chronologically by dates cases filed. Indexed alphabetically by names of defendants. Handwritten. Average 300 pages. 18 x 12 x 1.5. 1 volume, 1853-1857, Attic store room; 3 volumes, 1885-1931, Probate court vault.

220. ADMINISTRATION DOCKET

1835—. 16 volumes. (1-13).

Docket of estates administered consisting of copies of applications for appointments as administrator or executor, general entries of appointments, and orders to file bond, showing case number, date application file, name of decedent, date of death, late residence, name of administration agent, names of appraisers, date of inventory and appraisement, appraised value of estate, names of heirs-at-law, degree of kinship, dates and titles of various petitions and orders filed, and date of final settlement. Also contains Guardian Docket, 1835-1857, entry 221. Arranged chronologically by dates applications filed. Indexed alphabetically by names of decedents showing names of administration agents; also separate index, entry 226. 1835-1852, handwritten; 1853—, handwritten on forms. Average 550 pages. 18 x 12 x 2. Probate court vault.

221. GUARDIANS' DOCKET

1858—. 6 volumes. (1-6). 1835-1857 in Administration Docket, entry 220.

Docket of guardianships consisting of copies of applications for appointment as guardian, journal entries of appointments, and orders to file bond, showing case number, names of guardian and ward, age of ward, names of parents, date application filed, date of appointment, date bond filed, amount of bond, names of sureties, estimated value of ward's real and personal estate, appraised value, dates of filing accounts, amount credited to ward, amount debited, and date of final settlement. Arranged chronologically by dates applications filed. For indexes, see entries 226, 247. Handwritten on printed forms. Average 550 pages. 18 x 12 x 3. Probate court vault.

222. WITNESS DOCKET

1907-1925. 1 volume.

Docket witnesses subpoenaed and appearing in civil and criminal cases, showing names of plaintiff and defendant, title of case, case number, date of trial, names of plaintiff's witnesses, of defendants witnesses, number of days in attendance, mileage, and total fee due. Arranged chronologically by trial dates. Indexed alphabetically by names of plaintiffs showing names of defendants. Handwritten on forms. 150 pages. 14 x 10 x 1. Probate court vault.

Court Proceedings

223. JOURNAL

1852—. 46 volumes. (1-46).

Copies of journal entries in civil matters consisting of applications for appointment and appointments of administrators, executors, trustees, guardians or assignees, approvals of bonds filed by administration appointees, orders to take inventory and appraisement, petitions to sell real estate, orders to sell chattels and real estate, approvals of sale, determinations of inheritance tax, orders to distribute proceeds, determinations of heirship, entries in adoption, lunacy, feeble-minded, and epileptic proceedings, entries and assignment actions (insolvent debtors), and appointments of members to board of county visitors, 1913—, and copies of reports of board of county visitors, 1913—, and appointment of member of park commission, 1936. Also includes entries in criminal cases, 1853-1857, 1885-1931, showing term of court, case number, names of plaintiff and defendant or principles, title of action, date of filing, title of entry, and text of entry. Arranged chronologically by dates filed. Indexed alphabetically by names of plaintiffs, decedents, wards, assignors, incompetents, defendants (criminal cases), or other principles. 1852-1910 handwritten; 1910—, typed. Average 600 pages. 18 x 12 x 3. 45 volumes, 1852-1939, probate courts' vault; 1 volume, 1939—, Probate court main office.

224. CIVIL RECORD

1853—. 27 volumes. (1-27).

Complete record of proceedings in civil cases consisting of copies of petitions, motions, affidavits, pleas, writs, court orders, and sheriff's returns, in cases pertaining to injunctions, condemnation proceedings, adoptions, assignments, change of name, lunacy, 1853-1874, feeble-minded, 1853-1904, 1913—, and all other matters except estates and guardianships, showing term of court, names of plaintiff and defendant or principles, title of case, case number, date case filed, brief testimony and trial proceedings, names of witnesses, names of jurors (if jury impaneled), and date case disposed of. Arranged chronologically by dates of filing cases. Indexed alphabetically by names of plaintiffs or other principles. 1853-1910. Handwritten; 1910—, typed. Average 600 pages. 18 x 12 x 3. 14 volumes, 1853-1899, juvenile courts; vault; 13 volumes, 1900—, Probate court vault.

For subsequent lunacy records, see entry 255; for prior and subsequent records of feeble-minded youths, see entry 256.

225. [CASE RECORDS, CIVIL]

1852—. 76 file boxes. (labeled by contained case numbers).

Original papers filed in all civil actions, except administration of estates and guardianships, consisting of petitions, answers, affidavits, motions, pleas, writs, court orders, sheriff's returns, and cost bills, showing title of paper, case number, names of litigants or principles, title of case, date issued, text of paper, date file, and volume and page numbers where recorded. All papers of each case filed together in a jacket, showing case number, names the litigants or principles, title of case, names of attorneys, date case filed, date case disposed of, volume and page numbers of Journal, entry 223, and civil records, entry 224. Also contains [Case Records, Lunacy], 1902—, entry 257. Arranged numerically by case numbers. For index, see entry 226. 1852-1919, handwritten on printed forms; 1915—, handwritten and typed on printed forms. 10.5 x 4.5 x 14. Probate court vault.

226. GENERAL INDEX TO FILES

[1835—]. 2 volumes. (1, 2).

Index to Case Records, Civil, entry 225, Estates, entry 251, Wards, entry 252, Estate Bonds, entry 237, and Guardian's Bonds, entry 238; also index to Civil Docket, entry 218, Administration Docket, entry 220, and Guardians' Docket, entry 221, showing names of decedent, ward, plaintiff, or other principal, administrator, executor, trustee, guardian, defendant, or other principal, case number, what docket, and volume and page numbers of records. Arranged alphabetically by names of decedents, wards, plaintiffs, or other principles. Handwritten on forms. Average 500 pages. 18 x 12 x 3. Probate court vault.

227. [CASE RECORDS, CRIMINAL]

1887-1931. 17 file boxes. Discontinued.

Original papers filed in criminal actions, consisting of affidavits of complaint, transcripts from magistrate's courts, petitions, pleas, motions, writs, court orders, sheriff's returns, and cost bills, showing title of paper, case number, name of defendant, offense, text of paper, date issued, date filed, volume and page numbers where recorded. All papers of each case filed together in a jacket, showing case number, name of defendant, names of attorneys, date case filed, date case disposed of, and volume and page numbers of Criminal Docket, entry 219. Arranged chronologically by dates disposed of. No index. 1887-1915, Handwritten on printed forms; 1916-1931, typed on printed forms. 9.5 x 5 x 12. Attic store room.

Wills and Determination of Heirship

228. WILL RECORD

1828—. 28 volumes. (1-28).

Record of wills filed consisting of copies of applications to admit to probate, journal entries admitting will to probate, and wills, showing date of application, date admitted to probate, case number, names of testator and executor, date of death of testator, late residence, directions for distribution of estate, names of legatees or devisees, names of witnesses, notarization, and date of will. Arranged chronologically by dates of applications. 1824-1844, indexed alphabetically by names of testators; for index, 1844—, see entry 229. 1828-1910, handwritten; 1911—, typed. Average 550 pages. 18 x 12 x 3. Probate court vault.

229. GENERAL INDEX TO WILLS

1844—. 2 volumes. (1, 2).

Index to Will Record, entry 228, showing case number, name of testator, name of executor, date probated, volume and page numbers of record, Administration Docket, entry 220, and Journal, entry 223. Arranged alphabetically by names of testators. Handwritten on forms. Average 450 pages. 16 x 11 x 2.5. Probate court vault.

230. [WILLS]

1829—. In Estates, entry 251.

Original wills and applications to admit will to probate showing date, name of testator, names of witnesses, and text of will.

231. HEIRSHIP RECORD

1932—. 1 volume. (1). Record initiated 1932.

Record of proceedings in determination of heirship consisting of copies of petitions to have heirship established, summonses on petitions, sheriff's returns, construction of wills, and journal entries of findings, showing case number, date petition filed, names of heirs, residents, name of decedent, date of death, late residence, and date of journal entry. Arranged chronologically by dates of filing petitions. Indexed alphabetically by names of heirs showing names of decedents. Handwritten on printed forms. 600 pages. 18 x 12 x 3. Probate court main office.

Estates and Guardianships

Appointments, Bonds, and Letters

232. ADMINISTRATORS BONDS AND APPOINTMENTS

1875—. 17 volumes. (5-17). Title varies: Record, Administrator's Bond and Letters; 18751891, 2 volumes; Administrator's Bonds and Letters, 1891-1894, 1 volume; Administrator's Bonds and Appointments, 1894-1911, 4 volumes; Administrator's Bonds and Letters, 1911-1932, 6 volumes.

Copies of applications for appointment as administrator, journal entries of appointments, notices of appointment, orders to file surety bonds, surety bonds, and letters of authority, showing case number, date application file, name of decedent, late residence, date of death, name of applicant for appointment, date of appointment, estimated value of estate real and personal, names of heirs-at-law, degree at kinship, amount of bond, names of sureties, and date letters of administration issued. Arranged chronologically by dates of filing applications. Indexed alphabetically by names of decedents showing name of administrators. Handwritten on printed forms. Average 560 pages. 18 x 12 x 3. 13 volumes, 1875-1932, probate court's vault; 4 volumes, 1932—, Probate deputy's office.

233. EXECUTOR'S BONDS AND APPOINTMENTS

1875—. 17 volumes. (5, 6, 7, & 8, 9-22). Title varies: Record, Executioner's Bonds and Letters, 1875-1894, 2 volumes; Executioner's Bonds and Appointments, 1894-1905, 2 volumes; Record, Bonds and Appointments Executioners and Administrator's Will Annexed, 1905-1919, 3 volumes. Copies of applications for appointment as executors of wills, journal entries of appointments, notices of appointments, orders to file surety bonds, surety bonds, and letters testamentary showing case number, date application filed, name of testator, late residence, date of death, name of applicant, date of appointment, estimated value of estate real and personal, names of devisees or legatees, relationship to testator, amount of bond, names of sureties, date bond filed, and date letters testamentary issued. Also contains Record of Bonds and Appointments D[e] B[onis] N[on]—W[ith] W[ill] A[nnexed], 1875-1918, entry 234. Arranged chronologically by dates of filing applications. Indexed alphabetically by names of testators showing names of executors. Handwritten on printed forms. Average 550 pages. 18 x 12 x 3. 15 volumes, 1875-1932, probate courts' vault; 2 volumes, 1933—, Probate deputy's office.

234. RECORD OF BONDS AND APPOINTMENTS D[e] B[onis] N[on]—W[ith] W[ill] A[nnexed]
1918—. 4 volumes)12A-15). 1875-1918 in Executors Bonds and Appointments, entry 233. Title varies: Record of Bonds and Appointments-Administrator- Will Annexed, 1918-1930, 2 volumes.

Copies of applications for appointment as administrator with will annexed, journal entries of appointments, notices of appointment, orders to file surety bonds, surety bonds, and letters of administration with will annexed, showing case number, date application filed, name of testator, late residence, date of death, name of applicant, date of appointment, estimated value of estate real and personal, names of heirs-at-law, legatees, or devisees, relationship to testator, amount of bond, names the sureties, date bond filed, and date letters of administration issued. Arranged chronologically by dates of filing applications. Indexed alphabetically by names of testators showing names of administrators. Handwritten on printed forms. Average 600 pages. 18 x 12 x 3. 2 volumes, 1918-1931, probate courts' vault; 2 volumes, 1931— , Probate deputy's office.

235. GUARDIANS' BONDS AND LETTERS
1875—. 11 volumes. (5-15). Title varies: Record, Guardian's Bonds and Letters, 1875-1894, 2 volumes; Record of Guardian's Bonds and Appointments, 1894-1907, 3 volumes.

Copies of applications for appointment as guardian of minors or incompetents, journal entries of appointments, orders to file surety bonds, surety bonds, and letters of guardianship, showing case number, date application filed, name of ward, age, if minor name of deceased parent, resident, name of applicant, date of appointment, estimated value of estate real and personal, amount of bond, names of sureties, dates bond filed, and date letters of guardianship issued. Arranged chronologically by dates of filing applications. Indexed alphabetically by names of wards showing names of guardians; also separate index, entry 247. Handwritten on printed forms. Average 550 pages. 18 x 12 x 3. 9 volumes, 1875-1934, probate courts' vault; 2 volumes, 1934—, Probate deputy's office.

236. BOND RECORD

1850-1851. 4 volumes. (1-4).

Record of appointments of administrators, executors, trustees, guardians, and assignees and of surety bonds filed including copies of legal notices of appointment, surety bonds, and letters of authority, showing case number, names of administration agent and decedent, ward, or assignor, date appointed, amount of bond, names of sureties, date bond filed, and date letters of authority issued. Arranged chronologically by dates of appointments. Indexed alphabetically by names of decedents, wards, and assignors showing names of administration agents. Handwritten on printed forms. Average 450 pages. 16 x 11 x 2.5. Probate court vault.

237. ESTATE BONDS

1840—. 12 file boxes. (labeled by contained case numbers).

Original surety bonds filed by administrators, executors, and trustees, showing case number, name of decedent, date of death, name of administrator or executor, amount of bond, names of sureties, conditions of bond, signatures of principal and sureties, date filed, volume and page numbers of Administration Docket, entry 220, and Administrator's Bonds and Appointments, entry 232, or Executor's Bonds and Appointments, entry 233. Arranged numerically by case numbers. For index see entry 226. 1840-1915, handwritten on printed forms; 1916—, typed on printed forms. 10.5 x 4.5 x 14. Probate court vault.

For other estate papers, see entry 251.

238. GUARDIAN'S BONDS

1830—. 8 file boxes. (labeled by contained case numbers).

Original surety bonds filed by guardians of minors and incompetents, showing case number, name of ward, if minor name of deceased parent, name of guardian, amount of bond, names of sureties, conditions of bond, signatures of guardian and sureties, volume and page numbers of Guardian's Docket, entry 221, and Guardian's Bonds and Letters, entry 235. Arranged numerically by case numbers. For index, see entry 226. 1830-1847, handwritten; 1848-1915, handwritten on printed forms; 1916—, typed on printed forms. 10.5 x 4.5 x 14. 5 file boxes, 1830-1902, Juvenile court vault; 3 file boxes 1903—, Probate court vault.

For other guardians' papers, see entry 252.

239. [MISCELLANEOUS BONDS]

1831-1926. 3 file boxes.

Original surety bonds filed by assignees, trustees, and appeal and injunction bonds, showing case number, title of case, names of principles, amount of bond, names of sureties, condition of bond, signatures of principals and sureties, date filed, and volume and page numbers where recorded. No obvious arrangement. No index. Handwritten and handwritten, on printed forms. 10.5 x 4.5 x 14. Probate court vault.

240. NOTICE RECORD

1878-1894. 1 volume. (1).

Record of publication of notices of appointment of administrators, executors, and guardians, showing case number, name of decedent or ward, name of administrative agent, date appointed, date notice of appointment issued, name of newspaper publishing notice, and date proof of publication filed. Arranged chronologically by dates of filing proofs. Indexed alphabetically by names of decedents or wards showing names of administrative agents. Handwritten on forms. 400 pages. 16 x 11 x 2. Probate court vault.

Inventories, Appraisements, and Claims

241. RECORD OF INVENTORIES

1853—. 38 volumes. (1-38).

Record of inventories and appraisements of assets of estates and guardianships consisting of copies of journal entries, orders to take inventory and make appraisal, notices of inventory and appraisement, and statements of inventory and appraisement, showing case number, name of decedent or ward, name of administrative agent, date of order to take inventory, names of appraisers, date of appraisement, itemized statement of inventory and appraisement, item, quantity, appraised value, total value all assets, itemized statement of claims of debts, names of creditors, amount, for what, total debts, date inventory and appraisement filed, and date approved. Arranged chronologically by dates of orders to take inventory.

Indexed alphabetically by names of decedents and wards showing names of administrative agents. 1853-1933, handwritten on forms; 1934—. Typed on forms. Average 625 pages. 18 x 12 x 3. 34 volumes, 1853-1923, juvenile court vault; 2 volumes, 1924-1934, Probate court vault; 2 volumes, 1934—. Probate deputy's office.

242. INVENTORY OF GUARDIAN STATEMENTS
1853—. 2 volumes. (1, 2).

Copies of guardian's statements of credits and debits, showing case number, date of guardian's appointment, names of ward and guardian, date inventory filed, appraised value of assets real and personal; credits showing date credited, amount, for what; debits showing date debited, amount, for what; statement of final accounts, total credit, total debits, credit balance, and date final account approved. Arranged chronologically by dates of appointments. Indexed alphabetically by names of wards showing names of guardians; also separate index, entry 247. 1853-1912, handwritten on forms; 1913—, typed on forms. Average 670 pages. 18 x 12 x 3.5. Probate court vault.

243. RECORD OF SCHEDULE OF DEBTS
1933—. 1 volume (1). Initiated 1933.

Record of debts and claims filed against the estates consisting of copies of journal entries of notices to file claims and notices of hearing on claims, itemized statement of claims filed, and journal entries of approval or rejection of claims, showing case number, date of notice to file claims, name of decedent, late residence, date of death, name of administrator or executor, claims itemized under the several schedules, names of creditors, amount of claim, for what, total amount of claims, amount allowed each item, total amount allowed, and date of journal entry approving claim. Arranged the chronologically by dates of notices to file claims. Indexed alphabetically by names of decedents. Typed on pregnant forms. 550 pages. 18 x 12 x 3. Probate court main office.

Sales

244. REAL ESTATE RECORD

1852—. 37 volumes. (1-37).

Record of sale of real estate in the administration of estates or guardianships consisting of copies of petitions to sell, notices of filing partitions to sell, orders to appraise, appointments of appraisers, administrators' and guardians' additional bonds in proceedings to sell real estate, orders of sale, reports of sale, sheriff's returns, and cost bills, showing case number, name of decedent, name of petitioner, date petition filed, names of appraisers, itemized statement of appraisal, date of additional bond, names of sureties, date sale order issued, description and location of tract, date of sale, to whom sold, amount of sale, term of sale, and date sale confirmed. Arranged chronologically by dates of filing petitions. Indexed alphabetically by names of decedents. 1852-1910, handwritten; 1911—, typed. Average 600 pages. 18 x 12 x 3. Probate court vault.

Accounts and Settlements

245. ROSTER OF SETTLEMENTS

1891-1896. 1 volume.

Record of due dates of settlements by the administrators, executors, guardians, and trustees, showing name and title of administrative agent, name of decedent or ward, address of agent, volume and page number of Administrative Docket, entry 220, or Guardians' Docket, entry 221, date settlement due, and date account filed. Arranged chronologically by dates settlements due. No index. Handwritten on forms. 300 pages. 18 x 12 x 1.5. Attic storage room.

246. ESTATES-RECORD OF ACCOUNTS

1865—. 28 volumes. (1-28).

Record of partial and final settlements of estates consisting of copies of journal entries of notices to file account, statements partial account, statements final account and settlement, affidavits of administrator or executor, and journal entries of notice of final settlement, showing case number, name of decedent, date of death, late residence, name of administrator or executor, date notice issued to file account, itemized statement of credits and debits partial accounts, itemized statement of credits and debits final account, and date final account approved. Arranged chronologically by dates of notices to file. Indexed alphabetically by names of decedents showing names of administrative agents. 1865-1912, handwritten on forms; 1913—, typed on forms. Average 600 pages. 18 x 12 x 3. 10 volumes, 1865-1896, Juvenile court vault; 18 volumes, 1897—, Probate court vault.

247. GENERAL INDEX, GUARDIANS' ACCOUNTS
[1847—]. 1 volume. (1).

Index to Guardians' Docket, entry 221, Guardians' Bonds and Letters, entry 235, Inventory of Guardians Statements, entry 242, Guardians' accounts, entry 248, guardians partial accounts, entry 249, and Guardians' Final Accounts, entry 250, showing names of ward and guardian, volume and page numbers of record. Arranged alphabetically by names of wards. Handwritten on forms. 600 pages. 18 x 12 x 3.25. Juvenile court vault.

248. GUARDIANS' ACCOUNTS
1847-1964. 16 volumes. (1-4, 9-20).

Contains: Guardians' Partial Accounts, entry 249; and Guardians' Final Accounts, 1847-1864, 1892—, entry 250. Arranged chronologically by dates notices issued. For index, see entry 247. Handwritten. Average 590 pages. 18 x 12 x 3. Juvenile court vault.

249. GUARDIANS' PARTIAL ACCOUNTS
1864-1887. 4 volumes. (5-8). 1847-1864, 1887—, in Guardians' Accounts, entry 248.

Records of partial accounts filed by guardians, showing case number, names ward and guardian, date notice issued to file partial account, date account filed, what account, itemized statement of credits and debits, date credited, amount, from what source, total credits, total debited, amount, for what, total debit, credit balance, and guardian's affidavit. Arranged chronologically by dates notices issued. For index, see entry 247. Handwritten. Average 580 pages. 18 x 12 x 3. Juvenile court vault.

250. GUARDIANS' FINAL ACCOUNTS
1864-1891. 6 volumes. (1-6). 1847-1864, 1892—, in Guardians' Accounts, entry 248.

Record of final accounts filed by guardians, showing case number, date notice issued to file final account, date account filed, names of ward and guardian, itemized statement of credits and debits, date credited, amount, from what source, total credits, date debited, amount, for what, total debits, credit balance, guardian's affidavit, and date account approved. Arranged chronologically by dates notices issued. For index, see entry 247. Handwritten. Average 590 pages. 18 x 12 x 3. Juvenile court vault.

Case Records

251. ESTATES

1829—. 657 file boxes. (labeled by contained case numbers).

Copies of papers issued and filed in administration of estates including applications for appointment as administrator or executor, journal entries of appointments, notices of appointments, orders to file surety bonds, letters of administration or testamentary, order to take inventory and appraise assets, appointments of appraisers, schedules of inventory and appraisement, orders to sell personal estates, sale bills, petitions to sell real estate, records of sale, schedules of debts, orders to distribute proceeds, accounts filed, final settlements, writs, sheriff's returns, coast bills, and journal entries discharging administrator or executor, showing case number, title and text of paper, dates issued and filed, names of decedent and administrator or executor, appraised value of estate, amount of sale bill, amount of debts, cost of administration, balance for distribution, names of distributees, relationship to deceased, and volume and page numbers of record or docket where recorded. Also contains [Wills], entry 230. All papers of each case filed together and a jacket, showing case number, names of decedent and administrator or executor, date case filed, date of final settlement, name of attorney, volume and page number of Administration Docket, entry 220, and Civil Docket, entry 218. Arranged numerically by case numbers. For index, see entry 226. 1829-1844, handwritten; 1845-1915, handwritten on printed forms; 1916—, typed on printed forms. 10.5 x 4.5 x 14. Probate court vault.

For surety bonds, see entry 237.

252. WARDS

1841—. 152 file boxes. (labeled by contained a case numbers).

Copies of papers issued and filed in guardianships of minors and incompetents including application for appointment as guardian, journal entries of appointments, notices of appointments, orders to file surety bonds, letters of guardianship, orders to take inventory and appraise assets, appointment of appraisers, schedules of inventory and appraisement, orders to file partial accounts, notices of filing accounts, writs, cost bills, sheriff's returns, and final settlements, showing case number, title of paper, name of ward, age, it minor name of deceased parent, name of guardian, dates of application and appointment, dates of issue and filing various papers, appraised value of estate, receipts and expenditures per partial accounts, and value of estate on final settlement. All papers of each case filed together in a jacket, showing case number, names of ward and guardian, date application for appointment filed, date guardianship terminated, volume and page numbers of Civil Docket, entry 218, and Guardians' Docket, entry 221. Arranged numerically by case numbers. For index, see entry 226. 1841-1845, handwritten; 1845-1915, handwritten on printed forms; 1916—, typed on printed forms. 10.5 x 4.5 x 14. Juvenile court vault.

For surety bonds, see entry 238.

Inheritance Taxes
(See also entries 351, 352, 432)

253. INHERITANCE TAX RECORD
1919—. 3 volumes. (1-3).

Record of inheritance tax assessments, showing case number, name of decedent, late residence, date of death, name of administrative agent, date case filed, value of estate as fixed by probate court, volume and page numbers of Civil Docket, entry 218, and Journal, entry 223, amount of claims and debts, cost of administration, net value of estate, names and addresses of heirs-at-law, legatees, and devisees, relationship to decedent, value of each distributee's share, amount of exemption, net amount subject to tax, amount of tax assessed, date tax accrued, and date paid. Arranged chronologically by dates cases filed. Indexed alphabetically by names of decedents. Typed on printed forms. Average 575 pages. 18 x 12 x 3. 2 volumes, 1919-1936, Probate court vault; 1 volume, 1937—, Probate deputy's office.

254. ESTATES NOT SUBJECT TO TAX
1919—. 1 volume. (1).

Records of estates exempt from inheritance tax, showing case number, name of the decedent, late residence, date of death, name of administrator or executor, date case filed, estimated value of estate, inventory value, value as fixed by court, amount of debts, administration cost, net value of estate, and total legal exemption. Arranged alphabetically by names of decedents and chronologically thereunder by dates cases filed. No index. Handwritten on forms. 300 pages. 18 x 12 x 1.5. Probate deputy's office.

Records of Incompetents

255. LUNACY RECORD

1875—. 6 volumes. (1-6).

Record of proceedings in lunacy complaints consisting of copies of affidavits of complaints, applications for admission to institution, warrants to arrest, medical certificates, inquest proceedings, journal entries of findings, orders to commit to institution, warrants to convey, receipts of admission to institution, and sheriff's returns, showing case number, date affidavit filed, name of patient, name of complaint, age of patient, birthplace, sex, color, marital status, name and next of kin, detailed report on medical examination, name of physician, brief of inquest proceedings, names of witnesses, date of order to commit, date conveyed, to what institution, dates of sheriff's returns, and amount of sheriff's fees. Arranged chronologically by dates of filing affidavits. Indexed alphabetically by names of patients. 1875-1920, handwritten on printed forms; 1921—, typed on printed forms. Average 300 pages. 18 x 12 x 1.5. Probate court vault.

256. RECORD OF FEEBLE-MINDED YOUTH

1905-1912. 1 volume. (1).

Record of proceedings in feeble-minded youth complaints consisting of copies of affidavits of complaints, applications for admission to an institution, warrants to arrest, medical certificates, inquest proceedings, journal entries of findings, orders to commit to institution, warrants to convey, receipts of a mission to institution, and sheriff's returns, showing case number, date affidavit filed, name of patient, name of complaint, age of patient, birthplace, sex, color, marital status, names of parents, guardian or next of kin, detailed report on medical examination, name of physician, brief of inquest proceedings, names of witnesses, date of order to commit, date conveyed, to what institution, dates of sheriff's returns, and amount of sheriff's fees. Arranged chronologically by dates affidavits filed. Indexed alphabetically by names of patients. Handwritten on printed forms. 150 pages. 18 x 12 x 1. Probate court vault.

For prior and subsequent records, see entry 224.

257. [CASE RECORDS, LUNACY]

1844-1901. 2 file boxes. 1902—, in [Case Record Civil], entry 225.

Original papers issued and filed and lunacy proceedings, consisting of affidavits of complaints, applications for admission to institution, medical certificates, orders for inquest, journal entries of findings, orders to commit, summonses, warrants to arrest and to convey to institution, receipts from superintendent of institution of admission, sheriff's returns, and cost bills, showing case number, dates of issue and of filing various papers, name of patient, age, birthplace, sex, color, marital status, name of next kin, detailed report of medical examination, date of inquest, date conveyed to institution, name of institution, name of superintendent, and itemized cost bill. All papers of each case filed together and a jacket, showing case number, name of patient, date affidavit filed, and volume and page numbers of Journal, entry 223. Arranged chronologically by dates affidavits filed. No index. Handwritten and handwritten on printed forms. 10.5 x 4.5 x 14. Probate court vault.

Naturalization
(See also entries 184-186)

258. DECLARATION OF INTENTION

1890-1906. 1 volume.

Copies of declarations of intention to become naturalized citizens filed by aliens, showing case number, name and address of declarant, age, birth date, birthplace, nativity, marital status, date and port of embarkation, port and date of entry, name of ruler of native land, and date declaration filed; copies of affidavits attested by two citizens as to length of residence and character of declarant, showing names of citizens. Arranged chronologically by dates filed. Indexed alphabetically by names of declarants. Handwritten on printed forms. 450 pages. 18 x 12 x 2.5. Probate court vault.

259. NATURALIZATION RECORD

1860-1905. 3 volumes,

Record of citizenship granted to aliens consisting of copies of applications for citizenship, oaths of allegiance, and certificates of citizenship, showing case number, date application filed, name of applicant, age, birth date, birthplace, nativity, marital status, names and addresses of dependents, date of arrival in the United States, name of ruler of native land, oath renouncing allegiance to ruler of native land and pledging allegiance to government of the United States, date of certificate of citizenship, certificate number, name of judge, name of naturalized citizen, volume and page number of Journal, entry 223. Arranged chronologically by dates applications filed. Indexed alphabetically by names of applicants. Handwritten on printed forms. Average 100 pages. 18 x 12 x .5. Probate court vault.

Vital Statistics

Births and Deaths ((See also entries 502, 504)

260. BIRTH AND DEATH RECORD
1867-1876. 1 volume. (1).

Record of birth reported (in front half of volumes), showing family name, Christan name, date of birth, sex, color, place of birth, name of father, maiden name of mother, residence of parents, by whom reported, and date reported; record of deaths (in back half of volume), showing name of deceased, date of death, age, birth date, birthplace, sex, color, cause of death, placed of death, marital status, by whom reported, and date reported. Arranged chronologically by dates reported. Indexed alphabetically by names of children or decedents. Handwritten on forms. 275 pages. 16 x 12 x 1.5. Probate court vault.

For subsequent records see entries 261, 262.

261. BIRTH RECORD
1877-1908. 4 volumes. (2-5).

Record of births reported, showing family name, Christian name, date of birth, sex, color, place of birth, name of father, maiden name of mother, residents of parents, and by whom reported. Arranged alphabetically by family names. No index. Handwritten on forms. Average 350 pages. 15 x 12 x 2. Probate court vault.

For prior records see entry 260.

262. DEATH RECORD
1877-1908. 4 volumes. (2-5).

Record of deaths reported, showing name of deceased, age, birthplace, sex, color, date of death, place of death, cause of death, if unnamed infant names of parents, occupation, by whom reported, and date reported. Arranged alphabetically by names of decedents. No index. Handwritten on forms. Average 350 pages. 15 x 12 x 2. Probate court vault. For prior records see entry 260.

Marriages

263. MARRIAGE RECORD

1841—. 22 volumes. (1-22).

Record of marriages authorized by license, showing date of application for license, license number, names and addresses of contracting parties, ages, occupation of each, names of parents of each party, and date license issued; copies of marriage certificates filed by officiating minister or magistrate showing certificate number, names of contracting parties, date married, name of minister or magistrate, and date filed; includes certificates of marriage by banns, showing dates of publishing banns, names contracting parties, date filed, and name of minister. Also contains: Record of Marriage Banns, 1843-1866, entry 264A; Minister's License, 1841-1864, entry 267. Arranged chronologically by dates of applications or filing notices of banns. For index, see entry 264. 1841-1863, handwritten; 1864—, handwritten on printed forms. Average 500 pages. 17 x 12 x 2.5. 21 volumes, 1841-1939, Probate court vault; 1 volume, 1939—, Probate deputy's office.

264. INDEX TO MARRIAGE RECORD

1841—. 5 volumes. (1-5).

Index to Marriage Record, entry 263, and record of Marriage Banns, entry 264A, direct on left-hand page, showing name of male, name of female, date license issued, and volume and page numbers of record; reverse on right-hand page, showing name of female, name of male, date license issued, volume and page numbers of record. Arranged alphabetically, direct, by names of males, reverse, by names of females. Handwritten on forms. Average 400 pages. 17 x 13 x 2. 3 volumes, 1841-1906, Probate court vault; 2 volumes, 1907—, Probate deputy's office.

264A. RECORD OF MARRIAGE BANNS

1867—. 2 volumes. (5.5, 6.5). 1843-1866 in Marriage Record, entry 263.

Copies of certificates of marriage solemnized after publication of banns, showing date of certificate, certificate number, names of contracting parties, name of minister performing the ceremony, date certificate filed, and date recorded. Also contains Minister's License, 1867-1878, entry 267. Chronological by dates filed. For index, 1867-1923, see entry 264; 1923—, indexed alphabetically by names of males showing names of females. 1867-1923, handwritten; 1923—, Handwritten on printed forms. Average 450 pages. 20 x 12 x 2.5. Probate court vault.

264B. MARRIAGE LICENSE

1858-1861. 1 volume.

Copies of marriage licenses issued, showing names of applicants, signatures of applicants, date of application, date issued, and signature of probate judge or deputy. Arranged chronologically by dates issued. No index. Handwritten on printed forms. 200 pages. 14 x 9 x 1. Probate court vault.

265. MARRIAGE CERTIFICATES

1841—. 14 file boxes. (dated).

Original certificates of marriage filed by minister or magistrates performing marriage ceremonies, showing certificate number, names of contracting parties, date of marriage, signature of minister or magistrate, date filed, and volume and page numbers of Marriage Record, entry 263; also includes original consents of parents or guardian to marriage of minors, showing date of consent, name and age of minor, name of other contracting party, signature of parents or guardian, and date filed. Arranged chronologically by dates filed. No index. Certificates, 1841-1852, handwritten; 1853—, handwritten on printed forms; consents, handwritten. 10 x 4.5 x 14. Probate court vault.

266. MARRIAGE CONSENTS

1861-1864. 1 volume.

Copies of written consents of parents or guardian to marriage of minors, showing name of parent or guardian, name of minor, name of other contracting party, date of consent, and date filed. Arranged chronologically by dates filed. No index. Handwritten on forms. 250 pages. 14 x 8 x 1.5. Attic store room.

Licenses and Permits

267. MINISTER'S LICENSE

1877—. 2 volumes. (2, 3). 1841-1864 in Marriage Record, entry 263. 1867-1878 in Record of Marriage Banns, entry 264A.

Copies of licenses issued to ordained ministers in Seneca County to solemnize marriage ceremonies or registered copies of licenses issued to ministers by foreign probate courts, showing license number, name and address of minister, church denomination, date ordained, date issued, county of issue, and date recorded. Indexed alphabetically by names of ministers. Handwritten on printed forms. Average 350 pages. 16 x 11 x 2. Probate court main office.

268. RECORD OF MEDICAL CERTIFICATES

1896—. 1 volume.

Copies of certificates issued on experience in the practice of medicine and surgery prior to 1896, or on graduation from an accredited college of medicine and an examination by the state board of medical examiners, 1896—, granting license to practice medicine and surgery, showing certificate number, name of licensee (if on experience prior to 1896 number years experience, medical school from which graduated or name of physician and surgeon trained under), medical school graduated from, date of graduation, date of examination, and date filed and recorded; also includes, 1916—, copies of certificates issued to graduate nurses and limited practitioners, granting license to practice, showing certificate number, name of nurse or practitioner, name of school or hospital of training (nurses), date of graduation, date of examination (for practitioners), name of school from which graduated, date of graduation, what degree, and dates filed and recorded. Arranged chronologically by dates filed. Indexed alphabetically by names of licensees. Handwritten on printed forms. 700 pages. 16 x 11 x 3.5. Probate deputy's office.

269. [PERMITS, DANCE HALL]

1917—. 1 file box.

Copies of permits issued to operate public dance halls, 1925—, showing permit number, to whom issued, location of hall (street address or township), date issued, and date of expiration; copies of revocation of public dance hall permits showing date issued, name and address of permit holder, location of hall, and reason for revocation. Also contains [Applications Clerk Hire], 1917—, entry 275. No obvious arrangement. No index. Typed and typed on printed forms. 10.5 x 4 x 14. Probate deputy's office.

Financial Records

270. CASH BOOK

1897—. 18 volumes. (Two unlabeled; 1-16).

Record of cash receipts and disbursements: Receipts, showing date received, name of payer, total amount, and for what; disbursements, showing date disbursed, name a payee, amount, and for what. Arranged chronologically by dates received. No index. Handwritten on forms. Average 300 pages. 18 x 12 x 1.5. 2 volumes, 1897-1906, Attic store room; 9 volumes, 1907-1926, Juvenile court vault; 6 volumes, 1927-1938, Probate court vault; 1 volume, 1938—, Probate court main office.

271. RECORD OF ACCRUED FEES

1907—. 17 volumes. (1-17).

Record of fees accrued in probate court, showing date accrued, case number, in what matter, to whom charged, total amount, amount of court, sheriff's, foreign sheriff's, witnesses, and sundry fees. Arranged chronologically by dates accrued. No index. Handwritten on forms. Average 300 pages. 16 x 11 x 1.5. 16 volumes, 1907-1938, Probate court vault; 1 volume, 1938—, Probate court 'main office.

272. RECEIPTS

1882—. 11 volumes. (labeled by contained receipt numbers).

Stubs, 1882-1904, and carbon copies, 1905—, of official receipts issued on payments into probate court, showing receipt number, date issued, case number, name of payer, amount, in what matter, and for what. Arranged numerically by receipt numbers. No index. Handwritten on printed forms. Average 375 pages. 15 x 9 x 2. 10 volumes, 1882-1938, Probate court vault; 1 volume, 1938—, Probate court main office.

Miscellaneous

273. RECORD OF UNCLAIMED DEPOSITS

1888—. 1 volume. (1). Last entry 1922.

Record of unclaimed deposits by banking institutions, showing name of banks, name of depositor, date of last deposit, date of last withdrawal, amount unclaimed, amount of interest accumulation, total amount, date of report, and name and title of bank official attesting report. Arranged chronologically by dates of reports. No index. Handwritten on printed forms. 250 pages. 15 x 10 x 1.5. Probate court vault.

274. POWERS OF ATTORNEY

1903—. 1 file box.

Copies of instruments delegating authority to act as agent for grantor, showing date of issue, names of grantor and agent, duties of agent, notarization, signatures of grantor and witnesses, and date filed; also contains revocation of power of attorney, showing date revocation issued, names of grantor and agent, statement of revocation, and date filed. Arranged chronologically by dates filed. No index. Handwritten and typed on printed forms. 10.5 x 5 x 14. Probate court main office.

275. [APPLICATIONS, CLERK HIRE]

1917—. In [Permits, Dance Hall], entry 269.

Copies of applications to county commissioners for supplementary appropriations for extra clerk hire, showing date of application, amount requested, number of extra clerks, and reason for request.

276. CORONER'S REPORTS

1902—. 3 file boxes. (dated).

Original inventories of effects found on dead bodies filed by coroner, showing case number, name of deceased, date of investigation, date of death, place of death, cause of death, itemized statement of personal effects found on body, names and addresses of relatives (if known), and date filed. Arranged chronologically by dates filed. No index. Handwritten on printed forms. 10.5 x 5 x 14. Probate deputy's office.

For other records, see entries 147, 148, 297.

277. TREASURY EXAMINATIONS

1867-1913. 2 file boxes.

Original reports of annual examinations of condition of county treasurer's account, showing period covered by report, date of examination, names of funds, amount credited each fund, sources of credit, total credit, amounts debited each fund, for what (as salaries, wages, material, supplies, bond, principle, interest), total debit, credit or debit balance, total credits all funds, total of deposits in county fund depositories, total withdrawals from depositories, balance or overdraft, amount of currency, gold, silver, checks in treasurer's safe, total in safe; names of examining committee, and date filed. Arranged chronologically by dates filed. No index. Handwritten on printed forms. 10.5 x 5 x 14. Probate court vault.

The juvenile court, though of uncertain origin, has been generally recognized as an American contribution to the administration of social justice. The establishment of such courts was the logical outcome of the practical philosophy of enlightened public men that child offenders against the law, or conventional social standards, should not be treated as criminals, but as unfortunates needing the help, supervision, and protection of the state.[1] Although the first separate court in the United States for the trial of juvenile offenders was established in 1899, in Chicago, Cook County, Illinois, by an act of the legislature of that state, the juvenile court was an institution of gradual growth. The Illinois experiment gave impetus to the children's movement in the middle west.[2]

The Ohio legislature was not slow in seeing the advantage of the Illinois experiment, and accordingly, in 1902, an act was passed creating the juvenile court in Cuyahoga County. Under this act all counties having a population of over 380,000 and an insolvency court were authorized, under an extension of the jurisdiction of this court to establish children's courts. The stipulations of this act excluded Seneca County. It gave the court jurisdiction of the trial of cases involving delinquent and neglected children; defined the terms "delinquent, dependent, and neglected;" authorized the appointment of a probation officer, and make it his duty to investigate the facts of cases coming before the court, and to take charge of the offender before and after trial. The clerk of the juvenile court was directed to keep a journal in which were to be recorded the minutes of the cases.[3] The judge of the insolvency court serving as juvenile judge served for a period of five years, and from 1935 the common pleas judge serving in such a capacity was to serve for six years.[4]

Two years after the establishment of the Cuyahoga County juvenile court, the general assembly provided by statute for the establishment of juvenile courts in the rural counties of the state which, because of their lack of population, were unable to create the newer agencies under the provisions of the act of 1902. Under the act of 1904 the judges of the court of common pleas, in counties wherein three or more common pleas judges held court currently, and the judges of the insolvency and superior courts where established, were authorized to designate one of their numbers as "juvenile judge."

---

1. Miriam Van Waters, *Youth in Conflict,* 147, 159, 161.
2. Edwin H. Sutherland, *Principles of Criminology,* 270-272.
3. *Laws of Ohio,* XCV, 785.
4. *Ibid.,* XCI, 845; CXVI, pt. ii, 157.

The court was given original jurisdiction in all cases involving neglected, dependent, and delinquent children under the age of sixteen years; and all children, who had been scheduled in the past for trial in a justice of the peace or police court were in the future to be tried before a juvenile judge. As under the act of 1902, the judge was authorized to appoint a probation officer, and the clerk of courts was directed to keep a journal of the minutes of each case.[5] The probate judge of Seneca County became juvenile judge under the provisions of the act of 1906.[6] In 1908 the court was given jurisdiction in cases involving minors under seventeen years of age, and such children as were brought before the juvenile judge were to become wards of the court until they had obtained the age of twenty-one years. The county commissioners were authorized to provide by lease or purchase, a "detention home" where neglected or dependent children might be detained pending the final disposition of their cases. The clerk of courts was directed to keep not only a journal, but also an appearance docket containing all orders, judgments, and findings of the court. It provided also for case studies to be made by the probation officer. Since 1937 a cashbook has been required to be kept. Records of the juvenile court are open only by order of the court to persons having a legitimate interest in them.[8] The age jurisdiction of the court was increased to eighteen in 1913.[9]

While provisions were being made for the establishment of juvenile courts, the legislature gave the court jurisdiction in cases involving adults who committed crimes against children or contributed to the delinquency of dependent children. Thus, in 1906 it was made a misdemeanor to contribute to the delinquency of a child under seventeen years of age.[10] Two years later the "lack of parental care" was defined and it was made a misdemeanor to fail to support a minor, or to cause him to engage in begging.[11] In 1913 "proper parental care" was defined by statute. By the provisions of this act the judges of the common pleas, probate, and where established, the insolvency and superior courts again designated the juvenile judge.[12]

---

5. *Laws of Ohio,* XCVII, 561.
6. *Ibid.,* XCVIII, 315.
7. *Ibid.,* XCIX, 192.
8. *Ibid.,* CXVII, 520.
9. *Ibid.,* CIII, 869.
10. *Ibid.,* XCVIII, 314.
11. *Ibid.,* XCIX, 193.
12. *Ibid.,* CIII, 872; CXIII, 471.

Marked progress has been made in the medical treatment of juveniles. While the act of 1913 authorized the juvenile judge to submit any child sentenced to an institution for correction to a mental test, the act of 1929 authorized him to submit any child coming before the court to a mental and physical test to be made by a physician or psychiatrist.[13] To further the scientific handling of children, the county commissioners were authorized, in the same year, to lease or construct a separate building to be known as the "juvenile court" which should be appropriately constructed, arranged, furnished, and maintained for the convenient and effective transaction of the business of the court, including adequate facilities for laboratories, dispensaries, or clinics for the scientific use of specialists attached to the court.[14]

One of the guiding principles of the court has been to make its "custody and discipline" of children approximate as nearly as possible that which should be given by their parents. In the case involving neglected or dependent children, not sentenced to state institutions, it has been the policy of the judges to assign children to private homes, and make arrangements for their adoption.

In 1913 the juvenile court was given the duty of administering mothers' pensions.[15] When the sections of the General Code[16] governing mother's pensions were repealed in 1936 with the acceptance of title IV of the Federal Social Security Act providing for aid to dependent children, the juvenile judge was designated as "county administrator."[17] When he serves in the capacity of county administrator, the judge is directed to utilize the service of the employees of the court exercising juvenile jurisdiction. In the performance of his duties the judge is authorized to compel the attendance of witnesses and the production of books, and may institute contempt proceedings against persons refusing to testify. Except for this, power s conferred upon a judge are administrative powers only.

Those entitled to aid under the act included, among others, a child residing in the state not less than sixteen years of age who has been deprived of parental support or care by reason of death, continued absent of a parent, or mental or physical incapacity of a parent. However, a child more than sixteen but less than eighteen years of age may receive aid at the discretion of the county administrator.

---

13. *Ibid.,* CIII, 872; CXIII, 471.
14. *Ibid.,* CXIII, 470.
15. *Ibid.,* CIII, 877.
16. G. C. Secs. 1683-2--1683-10.
17. C.C. sec. 1359-31. See this section for exceptions to the general provision.

Application for aid is made to the court by the parent or a relative, with whom the child must be living. Before aid is granted, a careful examination of the home is made by the employees of the court. If the child is found to be eligible, the court may grant such amount as is deemed proper. The amount of aid payable to any child is determined on the basis of actual needs "and shall be sufficient to provide support and care requisite for health and decency." In the event aid is granted, the home of such a child must be visited four times during each year. Each month the county auditor issues warrants upon the county treasurer for the pavement of the warrants certified by the court. The decisions of the juvenile judge are subject to abrogation or modification by the department of public welfare. Any person attempting to receive aid on behalf of any child not entitled to such aid is deemed guilty of a misdemeanor and upon conviction may be punished by fine or imprisonment, or both.[18]

The juvenile court at Cuyahoga County is the only independent juvenile court in the state. There are seven other juvenile courts in Ohio attached to the court of domestic relations. In Seneca County, as in other counties where there is neither an independent juvenile court nor a court of domestic relations, the probate judge serves as ex-officio judge of the juvenile court under the provision of the act of April 29, 1937,[19] which repealed the act of 1913 which had provided for the designation of a juvenile judge by the judges of other courts in the county.[20]

---

18. G. C. secs. 1359-31–1359-45; *Laws of Ohio,* CXVI, pt. ii, 188-195.
19. G. C. sec. 1639-7.
20. See P. 130. *Laws of Ohio,* CIII, 868.

Court Proceedings

(See also entries 283, 286)

278 JUVENILE APPEARANCE DOCKET

1906—. 5 volumes. (1-5). Title varies: Juvenile Record, 1906-1918. 1 volume.

Docket of cases filed in juvenile court, showing case number, name of juvenile delinquent or dependent, adult offender, or application for mothers' pension, 1914-1936, nature of case, date case filed, dates and titles of various papers filed, name of complainant, date of hearing, date case disposed of, how case disposed of, volume and page numbers of Juvenile Journal, entry 279. Serves as an index to [Original Papers], entry 280, by showing case numbers. Arranged numerically by case numbers. Indexed alphabetically by names of juveniles, adult offenders or applicants. Handwritten on forms. Average 300 pages. 17 x 12 x 1.5. Juvenile court office.

279. JUVENILE JOURNAL

1906—. 4 volumes. (1-4).

Copies of journal entries in juvenile cases and record of proceedings: juvenile offenders, showing case number, name of juvenile, nature of case, name of complainant, date case filed, dates of entries, date of hearing, names of parents or guardian, age of juvenile, sex, color, report on medical examination, report of juvenile officers investigation, name of school attended, name of teacher, grade, family history, brief of hearing, date case disposed of, and how disposed of; adult offenders, showing case number, name of offender (adult), offense charged, date case filed, date case disposed of, and how disposed of; mothers' pensions, showing case number, name of applicant, date application filed, report of investigation on application, name and ages of dependent children, entry of approval or rejection of application, amount of grant, and date effective. Arranged chronologically by dates filed. Indexed alphabetically by names of principles. 1906-1917, handwritten; 1918—, typed. Average 500 pages. 18 x 12 x 2.5. Juvenile court office.

280. [ORIGINAL PAPERS]

1906—. 15 file boxes. (labeled by contained case numbers).

Original papers issued and filed in juvenile cases, consisting of affidavits of complaints, pleas, motions, petitions, juvenile officers reports, reports of medical examinations, notice to parents or guardian and to board of county visitors, writs, court orders, sheriff's returns, and cost bills, showing title of paper, case number, name of principal, nature of case, date issued, text of paper, date filed, and volume and page numbers of Juvenile Appearance Docket, entry 278 and Juvenile Journal, entry 279. Arranged numerically by case numbers. For index, see entry 278. 1906-1917, handwritten on printed forms; 1917—, typed on printed forms. 10.5 x 4.5 x 14. Juvenile court vault.

281. CASE HISTORY

1932—. 3 file drawers. (labeled by contained letters of alphabet).

Case and family histories of each delinquent or dependent child coming under jurisdiction of juvenile court, showing case number, date referred, name and address of child, age, birth date, birthplace, sex, color, nationality, name of school attended, name of teacher, grade, names and addresses of parents or guardian, ages of parents, nativity, education, number of children in family, marital status of parents, cause of dependency or delinquency, and other data pertinent to individual case, status of case, and if disposed of manner of disposition. Arranged alphabetically by surnames or juveniles. No index. Handwritten and typed on printed forms. 12 x 16 x 24. Juvenile court vault.

282. RECORD OF DELINQUENTS

April 1938—. 1 file box.

Record of delinquents, showing method of disposition (official or unofficial), date referred, date of disposition, volume and page numbers of Juvenile Appearance Docket, entry 278, name of child, address, sex, birth date, county and state of birth, race, religion, name of school, mother tongue,TSTShether or not child is attending school, parents' names and addresses, age, county and date of birth, religion, church attendance, school grade completed, whereabouts of child when referred, history of delinquency, by whom referred, reason referred, and status of case. Arranged alphabetically by names of delinquents. No index. Handwritten on printed forms. 6.25 x 8 x 16. Juvenile court vault.

Dependents

(See also entries 278-281, 287, 288)

283. RECORD OF DEPENDENTS

April 1938—. 1 file box.

Record of dependent, neglected, and crippled children, showing date referred, method of disposition (official or unofficial), date of disposition, volume and page number of Juvenile Appearance Docket, into 278, name of child, sex, date of birth, verification of birth, address, county and state of birth, mother tongue, religion, church attendance, Sunday school attendance, name of school, grade completed, whether or not child attends school, if not in school, reason why, parents name and addresses, school grade completed, whereabouts of child when referred to, marital status a child's parents when referred to, reason referred, status of case, how disposed of, and place of commitment. Arranged alphabetically by names of dependent children. No index. Handwritten on printed forms. 6.25 x 8 x 16.25. Juvenile court vault.

284. RECORD OF BOARDING HOMES

1933—. 2 volumes.

Record of private homes approved for boarding and care of dependent children, showing name and address of owner, date of application, and date approved; record of placement of children in boarding homes, showing name of child, age, birth date, date placed in home, date removed or released from home, reason for removal or release, and boarding rate per week; record of payments to owners of boarding homes,[1] showing name of owner, year, month, and amount paid each month; record of payments to charitable institutions for care of dependent children from Seneca County, showing name and address of institution, names of children, date of payment, and amount of payment; record of expenditures for care of crippled children, showing name of child, age, date of birth, sex, color, names of parents or guardian, date placed in institution, name of institution, nature of deformity, date released, and amount of monthly payments to institutions;

---

1. Seneca county does not have a county children's home. Orphan and dependent children are placed in private boarding homes approved by juvenile court, and occasionally a child is placed in the children's home of one of the adjoining counties. The plan followed for many years passed by the juvenile authorities have been to get the children in homes on trial, with the view of adoption and the plan has been very successful as the ratio of adoptions is quite high.

Record of expenditures for clothing, medical and dental care, and miscellaneous items for dependent children. Arranged by subjects and chronologically thereunder by dates of applications, placements, or payments. No index. Handwritten on printed forms. Average 150 pages. 11.5 x 14.5 x 1. Juvenile court vault.

285. MOTHERS' PENSIONS

1914-1936. 4 file boxes. (labeled by contained letters of alphabet).

Original papers relative to mothers' pensions consisting of applications, reports on investigations, journal entries approving the applications, revising grants and termination of grants, showing case number, date filed, name and address of applicant, names and ages of dependent children, case history, date of approval, amount of grant, and volume and page numbers where recorded. All papers of each case filed together in a jacket, showing case number, name of client, date approved, volume and page numbers of Juvenile Appearance Docket, entry 278, and Juvenile Journal, entry 279. Arranged to alphabetically by names of clients. No index. Handwritten and typed on printed forms. 10.5 x 4.5 x 14. Juvenile court vault.

Financial Records

286. JUVENILE COURT CASH BOOK

1937—. 1 volume.

Record of receipts and disbursements: Receipts, showing date received, case number, name of payer, to whom due, amount, amount credited to county fund, probation officer, sheriff, witness, and deposit or cost or sundries; disbursements, showing date disbursed, name of payee, for what, and amount. Arranged chronologically by dates received and disbursed. No index. Handwritten on forms. 300 pages. 18 x 13 x 1.5. Probate courts' main office.

Aid to Dependent Children
(See also entries 283-186, 370, 371)

287. REGISTER OF CASES

1936—. 1 volume.

Register of applications for aid to dependent children, showing name of applicant, case number, date application filed, number of dependent children, date application approved, date denied, reason for denial, amount of monthly grant, date grant revised, amount of revised grant, reason for revision, date case closed, and reason for closing case. Arranged alphabetically by names of applicants. No index. Handwritten and typed on forms. 70 pages. (Loose-leaf binder). 11.5 x 17.5 x .5. Bureau of Public Assistance Office, 76 ½ South Washington Street, Tiffin.

288. CASE RECORD
1936—. 1 file box.

Case papers pertaining to aid to dependent children cases. Papers of each subject filed together in a folder. Contains: (a) Applications filed by mothers for aid to dependent children, showing application number, name and address of applicant, age, color, name of husband, marital status of applicant, names and ages of dependent children, birth dates, length of residence in county, in state, former residence, income, and date filed. (b) Investigation reports on applications for aid to dependent children, showing application number, (case number), name and address of applicant, color, nativity, marital status of applicant, education, religion, names and ages of dependent children, names and addresses of relatives, amount of income, home conditions, health record of family, life insurance analysis, estimated weekly budget necessary, and date of investigation. (c) Social data or case history of client, showing case number, name and address of client, age, color, nativity, length of residence in county, date of marriage, name of husband, place of marriage, age when married, maiden name, marital status, family history, income, from what source, names and birth dates of dependent children, date of application, date approved, date aid effective, and amount of grant. (d) Verifications of birth of dependent children, showing name of client, case number, name of child, date of birth, place of birth, and name of attending physician; verification of death, or imprisonment of husband, showing name of client, name of husband, date of death or imprisonment, and name and address of person attesting verification; verification of marriage showing case number, name of client, name of husband, age of each, client's maiden name, date of marriage, place of marriage, name of minister or magistrate performing ceremony; verification of divorce, showing case number, what court, volume and page numbers of court records, date of divorce decree, and grounds on which granted. (e) Face sheet of names and ages of dependent children in care of client, showing case number, name of client, date of application, date of grant, date grant effective, amount of grant, date grant revised, amount of revised grant, reason for revision, and names of persons or social organizations interested in case. (f) School reports from teachers and superintendents of schools, showing case number, name of child, name of school, name and address of mother, record of school attendance, grade in school, average grades, special aptitudes or difficulties, child's attitude towards school, amount of school relief granted, nature of relief granted, scholarships granted, by whom granted, name of teacher, name of superintendent, and date report filed. (g) Health records of dependent children, showing case number, name of client, name and age of child, birth date, date on physical examination, improvement over previous examination, medical history (illness, accident), record of vaccinations and immunizations, dates of examinations, and name of physician and nurse. (h) Copies of notices to applicant of approval of grant, showing case number, name and address of applicant, names and ages of dependent children, amount of monthly grant, date grant effective, and date of notice. (i) Copies of notices to client of modification of grant, showing case number, name and address of client, names and ages of dependent children, amount of original grant, amount of grant revised, date revision effective, reason for revision, and date of notice. (j) Copies of notices to client of termination of grant showing, case number, name and address of client, names of dependent children, date of application, date approved, amount of grant, date of first payment, date termination effective, date of last payment, amount of last payment, reason for termination, and date of notice. Arranged by subjects, each subject in a separate folder; and numerically thereunder by case numbers. For index, see entry 289. Typed on printed forms. 12 x 14 x 26. Bureau of Public Assistance Office, 76 ½ South Washington Street, Tiffin.

289. INDEX, AID TO DEPENDENT CHILDREN
1936—. 1 file drawer.

Index to Case Records, entry 288, showing name of client, case number, names and ages of children, name of father, marital status of client, date of application, date approved, amount of monthly grant, date grant revised, amount of revised grant, date case closed, and reason for closing. Arranged alphabetically by names of clients. Typed on printed forms. 5.5 x 8 x 20. Bureau of Public Assistance Office, 76 ½ South Washington Street, Tiffin.

290. [MINUTES ADMINISTRATION AND FINANCIAL RECORDS]
1936—. 1 file drawer.

Records of aid to dependent children pertaining to administration and finance consisting of: (a) Copies of minutes of meetings of board of public assistance, showing date and place of meeting, names of members present, motions and resolutions introduced and acted on, yay and nay votes, and recommendations for administration of bureau. (b) Copies of quarterly reports to county auditor and state department of public welfare, division of charities, showing period of report, case number, amount of monthly grant, estimate of medical and hospitalization expenses, total amount each case, total for quarter, and date of filing. (c) Copies of monthly statistical reports to state department of public welfare, division of charities, showing year, month, number of applications filed, number of applications rejected, number of applications continued, number of individuals granted aid, number of closed cases, number of grants revised, number of grants increased, number reduced, total cases receiving aid, total individuals (children) receiving aid, total amount of grants for month, total monthly grants, and date filed. (d) Copies of quarterly reports on cost of administration to state department of public welfare, division of charities, showing year, period of report, total cost for quarter, amount for salaries, amount for travel, amount for office expense, amount for miscellaneous expenses, and date filed. (e) Copies of pay rolls and administration of aid to dependent children, showing year, month, name and title of classification of employee, number hours worked, pay rate, amount due, and total pay roll for month. (f) Carbon copies of vouchers issued authorizing county auditor to issue warrant to client for monthly grant, showing voucher number, date issued, case number, name of client, names and ages of children, and amount authorized. Arranged by subjects, each subject in separate folder except vouchers (2 bundles). No index. 11.5 x 14.4 x 24. Bureau of Public Assistance Office, 76 ½ South Washington Street, Tiffin.

Jury commissioners were first authorized for Hamilton and Cuyahoga County in 1881.[1] In 1890 provision was made for the appointment of jury commissioners in counties having a city of the first class or of the first grade second class.[2] In 1891 the judges of the court of common pleas in counties having a city with a population of not less than 33,000 nor more than 50,000 were authorized to appoint four residents of the county to serve as a jury commission for a one-year term. The limitations of these acts excluded Seneca County. It was the duty of this commission to determine the qualifications and fitness of persons to be selected as jurors.[3] Three years later, in 1894, the provisions of the act were extended to Seneca County and all other counties in the state except Cuyahoga, Franklin, Hamilton, Lucas, Montgomery and Mahoning.[4] In 1902 the statute was amended to include all counties.[5] In 1913 the number of jury commissioners in each county was reduced to two.[6]

The jury code, which became effective August 2, 1931, provided for a jury commission of the same number and same qualifications previously specified, to hold office at the pleasure of the court, and to meet and select prospective jurors, both grand and petit, for the ensuing year from a list provided by the board of elections.[7] At the beginning of each year the commissioners are required to make up a new and complete jury list, known as the annual jury list, arranged alphabetically by precincts, districts, and townships, recording the name, occupation, business address, and residence of each prospective jour, and to prepare an index to this list. A duplicate list is certified by the commissioners and filed in the office of the clerk of court of common pleas.[8]

The jury commissioners select prospective jurors for civil and criminal cases as well as for the grand jury. They select jurors for the probate court, juvenile court, and other minor courts.

---

1. *Laws of Ohio,* LXXVIII, 95.
2. *Ibid.,* LXXXVII, 327.
3. *Ibid.,* LXXXVIII, 200.
4. *Ibid.,* XCI, 176.
5. *Ibid.,* XCIV, 3.
6. *Ibid.,* CIII, 513; CVI, 106.
7. *Laws of Ohio,* CXIV, 193-213.
8. *Ibid.,* CXIV, 205.

291. RECORD

1932—. 1 volume.

Copies of minutes of meetings of the jury commission, showing date and place of meeting, names of members present, common pleas court journal entry to draw jury venire, and list of names and addresses of electors drawn for grand and petit jury duty. Arranged chronologically by dates of meetings. No index. Handwritten. 420 pages. 16 x 11 x 2. Clerk of courts' main office.

292. CERTIFIED LISTS

1931—. 1 file box.

Original list of electors eligible for jury duty certified to jury commission by the county board of elections, showing year, name of township, municipality, city ward number, precinct number or letter, name and address of elector, and date certified. Arranged chronologically by date certified. No index. Typed on forms. 10.5 x 4.5 x 14. Clerk of courts' file room.

For clerk of courts' copies, see entry 124.

The grand jury, sometimes called the palladium of English liberty, has its function the preliminary examination of persons charged with a capital or other infamous crime. The right, guaranteed by the Federal Constitution, to an examination by grand jury, is recognized in the provisions of the Ohio Constitution of 1802 and 1851 and in the amendments of 1912.[1]

Under the present system, which does not differ in detail from that inaugurated in the early days of the state's history, the grand jury is composed of fifteen members, resident electors of the county having "the qualifications of jurors."[2] It is the duty of the grand jury "to inquire of and present all offenses committed in the county in and for which it was empaneled and sworn."[3] The proceedings of the grand jury are secret and each juror is required to take an oath to preserve such secrecy. Moreover, no grand juror may be required to reveal the way he or other grand jurors voted.[4]

The grand jurors are aided in their investigations by the county prosecuting attorney, who, since 1869, has been authorized by statute to present evidence before this body and compel the attendance of witnesses against whom he may institute contempt proceedings if they refuse to testify.[5] The prosecuting attorney must leave the room before the jurors begin the expression of their views or before a poll is taken. The courts have decreed, however, that the mere presence of the prosecuting attorney in the room during the deliberation is "not sufficient to sustain a plea in abatement."[6] Since 1902 the official court stenographer of the county may take shorthand notes of the testimony and furnish a transcript to the prosecuting attorney at his request. This reporter, like the prosecuting attorney and his assistants, is required to retire from the jury room before the grand jury begins its deliberations.[7]

At least twelve of the fifteen jurors must concur in finding an indictment.[8] Indictments found by the grand jury are presented by the foreman to the court and are filed with the clerk of courts.[9]

---

1. *Ohio Const. 1851,* Art. I, sec. 10.
2. G. C. sec. 13436-2.
3. G. C. sec. 13436-5.
4. G. C. sec. 13436-16.
5. See p. 147.
6. See *State of Ohio* v. *William Stichteneth,* 8 N. P., n. s., 297-339.
7. G. C. sec. 13436-8.
8. G. C. sec. 13436-17.
9. G. C. sec. 13436-21.

No grand juror or officer of the court is permitted to disclose that a person has been indicted before such indictment is filed and case docketed.[10] Any incarcerated person charged with an indictable offense who has not been indicted during the term of the court at which he is held to answer is discharged.[11]

Since 1869 it has been the duty of the grand jury to visit the county jail once at each term of court at which they may be in attendance, examine its state and condition and inquire into the discipline and treatment of prisoners, and return a written report to the court.[12]

The majority of contemporary opinion holds that the grand jury, although still defended as a safeguard against oppressive prosecution, seems to be of little usefulness in the administration of modern criminal justice. It is argued that the grand jury not only delays the prosecution of criminal offenses but makes it impossible to place responsibility for neglect of duty, and is, in many instances a rubber stamp for the opinions of the county prosecuting attorney.

The grand jury keeps no separate records; for clerk of courts jury dockets, see entries 118, 119; jury list, entries 124, 291, 292; jury witnesses, entry 123; grand jury reports to common pleas court, entry 187.

---

10. G. C. sec. 13436-15.
11. G. C. sec. 13436-23.
12. G. C. sec. 13436-20.

PETIT JURY

The petit jury, like the grand jury, had its origin in England during the reign of Henry II.[1] The right of trial by jury, guaranteed by the Federal Constitution, was included in each of the Ohio constitutions. At any trial, in any court, for the violation of a statute of the state of Ohio, or any ordinance of any municipality, except in cases where the penalty involved does not exceed a fine of fifty dollars, the accused is entitled to a trial by jury.[2]

---

1. Adams, *op. cit.,* 116.
2. G. C. sec. 13443.

Except in the method of selecting prospective jurors, the petit jury has remained unchanged for over 134 years. At each session of the court the jury commissioners[3] select not less than fifty nor more than seventy-five names for jury service. A venire is issued to the county sheriff for persons whose names are so drawn to appear on the day fixed for the trial.[4] From the persons so summoned a jury of twelve is empaneled. The county prosecuting attorney and the defense council may, in capital cases, peremptorily challenge six of the jurors. In other cases, four peremptory challenges are allowed.[5] Other challenges, alternately made, may be made for reasons prescribed by statute.[6]

When the case is submitted, the jury may decide the question before it in court, or retire to deliberate. Upon retiring, the jury members must be kept together at a convenient place by an officer of the court until they agree upon the verdict or are discharged by the court. The court may permit them to separate at night.[7] If the jurors disagree as to testimony, or desire to be further instructed on the law in the case, they may request the officer in charge to conduct them to the court for additional information.[8] In civil actions a jury renders a written verdict upon the concurrence of three-fourths or more of its members. This verdict is signed by each juror concurring therein.[9]

Under the criminal code adopted in 1929 the accused may waive his rights to a jury trial in favor of a trial by a judge. This procedure, although criticized by some, is considered by others to be a logical step in the administration of criminal justice in a modern state.

The petit jury keeps no separate records; for the clerk of courts' jury dockets, see entries 118, 120, 121; for jury list, see entries 124, 291, 292.

---

3. See p. 141.
4. G. C. sec. 13443-1.
5. G. C. secs. 13443-4, 13443-6.
6. G. C. sec. 13443-8.
7. G. C. sec. 11420-3.
8. G. C. sec. 11420-6.
9. G. C. sec. 11420-9.

The office of county prosecuting attorney, unlike those of the sheriff and coroner, is one of the relatively newer agencies in the administration of criminal justice. Established in America by the English during the colonial period, it offers a striking difference in the development of American criminal procedure as contrasted with English procedure for criminal prosecutions were usually instituted by private persons. As developed in recent years, the office of prosecuting attorney has become one of the state's most important agencies in its defense against modern crime.

The acts of the Northwest Territory placed the responsibility for criminal prosecutions upon the attorney general, who, in turn, appointed and commissioned persons to prosecute cases in their respective counties.[1]

While the act of the Northwest Territory outlined the local institutions for the newer states, the constitution of Ohio contained no provision for a prosecutor, leaving the creation of the office to the discretion of the legislature. In 1803, during the first session of the legislature, an act was passed authorizing the supreme court to appoint in each county an attorney to prosecute cases on behalf of the state.[2] Two years later, the appointing power was vested in the court of common pleas.[3] The office remained an appointive one until 1933 when the electorate of the county was directed to choose a prosecuting attorney in each county for a two-year term.[4] The act of 1852 left the office elective and the term unchanged, but in 1881 the term of office was set at three years, and in 1906 it was reduced to two years, and in 1936 increased to four years.[5]

Under the present system the prosecuting attorney is elected for a four-year term.[6] He is required to give bond of not less than one thousand dollars conditioned for the faithful performance of the duties of his office. If the office becomes vacant the court of common pleas is authorized to appoint a successor.[7]

---

1. Chase, *op. cit.,* I, 287, 348.
2. *Laws of Ohio,* I, 50.
3. *Ibid.,* III, 47.
4. *Ibid.,* XXXI, 13-14; Chase, *op. cit.,* III, 1935.
5. *Laws of Ohio,* LXXVIII, 260; XCVIII, 271-272; CXVI, pt. ii, 184.
6. G. C. sec. 2909.
7. G. C. secs. 2911, 2912.

The county prosecuting attorney is authorized to appoint clerks, assistants, and stenographers, and to fix their salaries subject to the approval of the county commissioners. Since 1911 he has been authorized to appoint a secret service agent or officer whose duty it is to aid him in the collection of evidence to be used in the trial of criminal cases and in matters of a criminal nature. The compensation of such an officer is determined by the court of common pleas.[8]

Most important among the duties of the prosecuting attorney are those connected with criminal prosecutions. Differing little from those of the early days of the office, these duties include the prosecution on behalf of the state of all complaints, suits, and controversies in which the state is a party, and such other suits, matters, and controversies as he is directed by law to prosecute within or without his county, in the probate court, court of common pleas, and court of appeals. In conjunction with the attorney general, he prosecutes cases in the supreme court which originated in his county.[9]

In felony cases, when a complaint is made to the prosecuting attorney, he is required to examine the evidence and determine if it is sufficient for prosecution. If he decides in the affirmative, he prepares the evidence for presentation to the grand jury.[10] If this body returns an indictment the prosecutor prepares to present the evidence in trial court. The court of common pleas may appoint an attorney to assist the prosecuting attorney in criminal cases.[11] In the case of conviction, the prosecuting attorney causes execution to be issued for the fines or costs and pays into the county treasury all moneys so received.[12] Without reference to the grand jury, the county prosecuting attorney may initiate prosecutions in misdemeanor cases in the court of common pleas by information.[13] After prosecution is inaugurated, he may eliminate the case without trial by means of the *nolle prosequi*. Although he is prohibited from enlisting the *nolle prosequi* without leave of the court on good cause shown, his requests are usually granted.[14]

---

8. G. C. secs. 2914, 2945-1.
9. G. C. secs. 2946.
10. See p. 144.
11. G. C. secs. 2948.
12. G. C. secs. 2916.
13. G. C. sec. 13437-34.
14. G. C. sec. 13437-32.

After prosecution has begun, it remains with the prosecuting attorney whether the case shall be pressed and steps taken that will lead to conviction.

Besides prosecution in criminal cases, the prosecuting attorney also acts in civil matters. He may bring suit in the name of the state when he is convinced that public money is being misapplied or is being illegally withheld or withdrawn from the county treasury. Moreover, he may bring suit against persons violating the obligations of contracts of which the county is a party, or when county property is being used or occupied illegally.[15]

In addition to these, other duties have been prescribed by statute. On the request of the judge having jurisdiction over juvenile cases, he must prosecute individuals for committing crimes against children.[16] Furthermore, when directed by the court of common pleas, he must prosecute persons for keeping a house of prostitution.[17] At the instance of the secretary of state, he must prosecute any officer who refused to furnished gratuitously statistical information for the use of that office.[18]

The prosecuting attorney has also served in an advisory capacity since 1906.[19] He acts as an advisor to all county boards and officials and to township officers who may require his opinion in writing on matters connected with their official duties.[20] In addition to this, he prepares official bonds for all county officers.[21]

The prosecuting attorney is required to make an annual report to the county commissioners stating the number of criminal prosecutions completed, the name or names of the party or parties to each, and the amount collected in fines and costs, and the amount forfeited.[22] Moreover, on the demand of the attorney general he must make an annual report on forms provided by the state on all criminal actions prosecuted by indictments in his county.[23]

All records are located in office of Robert C. Carpenter, prosecuting attorney, 90 ½ South Washington Street, Tiffin, Ohio.

---

15. G. C. sec. 2921.
16. G. C. sec. 1639-42.
17. G. C. secs. 6212-5, 6212-7.
18. G. C. sec. 174.
19. *Laws of Ohio,* XCVIII, 160-161.
20. *Ibid.,* LXXVIII, 120; G. C. sec. 2926.
21. G. C. sec. 2920.
22. *Laws of Ohio,* LXXVIII, 120; G. C. sec. 2926.
23. G. C. sec. 2825; *Laws of Ohio,* XC, 225.

293. CASES

1917—. 3 file drawers.

Original records pertaining to prosecution of criminal cases and other matters including pending and closed cases consisting of affidavits, complaints, and sworn statements, showing title of each case, charge, date of crime, name of defendant, names of witnesses, grand jury testimony, and case number. Arranged alphabetically by names of defendants. No index. Handwritten and typed on printed forms. 13.5 x 15.25 x 25.

294. CORRESPONDENCE

1937—. 1 file drawer.

Correspondence relative to criminal prosecutions and with persons on probation showing date of correspondence, name of principal, and text of correspondence. Arranged alphabetically by names of principals. No index. Typed. 13.5 x 15.5 x 25.

295. MISCELLANEOUS PAPERS

1916—. 6 file boxes.

Record of cases tried and disposed of by prosecuting attorney including indictments, showing name of defendant, date of indictment, and offense; also coroner's papers, showing name of decedent, date of death, and cause; also grand jury papers showing name of defendant, verdict, and date of verdict. Arranged alphabetically by subject and chronologically thereunder by dates of filing. Handwritten on printed forms. 11 x 5 x 15.5.

CORONER

The office of coroner, next to that of sheriff the oldest county office in America, had its inception in England during the latter part of the twelfth century when the coroner kept a record of the activities in the county, especially in regard to the administration of criminal justice. At the end of the thirteenth century it was his duty to make inquests whenever there was a sudden death in the shire, and the results were recorded in the coroner's rolls and presented to the justices when they made their eyre.[1]

This office, transplanted to America during the colonial period, was continued by the states, and was adopted by the territory of which the state of Ohio was then a part. An ordinance of the Northwest Territory published in 1788 authorized the governor to appoint a coroner in each county within the territory. This act, together with a supplementary act of 1785 adopted from the Massachusetts Code, fixed the power and duties of the coroner. He was empowered to do any act which, by previous legislation had been delegated to the sheriff, and was given the ancient duty of English coroners in holding preliminary investigations over the bodies of all persons found within his county, who was believed to have died by violence or casualty.[2]

The Ohio Constitution of 1802 continued the historic office, making it elective for a two-year term.[3] A statute of 1805 defined the duties and authority of the coroner which, in the main were comparable with those prescribed in the territorial code, except that he was denied the privilege of concurrent jurisdiction with the sheriff.[4] The coroner was required to post bond with the county commissioners, which was to be recorded in the record of their proceedings. The act further provided that the coroner should receive his remuneration from fees, and that if the office of sheriff were to become vacant the corner was to execute temporarily the duties of the sheriff.[5] The latter provision remain active until its abrogation in 1887.[6]

---

1. Pollock and Maitland, *op. cit.,* I, 519; II, 641.
2. Pease, *op. cit.,* 24-25, 272-275.
3. *Ohio Const. 1802,* Art. VI, sec. 1.
4. *Laws of Ohio,* III, 156-161.
5. *Ibid.,* III, 158-161.
6. *Ibid.,* LXXXIV, 208-210.

The constitution of 1851 and the constitutional amendments of 1912 left the duties of the coroner unchanged and it was not until recent years when he became an aid in the scientific detection of crime that laws have been passed which materially affect his office. By the legislative act of 1921 the coroner was made official custodian of the morgue in counties where a morgue is maintained. The same act provided that only licensed physicians were eligible to the office in counties having a population of 100,000 or more,[7] and in 1937 such restrictions was extended to all counties.

The coroner is required to draw up and subscribe his findings of facts, in inquests and autopsies and to report them to the clerk of courts. This record contains a detailed description of the body over which the inquest has been held and a statement of the coroner's findings as to the cause of death.[9] He is required also to return to the probate court an inventory of articles of the property found on or about the body and to preserve such property until the proper distribution may be made.[10] All records are open to the public inspection.[11]

In 1936 the tenure of office of the coroner was extended from two to four years.[12]

Records are located in the office of Dr. William H. Benner, Coroner, Tiffin, Ohio.

---

7. *Ibid.,* CIX, 543-544.
8. *Ibid.,* CXVII, 43.
9. G. C. secs, 2856, 2857.
10. G. C. sec, 2859.
11. G. C. sec. 2856-2.
12. G. C. sec. 2823.

296. ANNUAL REPORT

1931—. 1 file box.

Copies of annual reports from coroner to county commissioners pertaining to inquest and investigations held and filed. Showing name of deceased, date of inquest and filing report, cause and place each death, and fees collected. Arranged chronologically by dates of reports. No index. Typed. 8 x 3 x 14.

For other records, see entries 147, 148, 276, 297.

297. CORONER'S INQUESTS AND FINDINGS

1927—. 2 file boxes.

Copies of coroner's inquest, findings, and investigations with cost bills attached, showing date of inquest, name of deceased, place of death, cause of death, date of post-mortem, names of witnesses, cost bill, and inventory of articles found on body. Arranged chronologically by dates of inquest. No index. Handwritten and typed on printed forms. 8 x 3 x 14.

For other records, see entries 147, 148, 276, 296.

The office of sheriff antedates the Norman Conquest. This official was enjoying great power and importance centuries ago, and was probably brought into the English system after a model which existed in Roman law. The name comes from the Saxon "shire-reeve" softened to "shireve," "shyrife," and finally to "sheriff." In ancient times he received his commission directly from the king and specifically represented the sovereign. Originally, the sheriff in England was a judicial as well as a ministerial officer. He once held court in the shire and exercise no inconsiderable jurisdiction. By the time of Lord Coke (1560-1634), the functions of the English sheriff had become standardized under three general heads: (1) to serve process by which a suit was begun; (2) to execute the decrees of the court; (3) to act as a conservator of peace within the county.[1]

The office appeared in America in modified form among the earliest colonial institutions, being created in Virginia in 1634, and in Massachusetts in 1654. This ancient office was continued by the states created after independence.[2] The office assumed a new significance in the latter part of the eighteenth century when a flood of colonists swept across the ineffective Allegheny barrier to establish homes in the Northwest Territory organized by congress in 1787. In the remote West the pioneers, far removed from the orderly legal processes and courts of the East, were subjected to the machinations of the lawless elements prevalent in every new community.

In 1792 the governor and judges of the Territory adopted an act providing for the appointment by the governor of a sheriff in each county and defining his duties.[3] This pioneer law clearly established three of the four major duties of the sheriff as they remain today, namely: Attendance upon the court; execution of writs, warrants, and the like; and policing and the arrest of criminals.

When Ohio entered the union as a state in 1803, the office of sheriff was continued by constitutional provision, and was made elected for a two-year term.[4]

Since that time relatively few changes have been made in the structural organization of the office.

---

1. Adams, *op.cit.,* 17-19; William A. Morris, "The Office of Sheriff in the Anglo-Saxon Period," *English Historical Review,* XXXI, (1916), 20-40; Raymond Moley, "The Sheriff and the Coroner" in *The Missouri Crime Survey,* pt. ii, 59-60.
2. For a comparative study of the sheriff in England in the Chesapeake colonies, see Cyrus Harreld Karraker, *The Seventeenth-Century Sheriff . . . 1607-1689.*
3. Pease, *op. cit.,* 8.
4. *Ohio Const. 1802,* Art. VI, sec. 1.

When a new county was erected the associate judges appointed a day on which the qualified voters met at the temporary seat of justice and elected a sheriff who served until the next general election.[5] Although the constitution of 1851 did not specifically provide for this office, it did declare that no person should be eligible to the office for more than four in any period of six years.[6] No county officer was to have a longer term than three years,[7] but the matter of removal from office was left to legislative action.[8] The limitation upon the consecutive terms which a sheriff might serve remained in force until 1933, when it was repealed by an amendment authorizing any county to adopt a charter form of government. The term of office remained at two years until 1936 when it was extended to four years.[9] The sheriff received his remuneration from fees until 1875. From 1875 to 1906 he received a definite salary based upon the population of the county at the federal census proceeding his election, plus a percentage of the fees collected.[10] Since 1906 the compensation has been derived entirely from a salary determined on a population basis.[11] In 1831, because of the increasing complexity of his duties, the sheriff was authorized to appoint, with the consent of the court of common pleas, one or more deputies, who like their superior, were required to give bond for the faithful performance of the duties of their office, and the sheriff was made liable for their neglect of duty or misconduct in office.[12]

The present organization of the office may be briefly summarized: The sheriff is elected for a four-year term,[13] can hold no other elected office at the same time, and may not practice law while in office.[14]

---

5. A. E. Gwynne, *Practical Treaties on the Law of Sheriff and Coroner with Forms and References to the Statutes of Ohio, Indiana, and Kentucky*, 3.
6. *Ohio Const, 1851,* Art. X, sec. 3.
7. *Ibid.,* Art. X, sec. 2.
8. *Ibid.,* Art. X, sec. 6.
9. *Laws of Ohio,* CXVI, pt. ii, 184.
10. *Ibid.,* III, 49; XXXIII, 18; LII, 86; LXXII, 126.
11. *Ibid.,* XCVIII, 95. The salary in Seneca County in 1939 was $2,545. Ohio Auditor of State, *Annual Report, 1939,* p. 379.
12. *Laws of Ohio,* XXIX, 410.
13. G. C. sec. 2823.
14. G. C. secs. 11, 1706, 2565, 2783, 2910.

He is required to give bond, the cost of which is paid by the county commissioners[15] who are also required to provide an office for the sheriff at the county seat, equipment, supplies, and other essentials of the office.[16] The commissioners also appropriate funds for the expenses incurred by the sheriff in carrying out the various duties of his office.[17] The sheriff may appoint a deputy or deputies, but all appointees must be endorsed by the local judge of the common pleas court, be electors of the county, and are not permitted to be a justice of peace or mayor.[18] Deputies are also forbidden to practice law while in office.[19] The sheriff fixes the salaries of the deputies, subject to the budget limitations of the county commissioners,[20] and shares with his deputies certain civil and criminal liabilities.[21] The salary of the sheriff based on the graded scale according to the population with a $6,000 yearly maximum is $2,545.[22] The office may be vacated by failure to give proper bond, non-acceptance, or death.[23] Vacancies are filled by the county commissioners.[24]

The sheriff may be removed for various financial defalcations,[25] for willfully refusing or neglecting his duty in criminal cases,[26] for malfeasance in office,[27] for permitting the lynching of a person in his custody.[28] In the latter case the governor conducts the hearing and may remove the sheriff. If for some reason the sheriff is unable to serve a court order the judge of common pleas court is authorized to make a temporary appointment for the position.[29]

---

15. G. C. sec. 2824.
16. G. C. sec. 2832.
17. G. C. sec. 2997.
18. G. C. secs. 1706, 2830.
19. G. C. sec. 1706.
20. G. C. sec. 2981.
21. Willis A. Estrich, ed., *Ohio Jurisprudence*, XXXVI, 660-672, 699-701.
22. G. C. secs. 2994, 2995, 2997; Estrich, *op. cit.*, XXXVI, 704-705; Ohio Auditor of State *Annual Report, 1939*, p. 379.
23. G. C. secs. 2827, 12196.
24. G. C. sec. 3036, 3049.
25. G. C. secs. 3036, 3049.
26. G. C. secs. 12850, 12851.
27. *Ohio Const. 1851,* (Amendment, 1912), Art. II, sec. 38.
28. *Laws of Ohio,* CI, 109.
29. G. C. sec. 2828.

The retiring sheriff is required to deliver to his successor all moneys, papers, books, and the like, as well as the custody of all the prisoners.[30]

Aside from his power to appoint deputies, the sheriff has other special powers which are largely the products of historical development. From earliest years the sheriff has been empowered to call to his aid such persons as he deemed necessary to perform his lawful duty in apprehension of criminals.[31] Thus the *posse comitatus* was at his disposal as it is today.[32]

The specific duties of the sheriff were and are prescribed by statute and may be classified under four main divisions: (1) attendance upon the courts; (2) executions of summonses, warrants, processes, and other writs; (3) control and responsibility in the care of the jail and courthouse; (4) policing the county and the arrest of criminals.

The territorial law of 1792 required the sheriff to attend upon the court of common pleas and the court of appeals during their sessions,[33] and this requirement has been carried over into the laws of Ohio,[34] the present duties of the sheriff in this respect are survivals from the provisions of this act. He is required to attend the county court of common pleas,[35] the appellate court,[36] and the probate court if required by the judge of that division.[37] The sheriff may adjourn the court of common pleas from day to day upon failure of the judge to appear at regularly scheduled sessions.[38]

The duty of the sheriff to execute all warrants, writs, and processes directed to him by the proper and lawful authority has also been operative since the territorial period.[39] At present he executes every summons, orders, or other process, and makes returns thereof as required by law.[40]

---

30. G. C. secs. 2842, 2843.
31. *Laws of Ohio,* III, 156-158; XXIX, 112-113.
32. G. C. sec. 2833.
33. Pease, *op. cit.,* 8.
34. *Laws of Ohio,* III, 156-158; XXIX, 112; LXXXII, 26.
35. G. C. sec. 2833.
36. G. C. secs. 1530, 2833.
37. G. C. sec. 2833.
38. G. C. sec. 2855.
39. Pease, *op. cit.,* 8; *Laws of Ohio,* III, 156-158; XXIX, 112; LXXXII, 26.
40. G. C. sec. 2834.

He executes processes from the probate, juvenile, common pleas, and appellate courts. Although the jury commission has supplanted the clerk of courts in the matter of selecting names of prospective jurors from the jury wheel, the sheriff's duties in this remained much as they were in the earlier years of his office. He also executes warrants issued by the governor of the state,[41] and serves writs and subpoenas issued by various state officers and boards.[42] In other words, the sheriff serves all the papers which concern the county as a unit of government and some for the state as well.

As early as 1805 the sheriff was made official custodian of the county jail.[43] Although the early statutes directed the county commissioners to provide dungeons for the incarceration of prisoners, the act of 1847 directed the sheriff to exercise reasonable care for the preservation of the life, health, and welfare of those committed to his care. He was and is authorized to transport prisoners to other counties for safekeeping.[44] Under the direction and control of the county commissioners the sheriff is also given charge of the courthouse.[45]

The sheriff has had extensive and important police powers since 1792 when the territorial act authorized him to keep and preserve the peace, and suppress affrays, routs, riots, unlawful assemblies, and insurrections; to apprehend, and confined in jail all felons and traitors; and to return persons who, having committed a crime in his county, had taken refuge in another.[46] During the legislative session of 1803 the general assembly passed an act defining the duties of the sheriff which were in all respects similar to the provisions inherited from the territorial code.[47] In the same year the sheriff was designated as the county's executioner, and was bound to carry out sentences of death by hanging when imposed by the courts upon those convicted of murder.[48] Public executions, the general rule during the earlier years, were abolished in 1844.[49]

---

41. G. C. sec. 118.
42. G. C. secs. 285, 346, 2709, *et al.*
43. *Laws of Ohio,* III, 157.
44. *Ibid.,* III, 157; XXIX, 112-113; XCIII, 131. For general provisions as to jail duties see G. C. secs. 3157-3176, *passim.*
45. G. C. sec. 2833.
46. Pease, *op. cit.,* 8.
47. *Laws of Ohio,* III, 156-158.
48. Chase, *op. cit.,* I, 442.
49. *Laws of Ohio,* XLII, 71.

In 1886 the sheriff's duties in disrespect were delegated to the warden of the Ohio penitentiary.[50]

An act of 1831, repealing the act of 1805 redefined the duties of the sheriff as a conservator of the peace in his county,[51] and his present duties in this respect are survivals from the provisions of this act.[52] Although the sheriff is still regarded as the chief peace officer in the county, many of his earlier duties in this respect have been abolished by the development of other agencies of law enforcement, notably the state highway patrol. On the other hand, the powers of the sheriff to suppress affrays, riots, and unlawful assemblies became especially important in times of strikes or threatened riots. On a properly issued warrant he may arrest any person charge with the probability of doing injury to another person or the property of another.[53] Moreover, since 1921 the sheriff has forwarded to the bureau of criminal identification fingerprints of all persons arrested for a felony,[54] and since 1913 has been authorized to arrest any person violating is parole.[55]

The present police powers of the sheriff are quite comprehensive. His jurisdiction is coextensive with the county, including all municipalities and townships, and he is a chief law-enforcement officer of the county. In municipalities the sheriff and mayor stand on an equality as law-enforcement officers so far as state laws are concerned, and neither is permitted to cast the burden of action upon the other.[56]

The sheriff has possessed and still processes many powers and duties which are miscellaneous in nature. As in England the sheriff, during the earlier years of his office, was required to notify the electors of his county of the time and place of holding elections. He was enjoined to furnish ballot boxes at the expense of the county, and hold special elections when so directed by the governor, and deliver the poll books to the Secretary of State.[57] Since 1891 these duties have been taken over by the board of elections.[58]

---

50. *Ibid.,* LXXXIII, 145.
51. *Ibid.,* XXIX, 112-113.
52. *Ibid.,* LXXXII, 26.
53. G. C. sec. 13428-1.
54. *Laws of Ohio,* CIX, 584; VX, 5.
55 *Ibid.,* CIII, 404.
56. Estrich, *op. cit.,* XXXVI, 645. For the most important police powers see G. C. secs. 2833, 3345, 4112, 12811.
57. *Laws of Ohio,* II, 88-90; III, 331-332.
58. See pp. 227, 228.

The sheriff also has many heterogeneous powers and duties regarding elections,[59] executive orders of the secretary of agriculture,[60] fish and game laws,[61] probation officers,[62] military census,[63] traffic rules and regulations, funds and deposits in court,[65] shanty boats, [66] and executive orders of the governor.[67]

The multiplicate duties of the sheriff have made it necessary to require many records of the business of the office to be kept. The sheriff has been required to keep a foreign execution docket since 1838,[68] a cash book since 1842,[69] and a jail register since 1843.[70] These records for Seneca County are extant for 1838, 1868, and 1843, to date respectively.[71] Indexes, direct and reverse, to the foreign execution docket were prescribed by the legislature in 1925.[72] Since 1843 he has been required to transmit annually the jail register, and certified copies, to the clerk of courts, the county auditor, and the secretary of state.[73] Since 1850 he has been required, on the first Monday of September in each year, to submit to the county commissioners a certified statement of all fines and costs collected during the year, and the amount of fees collected and paid to the clerk of courts of common pleas.[74]

---

59. G. C. secs. 4785-124, 4829.
60. G. C. sec. 1110.
61. G. C. secs. 1434, 1441, 1444, 1451.
62. G. C. sec. 1639-19.
63. G. C. sec. 5188-5.
64. G. C. sec. 7251-1.
65. G. C. sec. 11900.
66. G. C. sec. 13403-1.
67. G. C. sec. 118.
68. *Laws of Ohio,* XXXVI, 18; LVII, 6; LXXXIV, 208.
69. *Ibid.,* XL, 25; LXV, 115; LXXXIV, 208; LXXXVI, 239.
70. *Ibid.,* XLI, 74.
71. See entries 298, 308, 304.
72. *Laws of Ohio,* CXI, 31.
73. Ibid., XLI, 74.
74. G. C. sec. 2844; *Laws of Ohio,* XLVIII, 66.

Thus, the modern sheriff keeps the following records: (1) a cashbook, which is a record of all moneys received from all sources; (2) a foreign execution and foreign summons docket, which is a record of executions and summonses from counties other than his own; (3) an accrued fee record, which is his statement to the county prosecuting attorney of fees, penalties and allowances due and unpaid for more than one year prior to January first; (4) a jail register; (5) a record which relates in detail to all money paid by him into the county treasury, which cross references to his own casebooks and dockets; (6) a record which is a statement to the county auditor of all fees and money received by the sheriff or due him, and (7) an annual financial report to the commissioners.[75]

---

75. G. C. secs. 2837, 2839, 2979, 3045, 3046, 3158, 2844.

Court Orders and Sales

298. FOREIGN EXECUTION DOCKET

1838—. 9 volumes. (3 unlabeled; 3-8).

Docket of execution issued to satisfy judgments rendered by other than Seneca County courts on lands or other property in Seneca County, showing date issued, from what county, date received, names of judgment creditor and debtor, title of case, case number, volume and page numbers of appearance docket (county of issue), date of judgment, nature of judgment, amount of judgment, rate of interest, date from which interest is to be computed, dates and copies of sheriff's returns, description and location of property levied on, date judgment satisfied, how satisfied, if sale on execution a clipped copy of legal notice of sale pasted in, showing date of sale, case number, names of litigants, description of property, terms of sale, dates of publication, name of newspaper; record of sale, showing date of sale, to whom sold, amount of sale, and itemized cost bill. Arranged chronologically by dates received. Indexed alphabetically by names of judgment creditors and showing names of debtors. 1838-1866, handwritten; 1866—, handwritten on printed forms. Average 300 pages. 16 x 11 x 1.5. Sheriff's office.

299. FOREIGN WRITS

1875—. 3 volumes. (two unlabeled; 2).

Register of writs issued by other than Seneca County courts on residents of Seneca County, showing date received, names of litigants, case number, kind of writ, court of issue, county, date served, date of sheriff's return, and amount deposited for sheriff's fee. Arranged by counties and chronologically thereunder by dates received. Indexed alphabetically by names of counties. Handwritten on forms. Average 360 pages. 16 x 12 x 2. Sheriff's office.

300. PARTITION RECORD

1875—. 7 volumes. (A-G).

Record of sales and distribution of proceeds and partition proceedings, showing case number, names of plaintiff and defendant, description of real estate sold, date order of sale received, date of sale, to whom sold, terms of sale, amount of sale, amount of first payment, amount of cost, taxes and other debits, date sale confirmed, date of distribution of proceeds, name of distributees, and amount to each. Arranged chronologically by dates orders of sales received. Indexed alphabetically by names of plaintiffs showing names of defendants. Handwritten on forms. Average 300 pages. 18 x 12 x 1.5. Sheriff's office.

301. LAND APPRAISALS AND SALES

1837-1841, 1853-1855, 1882-1887, 1899-1901, 1914—. 5 file boxes.

Copies of appraisement schedules returned by appraisers, clipped copies of legal notices of sales, record of sale of lands and partition and foreclosure proceedings, showing name of appraisers, date of appraisal, brief description of lands, itemized statement of appraisal, and date filed; notices, showing case number, names of litigants, date and place of sale, description and location of lands, amount of appraisal, terms of sale, dates of publication, and name of newspaper; sales record, showing date of sale, to whom sold, amount of sale, and date sale confirmed. All papers of each case banded together. Arranged chronologically by dates of filing appraisal schedules. No index. Handwritten on printed forms. 10.5 x 4.5 x 14. Sheriff's office.

302. CONFIRMATION OF SALE AND ORDER TO DISTRIBUTE

1916—. 3 file boxes.

Original orders issued by common pleas court confirming sale of lands and distributing proceeds of sale and partition and foreclosure proceedings, showing date of order, case number, names of litigants, title of case, volume and page numbers [Common Pleas], Journal, entry 174; amount of sale, amount to county treasurer for taxes, amount to clerk of courts for all cost, amount to mortgage, lien, or other claim, names of payees, amount to other distributees, name of distributees, and copy of journal entry ordering county recorder to release mortgage. Arranged chronologically by dates of orders. No index. Typed on printed forms. 10.5 x 4.5 x 14. Sheriff's office.

303. ORDERS OF SALE DOCKET

1879-1884. 1 volume.

Docket of sales of lands and foreclosure proceedings, showing case number, names of plaintiff and defendant, title of case, date order to sell received, volume and page numbers of Appearance Docket, entry 162; names of appraisers, date of appraisement, and amount of appraisement; clipped copies of legal notices of sale showing, case number, names of litigants, title of case, date and place of sale, to whom sold, amount of sale, amount of first payment, amount deducted for taxes due, amount for court cost,, amount due on mortgage, and date of settlement. Arranged chronologically by dates orders of sale received. Indexed alphabetically by names of plaintiffs showing names of defendants. Handwritten. 360 pages. 16 x 11 x 2. Sheriff's office.

Record of Prisoners and Fugitives

304. JAIL REGISTER

1843—. 7 volumes. (1, 2, 2-6).

Register of commitment to county jail, showing consecutive number, name of prisoner, age, sex, color, birth date, birthplace, nativity, physical description, offense, date committed, by what authority committed, number of days in jail, date released, and by what authority released. 1843-1922, arranged chronologically by dates committed; 1923—, arranged alphabetically by names of prisoners. No index. Handwritten on forms. Average 380 pages. 18 x 13.5 x 2. County jail office.

305. MITTIMUS

1932—. 1 letter file.

Original warrants issued by magistrates or common pleas judge ordering commitment of persons convicted of misdemeanors to county jail, showing date issued, name of person committed, offense, from what court, sentence, and name and title of judicial official. Arranged alphabetically by names of persons committed. No index. Handwritten and typed on printed forms. 12 x 11.5 x 2.5. County jail office.

306. [CASE RECORDS]

1925—. 1 file drawer.

Case record and identification data of each person convicted of a felony and committed to a state penal institution, showing name, aliases, offense, date and place offense committed, date sentenced, sentence, date conveyed to an institution, and name of institution; identification data, showing name, age, sex, color, nationality, previous police records, physical description, scars or marks, fingerprints and classification, photographs front and profile views. Arranged alphabetically by names of prisoners. No index. Typed and typed on printed forms. 10 x 11.5 x 15. County jail office.

307. [FUGITIVE RECORDS]

1934—. 1 file drawer.

Copies of notices from law enforcement agencies of wanted suspects or fugitives; showing for what wanted, name, aliases, last known address, age, physical description, photographs, fingerprint classification (if on file), reason wanted, and name and address of agency to be notified if apprehended. Arranged alphabetically by names of futurities. No index. Printed. 9 x 12 x 15. Sheriff's office.

Financial Records

308. SHERIFF'S CASH BOOK

1868—. 6 volumes. (1-3; 3-5).

Record of cash received and disbursements; receipts, showing year, date received, in what matter, name of payer, amount, amount credited sheriff's fees, court costs, taxes, and judgments; disbursements, showing date disbursed, name of payee, amount, and for what. Arranged chronologically by dates received and disbursed. Indexed alphabetically by names of payers. Handwritten on forms. Average 430 pages. 18 x 12 x 2.25. Sheriff's office.

309. SHERIFF'S RECORD OF ACCRUED FEES

1907—. 6 volumes. (1-6).

Record of fees accrued, showing date of accrual, case number, in what matter, to whom charged, total amount, due from civil case, criminal case, due from county, due from juvenile and probate court, and date paid. Arranged chronologically by dates of accrual. No index. Handwritten on forms. Average 275 pages. 18 x 12 x 1.5. Sheriff's office.

310. FEE BOOK

1887-1893, 1904-1907. 4 volumes.

Record of fees taxed for official services, showing date of entry, case number, names of litigants, title of case, in what court, amount, for what service, and date paid. Arranged chronologically by dates of entries. No index. Handwritten on forms. Average 280 pages. 16 x 11 x 1.5. Sheriff's office.

311. SHERIFF'S EXPENSE ACCOUNT

1922-1924. 1 volume.

Record of expenses incidental to routine duties of office, showing date of entry, amount expended, for what, and what matter; also includes record of impounded dogs redeemed, 1923, showing name of person redeeming dog, date of entry, description of dog, and amount of costs and fees collected. Arranged chronologically by dates of entries. No index. Handwritten on forms. 200 pages. 14 x 10 x 1. Sheriff's office.

Miscellaneous

312. COMPLAINTS AND REPORTS

1935—. 1 file box.

Register of complaints relative to law violations filed with sheriff, showing date filed, name of informer, nature of complaint, notation of officer investigating as to findings, action taken; also register of motor vehicle accidents, showing date and hour of accident, place of accident, names of drivers of vehicles, license numbers, make of vehicles, names of persons involved in accident, notation as to deaths or injuries, cause of accident, names of witnesses, and name of officer investigating. Arranged alphabetically by names of informers or vehicle drivers. No index. Typed on printed forms. 7 x 9 x 12. Sheriff's office.

313. BRANDS AND TATTOO MARKS

1935—. 1 file box.

Register of livestock and poultry identification marks, showing name and address of owner, registration number, facsimile of brand of tattoo mark, and date filed. Arranged alphabetically by names of owners. No index. Handwritten on printed forms. 4.5 x 6 x 5. Sheriff's office.

314. POUND KEEPER'S RECORD

1918-1923. 1 volume.

Record of unlicensed dogs impounded, showing date seized, description of dog, name of owner (if known), date dog will be destroyed if not claimed, date of dog disposed of, and how disposed of. Arranged the chronologically by dates seized. No index. Handwritten on forms. 100 pages. 16 x 11 x .5. Sheriff's office.

315. [MISCELLANEOUS]

1885-1887, 1899-1904, 1921—. 1 file box.

Original orders to sheriff, 1885-1887, from county commissioners authorizing judge to release prisoners confined in county jail, showing date of release, name of prisoner, by what authority committed, offense, sentence, days served, by what authority released; original orders of attachment on judgments, 1899-1904, showing date of order, names of judgment creditor and debtor, amount of judgment, description of property attached, date writ served; annual statistics of county jail commitments and discharges, 1921—, showing year, number of prisoners committed, number white, number colored, number all other, number male, number female, number native born, number born in other states, number foreign born, number illiterate, number elementary school education, number high school or higher education, number under 21 years of age, number of each class of misdemeanor, average number of days of sentence, average number days served, number of deaths, cause of death, total number of meals served, cost per meal, and total cost; also includes orders of attachment and garnishee, 1899-1904, showing date of order, from what court, names of debtor and creditor, amount of judgment, date order received, and date served. No obvious arrangement. No index. Handwritten on printed forms. 10.5 x 4.5 x 14. Sheriff's office.

The county dog warden, appointed by and responsible to the county commissioners, had as his duty the enforcement of the provisions of the General Code relative to licensing dogs, the impounding and destruction of unlicensed dogs, and the payment of compensation for damage to livestock inflicted by dogs. This officer, like other county officials, is required to give bond conditioned for the faithful performance of the duties of his office. This bond, in the sum of not less than $500 nor more than $2,000 is filed with the county auditor. His compensation and tenure, like that of his deputies, is determined by the county commissioners.[1]

In Seneca County the duties of dog warden were performed by the sheriff from 1917 to 1927 as provided by statute.[2] In 1927 the commissioners were authorized to appoint a dog warden.[3] Accordingly, the commissioners appointed a special deputy sheriff who served both as dog warden and road patrol.[4] This arrangement was continued until October 1936 when the dog warden was made a separate office.[5]

The warden is required to make a record of all dogs owned, kept, or harbored in the county; to patrol the county; and to seize and impound dogs more than three months of age found not wearing a valid registration tag. The latter provisions do not apply, however, to dogs kept in regularly licensed kennels. Moreover, he is required to make weekly written reports to the county commissioners of all dogs seized, impounded, redeemed, and destroyed. Then, too, he is required to report all claims for damages to livestock inflicted by dogs.

The dog warden and his deputies have, in the performance of their legal duties, the same "police powers" as are conferred by statute upon sheriff's and police. They may summon the assistance of bystanders in performing their duties, serve writs and other legal processes issued by any court in the county with reference to enforcing the provisions of the laws relating to dogs.[6]

The dog warden of Seneca County does not keep any records. For records in other offices, see entries 8, 311, 314.

---

1. G. C. sec. 5652-7.
2. *Laws of Ohio,* CVII, 535.
3. *Ibid.,* CXII, 348.
4. Commissioners' Journal, XXXIII, 237.
5. *Ibid.,* XXXIV, 541.
6. G. C. sec. 5652-7.

The first Ohio Constitution, adopted in 1802, did not provide for the office of county auditor and it was not until 1820 that the general assembly by joint resolution appointed an auditor in each county for a one-year term.[1] In 1821 the office became elective and the term was fixed at one year.[2] In 1831 the term was set at two years, in 1877 at three years, in 1906 reduced to two years, and in 1919 extended to four years.[3]

The county auditor is required to take oath and give bond for faithful performance of the duties of his office; to preserve all copies of entries, surveys, extracts, and other documents transmitted to his office from the state auditor; and to transfer to his successor all books, records, maps, and other papers pertaining to his office.[4] With the approval of the county commissioners he is authorized to appoint deputies, for whose official acts he and his sureties are held liable; the record of these appointments which has been required to be filed with the county treasurer since 1869[5] was not located in the inventory of the Seneca County treasurer's office. If the office of each county auditor falls vacant the county commissioners are authorized to appoint a successor.[6]

The first auditor in each county was required to list all lands in his county subject to taxation. From this list and one submitted to him by the county commissioners and one from the state auditor, the county auditor was directed to make a tax duplicate to be kept in a book for that purpose, and to give a copy of the list to the tax collector.[7] The auditor was also directed to compile from the treasurer's duplicate a list of lands on which taxes were delinquent, and if such lands were sold for taxes to grant a deed to the purchaser.[8]

Subsequent legislation expanded and itemized the duties of the auditor in regard to taxation; with modifications to meet modern requirements these duties have continued much as they were doing the earlier years of his office.

---

1. *Laws of Ohio,* XVIII, 72.
2. *Ibid.,* XIX. 116.
3. *Ibid.,* XXIX, 280; LXXIV, 381; XCVIIII, 271; CVIII, pt. ii, 1294.
4. *Ibid.,* XIX, 116; LXVII, 103; G. C. secs. 2559, 2582.
5. *Laws of Ohio,* LV, 20; LXVI, 35; G. C. sec. 2563.
6. G. C. secs. 2579, 2580, 2990, 2996.
7. *Laws of Ohio,* XVIII, 79.
8. *Ibid.,* XVIII, 82; XIX, 115.

During the 1840s the office of county assessor was abolished and provision was made for township assessors whose duty it was to list all taxable property and make a return to the auditor.[9] Since 1874 the auditor is required by statute to keep a book in which he lists additions to in deductions from the amount of tax assessed.[10] In 1915 he was made chief assessing officer of the county.[11]

The county auditor has been a member and serves as the secretary of the county budget commission since it's beginning in 1911, and his duties include keeping full and accurate records of the proceedings of that body. For the purpose of adjusting the tax rates and fixing the amount to be levied each year the commissioners are governed by the amount of taxable property as shown on the auditor's tax list for the current year. He submits to the commissioners the annual tax budget given him by each taxing authority of each subdivision, together with an estimate of any tax levy prepared by the state auditor, and such other information as the budget commission may request or the state tax commission require.[12]

Tax settlements have been made annually until 1858 when the auditor was required to make semiannual settlement with the treasurer to acertain the amount of taxes with the treasurer is to stand charged.[13] Since 1904 liquor, cigarette, and inheritance taxes have constituted separate funds. All other taxes are credited to the general fund.[14]

Since 1831 the county auditor has kept in an account current with the county treasurer showing the payments of moneys into the treasury, listing the date, by whom paid, and to which fund. On receiving the treasurer's daily statement the auditor enters on his account current the amount as a charge to the treasurer.[15] Another important function of the county auditor is the approval before payment of bills and other claims against the county. Since 1831 he is authorized to issue, on presentation of proper voucher, all warrants on the county treasurer for moneys payable from the county treasury; and to preserve all warrants, showing the number, date of issue, amount for which drawn, in whose favor, and from which fund.[16]

---

9. *Ibid.,* XXXIX, 22-25.
10. *Laws of Ohio,* LXXI, 30.
11. *Ibid.,* CVI, 246.
12. G. C. sec. 5625-19; *Laws of Ohio,* CXII, 402.
13. G. C. sec. 2596; *Laws of Ohio,* LV, 62; LVI, 132; LXXVIII, 226.
14. *Laws of Ohio,* XCVII, 457.
15. *Ibid.,* XXIX, 280-291; LXVII, 103.
16. G. C. sec. 2570; *Laws of Ohio,* XXIX, 280-291; LXVII, 103.

County money due the state is paid on warrant of the state auditor. Since 1904 a bill or voucher for payment from any fund controlled by the county commissioners or board of county infirmary directors is filed with the county auditor and entered in a book for that purpose at least five days before its approval for payment by the commissioners, and when approved the date is entered opposite the claim.[17]

Beside approving bills and claims against the county, the auditor in 1835 was given the duty of certifying all moneys, except collections on the tax duplicate, into the county treasury, specifying by whom paid and the fund to which such payment is credited. Such moneys he charges to the treasurer and keeps a duplicate copy of the statement in his office. Since 1835 all costs collected in penitentiary cases which have been or are to be paid to the state have been certified into the treasury as belonging to the state.[18]

In 1902 the legislature provided for system of uniform accounting and auditing of all public offices, and for the annual examination of their finances, under the direction of a bureau of inspection in the office of the state auditor.[19] Since 1904 the county auditor has been required to report to the commissioners on the state of county finances; on the first business day of each month he prepares in duplicate a statement of the county finances for the proceeding month, compares it with the treasurer's balance, and submits it to the commissioners who post one copy of it in the auditor's office for thirty days for public inspection.[20]

During the development of the office additional duties in great diversity have been delegated to the county auditor. Since 1833 he has been authorized to discharge prisoners jailed for nonpayment of any fine or amercement due the county when in his opinion the amount cannot be collected.[21] In 1838 an act was passed making him county superintendent of schools. He was relieved of this duty in 1848 when a county superintendent of schools was authorized in each county.[22] Since 1846 he has served as a sealer of weights and measures, is responsible for the preservation of the copies of the original standards delivered to his office, and enforces in his county all state laws regulating weights and measures.[23]

---

17. *Laws of Ohio,* XCVII, 25; CVIII, pt. i, 272.
18. *Ibid.,* XXXIII, 44; LXVII, 103.
19. *Ibid.,* XCV, 511-515.
20. *Ibid.,* XCVII, 457.
21. G. C. sec. 2576; *Laws of Ohio,* XXXI, 18; LXVII, 103.
22. See pp. 254, 255.
23. G. C. sec. 2615; *Laws of Ohio,* XLIV, 55; LVIII, 78; CI, 234.

In 1861 he was authorized to report to the state auditor statistics concerning the deaf, dumb, blind, insane, and idiots in his county, with the names and addresses of their parents or guardians.[24] In 1869, he was authorized to report to the same officer statistics concerning livestock in his county as returned to his office by assessors, and an abstract of the funded indebtedness of his county, and of each township, city, village, and school district.[25] Since 1827 he has been authorized to issue licenses to traveling public shows and exhibitions, although municipal authorities may impose an additional license.[26] In 1862 he was authorized to issue peddlers' licenses to persons who filed a statement of stock in trade in conformity with the law requiring the listing of such stocks for taxation, and since 1817 he has issued dog licenses.[27] The auditor has issued licenses to wholesale and retail dealers in cigarettes since 1893,[28] in brewers' wort and malt since 1933,[29] and cosmetic licenses from August 1, 1933 to June 30, 1936.[30]

The auditor of Seneca County served as clerk to the board of county commissioners from 1821 to 1937.[31] His duties included keeping an accurate record of their proceedings and preserving all documents, books, records, maps, and papers which were required to be filed and his office.[32] From 1850 to 1927 he was official custodian of the reports submitted to the commissioners by the prosecuting attorney, the clerk of courts, the sheriff, and the treasurer; These reports were required to be recorded by the auditor in books kept especially for that purpose.[33] The original reports are extant in Seneca County from 1910 to date.[34] Copies of the reports are found from 1871 to date.[35]

The county auditor is a member of the county board of revision established in 1825, secretary of the budget commission, and serves as a trustee and the secretary of the board of trustees of the sinking fund established in 1919.[36]

---

24. *Laws of Ohio,* LVIII, 40.
25. G. C. sec. 2604.
26. Chase, *op. cit.,* III, 1582; *Laws of Ohio,* XXIX, 446; G. C. secs. 6374, 6375.
27. *Laws of Ohio,* LIX, 67; LXXIX, 96; CVII, 534.
28. G. C. sec. 5894-5.
29. G. C. sec. 5545-5.
30. *Laws of Ohio,* CXV, 649; CXV, pt. ii, 83; CXVI, pt. ii, 323.
31. *Ibid.,* XIX, 147; Commissioners' Journal, XXXIX, 469.
32. G. C. sec. 2566.
33. G. C. sec. 2504; R. S. Sec. 886; *Laws of Ohio,* XLVIII, 66.
34. See entry 6.
35. See entry 1.
36. See pp. 215, 217, 218, 221.

Property Transfers
(See also entries 43-84)

316. TRANSFER RECORD
1844-1905. 49 volumes. (dated).
Record of transfers of real property, showing names of grantor and grantee, date of transfer, location of property, lot number, and name of subdivision. Arranged chronologically by dates of transfers. No index. Handwritten. Average 200 pages. 18.5 x 11.5 x 1.5. Auditor's vault.

For subsequent records, see entry 332.

317. LIST OF TRANSFERS
1913, 1924. 2 volumes.
Memorandum of transfers of real property, showing names of present and former owners, date of transfer, lot number, location of property, acreage, consideration, new valuation, and old valuation. Arranged alphabetically by townships, villages, and city wards and alphabetically thereunder by names of owners. No index. Handwritten on printed forms. Average 290 pages. 19 x 13.5 x 2. 1 volume, 1913, state examiner's office. 1 volume, 1924. Auditor's vault.

318. RECORD OF DEEDS
1838—. 1 volume (1). Last entry 1926.
Record of auditor's deeds to property sold for delinquent taxes, showing name of owner, date of sale, name of purchaser, description of land, amount of delinquent taxes, to whom deed made, date of deed, and signature of auditor. Arranged chronologically by dates of deeds. No index. Handwritten. 600 pages. 16.5 x 13 x 3. Auditor's vault.

319. TAX SALE CERTIFICATES
1883-1925. 1 file box.
Copies of certificates of title to land sold for delinquent taxes, showing name of owner, name of allotment, original lot number, sub-lot number, what part of sub-lot owned, name of street, to whom sold, redemption if any, and to whom assigned. Arranged chronologically by dates of certificates. No index. Handwritten. 11 x 5 x 15.5 Auditor's office.

Plats and Maps

(See also entries 73, 75-77, 79-83, 545, 548-551)

320. PLATS

n, d., 1900, 1910, 1931—. 60 volumes, 1 file box. 39 volumes subtitled by names of divisions.

Copies of plats and maps showing name of township, section numbers, names of subdivision, boundary lines, boundary lines and land tracts and lots, names of owners of land tracts and out-lots, number of acres, in-lot of dimensions, lot numbers, roads, streets, alleys, railroads, streams and watercourses, and date prepared. Volumes, 1931, corrected to date. 1 file box, 1910, contains surveyor's tracings of plats of townships, prepared by county engineering department. Scale 1 inch equals 100 feet. Townships arranged numerically by section numbers, towns and villages by original plats and additions. No index. Hand drawn, black on white. Volumes average 38 pages. 17 x 21 x 1; file box, 10.5 x 5 x 14. 21 volumes, n. d., county sealer's office; 39 volumes, 1 file box, 1900, 1910, 1931—, Auditor's vault.

321. SCHOOL DISTRICT PLATS

1856—. 3 file boxes.

Original plats and tracings of school districts, showing lands transferred from one district to another, petitions for transfer to another district, and record of real estate appraisement, showing year, name of township, school district, boundary lines of district with shaded lines indicating boundary of portions transferred, boundary lines of farm tracts and lots, area, names of owners, roads, and streams, and school lands designated; appraisements of transferred lands, showing name of owner, range, township, and section numbers, name of school district, number of acres, and appraised value. Plats and tracings prepared by county engineering department. No obvious arrangement. No index. Plats and tracings hand drawn, black on white; appraisements, handwritten 10.5 x 5 x 14. Auditor's vault.

322. SECTIONAL MAPS

1900. 15 volumes. Subtitled by names of townships.

Copies of original government surveys, showing section and quarter section lines, Indian reservation boundaries, boundary lines of tracts and lots, area, names of owners, roads, railroads, streams, width of railroad right of way, public roads, and drainage ditches. Prepared by county engineering department. 1 inch equals 10 chains. Arranged numerically by section numbers. No index. Hand drawn. Average

80 pages. 17.5 x 13 x 1.5. State examiner's office.

Tax Records
(See also entries 420-443)

Tax Levies and Rates

323. TAX LEVIES
1892-1900, 1902, 1909-1913. 6 file boxes.
Original certificates of approval of budgets and levies by school boards, township trustees, and municipal councils for general taxes and special assessments, showing year, name of taxing district, total property value, total estimated expenditures, special assessments, total revenue required, and date filed. Arranged chronologically by dates filed. No index. Handwritten on printed forms. 10.5 x 5 x 14. Auditor's vault.

324. TAX RATE
1924-1938. 5 volumes. (3; 4 unlabeled)
Record of tax rates for various taxing districts, showing year, name of taxing district, name of fund or special assessment, rate for each fund, and total tax rate. Arranged chronologically by years and alphabetically thereunder by names of taxing districts. No index. Handwritten on forms. Average 50 pages. 6.5 x 4 x .5. Auditor's vault.

Tax Appraisements and Assessments

325. REAL ESTATE APPRAISEMENTS
1870, 1910. 30 volumes. Two subtitled Adams to Liberty; twenty-eight, 1910, by names of taxing districts.
Record of decennial appraisement of real estate for taxation, showing name of taxing district, name of property owner, description and location of tract or lot, lot number or number of acres, building value, land value, and total value. Arranged alphabetically by names of taxing districts and alphabetically thereunder by names of property owners. No index. Handwritten on forms. 2 volumes average 1000 pages, 18 x 13 x 4.5. 28 volumes average 100 pages, 17 x 14 x .5. State examiner's office.

326. REAPPRAISMENT OF REAL PROPERTY

1925, 1931. 10 volumes. Subtitled by names of taxing districts.

Record of appraisement a real property for taxation, showing name of taxing district, name of property owner, number acres or lot number, location and description, valuation, unit value, amount of appraisement, and total land and building valuation. Arranged alphabetically by names of taxing districts and thereunder by names of property owners. No index. Typed on forms. Average 250 pages. 18 x 17.5 x 2. Auditor's vault.

327. [APPRAISEMENT]

1937. 1 file box. (labeled by names of taxing districts).

Appraisements of new buildings and improvements only, showing name of city and ward number, village or township, name of taxing district, name and address of owner, number of acres or lot number, number improvements reported since 1931, kind of improvement, year built, owners estimate of cost, appraiser's value, value by board of revision, signatures of appraisers, and remarks. No obvious arrangement. No index. Typed on printed forms. 14 x 16.5 x 18.75. Auditor's vault.

328. [SPECIAL ASSESSMENTS PUBLIC IMPROVEMENTS]

1910. 1 file box.

Record of special assessments on real estate for owner's share of cost of public improvements, showing name of taxing district, year, name of property owner, name of subdivision, what improvement, lot number, sublet number, value, amount assessed; also includes copies of complaints of property owners to board of equalization, showing names of taxing district, name of owner, amount assessed, what improvement, grounds of complaint, and date filed. No obvious arrangement. No index. Handwritten. 4.5 x 10.5 x 3.25. Auditor's vault.

329. SPECIAL TAX CERTIFIED OR COLLECTION

1910-1930. 3 file boxes.

Special assessments for owner's share of cost of public improvements, certified to county auditor by municipal and township clerks for collection, showing name of township or municipality, date filed, what improvement, name of property owner, range, township, section or lot numbers, number of acres, foot frontage, total assessment, and amount of each installment. Arranged alphabetically by names of townships and municipalities and alphabetically thereunder by names of property owners. No index. Handwritten on forms. 10.5 x 5 x 14. Auditor's vault.

Tax Returns

330. INDIVIDUAL TAX RETURNS

1932—. 20 file drawers. (dated).

Original returns of chattels filed by owners, showing year, name of taxing district, name and address of property owner, itemized list of chattels, number of each item, unit value, total value, grand total value all items, notarization, signature of owner, and date filed; also includes certificates of advance payment of tax assessments attached to return, showing certificate number, name and address of taxpayer, name of taxing district, property value general personal property, tax rate, amount of assessment, property value each class of classified chattels (intangibles), tax rate each class, amount of assessment, total tax assessed, amount of advanced payment, balance due, and date of payment. Also contains property; Settlement of Estates, 1932-1933, entry 331. Arranged chronologically by years and alphabetically thereunder by taxing districts and alphabetically thereunder by names of owners. No index. Returns, handwritten on printed forms; certificates, typed on printed forms. 11 x 16 x 27. Auditor's main office.

331. PROPERTY, SETTLEMENT OF ESTATES

1934—. 1 file box. 1932-1933 in Individual Tax Returns, entry 330.

Original statements by administrators and executors of estates of chattel property certified by probate court, showing name of decedent, case number, date of death, name of taxing district, name of administrator or executor, itemized list of chattels, number of each item, unit value, total value, total value all items, and dates certified and filed. Arranged chronologically by dates filed. No index. Handwritten on printed forms. 10.5 x 5 x 14. Auditor's private office.

Tax List, Duplicates, and Abstracts

332. AUDITOR'S DUPLICATE

1840—. 313 volumes (dated). Title varies: Tax Duplicate, 1840-1905, 153 volumes.

Auditors duplicate of taxes assessed on real estate, and special assessments of property owners share of public improvements, annual duplicate, 1840-1858, semiannual duplicate, 1859—, showing year, name of taxing district, name of property owner, range, township, section or lots numbers, description of tract or lot, number of acres, assessed value, amount of tax assessed, amount of delinquent tax, amount of special assessment, total due, and date due; also includes, 1925—, record of real property transfers, showing date of transfer and name of grantee; personal property duplicate, 1840-1931, showing year, name of taxing district, name of property owner, property value, amount of tax assessed, amount delinquent tax, total due, and date due. Arranged alphabetically by the names of taxing districts and alphabetically thereunder by names of property owners. No index. Handwritten on forms. Average 400 pages, 18 x 12 x 2.5. 153 volumes, 1840-1905, Attic store room; 145 volumes, 1906-1936, Auditor's vault; 15 volumes, 1937—, Auditor's main office.

For prior records of real property transfers, see entry 316; subsequent personal property, entries 338, 339; separate records of delinquent taxes, entry 344, 350.

333. ABSTRACT OF REAL PROPERTY
1914. 1 volume.

Abstract of real property tax assessments, showing name of taxing district, number acres cultivated, pasture and wood and waste lands, assessed value, building value, value farm tracts and buildings, value city and town lots, building value, total value, total value real property each taxing district, total land value all taxing districts, total building value all taxing districts, and grand total value land and buildings. Arranged alphabetically by names of taxing districts. No index. Handwritten on forms. 100 pages. 18 x 14 x .5. State examiner's office.

334. EXEMPT PROPERTY LIST
1937—. 1 volume.

List of real property exempt from taxation (public owned lands, churches, hospitals, cemeteries, charitable agencies), showing name of owner, name of taxing district, range, township, section or lot numbers, description of tract or lot, number of acres, appraised value, and date entered. Arranged alphabetically by names of owners. No index. Typed on printed forms. 100 pages. 14 x 17 x .5. Auditor's vault.

335. AUDITOR'S ROAD DUPLICATE
1917—. 3 volumes. (1, 2, 2).

Duplicate of special assessments on abutting lands and lots or owner's share of cost of public improvements (roads and streets), showing year, name of taxing district, name of improvement, name of owner, range, township, section or lot numbers, description of tract or lot, foot frontage, total assessment, amount of annual or semiannual installment, and date due. Arranged alphabetically by names of improvements and alphabetically thereunder by names of property owners. No index. Typed on forms. Average 300 pages. 16 x 22 x 1.5. Auditor's vault.

336. AUDITOR'S DITCH DUPLICATE
1905-1929. 3 volumes.

Duplicate of special assessments on lands and lots for owner's share of cost of construction of drainage ditches, showing year entered, name of ditch, name of taxing district, name of property owner, range, township, section, or lot numbers, description of tract or lot, number of acres, number of acres assessed, total assessment, amount of each annual or semiannual installment, and date due. Arranged chronologically by dates of entries. Indexed alphabetically by names of property owners. Handwritten on forms. Average 280 pages. 20 x 14 x 1.5. 1 volume, 1905-1913, State examiner's office; 2 volumes, 1913-1929, Auditor's vault.

337. AUDITOR'S LIQUOR TAX DUPLICATE
1918-1929. 1 volume.

Duplicate license assessments to traffic in intoxicating liquor, showing name of licensee or violator, name of town or township, business address, name of owner of real estate, description of real estate, date of assessment, amount of assessment, penalty, and date due. 1920-1929 entries are of penalty assessments for Dow tax against violators of prohibition statutes. Arranged alphabetically by names of towns and townships and chronologically thereunder by dates of assessments. No index. Typed on forms. 140 pages. 18 x 14 x 1. Auditor's vault.

338. AUDITOR'S GENERAL TAX LIST
1932. 1 volume. Discontinued.

List of general personal property (tangibles) tax assessments, showing year, name of taxing district, name of property owner, property value, tax rate, amount of tax assessed, amount of advanced payment, balance due, and advanced payment certificate number. Arranged alphabetically by names of taxing districts and alphabetically thereunder by names of property owners. No index. Typed on printed forms. 300 pages. 12 x 16 x 1.5. Auditor's vault.

For prior records, see entry 332.

339. AUDITOR'S CLASSIFIED TAX LIST
1932. 1 volume. Discontinued.

List of classified personal property (intangibles) tax assessments, showing year, name of taxing district, name of property owner, property value, tax rate, amount of tax assessed, amount of advance payment, balance due, and advance payment certificate number. Arranged alphabetically by names of taxing districts and alphabetically thereunder by names of property owners. No index. Typed on printed forms. 100 pages. 12 x 15 x .5. Auditor's vault.

Auditions, Deductions, and Refunds

340. ADDITIONS AND REFUNDS
1924—. 4 volumes. (2-5). Title varies: Additions and Deductions, 1924-1931, 1 volume.

Record of additions to or deductions from property values on tax duplicate, showing name of property owner, range, township, section or lot numbers, description of tract, property value, amount added or deducted, revised value, and reason for revision. Arranged chronologically by dates of revisions. No index. Handwritten on forms. Average 200 pages. 18 x 12 x 1. Auditor's vault.

341. ADDITION CERTIFICATES
1931—. 2 volumes. (labeled by contained certificate numbers).

Carbon copies of auditor's certificates of additions to property value for taxation, showing certificate number, date issued, name of property owner, name of taxing district, description and location of tract, amount of addition, and reason for addition. Arranged numerically by certificate numbers. No index. Handwritten on printed forms. Average 200 pages. 17 x 10 x 1. 1 volume, 1931-1935, Auditor's vault; 1 volume, 1935—, Auditor's main office.

342. REMITTER ORDERS
1931—. 4 volumes. (One unlabeled; 2-4).

Carbon copies of auditor's orders to treasurer to remit stated amount on property valuation, showing order number, date issued, name of property owner, name of taxing district, description and location tract, amount remitted, and reason for reduction. Arranged numerically by ordered numbers. No index. Handwritten on printed forms. Average 150 pages. 17 x 10 x 1. 2 volumes, 1931-1936, Auditor's vault; 2 volumes, 1936—, Auditor's main office.

343. REFUNDERS

1889-1897. 1 volume. (1).

Record of refund orders issued by auditor to treasurer on liquor tax assessments, showing order number, date of order, name and address of payee, amount of refund, and reason for refund. Arranged numerically by ordered numbers. No index. Handwritten on forms. 320 pages. 16 x 11.5 x 1.5. Attic store room.

Delinquent Taxes

344. AUDITOR'S DELINQUENT LAND LIST

1905—. 4 volumes. (dated). Title varies: Delinquent List, 1905-1931, 3 volumes.

List of delinquent lands and lots, showing year, name of taxing district, name of property owner, range, township, section or lot numbers, description of tract or lot, number of acres, assessed value, amount of tax assessed, years delinquent, penalty, and total due. Arranged chronologically by years, alphabetically thereunder by names of taxing districts and alphabetically thereunder by names of owners. No index. 1905-1912, 1916—, handwritten on forms; 1913-1916, typed on forms. Average 450 pages. 18 x 12 x 2.5. 1 volume, 1905-1912, State examiner's office; 3 volumes, 1913—, Auditor's vault.

For other prior records, see entry 332.

345. AUDITOR'S RECORD OF QUADRENNIAL CERTIFICATES–UNREDEEMED DELINQUENT LANDS

1918-1930. 1 volume.

Record of quadrennial certificates to state auditor of unredeemed delinquent lands and lots, showing date issued, name of delinquent owner, name of taxing district, certificate number, description and location of tract, assessed value, and years delinquent, amount of delinquent tax, amount of penalty, and total due. Arranged numerically by certificate numbers. No index. Handwritten on forms. 200 pages. 17 x 12 x 1.25. Auditors' vault.

346. AUDITOR'S RECORD OF TRIENNIAL CERTIFICATES–DELINQUENT LANDS

1931—. 1 volume.

Record county auditor's triennial certificates to prosecuting attorney of delinquent lands and lots, showing certificate number, name of delinquent owner, description and location of tract, years delinquent, amount of delinquent tax, amount of penalty, total due, and date certified. Arranged numerically by certificate numbers. No index. Handwritten on forms. 280 pages. 16 x 15 x 1.5. Auditor's vault.

347. DELINQUENT LIST ADVERTISED
1899-1916. 1 volume.

List of lands and lots advertised delinquent, showing year, name of taxing district, name of owner, description and location of tract, number of acres, assessed value, amount of delinquent tax and penalty, and date advertised. Arranged alphabetically by names of taxing districts and alphabetically thereunder by names of owners. No index. Handwritten on forms. 400 pages. 17 x 14 x 2. State examiner's office.

348. DELINQUENT TAX SALE RECORD
1841—. 3 volumes. (dated). Last entry 1917.

Record of delinquent lands and lots sold at public sale, showing year; name of taxing district, name of delinquent owner, description and location of tract, amount of delinquent tax and penalty, amount of cost, date sold, to whom sold, amount sold for, and date redeemed or auditor's deed executed. Arranged chronologically by years, alphabetically thereunder by names of taxing districts and alphabetically thereunder the names of delinquent owners. No index. Handwritten on forms. Average 560 pages. 18 x 12 x 3. Auditor's vault.

349. DELINQUENT TAX SALE RECORD
1841—. 3 volumes. (dated). Last entry 1917.

Record of delinquent lands and lots sold at public sale, showing year; name of taxing district, name of delinquent owner, description and location of tract, amount of delinquent tax and penalty, amount of cost, date sold, to whom sold, amounts sold for, and date redeemed or auditor's deed executed. Arranged to chronologically by years, alphabetically thereunder by names of taxing districts and alphabetically thereunder by names of delinquent owners. No index. Handwritten on forms. Average 560 pages. 18 x 12 x 3. Auditor's vault.

350. AUDITOR'S DELINQUENT PERSONAL TAX LIST
1904 —. 3 volumes. (1-3).

List of delinquent personal property taxes, showing year, name of taxing district, name of owner, property value, amount of tax assessed, amount of penalty, total due, and date paid; 1932—, accumulated delinquent taxes and penalties shown.

Arranged chronologically by years, alphabetically thereunder by taxing districts and thereunder by name of owners. No index. Handwritten on forms. Average 500 pages. 17 x 12 x 2.5. 1 volume, 1904-1913, State examiner's office; 2 volumes, 1914—, Auditor's vault.

For prior records, see entry 332.

Inheritance Taxes

(See also entries 253, 254, 432)

351. AUDITOR'S INHERITANCE TAX CHARGES

1920—. 1 volume.

Record of inheritance taxes charged, showing name of decedent, case number, date of death, date return filed, value of estate as fixed by probate court, net amount taxable, amount of tax as determined by probate court, to whom charged, date paid, amount of discount or interest, and amount paid. Arranged chronologically by dates filed. Indexed alphabetically by names of decedents. Handwritten on printed forms. 450 pages. 11.5 x 12 x 2.5. Auditor's vault.

352. PROBATE COURT PAPERS [Inheritance Tax Returns]

1920—. 10 file boxes.

Original papers filed by probate court relative to inheritance tax determination and charges, consisting of journal entries of appointment of appraisers, orders to appraise assets of estate, inventories and appraisements, and decedent, date of death, name of administrative agent, case number, volume and page number of Journal, entry 223, date appraiser appointed, name of appraisers, date of appraisal, itemized statement of inventory and appraisal of assets, total appraised value, total amount realized on sale of assets, amount of administrative cost, amount of debts and claims allowed, net amount subject to tax, names of heirs-at-law or legatees, to whom tax charged, and date filed. Arranged chronologically by dates filed. No index. Handwritten on printed forms. 10.5 x 5 x 14. 5 file boxes, 1920-1931, Auditor's vault; 5 file boxes, 1931—, Auditor's main office.

Settlements

353. RECORD OF ABSTRACT AND SETTLEMENT SHEETS
1885, 1893—. 5 volumes, 5 folders. (dated).

Annual abstracts of real and personal property valuations all classes, showing year, name of taxing district, class of property, total evaluation of each class, and grand total; abstract of school statistics reported to state auditor, showing year, name of school district, number of school buildings, number of school rooms, number of teachers, and average monthly enrollment of pupils; abstract of acres, land value, building value, total value, tax rate, and amount of tax assessed; record of semi-annual settlements with townships, corporations, and school districts, showing year, settlement period, name of subdivision, total property value, tax rate, amount of tax assessed, amount collected, date of settlement with subdivision fiscal officer, dates and amounts of advance draws made by subdivision, date of final settlement, and amount remaining in county treasury to credit of subdivision. Arranged chronologically by settlements periods. No index. 1885, 1893-1919, handwritten on printed forms; 1920—, typed on printed forms. Volumes average 150 pages. 23.5 x 17.5 x 1; folders, 18 x 24. 1885, 1893-1930, 5 volumes, County sealer's office; 1931—, 5 folders, Auditor's vault.

354. SCHOOL SETTLEMENT
1914—. 2 volumes, 1 file box.

Record of semiannual settlements with school treasurers, showing name of township or corporation, settlement period, total property valuation in subdivision, amount of school tax levied, amount of tax collected, amount from sources other than taxes, total amount credited to subdivision, amount of advance draw, amount due subdivision on final settlement, auditor's warrant number, and date of settlement. Arranged chronologically by dates of settlements. No index. Handwritten on printed forms. Volumes average 250 pages. 18 x 12 x 1.5; file drawer, 12 x 14 x 26. 2 volumes, 1914-1929, Auditor's vault; 1 file drawer, 1930—, Auditor's main office.

355. COLLECTIONS
1929—. 6 file boxes.

Auditor's data on treasurer's semiannual tax collections, showing collection period, name of taxing district, total tax levied on real and personal property, special assessments, total amount collected, amount delinquent taxes and penalties collected, amount of inheritance taxes collected, amount of cigarettes taxes collected, total taxes collected, and amount to be credited to subdivision. Arranged chronologically by collection periods. No index. Handwritten on forms. 10.5 x 5 x 14. Auditor's vault.

356. ADVANCE REQUESTS

1932—. 1 file box.

Original request filed by township trustees, corporation councils, and boards of education for advanced funds on anticipated tax collections, showing name of subdivision, date of request, amount requested, to be credited to what fund or funds, signature of subdivision clerk, and date filed. Arranged chronologically by dates filed. No index. Handwritten on printed forms. 10.5 x 5 x 14. Auditor's private office.

357. RECORDS OF DISTRIBUTION OF MOTOR VEHICLE LICENSE TAX

1927-1930. 1 volume. Discontinued; law repealed.

Record of distribution to subdivisions of motor vehicle license fees, showing date, name of subdivision, number of vehicles licensed, total fees, and amount of fees allotted to subdivision. Arranged alphabetically by names of subdivisions and chronologically thereunder by dates of distribution. No index. Handwritten on forms. 280 pages. 16 x 11 x 1.5. Auditor's vault.

Financial Records

Appropriations

358. APPROPRIATION LEDGER

1916—. 12 volumes. (dated).

Record of appropriations, showing name of fund, date credited, amount of credit, source of credit, authorization, debit certification, credit adjustment, amount of unencumbered balance; also includes debits, showing date of debit, and name of account. Arranged alphabetically by names of funds. No index. Handwritten on forms. Average 500 pages. 11.5 x 14.5 x 2. Auditor's vault.

Bills and Claims

359. RECORD OF BILLS FILED

1913—. 6 volumes. (3-8).

Auditor's docket of bills filed for commissioners' approval, showing date filed, bill number, name of creditor, amount, for what, date of bill, amount approved, date paid, and warrant number. Arranged numerically by bill numbers. No index. Handwritten on forms. Average 600 pages. 18 x 13 x 3. Auditor's vault.

360. BILLS

1932—. 85 file boxes. (dated).

Original bills filed by creditors for materials, supplies, and labor, with commissioners' voucher for payment attached, showing bill number, date of bill, name and address of creditor, itemized statement of claim, total amount, for what, date filed, voucher number, date issued, name of payee, bill number, amount, and for what. Arranged chronologically by dates of vouchers. No index. Handwritten and typed on forms. 10.5 x 5 x 14. 60 file boxes, 1932-1936, auditor's vault; 25 file boxes, 1936—, Auditor's main office.

361. [MISCELLANEOUS BILLS]

1934—. 1 file box.

Original bills filed by state department of public welfare, division of charities, for cost of maintenance of inmates from Seneca County in state institutions, including care of crippled children, showing date of bill, bill number, date filed, name and address of creditor, itemized statement, total amount, for what, date approval for payment, and amount approved. Also includes auditor's salary, jail matron's salary, wages of employees, division of aid for the aged, medical services, charity cases, and cost of publishing legal notices of delinquent tax sales. Arranged chronologically by dates approved for payment. No index. Handwritten and typed on forms. 10.5 x 5 x 14. Auditor's main office.

362. REGISTER OF SHEEP CLAIMS

1909—. 2 volumes. (2, 3).

Record of claims filed for compensation for sheep or other domestic animals killed or injured by dogs, showing date claim filed, claim number, name and address of claimant, name of township, number of animals killed, number injured, general damage, amount allowed by appraisers, and names of appraisers. Arranged chronologically by dates claims filed. No index. Handwritten on forms. Average 270 pages. 16.5 x 17 x 1.5. Auditor's vault.

General Accounts

363. LEDGER

1858-1962, 1886—. 9 volumes. (dated).

Ledger of credits and debits various county funds, showing name of fund, amount of credit, date of credit, amount of debit, date of debit, credit balance, and debit balance. Arranged alphabetically by names of funds and chronologically thereunder by dates of credits and debits. No index. Handwritten on forms. Average 650 pages. 18 x 13 x 3.5. Auditor's vault.

364. RECEIPTS JOURNAL

1935—. 2 volumes.

Record of receipts into county treasury the general property tax, depository interest, cigarette tax, special assessments for ditch purposes, road assessment, township levy, school levy, State of Ohio sales tax, malt tax, auditor's fees, treasurer's fees, probate judge's fees, clerk of courts' fees, county, home receipts, justices', and mayor's fees, police court fees, and miscellaneous sources credited to the various county funds, showing date received, amount, from what source, and to what fund or account credited. Arranged alphabetically by names of funds and accounts and chronologically thereunder by dates received. No index. Handwritten on forms. Average 100 pages. 15 x 11.5 x 1. Auditor's vault.

365. AUDITOR'S JOURNAL OF WARRANTS ISSUED

1897—. 12 volumes. (8-11, 1-6; 2 unlabeled). Title varies: Warrant Register, 1897-1903, 4 volumes.

Records of auditor's warrants issued for payment of approved bills and claims showing date issued, warrant number, name of payee, amount, for what, and what fund debited. Also contains court warrants issued, 1897-1903, entry 366. Arranged numerically by warrant numbers. No index. Handwritten on forms. Average 475 pages. 18 x 13 x 2.5. 7 volumes, 1897-1900, 1904-1930, State examiner's office; 2 volumes, 1900-1903, County sealer's office; 1 volume, 1931-1933; Auditor's vault; 1934—, Auditor's main office.

366. COURT WARRANTS ISSUED

1904—. 4 volumes. (1-4). 1897-1903 in Auditor's Journal of Warrants issued, entry 365.

Records of court warrants issued on certification by clerk of courts and probate judge for fees due, showing date of issue, warrant number, name of payee, amount, for what service, what court, and fund debited. Arranged numerically by auditors court warrant numbers. No index. Handwritten on forms. Average 240 pages. 18 x 12 x 1.5. 2 volumes, 1904-1916, State examiner's office; 1 volume, 1917-1932, Auditor's vault; 1 volume, 1933—, Auditor's main office.

367. TREASURER'S RECEIPTS

1935—. 1 file box.

Copies of treasurer's receipts to state treasurer for Seneca County's allotment of relief funds from excise taxes, showing receipt number, date of receipt, amount, from what source, state auditor's warrant number, and treasurer's signature. Arranged chronologically by dates of receipts. No index. Handwritten on printed forms. 10.5 x 5 x 14. Auditor's main office.

Special Accounts

368. AUDITOR'S RECORD, SOLDIERS' RELIEF

1908—. 3 volumes.

Record of payments to soldiers, sailors, or dependents of deceased veterans, showing name and address of recipient, amount of grant, date paid, and warrant number. Arranged alphabetically by names of recipients. No index. Handwritten on forms. Average 320 pages. 18 x 14 x 1.5. 1 volume, 1908-1917, State examiner's office; 1 volume, 1918-1933, Auditor's vault. 1 volume, 1933—, Auditor's main office.

For other related records, see entry 525.

369. MOTHERS' PENSION RECORD

1914-1936. 1 volume. (1). Discontinued; superseded by Aid to Dependent Children.

Record of payments of mothers' pensions, showing name and address of recipient, amount of monthly grant, date paid, and warrant number. Arranged alphabetically by names of recipients. No index. Handwritten on forms. 100 pages. 17.5 x 17.5 x .5 Auditor's main office. For subsequent records, see entry 370.

370. RECORD OF DEPENDENT CHILDREN

1936- September 1939. 1 volume.

Record of payments to mothers of dependent children, showing name and address of recipient, case number, number of dependent children, amount of monthly grant, date paid, warrant number, notation of reason for increase or reduction of monthly grant; also includes ledger record of funds received from federal, state, and local sources, showing dates credited, from what source, amount, to what fund credited, total amount of payments each month for aid, for administration expense, for emergency aid (medical care), and balance each month. Payments arranged alphabetically by names of recipients; legend record, chronologically by monthly entries. No index. Handwritten on forms. 150 pages. 14 x 19 x 1. Auditor's main office.

For prior record of payments, see entry 369; for subsequent records, c entry 371.

371. AID TO DEPENDENT CHILDREN

October 1939—. 1 file box.

Record of monthly payments to mothers of dependent children certified eligible to receive aid by administrator of aid to dependent children showing month, name of recipient, case number, amount of grant, date paid, and warrant number. Arranged chronologically by months. No index. Typed on printed forms. 10.5 x 5 x 14. Auditor's main office.

For prior records, see entry 370.

372. BLIND RELIEF RECORD

1911—. 1 volume. (1), 1 file box.

Record of quarterly or monthly payments to blind residents, showing month, name and address of recipient, case number, amount of quarterly or monthly grant, date paid, and warrant number. 1911- June 1936 arranged alphabetically by names of recipients; July 1936—, arranged chronologically by months and alphabetically thereunder by names of recipients. No index. Handwritten on forms. Volumes, 190 pages. 17 x 15 x 1; file box, 10.5 x 5 x 14. Auditor's main office.

For prior records of blind relief payments, see entry 529.

373. RECEIPTS AND EXPENDITURES [Aid For The Blind]

July 1936—. 1 folder.

Original monthly reports from administrator of aid for the blind to county auditor, showing amount on hand at beginning of month, amount of local, state, and federal funds received during month, and total credits; also includes record of expenditures, and warrants issued for aid, for medical care, for administration, total expenditures, and balance on hand at the end of month; administration expenditures, showing amounts for salaries, travel, office expense, and miscellaneous expense; also unredeemed warrants reported, showing name of payee, warrant number, amount, date issued, and date certified by county auditor. Arranged chronologically by months. No index. Typed on printed forms. 11 x 8.5. Auditor's main office.

374. AUDITOR'S FEES

1907—. 2 volumes. (1, 2).

Record of fees for official services, showing date of service, to whom charged, amount of fee, for what, and remarks. Also contains Record of Transfer Fees, 1907-1926, entry 375. Arranged chronologically by dates of service. No index. Handwritten on forms. Average 240 pages. 16 x 11 x 1.5. 1 volume, 1907-1926, Auditor's vault; 1 volume, 1927—, Auditor's main office.

375. RECORD OF TRANSFER FEES

1927—. 1 volume. (1). 1907-1926 in Auditor's Fees, entry 374.

Record of fees for transferring title of ownership to real estate, showing date transferred, needs of grantee and grantor, location of tract or lots, and amount of fee. Arranged chronologically by dates of transfers. No index. Handwritten on forms. 300 pages. 14 x 9.5 x 1.5. Auditor's main office.

376. RECORD OF UNCLAIMED COSTS

1903—. 1 volume. (2).

Record of witness and jury fees unclaimed and paid into county treasury as certified by clerk of courts and probate judge, showing date certified, name of person to whom due, amount due, for what service, what court, certificate number, and date certificate issued for recovery. Arranged chronologically by dates certified. No index. Handwritten on forms. 250 pages. 18 x 12 x 1.5. Auditor's vault.

377. CERTIFICATES–UNCLAIMED COST
1897—. 1 file box.

Original certificates issued by clerk of courts and probate judge for fees and costs unclaimed and paid into county treasury, showing certificate number, what court, date issued, name of person to whom due, amount, for what service; also includes certificates issued for recovery of unclaimed fees and cost, showing certificate number, date issued, what court, name of payee, amount, and for what service. Chronologically by dates of certificates. No index. Handwritten on printed forms. 10.5 x 5 x 14. Auditor's main office.

378. AUDITOR'S SINKING FUND RECORD
1914-1923. 1 volume.

Record of debenture bonds issued to provide funds to finance costs of public improvements, showing date of issue, purpose of issue, amount of issue, date of maturity of issue, rate of interest, amount of special tax levy or provision for other income to retired bonds. Arranged the chronologically by dates of issue. No index. Handwritten on forms. 170 pages. 19 x 14 x 1. Auditor's vault.

379. LEDGER [Infirmary]
1897-1912. 1 volume.

Record of accounts with other counties for the care of inmates at the Seneca County home, showing name of county, name of inmate, amount and date debited, amount and date paid, balance due. Alphabetical by names of counties and chronologically thereunder by dates debited. No index. Handwritten on forms. 224 pages. 14.5 x 9 x 1.25. Auditor's vault.

380. AUDITOR'S PAY ROLL RECORD OF PUBLIC EMPLOYEE'S RETIREMENT FUNDS
1938. 1 volume.

Auditor's account with each county employee who is a member of the Public Employees Retirement System, showing name, membership number, title or classification, what office or department, changes in pay-roll status (or other changes), service credit prior to January 1, 1935, amount of salary or wage, January 1, 1935 to June 30, 1938, pay-roll period, time worked in hours, days, weeks or months, base rate of pay, maintenance value of this period, or other allowance, amount earned per base rate, deductions, and net pay-roll amount. Arranged alphabetically by names of members. No index. Typed on printed forms. 250 pages. 10 x 12.75 x 1.5. Auditor's vault.

381. PUBLIC EMPLOYEE'S RETIREMENT REPORTS
1938—. 1 volume.

Copies of semi-monthly reports, accompanied by remittances, submitted by county auditor to Public Employment Retirement System of employment data pertaining to county personnel, showing name, date of payroll period, names and title of employees, name of office, department, board, commission, or institution, number of hours of work performed, base rate of pay, variations in base rate of pay, amount earned, and amount of deductions on certification of county auditor, director of finance, or other responsible official. Arranged chronologically by dates of pay-roll period. No index. Typed on printed forms. 220 pages. 15 x 18 x 1.25. Auditor's vault.

382. SALARY RECORD
1914-1925. 1 volume. (1).

Record of salaries of each county official with annual budget for wages and salaries of employees each department, showing year, name of office or department, salary of official, and amount of budget for deputy and clerk hire for year. Arranged chronologically by years and alphabetically thereunder by names of offices and departments. No index. Handwritten on forms. 100 pages. 14 x 13 x .75. Auditor's vault.

Pay-ins

383. AUDITOR'S JOURNAL OF PAYMENTS
1904—. 6 volumes. (1-6).

Record of pay-in orders issued authorizing county treasurer to receive payment (except taxes), showing date of order, order number, name of payer, amount, for what, and what fund credited. Arranged numerically by order numbers. No index. Handwritten on forms. Average 300 pages. 20 x 17 x 1.5. 2 volumes, 1904-1916, county sealer's office; 3 volumes, 1917-1934, Auditor's vault; 1 volume, 1934—, Auditor's main office.

384. PAY-IN ORDERS

1930—. 5 volumes. (labeled by contained order numbers).

Stubs of auditor's pay-in orders issued, showing order number, date issued, name of payer, amount, for what, and what fund credited. Arranged numerically by order numbers. No index. Handwritten on forms. Average 250 pages. 15.5 x 10 x 1.5. 4 volumes, 1930-1937, Auditor's vault, 1 volume, 1938—, Auditor's main office.

385. TREASURER'S RECEIPTS

1932—. 2 file boxes.

Duplicate copies of treasurer's receipts for money paid into county treasury on auditor's pay-in orders, showing receipt number, date of receipt, name of payer, amount, for what, what fund credited, pay-in order number, and signature of treasurer or deputy. Arranged numerically by receipt numbers. No index. Handwritten on printed forms. 10.5 x 5 x 14. Auditor's main office.

Vouchers and Warrants

386. VOUCHERS AND WARRANTS

1934—. 11 cartons, 4 file drawers.

Original vouchers with auditor's warrants (redeemed) attached for expenditures for emergency relief, showing voucher number, date issued, name and address of vendor or payee, name and address of client, case number, amount of voucher itemized, signature and title of disbursing official, warrant number, date of issue, name of payee, amount, for what, what fund debited, name of relief client, signature of auditor, and date redeemed. Arranged chronologically by dates redeemed. No index. Typed on printed forms. Cartons, 10 x 12 x 15; file drawer, 11 x 12 x 24. 11 cartons, 1934-1938, Attic store room; 4 file drawers, 1938—, Auditor's office.

387. [REDEEMED WARRANTS]

1932—, 44 file boxes. (dated).

Original warrants issued by auditor for payment of approved bills and claims and redeemed by county treasurer, showing warrant number, date issued, name of payee, amount for what, what fund debited, signature of auditor, and date redeemed. Arranged chronologically by dates redeemed. No index. Handwritten on forms. 10.5 x 5 x 14. Auditor's vault.

388. WARRANTS

1910—. 13 volumes. (labeled by contained warrant numbers).

Carbon copies of auditor's warrants issued, showing warrant number, date issued, name of payee, amount, for what, what fund debited, and signature of auditor. Arranged numerically by warrant numbers. No index. Handwritten on printed forms. Average 650 pages. 19 x 10 x 3.5. 12 volumes, 1910-1939, Auditor's vault; 1 volume. 1939—, Auditor's main office.

Licenses and Permits

389. APPLICATIONS, DOG LICENSE

1930—. 8 bundles, 3 file boxes.

Original applications for dog licenses, showing application number, date of application, name and address of applicant, description of dog, tag number, license fee, and signature of applicant. Arranged numerically by application numbers. No index. Handwritten on printed forms. Bundles, 4 x 3.5 x 7; file boxes, 10.5 x 5 x 14. 8 bundles, 1930-1934, Auditor's vault; 3 file boxes. 1934—, Auditor's main office.

390. DOGS AND KENNEL LICENSE

1933—. 8 file drawers. (dated and labeled by container letters of alphabet).

Copies of dog and kennel licenses issued, showing license number, date issued, name and address of owner, description of dog, tag number assigned, and license fee; kennel license, showing license number, date issued, name and address of owner, number of dogs, breed, tag numbers assigned, and license fee. Arranged chronologically by years and alphabetically thereunder by names of owners. No index. Handwritten on printed forms. 5.5 x 10 x 17. Auditor's main office.

391. APPLICATIONS VENDORS' LICENSE

1935—. 1 file drawer.

Original applications by retail merchants for vendor licenses (sales tax), showing application number; name and business address of applicant; date of application, kind of business, code number, and signature of applicants. No index. Handwritten on printed forms. 10 x 15 x 18.5. Auditor's main office.

392. VENDOR'S LICENSE

1935—. 35 volumes.

Copies of license issued to retail vendors, showing license number, name and business address of vendor, kind of business, code number, date issued, license fee, and signature of auditor. Arranged numerically by license number. No index. Handwritten on printed forms. Average 150 pages. 7 x 8.5 x 1. Auditor's main office.

393. [VENDOR'S LICENSE DATA]
1935—. 1 file box.

Record of cancellations of licenses, legal status change, license issued incorrectly, license not required, showing name of vendor, application or license number, license not required, showing name of vendor, application or license number, reason for cancellation or change of status, and date of cancellation or status change. Arranged alphabetically by names of applicants or vendors. No index. Handwritten on printed forms. 10.5 x 5 x 14. Auditor's main office.

394. LISTS OF LICENSED VENDORS
1935—. 1 file drawer.

List of vendors' licenses issued each week, showing name and business address of vendor, license number, code number, and date issued. Arranged chronologically by dates of weeks and numerically thereunder by license numbers. Handwritten on forms. 10 x 15 x 18.5. Auditor's main office.

395. PEDDLERS' LICENSE
1933—. 1 volume.

Stubs of licenses issued to army and navy veterans to peddle merchandise at retail, showing license number, date issued, name and address of peddler, discharge number of veteran, and license fee. Arranged numerically by license numbers. No index. Handwritten on printed forms. 250 pages. 14.5 x 8.5 x 1.5. Auditor's main office.

396. CIGARETTES LICENSE
1930—. 7 bundles, 3 volumes.

Duplicate copies of cigarette traffic licenses issued to dealers, showing license number, wholesale or retail dealer, home and business address of dealer, year of license, date issued, amount of fee, and signature of auditor. Arranged numerically by license numbers. No index. Handwritten on printed forms. Bundles, 8.5 x 10.5 x 1.5; volumes average 200 pages. 8.5 x 10.5 x 1.5. 7 bundles, 1930-1936, Auditor's vault; 3 volumes, 1937—, Auditor's main office.

397. LICENSES

1933-1934. 1 file box. Discontinued; law repealed.

Original applications for cosmetic dealers' and beverage dealers' licenses, showing application number, date of application, name and business address of applicant, kind of business, and signature of applicant; also carbon copies of cosmetic dealers' and beverage dealers' licenses issued, showing license number, date issued, name and business address of dealer, kind of business, and license fee. Arranged numerically by application and license numbers. No index. Handwritten on printed forms. 10.5 x 5 x 14. Auditor's vault.

398. BEER, MALT AND WORT DEALER'S LICENSE

1933—. 2 volumes.

Carbon copies of malt and wort licenses issued, showing license number, name and business address of dealer, date issued, kind of business, and license fee. Also includes copies of beer licenses, 1933-1934. Arranged numerically by license numbers. No index. Handwritten on printed forms. Average 400 pages. 9.5 x 14 x 3. Auditor's main office.

Reports and Statements

(See also entries 5-9, 25)

399. AUDITOR'S ANNUAL FINANCIAL REPORTS

1905—. 1 file drawer.

Copies of auditor's annual financial reports on receipts and expenditures, showing year, names of funds, offices and departments, balance each fund at beginning of year, total balance, credit each fund, source of credit, total credits all funds; also expenditures classified each fund (salaries, wages, materials, supplies, principal on bonds, interest), total expenditures each fund, total expenditures all funds, balance or deficit each fund, total credit or debit balance, and date of report. Arranged chronologically by years. No index. Handwritten and typed on printed forms. 5.5 x 11 x 18. Auditor's main office.

400. TREASURER'S DAILY STATEMENTS

1933—. 4 file drawers.

Daily financial statements from county treasurer: receipts, showing date, names of funds, balance at beginning of day, receipts each fund, source of receipts, total receipts; expenditures, showing name of fund, amount, name of payee, for what, total expenditures all funds, balance each fund, and total balance. Arranged chronologically by daily reports. No index. Handwritten on printed forms. 4 x 10 x 16. Auditor's main office.

401. FINANCIAL REPORTS
1850-1953, 1920—. 4 file boxes, 1 file drawer.

Original reports from county officials and department heads of receipts and expenditures, showing period covered by report, name of office or department, receipts itemized, total receipts (fees), expenditures itemized (salaries, wages, supplies), total expenditures, and date filed. Arranged chronologically by dates filed. No index. 1850-1853, handwritten on printed forms; 1920—, typed on printed forms. File boxes, 10.5 x 5 x 14; file drawer, 11 x 14 x 26. 1 file box, 1850-1853, Auditor's vault; 3 file boxes, 1 file drawer, 1920—, Auditor's main office.

402. STATISTICAL REPORTS
1889—. 2 file drawers.

Copies of auditor's annual reports to state auditor of sheep killed or injured by dogs, showing year, number of sheep killed, appraised value, number injured, appraised value, general damage allowed, total amount allowed, and date of report; original reports, 1891, 1900, from state board of equalization, showing amount of taxes assessed (real and personal property) as returned to state auditor for each taxing district, amount as revised by state board of equalization; copies of auditors annual reports to state department of education, 1937—, showing year, number of school districts, number of school buildings, number of elementary school buildings, number of high school buildings, number of elementary teachers, number of high school teachers, average monthly wage of teachers, number of elementary pupils, number high school pupils, amount of indebtedness each district, estimated value of school property (real estate, building and equipment each district), date of report; copies of annual reports to state tax commission 1918—, showing names and business addresses of individuals and firms trafficking in cigarettes, date of report; copies of quarterly reports to state auditor, 1938—, of federal and state funds allocated to aid dependent children and aid to the blind, showing quarter, amount of federal funds, amount of state funds, total amount, dates of reports; original statements from state auditor, 1937—, on distribution of excise tax receipts to Seneca County to be credited to relief funds, showing year, amount, from want source, total amount, and date filed; copies of auditor's annual reports to state auditor, 1937—, on number of wort and malt dealers licenses and vendors' licenses issued; auditors copy of statement to clerk of city of Fostoria, 1937, of delinquent special tax assessments (street paving and sewers), showing lot number, foot frontage, name of owner, amount delinquent, and date filed. Arranged chronologically by dates of reports or of filing. No index. Handwritten and typed on printed forms. 11 x 14 x 26. Auditor's main office.

403. MAGISTRATES REPORTS
1928—. 1 file box.
Original annual reports from magistrates of fines and costs assessed and collected (criminal cases), showing year, what court, township or corporation, name of magistrate, name of defendant, charge, amount of fine, amount of cost assessed, amount collected, dates paid, and date of report. Arranged chronologically by dates of reports. No index. Handwritten on printed forms. 10.5 x 5 x 14. Auditor's main office.

404. ENGINEER'S REPORTS
1937—. 2 file boxes.
Original monthly pay-roll reports filed by county engineer, showing month, year, name of employee, classification, wage rate, number hours, total due, and total amount of pay-roll; engineer's monthly reports of expenditures for maintenance of highways, showing month, year, expenditures for material, for labor and supervision, and total for month. Arranged chronologically by years and thereunder by months. No index. Typed on forms. 10.5 x 5 x 14. Auditor's main office.

405. BOARD OF EDUCATION REPORTS
1923—. 2 file boxes.
Original annual reports for local boards of education, showing town, township, year, total receipts all sources, total expenditures classified (salaries, wages, transportation, repairs, incidentals), number elementary teachers, number high school teachers, number elementary pupils, number high school pupils, and date filed. Arranged chronologically by dates filed. No index. Handwritten on printed forms. 10.5 x 5 x 14. Auditor's vault.

406. SCHOOL TREASURER'S REPORTS
1927—. 2 file boxes.
Original semiannual reports from township clerk-treasurers of condition of school funds, showing name of township, semiannual period, total receipts all sources,

amount credited each fund, amount of disbursements each fund, total disbursements, credit or debit balance each fund, total credit or debit balance, total bonded indebtedness, and date filed. Arranged chronologically by dates filed. No index. Handwritten on printed forms. 10.5 x 5 x 14. Auditor's main office.

407. SCHOOL EXAMINER'S REPORTS

1904-1933. 2 file boxes. Discontinued; law repealed.

Original quarterly reports from board of school examiners, showing quarter, number applicants examined, and total fees; amount expended for examiner's salary, advertising, printing, rent, incidentals, total expenditures, and date filed; also annual financial report of teachers' institute fund, showing year, receipts itemized, total receipts, expenditures itemized, total expenditures, balance, and date filed. Arranged chronologically by dates filed. No index. Handwritten on printed forms. 10.5 x 5 x 14. Auditor's vault.

408. TOWNSHIP AND CORPORATION SCHOOL CLERK-TREASURERS

1938—. 1 file box.

Reports for township and corporation clerks of names of board of education clerk-treasurers, showing name of township or corporation, name and address of clerk-treasurer, date of beginning of term of office, date bond filed, amount of bond, names of sureties, and date report filed. Arranged chronologically by dates reports filed. No index. Handwritten and typed on printed forms. 10.5 x 5 x 14. Auditor's main office.

409. STATE EXAMINER'S FINDINGS

1918—. 4 file boxes. 2 subtitled, School Districts; 2, Townships.

Copies of findings by state examiners of school and township officials' accounts, showing name of school district or township, names of fiscal officials, township trustees, and justices of the peace, total amount of funds received during period of the report, total legal expenditures, total illegal expenditures (if any), name of official against whom finding made, total amount of fines and costs imposed by justice of the peace, total amount of fines and costs collected, total amount of fines and costs accounted for, amount of findings against justice (if any), date of examination, and date report filed. Arranged chronologically by dates filed. No index. Handwritten on printed forms. 10.5 x 5 x 14. Auditor's main office.

410. STATE HIGHWAY DEPARTMENT REPORTS

1922-1930. 2 file boxes. Discontinued.

Reports of pay rolls on state highway work in county, showing date of report, pay-roll number, type of work, name of township, date of pay-roll, section number, total time, rate of pay, amount shared by county and state, and pay-roll approvals; also includes resolutions and applications of county commissioners applying for state aid; resolutions of township trustees approving schedule of assessments for property owner's share and township's share of cost of location and construction of improved roads; also copies of approved estimates of state highway department to county auditor cost of improvement by county-state highways. Arranged chronologically by dates of reports. No index. Handwritten on printed forms. 10.5 x 5 x 14. Auditor's vault.

411. INDEBTEDNESS REPORTS

1828—. 1 file box.

Original reports by subdivisions and school districts of bonded indebtedness, showing year, name of subdivision or school district, total property value (tax assessment value), total bonded debt, date of maturity of issue, date issue, interest rate, and date filed. Arranged chronologically by dates filed. No index. Handwritten on printed forms. 10.5 x 5 x 14. Auditor's vault.

Bonds

(See also entries 453-455)

412. RECORD OF BONDS

1929-1933. 1 volume.

Copies of surety bonds filed by sheriff, treasurer, coroner, showing name and title of official, amount of bond, name and address of surety (bonding company), terms of obligation, copy of prosecuting attorney's certificate of legality of bond, commissioners' approval, date of bond, and dates filed and recorded. Arranged chronologically by dates recorded. Indexed alphabetically by names of officials. Handwritten on printed forms. 400 pages. 16 x 11 x 2. Auditor's vault.

413. SURETY BONDS

1919—. 1 file box.

Original surety bonds filed by various county officials (elected and appointed), showing name and title of official, amount of bond, name and address of surety (bonding company), terms of obligation, prosecuting attorney's certificate of the legality and commissioners' approval, date of bond, and date filed. Arranged alphabetically by names of officials. No index. Typed on printed forms. 10.5 x 5 x 14. Auditor's vault.

414. SCHOOL CLERK-TREASURER'S BONDS
1921—. 2 file boxes.

Original bonds filed by township and corporation boards of education clerk-treasurers, showing name of subdivision, name of official, amount of bond, names of sureties, terms of obligation, date of bond, and date filed. Arranged chronologically by dates filed. No index. Handwritten and typed on printed forms. 10.5 x 5 x 14. Auditor's main office.

415. RECORD OF BONDS
1884—. 3 volumes. (1-3).

Record of bonds issued on authorization of county commissioners to provide funds to finance construction of public improvements or fund deficits, showing date of issue, name of issue, purpose of issue, total amount of issue, denomination of bonds, serial numbers, date of maturity, interest rate, and interest due dates. Arranged chronologically by dates of issue. No index. Handwritten on forms. Average 130 pages. 16 x 11 x 1. Auditor's vault.

Miscellaneous

416. RECORD OF BUILDING NOTICES
1919-1920. 1 volume.

Records of auditor's permits issued for construction or remodeling of buildings outside of municipalities, showing date of issue, permit number, name of property owner, range, township, and section numbers, description of tract or lot, description of proposed new building or remodeling, and estimated cost. Arranged alphabetically by names of property owners. No index. Handwritten on forms. 250 pages. 18 x 12 x 1.5. Auditor's main office.

417. APPOINTMENTS

1921—. 2 file boxes.

Record of appointments of deputies to various county offices except sheriff's showing name of office, name of appointee, monthly salary, amount of bond (if bonded), date of appointment, and name of department head(county official); also includes copies of applications from various county officials to county commissioners for additional allowances for extra clerk hire, showing date of application, name of department, name of official, amount requested, reason extra clerks needed, and date filed. Arranged chronologically by dates of appointments or dates filed. No index. Handwritten and typed on printed forms. 10.5 x 5 x 14. Auditor's main office.

418. ENUMERATION OF SCHOOL AGE YOUTH

1915—. 2 file boxes.

Original annual enumeration list of school-age youth, showing name of school district, name of township or corporation, year, name of youth, age, date of birth, sex, name and address of parent or guardian, name of enumerator, and date list filed. Arranged chronologically by years. No index. Handwritten on printed forms. 10.5 x 5 x 14. 1 file box, 1915-1933, auditor's main office; 1 file box, 1934—, Auditor's private office.

Weights and Measures

419. RECORD OF INSPECTIONS

1927-1931, 1937—. 17 volumes.

Record of inspections by sealer of weights and measures of weighing measuring devices, showing date of inspection, name and address of owner of device, kind of business, number of weighing devices inspected, kind of scale, name of manufacturer, if approved or condemned, recommendations to owner, number of measuring devices inspected, type and capacity of each, if approved or condemned, recommendations to owner, and amount of fee. Arranged chronologically by dates of inspections. No index. Handwritten on printed forms. Average 250 pages. 14 x 9 x 1.5. County sealer's office.

The office of county treasurer was established by an act of the Northwest Territory in 1792 and continued by the State of Ohio.[1] Although the constitution of 1802 made no provision for the office of county treasurer, it was created by the legislative act of 1803.[2] The treasurer, appointed by the associate judges in 1803 and by the county commissioners in 1804, was required to take an oath and give bond for the faithful performance of the duties of his office, and was subject to removal by the appointing power.[3] The treasurer remained an appointive official until 1827 when the office became an elective one by popular vote in the county.[4] Although it did not specifically create the office, the constitution of 1851 stated that no person shall hold the office of treasurer for more than four years in any six. This provision was repealed in 1933 by an amendment authorizing any county to adopt a charter form of government.[5] Interpreting the constitutional provision, the legislature fixed the term of office at two years in 1859.[6] The term of office continued at two years until 1936 when it was extended to four years.[7] Until 1906 the county treasurer received his remuneration from fees; since that date his salary has been determined by law according to the population of the county.[8] In 1939 the Seneca County treasurer's salary was $3,390.[9]

The duties of the treasurer were defined by statute in the earlier period and specified in detail by the acts of 1827 and 1831 repealing previous acts. The provisions of the latter acts, although subject to amendment and repeal, furnished the foundation for subsequent legislation and laid the basis for the present duties of the treasurer, which did not differ greatly from those prescribed by earlier statutes.

In 1803 the treasurer was given his present duty of giving public notice of the tax duplicate.

---

1. Pease, *op. cit.*, 68-69.
2. *Laws of Ohio,* I, 97.
3. *Ibid.*, I, 97-98; II, 154.
4. *Ibid.*, XXV, 25-32.
5. *Ohio Const. 1851,* Art. X, sec. 3 (Amendment, 1933).
6. *Laws of Ohio,* LVI, 105.
7. *Ibid.*, CXVI, pt. ii, 184.
8. *Ibid.*, XCVIII, 89.
9. Ohio Auditor of State, *Annual Report,* 1939, p. 369.

On receiving from the county auditor a duplicate of the taxes assessed upon the property of the county, the treasurer prepares and post notices in three places in each township including the place and which elections are held; and inserts the notice for six consecutive weeks in the newspaper having the largest circulation in the county.[10] He receives money in payment of taxes levied for the county, for the state, and for other purposes, and gives the payer a receipt.[11] In the earlier years of the office the treasurer was required to give announcement of the time he would be in the respective townships of the county and in his office at the seat of justice to receive tax collections. Since 1858 the treasurer has been authorized to prescribe the semiannual payment of taxes or assessments levied upon real estate.[12] Moreover, since 1908, the commissioners have been authorized to extend the time of paying taxes for not more than 30 days after the time fixed by law.[13]

After each semiannual collection of taxes, the treasurer is required to report to the auditor, showing the amount of taxes received at each taxing district in the county since the last settlement. Since 1904 the semiannual settlements have been made under the heads of liquor, cigarette, inheritance, delinquent personal, road, and general taxes. The treasurer keeps his accounts in books which enable him to compile such reports.[14]

After the taxes are collected and immediately after each settlement with the county auditor, the county treasurer, upon the presentation of proper warrant from the auditor, pays to the township treasurer, city or village treasurer, the treasurer of the school district, or treasurer of any "legally constituted board authorized by law to receive the funds or proceeds of any special tax levy," or other officer delegated with authority to receive such funds, all money in the treasury belonging to such boards and subdivisions.[15] In addition, after the treasurer has made each settlement with the county auditor, he is required to pay to the state treasurer, on warrant from the state auditor, "the full amount of all sums" found by the latter to belong to the state.[16]

---

10. *Laws of Ohio,* I, 98; XXIX, 291; LII, 124.
11. G. C. sec. 2650; *Laws of Ohio,* XXIX, 292; LXXVI, 70; LXXXV, 327.
12. *Laws of Ohio,* LV, 62; LVI, 101.
13. *Ibid.,* XCIX, 435; CXIV, 730; CXV, pt. ii, 226.
14. G. C. sec. 2643; *Laws of Ohio,* XXIX, 296; XCVII, 458.
15. G. C. sec. 2689; *Laws of Ohio,* LVI, 101.
16. *Laws of Ohio,* LVI, 101; CXIV, 732.

Another function of the county treasurer, which had its inception in the earlier years of the office, is the collection of delinquent taxes. It was and is his duty to assess a penalty on the tax duplicate for nonpayment of taxes–which penalty when collected, is paid to the treasurer's fund. If the treasurer is unable to collect the delinquent taxes, he is authorized to apply to the clerk of courts of common pleas who serves notice to show cause why such taxes were not paid. The court may enter a rule against the delinquent taxpayer for the payment and cost and enforce it by attachment.[17]

During the last decade provision has been made for the installment payment of delinquent taxes without interest or penalty. In 1931 it was provided that the delinquent taxes, assessments, and penalties charged on a tax duplicate against any entry of real estate might be paid in installments during five consecutive semiannual tax paying periods, "whether such real estate had been certified as delinquent or not."[18] The Whittemore act, passed as an emergency measure in 1933, provided for the collection in installments, without interest or penalty, of delinquent real estate assessments. Anyone electing to pay such delinquent real property taxes and assessments in installments pursuant to this act may, at any installment period, pay the entire unpaid balance, in which event no interest shall be charged or collected on the amount so paid. In 1934 the benefits of the act were extended to include delinquent personal and classified taxes.[19] With slight alterations the law was re-enacted in 1935 and again in 1936.[20] An act was passed in February 1937 providing for the settlement of taxes delinquent prior to 1936 without interest or penalty in one payment or in ten annual installments and re-enacted in February 1938.[21]

The county treasurer has charge of the funds collected by taxes, and also of other funds belonging to the county. Although earlier acts made provision for storage vaults in the county treasury for county deposits, the commissioners have been authorized, since 1894, to receive sealed bids for the deposit of county funds; and the banks or trust companies offering the highest rate of interest are selected as the county depositories.[22]

---

17. G. C. sec. 2662; *Laws of Ohio,* LVI, 175; XCIX, 435.
18. G. C. sec. 2672; *Laws of Ohio,* CXIV, 827.
19. *Laws of Ohio,* CXV, 161-164; CXV, pt. ii, 230, 332.
20. *Ibid.,* CXVI, 199, 468; CXVI, pt. ii, 14-21.
21. *Ibid.,* CXVII, 32, 832.
22. *Ibid.,* XCI, 403; CII, 59; CXV, pt. ii, 215.

The treasurer is required to keep an account current with the county auditor– a practice which originated in 1831. Each day the treasurer makes a statement to the county auditor for the previous day's business showing the amount of taxes received on auditor's drafts, the amount received from other sources, together with the amount of money deposited in the depository, the total amount paid out by check and by cash, and the balance in the treasury.[23]

The treasurer as well as the sheriff, the prosecuting attorney, and the clerk of courts, has been required since 1850 to report annually to the county commissioners.[24] Since 1874 the county auditor and county commissioners have been required to make a thorough examination of all books, vouchers, accounts, moneys, bonds, securities, and other property in the treasury at least every six months.[25] Besides being under the supervision of the county commissioners and county auditor, the treasurer is subject to the supervision of the state auditor. In 1902 an act was passed providing for a uniform system of accounting and auditing for all public offices in the state, under the direction of a bureau of inspection in the office of the state auditor, and for the annual examination of the finances of all public offices.[26]

The treasurer is a member of the budget commission, the county board of revision, and serves as a trustee of the sinking fund.[27] Since the early days of the office the treasurer has been the official custodian of the bonds furnished to the state by the county auditor, county commissioners, and other officials. Since 1869 he has been required to record and preserve a record of the deputies appointed and removed by the county auditor,[28] but such record was not found in Seneca County.

Like other county officials, the treasurer is required at the expiration of his term to turn over to his successor all books, papers, moneys, and records after appertaining to his office.[29]

---

23. G. C. sec. 2642; *Laws of Ohio,* XCVII, 457.
24. G. C. sec. 2504.
25. G. C. sec. 2699; R. S. sec. 1129; *Laws of Ohio,* LXXI, 137.
26. G. C. sec. 2641; *Laws of Ohio,* CVIV, 728; XCV, 511-515.
27. G. C. secs. 5625-19; 2976-18; 5580.
28. G. C. sec. 2563; *Laws of Ohio,* LXVI, 35.
29. G. C. sec. 2639.

Tax Records
(See also entries 323-350)

Text List and Duplicates

420. TREASURER'S DUPLICATE OF REAL PROPERTY

1845, 1921—. 195 volumes. (dated). Subtitled by names of taxing districts. Duplicates of taxes assessed on real property, showing year, name of taxing district, name of property owner, description of property and location of tract or lot, number of acres or lot number, property valuation, amount of tax assessed, amount of delinquencies and penalties, total due, and total paid; notation of accounts and payments under Whittemore plan 1933—, personal property, 1845, 1921-1931, showing year, name of taxing district, name of property owner, property valuation, amount assessed, amount of delinquent tax and penalties, and date paid. Arranged alphabetically by names of taxing districts and alphabetically thereunder by names of owners. No index. 1845, handwritten on printed forms; 1921—, typed on printed forms. 1 volume, 1845, 365 pages. 13 x 8.25 x 2.5; 194 volumes, 1921—, average 175 pages. 16 x 17 x 2. 1 volume, 1845, Treasurer's vault. 2; 194 volumes, 1921—, Treasurer's vault 1.

For subsequent record personal property taxes, see entries 423, 424; for delinquencies, see entry 427.

421. TREASURER'S SPECIAL DUPLICATE OF ROAD TAXES

1917—. 3 volumes.

Duplicate of special taxes assessed on lands and lots for owner's share of cost of improvement of public roads, showing name of improvement, name of taxing district, name of owner, description and location of tract or lot, total assessment, amount of each annual installment, amount delinquent, and date paid. Arranged alphabetically by names of ditches and alphabetically thereunder by names of property owners. No index. Typed on printed forms. 342 pages. 20 x 14.5 x 2. Treasurer's main office.

423. GENERAL TANGIBLE TAX LIST

1932—. 8 volumes. (dated).

List of general personal tangible taxes, showing name of taxing district, tax rate, name and address of taxpayer, property value, amount of assessment, penalty assessment, total tax for year, amount of advanced payment, advance payment certificate number, amount of unpaid taxes for the year, and remarks. Arranged alphabetically by names of taxing districts and alphabetically thereunder by names of taxpayers. No index. Typed on forms. Average 500 pages. 18.25 x 17.25 x 2.5. Treasurer's vault 1.

For prior personal taxes, see entry 420.

424. INTANGIBLE TEXT LIST
1932—. 8 volumes. (dated).

List of intangible classified tax assessments, showing name of taxing district, name and address of taxpayer, property value each class of property, tax rate, amount of assessment, total assessment, amount of advanced payment, advance payment certificate number, amount of unpaid taxes, and remarks. Arranged alphabetically by names of taxing districts and alphabetically thereunder by names of taxpayers. No index. Typed on printed forms. Average 400 pages. 16 x 19 x 2. Treasurer's vault 1.

For prior personal taxes, see entry 420.

425. TREASURER'S CIGARETTE TRAFFIC TAX DUPLICATE
1921-1931. 1 volume.

Treasurer's duplicate of licenses to traffic in cigarettes, showing name and business address of licensee, name of owner of real estate, description of real estate, amount of assessment, penalty, total amount, and date paid. Arranged chronologically by dates of payments. No index. Typed on printed forms. 100 pages. 18 x 18 x .75. Treasurer's main office.

426. TREASURER'S LIQUOR TAX DUPLICATE
1887-1888, 1898-1929. 2 volumes.

Duplicate of liquor traffic license assessments, showing name and address of licensee, name of town or township, name of owner of real estate, description and location of real estate, amount of assessment, date due, penalty, and date paid. Entries, 1920-1929, are records of Dow tax penalty assessments on conviction of violation of prohibition statutes. Arranged alphabetically by names of towns and townships and alphabetically thereunder by names of licensees. No index. Handwritten on forms. Average 100 pages. 16 x 17 x .75. 1 volume, 1887-1888, Attic store room; 1 volume, 1898-1929, Treasurer's main office.

Delinquent Taxes

427. DELINQUENCIES
1892-1894. 3 volumes. (dated).

Record of real and personal property tax delinquencies; real, showing year, name of taxing district, name of property owner, range, township, section or lot numbers, description of tract, number of acres, assessed value, amount of delinquent tax, penalty, and total due; personal property, showing value, amount of delinquent tax, penalty, and total due. Arranged alphabetically by names of taxing districts and alphabetically thereunder by names of property owners. No index. Handwritten on forms. Average 215 pages. 14 x 9 x 1.25. Attic store room.

For other records of delinquencies, see entry 420; for personal property, see entry 430.

428. TREASURER'S RECORD OF QUADRENNIAL CERTIFICATES, UNREDEEMED LANDS
1918-1930. 1 volume.

Copies of quadrennial certificates of delinquent lands and lots, showing certificate number, date issued, name of delinquent owner, name of taxing district, description and location of tract, assessed value, years delinquent, amount of delinquent tax, amount of penalty, and total amount due. Arranged numerically by certificate numbers. Indexed alphabetically by names of owners. Handwritten on printed forms. 350 pages. 17.5 x 12 x 2. Treasurer's vault 1.

429. TREASURER'S TRIENNIAL CERTIFICATES
1931—. 1 volume.

Copies of triennial certificates to prosecuting attorney of delinquent lands and lots, showing certificate number, date issue, name of delinquent owner, name of taxing district, description and location of tract, assessed value, years delinquent, amount of delinquent tax, penalty, and total due. Arranged numerically by certificate numbers. Indexed alphabetically by names of owners. Handwritten on printed forms. 300 pages. 15 x 11 x 2. Treasurer's vault 1.

430. TREASURER'S DELINQUENT PERSONAL TAX LIST
1912-1935. 2 volumes. (dated).

List of delinquent personal taxes, showing year, name of taxing district, name of property owner, property value, amount of delinquent tax, penalty, and total due.

Arranged chronologically by years, alphabetically thereunder by names of taxing districts and alphabetically thereunder by names of owners. No index. Handwritten on forms. Average 300 pages. 18 x 12 x 1.5. Treasurer's main office.

For prior records, see entry 427.

431. TREASURER'S CUMULATIVE DELINQUENT DUPLICATE
1932—. 2 volumes.

Duplicate of accumulated delinquent personal taxes, showing year, name of owner, name of taxing district, years delinquent, amount of delinquent taxes, penalty, total amount due, and date paid. Arranged chronologically by years, alphabetically thereunder by names of taxing districts and thereunder by names of owners. No index. Handwritten on forms. Average 350 pages. 10 x 14 x 2. Treasurer's main office.

Inheritance Taxes (See also entries 253, 254, 351, 352)

432. TREASURER'S INHERITANCE TAX CHARGES
1921—. 2 volumes.

Record of inheritance tax payments, showing date paid, name of decedent, to whom tax charged, date certified to auditor, amount of tax charged, amount of discount allowed or interest charged, net amount due, date paid, and auditor's pay-in-order number. Arranged chronologically by dates of payments. No index. Handwritten on forms. Average 200 pages. 16 x 11 x 1.25. Treasurer's vault 1.

Excise Tax Stamps

433. INVENTORY AND SALES RECORD SALES TAX STAMPS
1935—. 2 bundles, 1 volume.

Record of sales tax stamps received, showing date, number each denomination, value, discount, net amount due state treasury; record of daily sales, showing date, name of purchaser, license number, code number, number each denomination, total value, amount of dealer's discount, and net amount collected; daily inventory, showing date, number each denomination received, number each denomination on hand at beginning of day, number each denomination sold, number each denomination on hand at close of day, total sales for day, amount dealer's discount, amount treasurer's commission, and net amount due to state treasurer. Arranged chronologically by daily entries. No index. Handwritten on printed forms. Bundles,

14 x 8 x 1; volume, 150 pages. 14 x 17 x 1. 2 bundles, 1935-1937, Treasurer's vault 1; 1 volume, 1937—, Treasurer's main office.

434. TREASURER'S RECORD OF CIGARETTE TAX STAMPS RECEIVED AND SOLD

1931—. 1 volume.

Record of cigarette excise tax stamps received and sold, showing date received, from whom, receipt or check number, quantity, and value; record of sales, showing date, to whom sold, quantity, value, amount of treasurer's commission, and total net amount due state treasurer. Arranged chronologically by dates of entries. No index. Typed on printed forms. 100 pages. 12 x 14 x 1. Treasurer's vault 1.

435. COUNTY TREASURER'S SALES REPORT OF WINE TAX STAMPS

1933-1934. 1 file box. (37).

Carbon copies of reports of sale of wine excise stamp tax sales, showing date of sale, to whom sold, quantity, amount of sale, amount of county treasurer's commission, net amount due from county to state treasurer, and date of report. Arranged chronologically by dates of reports. No index. Handwritten on printed forms. 10.5 x 5 x 14. Treasurer's vault 1.

436. TREASURER'S SALES REPORT OF MALT AND WORT STAMPS

1933-1935. 1 file box. (39).

Carbon copies of reports to state treasurer on sale on malt and wort excise tax stamps, showing date of sale, to whom sold, amount of sale, amount of treasurer's commission, net amount due state treasurer, and date of report. Arranged chronologically by dates of reports. No index. Handwritten on printed forms. 10.5 x 5 x 14. Treasurer's vault 1.

437. TREASURER'S SALES REPORT OF BEVERAGE TAX STAMPS AND CROWNS

1933-1935. 1 file box. (38).

Carbon copies of reports to state treasurer on sale of beverage excise tax stamps, showing date of sale, to whom sold, quantity, amount of sale, amount of treasurer's commission, net amount due state treasurer, and date of report. Arranged chronologically by dates of reports. No index. Handwritten on printed forms. 10.5 x 5 x 14. Treasurer's vault 1.

438. TREASURER'S SALE REPORT OF COSMETIC TAX STAMPS
1933-1934. 1 file box. (36).
Carbon copies of reports to state treasurer on sale of cosmetic excise tax stamps, showing name of licensee, business address, date of purchase, quantity, amount of sale, amount of treasurer's commission, net amount due state treasurer, and date of report. Arranged chronologically by dates of reports. No index. Handwritten on printed forms. 10.5 x 5 x 14. Treasurer's vault 1.

Tax Collections

439. RECORD OF COLLECTIONS
1887-1902. 4 volumes.
Records of semiannual collections of real and personal property taxes, showing year, collection period, name of taxpayer, name of taxing district, description of real property, amount of tax assessed, and date paid. Arranged chronologically by collection periods and chronologically thereunder by dates of payments. No index. Handwritten on forms. Average 600 pages. 16 x 11 x 3. Attic store room.

For subsequent records, see entry 444.

440. DELINQUENT COLLECTIONS
1882-1887. 1 volume. (2).
Record of collections of delinquent real and personal taxes, showing year, name and address of taxpayer, name of taxing district, amount collected, date of collection, and name of collector. Arranged chronologically by dates collected. No index. Handwritten on forms. 385 pages. 16 x 11 x 2. Attic store room.

441. TREASURER'S CIGARETTE TAX COLLECTIONS
1930—. 1 volume. (2).
Record of cigarette traffic license tax collections, showing date collected, receipt number, name of town or township, name of dealer, and amount collected. Arranged chronologically by dates collected. No index. Handwritten on forms. 200 pages. 18 x 12 x 1. Treasurer's main office.

442. TAX PAID RECEIPTS
1928—. 8 file drawers.
Stubs of receipts for taxes paid including personal property, 1928-1931, showing the receipt number, year, collection period, name of taxing district, name of

property owner, description and location of real property, assessed value, amount of tax assessed, and date paid. Arranged chronologically by collection periods and numerically thereunder by receipt numbers. No index. Handwritten on printed forms. 7 x 14 x 18. Treasurer's vault 1.

443. PERSONAL PROPERTY RECEIPTS
1932—. 4 file drawers. (dated).

Carbon copies of receipts for personal property taxes paid, showing receipt number, assessment certificate number, name of taxpayer, name of taxing district, property value, tax rate, tax assessed, property value each class of classified (intangible) property, tax rate, tax assessed, total tax due, amount of advance payment, balance due, and date paid. Arranged chronologically by years and numerically thereunder by receipt numbers. No index. Handwritten on printed forms. 7 x 14 x 18. Treasurer's main office.

Financial Records

444. TREASURER'S DAILY CASH BALANCE
1886-1890, 1904—. 11 volumes. (1886, 1-10). Title varies: Treasurer's Cash Book, 1886-1890, 1904-1917, 5 volumes.

Record of cash receipts into treasury and disbursements; receipts, showing year, date paid in, balance carried forward, amount general taxes, liquor, cigarette, delinquent tax collections, inheritance tax, excise tax stamp taxes, 1933—, auditor's miscellaneous pay-in orders, total daily receipts; disbursements classified (amounts for salaries, wages, materials, supplies, settlements and subdivisions, bond principal interest), total daily expenditures, and balance. Chronological by daily entries. No index. Handwritten on forms. Average 400 pages. 18 x 12 x 2. 9 volumes, 1886-1890, 1904-1933, Attic store room; 2 volumes, 1934—, Treasurer's main office.

For separate record of tax collections, see entry 439.

445. TREASURER'S LEDGER
1858-1864, 1904—. 7 volumes. (2 unlabeled; 1-5).

Treasurer's fund ledger, showing year, name of fund, date credited, amount credited, date and amount debited, monthly balance, credit or debit balance each fund. Chronological by dates of credits and debits. No index. Handwritten on forms. Average 600 pages. 18 x 12 x 3. 5 volumes, 1858-1864, 1904-1926, Attic store room; 2 volumes, 1926—, Treasurer's main office.

446. DAILY DEPOSITORY RECORD

1924—. 2 volumes. (1 unlabeled; 2).

Record of accounts with various depository banks, showing date of deposit, amount of deposit, and drafts and balances of activity and inactive funds. Arranged chronologically by dates of entries. No index. Handwritten on forms. Average 200 pages. 14.5 x 9.5 x 1.25. Treasurer's main office.

447. TREASURER'S ACCOUNT NUMBER 5

1895-1904. 1 volume.

Treasurer's account with state funds; receipts, showing year, name of fund, amount credited to fund, and source of receipt; disbursements, showing date, amount, name of payee, for what, and monthly balance. Arranged chronologically by dates of receipts and disbursements. For index, see entry 448. Handwritten on forms. 700 pages. 16 x 12 x 3.5. State examiner's office.

448. INDEX TO TREASURER'S ACCOUNTS NUMBER 5

1895-1904. 1 volume.

Index to treasurer's account number 5, entry 447, showing year, name of fund, and page number of record. Arranged alphabetically by names of funds. Handwritten on forms. 50 pages. 15 x 10 x .25. State examiner's office.

449. TOWNSHIP BOOK

1842-1949. 1 volume.

Record of county treasurer's accounts with the various townships, 1842-1849, showing name of township, date of entry, amount credited to township account, source of credit, date paid to township treasurer, amount paid, and balance to credit of township and county treasury; also includes record of redeemed orders on ditch, bridge, county building, and infirmary funds, 1874, showing name of fund, date redeemed, order number, name a payee, amount, and for what. Accounts, arranged alphabetically by names of townships and chronologically thereunder by dates of entries; orders redeemed, arranged chronologically by dates redeemed. No index. Handwritten. 225 pages. 14 x 9 x 1.25. Attic store room.

450. TREASURER'S JOURNAL OF WARRANTS REDEEMED
1914—. 16 volumes. (11-26).

Treasurer's record of auditor's general warrants redeemed, showing date redeemed, warrant number, name of payee, amount, for what, and what fund debited. Arranged chronologically by dates redeemed. No index. Handwritten on forms. Average 400 pages. 18 x 12 x 2. 14 volumes, 1914-1937, Attic store room; 2 volumes, 1937—, Treasurer's main office.

451. RECORD OF COURT WARRANTS REDEEMED
1904—. 5 volumes. (1-5).

Treasurer's record of auditor's court warrants redeemed, showing date redeemed, warrant number, name of payee, amount, for what service, what court, and what fund debited. Arranged chronologically by dates redeemed. No index. Handwritten on forms. Average 240 pages. 18 x 12 x 1.5. 3 volumes, 1904-1926, Attic store room; 2 volumes, 1926—, Treasurer's main office.

452. TREASURER'S JOURNAL OF RECEIPTS
1904—. 7 volumes. (1-7).

Treasurer's record of receipts into treasury on auditor's pay-in orders, showing date paid in, pay-in-order number, name of payer, amount, for what, and what fund credited. Arrange numerically by pay-in order numbers. Handwritten on forms. Average 200 pages. 19 x 16 x 1.25. 5 volumes, 1904-1931, Attic store room; 2 volumes, 1932—, Treasurer's main office.

Bonds

(See also entries 412-415)

453. OFFICIAL BONDS
1834-1884, 1922—. 2 volumes.

Copies of surety bonds of elected or appointed county officials, showing name of principal and sureties, what office, amount of bond, date witnessed, condition of obligation, prosecuting attorney's certificate, approval of county commissioners, oath of office, and dates filed and recorded. Arranged chronologically by dates recorded. Indexed alphabetically by names of officials. Handwritten on printed forms. Average 400 pages. 9.5 x 7.5 x 1.5. 1 volume, 1834-1884, Treasurer's vault 2; 1 volume, 1922—, Treasurer's vault 1.

454. RECORD OF TOWNSHIP CLERK'S BONDS
1923—. 1 volume.

Copies of bonds of township clerks, showing names of principals and sureties, name of township, amount of bond, date witnessed, conditions of obligation, approval of township trustees, oath of office, and dates filed and recorded. Arranged chronologically by dates recorded. Indexed alphabetically by names of clerks. Handwritten on printed forms. 400 pages. 14 x 8.5 x 2. Treasurer's vault 1.

455. [Redeemed] BONDS
1917-1926. 1 file box.

Redeemed bonds authorized by county commissioners to provide funds to finance road improvements, showing bond number, amount of bond, rate of interest, name of road or highway, date principal is due, date interest is payable, date paid, warrant number, and signatures of auditor and commissioners. No obvious arrangement. No index. Typed on printed forms. 10.5 x 5 x 14. Treasurer's vault 1.

A budget commission functions in Seneca County under the act of 1911, which authorized the establishment in each county of a budget commission to be composed of the county auditor, the mayor of the largest municipality, and the prosecuting attorney.[1] In 1915 the county treasurer replaced the mayor as a member of the commission.[2] It was not until after the World War when county expenditures steadily increased, that the importance of improving methods of finance were forcibly brought to the attention of the legislature. This need was met in 1923 by enlarging the powers and minutely prescribing the duties of the budget commission. As in 1915 the county auditor, county treasurer, county prosecuting attorney were made ex-officio members of the commission.[3] Under the present law, passed in 1927, the commission, consisting as before of the county auditor, the county treasurer, and the county prosecuting attorney, receives and examines the annual budget of the county, municipal, township, and school authorities, with an estimate of the amount to be raised for state purposes in each subdivision.[4] If the total amount exceeds the sum authorized to be raised, the commission adjusts the amount to be raised and may change and revise the estimates. The commission may reduce all items in the budget, but it is prohibited from increasing the total of any budget or any item.

The adjusted budget is certified to the taxing authority in each subdivision. If the work of the commission is satisfactory, each taxing authority by ordinance or resolution authorizes the necessary tax levies and certifies them to the county auditor. On the other hand, the taxing authority in any subdivision may appeal, through its fiscal officer from the decision of the budget commission to the state tax commission of Ohio, which is empowered to adjust the estimates of revenues and balances in fixing the tax rates.[5]

The county auditor, as secretary to the commission, is required to keep a full and accurate record of the proceedings of the commission.[6]

---

1. *Laws of Ohio,* CII, 271.
2. *Ibid.,* CV I, 180.
3. *Ibid.,* CX, 469. Under the provisions of this act elective commissioners might be substituted for the ex-officio members, at the option of the electors of the county.
4. *Laws of Ohio,* CXIi, 399.
5. G. C. secs. 5625- 25 , 5625- 28.
6. G. C. sec. 5625-19.

456. RECORD [Budget Commissioners Minutes]
1928—. 1 volume.

Minutes of county budget commission, showing date and place of meeting, names of members present, record of budget request by county commissioners, township trustees, corporation councils, and boards of education, showing name of subdivision, total property valuation for taxation, expenditures during past year, estimated requirements outside of bond retirement and interest for current year, and amount of budget itemized by funds for county and each subdivision as set by commission. Arranged chronologically by dates of meetings. No index. Typed. 300 pages. 16 x 11 x 1.5. Auditor's vault.

457. BUDGET REQUEST
1925-1926, 1936—. 1 file box, 1 file drawer.

Original request filed by county commissioners, township trustees, corporation councils, and boards of education with the budget commission, showing year, name of subdivision, total value of taxable property, total expenditures during past year itemized by funds, estimated amount required for each or current year, total amount requested, signature of clerk and president of legislative body, and date filed. Arranged chronologically by years. No index. Handwritten and typed on printed forms. File box, 10.5 x 5 x 14; file drawer, 11 x 14 x 26. Auditor's main office.

458. AUDITOR'S CERTIFICATES
1934—. 1 file box.

Original certificates from county auditor to budget commission of amounts available from all sources for each subdivision, showing year, name of subdivision, total property value for taxation, and balance each fund at end of past year. Arranged chronologically by years. No index. Typed on printed forms. 10.5 x 5 x 14. Auditor's private office.

The county board of revision, the object of which was to correct some of the defects and inequities of tax assessments, was established by the legislature in 1825. The first board of revision, or equalization as it was sometimes called, was composed of the county commissioners, the county auditor, and the assessor. The board was authorized to meet at the seat of justice on the first Monday in June annually " to hear and determine the complaint of any owner of property listed and valued by the assessor . . . and shall correct any list or valuation made by the assessor, either by adding to or deducting from valuation."[1] the act of 1831, repealing the act of 1825, left the duties and personnel of the board unchanged.[2]

In 1859 the legislature made for provision for two county boards of equalization. One board, composed of the county auditor and the county commissioners, was directed to meet annually for the purpose of equalizing real and personal property, and moneys and credits in the county. The other board, composed of the county auditor, the county surveyor, and the county commissioners, was authorized to meet sexennially for the same purpose.[3]

The act of 1863 amending the act of 1859, left the personnel and duties of the annual county board unchanged. The second county board, although continuing without alteration and compensation or duties, was directed to meet decennially, rather than sexennially.[4] The legislative act of 1868, amending the act of 1863, left the membership of the annual and special boards, as well as their duties, practically unchanged.[5]

The annual and special boards of equalization were abolished, when, in 1913, the tax commission of Ohio was given the task of supervising the assessment of real and personal property in the state.[6] Under this arrangement each county constituted a district. In Seneca County and in each district containing less than 60,000 inhabitants, there was to be appointed by the governor one state tax commissioner. In all other districts that were appointed, in the same manner, two state deputy tax commissioners. In each district there was appointed a district board of complaints.

---

1. *Laws of Ohio,* XXIII, 64.
2. *Ibid.,* XXIX , 278.
3. *Ibid.,* LVI, 193- 194.
4. *Ibid.,* LX , 57, 59.
5. *Ibid.,* LXV, 168-170.
6. See also pp. XLVI, XLIX

This board, appointed by the state tax commission with the consent of the governor, took over the duties and powers formerly vested in the board of equalization. The county auditor, made secretary to the board of complaints, was required to present at each meeting in person or by deputy, and keep an accurate record of the proceedings to be kept in a book for that purpose.[7] Moreover, the board was directed to take full minutes of all evidence given before it and might have such evidence taken in shorthand and extended into typewritten form. The auditor was required to preserve in his office separate records of all meetings and documentary evidence offered in each complaint.[8]

This arrangement, after being in operation for two years, was obligated by the legislature in 1915. In that year the county auditor, under the supervision of the tax commission of Ohio, became the chief assessing officer in the county. The county treasurer, the county prosecuting attorney, the probate judge, and the president of the county commissioners were to serve as a board for the purpose of appointing three members to constitute a board of revision. The county auditor was again made secretary of the board and was directed to keep a record of the proceedings and to preserve in his office a separate record of all minutes and documentary evidence offered in each complaint.[9]

Under the present system, inaugurated in 1917, the county treasurer, the county auditor, and the president of the county commissioners constituted a board of revision. This board organizes annually, on the second Monday in June, by electing a chairman for the ensuing year. The county auditor serves as secretary of the board.[10] The county board of revision may, with the consent and approval of the tax commission of Ohio, employ experts, clerks, and other employees.[11]

The duties of the board, not differing in details from those prescribed in 1825, included the hearing of all complaints relating to valuation or assessments of both real and personal property as it appears upon a tax duplicate of the "then current year." The board is authorized to investigate all complaints and may increase or decrease any valuation or correct any assessment complained of, or may order a reassessment by the original assessing official.[12]

---

7. *Laws of Ohio,* CIII, 791.
8. *Ibid.,* CIII, 794.
9. *Ibid.,* CVI, 254-258.
10. G. C. sec. 5580.
11. G. C. sec. 5587.
12. G. C. sec. 5597.

However, no valuation is increased without giving notice to the person in whose name the property affected is listed.[13] The board of revision, in all respects, is governed by the laws relating to the valuation of real property and makes no change of any valuation " except in accordance with such laws."[14]

On the second Monday in June, annually, the county auditor lays before the board of revision the statements and returns of assessments of any personal property for the current year, and the board proceeds to review the returns. On the first Monday in July, annually, the auditor lays before the board the returns of assessments of any real property for the current year. The board of revision reviews the assessments and certifies its action to the county auditor who corrects the tax list and duplicate according to the additions and deductions ordered by the board. The auditor is prohibited by statute for making up his tax list and duplicate until the board has completed its work and has submitted to him all returns laid before it with revisions.[15] But in the event the tax duplicate has been delivered to the county treasurer, the auditor is required to certify such corrections to him and enter such corrections in his tax duplicate.[16]

In its investigations the board may examine, under oath, persons as to their or others' real property. In the event witnesses fail to appear or refuse to testify, the board through its chairman is authorized to make a complaint in writing to the probate judge, who, by statute, is directed to institute proceedings against them.[17] The decisions of the board are subject to appeal to the tax commission of Ohio, within thirty days after a decision is served.[18]

The secretary of the board is required to keep " an accurate record of the proceedings of the board in a book to be kept for that purpose."[19] The county auditor, as in 1913, is required to preserve in his office separate records of all minutes and documentary evidence offered in each complaint.[20] The records of the board are open to the inspection of the public.[21]

---

13. G. C. sec. 5599.
14. G. C. sec. 5596.
15. G. C. sec. 5605.
16. G. C. sec. 5602.
17. G. C. sec. 5596.
18. G. C. sec. 5610.
19. G. C. sec. 5592.
20. G. C. sec. 5603.
21. G. C. sec. 5591.

459. MINUTES OF DECENNIAL BOARD OF EQUALIZATION
1910. 1 volume. (2).

Copies of minutes of meetings of decennial board of equalization, showing date and place of meeting, and names of members present; record of complaints on assessment values of property for taxation filed by owners, showing name of owner, description and location of property, assessed value, reason of complaint, action by board, and amount of deduction on valuation, no change, or amount of addition to valuation ordered. Arranged chronologically by dates of meetings. No index. Handwritten. 400 pages. 18 x 12 x 2. County sealer's office.

460. MINUTES OF CITY BOARD OF REVIEW
1910-1911, 2 volumes. 1 subtitled Tiffin; 1, Fostoria.

Copies of minutes of meetings of city boards of review, cities of Tiffin and Fostoria, showing date and place of meeting, names of members present, notices of hearing on complaints filed on assessment values of real estate, names of complainants, lot number, description of lot, foot frontage, and assessed value; record of action by board on complaints, showing amount of deduction or addition to value, or no revision ordered. Arranged chronologically by dates of meetings. No index. Handwritten. Average 300 pages. 16 x 11 x .5. County sealer's office.

461. [MINUTE BOOK BOARD OF REVISION]
1914—. 1 volume,

Minutes of board of revision, showing date and place of meeting, names of members present, copies of complaints filed, tax assessments, names of complainants, description and location of property, nature of complaint, action of board on complaint giving amount of deduction, or no revision, or amount of addition to assessment. Arranged chronologically by dates of meetings. No index. Typed. 300 pages. 16.5 x 11 x 1.5. Auditor's vault.

462. COMPLAINTS
1914—. 3 file boxes.

Original complaints filed by property owners of assessment values on real and personal property, showing name of complainant, description and location of real estate or description of personal property, appraised or assessed value, amount of reduction asked, reason for reduction, and date filed. Arranged chronologically by dates filed. No index. Handwritten on printed forms. 10.5 x 5 x 14. Auditor's vault.

The board of trustees of the sinking fund, composed of the prosecuting attorney, auditor, and treasurer, was authorized in 1919 in Seneca County and in each county owing a bonded debt. The county prosecuting attorney serves as president of the board and the auditor as secretary. It is the duty of the trustees to provide for the payment of all bonds issued by the county and the interests maturing thereon.[1]

Since 1919 all bonds issued by the county had been required to be recorded in the office of the trustees of the sinking fund, and to bear a stamp containing the words "Recorded in the office of the sinking fund trustees" and be signed by the secretary before they became valid in the hands of any purchaser. In 1921 the act was amended to allow such recording and authenticating to be performed by the county treasurer and in 1935 these provisions were abrogated by the legislature.[2]

On or before the first Monday in May of each year, the trustees certified to the county commissioners the rate of tax necessary to provide a sinking fund both for the payment at maturity bonds heretofore issued by the county and for the pavement of interest on bonded indebtedness. The amount certified by the trustees is set forth without diminution in the annual budget of the commissioners.[3] Then, after each semiannual settlement of taxes and assessments, the county auditor reports to the trustees the amount of money in the treasury of the county charged to the credit of the sinking fund. Money is drawn from the county treasury for investment or disbursement by the issuance of a voucher signed by all the members of the board and directed to the county auditor. The trustees are directed, by statute, to invest all money subject to their control in United States bonds, Ohio bonds, or bonds of a municipal corporation, school district, township, or county in the state.

The board members are required to keep "a full and complete record of their transactions, a complete record of the funded debt of the county specifying the dates, purposes, amounts, numbers, maturities, and rates of maturities of interest and installments thereof, and where payable, and an account exhibiting the amount held in the sinking fund for the payment thereof." [4]

---

1. G. C. secs. 2976-18, 2976-19.
2. *Laws of Ohio,* CIX, 16; CXVI , 442.
3. G. C. sec. 2976-26.
4. G. C. sec. 2976-24.

The meetings of the trustees are open to the public. All questions relating to the purchase or sale of securities for the payment of bonds or interests are decided by a yea and nay vote, which is recorded in their journal.

463. JOURNAL

1921—. 1 volume. (1).

Minutes of sinking fund trustees, showing date and place of meeting, names of members present; record of bond issues approved and sold, showing authority, for issue, name, purpose, and amount of issue, denomination of bonds, serial numbers, date of maturity of issue, interest rate, interest due dates, where payable, to whom sold, number of bonds, serial numbers, par value, date of sale, and amount of premium. Arranged chronologically by dates of meetings. No index. Typed. 500 pages. 16 x 11 x 2.5. Auditor's vault.

(State Deputy Supervisors of Elections)

The responsibility for supervising and conducting elections in the county is delegated to the state deputy supervisors of elections–the county board of elections. This board, created by the legislature in 1891 and consisting of four qualified voters in the county, is appointed for a four-year term by the secretary of state, who, by virtue of his office, is the chief election official of the state.[1] On the first day of March in the even-numbered years, the secretary of state appoints two board members, one of whom is from the political party which polled the highest number of votes in the state for the office of governor at the last proceeding state election, and the other from the political party which polled the next highest vote at such elections.[2] The board members may be removed by the secretary of state for the neglect of duty, malfeasance, misfeasance in office, for willful violation of the election laws, or for other good and sufficient causes.[3] The compensation of the members is determined on the basis of population of the county and is paid by the county.[4] Similarly the expenses of the county board are paid from the county treasury, "in pursuance of appropriations by the county commissioners," in the same matter as other expenses are paid.[5]

The persons so appointed by the secretary, meeting five days after their appointment, select one of their members as chairman and a resident elector of the county who is not a member of the board as clerk.[6] The board is vested with authority to establish, define, and provide election precincts; fix places of registration; provide for purchase, preservation, and maintenance of voting booths, ballot boxes, books, maps, flags, blanks, card of instruction, and other equipment used in registration; and to issue rules, regulations, and instructions not inconsistent with the law or contrary to the rules and regulations as established by the chief election official.[7]

---

1. *Laws of Ohio,* LXXXVIII, 449.
2. G. C. sec. 4785- 8. For the method of appointment when the term of each of the four members of the board expires on the same date see G. C. sec. 4785-8a.
3. G. C. sec. 4785-11.
4. G. C. sec. 4785-18.
5. G. C. sec. 4785-20
6. G. C. sec. 4785-10.
7. G. C. sec. 4785-13.

Besides providing places of voting and equipment, the board is authorized to appoint clerks and other officers of elections. On or before the fifteenth day of September before each November election the board by a majority vote is authorized, after careful examination and investigation as to their qualifications, to appoint to each precinct six "competent persons, four as judges and two as clerks, who shall constitute the election officers of such precincts." Not more than two of the judges and one of the clerks, states the law, "shall be members of the same political party." Precinct election officers, appointed for a one-year term, may be removed by the board for neglect of duty, malfeasance, or misconduct in office.[8]

The county board of elections is authorized to receive and examine nominating petitions and to certify their sufficiency and validity. They receive the election returns, canvas the returns, then make abstracts therefrom and transmit them to the proper authorities. They issue certificates of elections on forms prescribed by the secretary of state and report annually to the same official, on forms prescribed by him, the number of voters registered, the elections held, votes cast, appropriations received, expenditures made, and such other information as the secretary of state may require. Moreover, the board prepares and submits to the property authorities a budget estimating the cost of elections for the ensuing year.[9]

Finally the board is empowered to investigate irregularities, non-performance of duty, or violation of election laws by election officials. For the purpose of conducting investigations they may administer oaths, issue subpoenas, summon witnesses, and compel the presentation of books, papers, and records in connection with any investigation and report the facts to the prosecuting attorney.[10]

The secretary of state, in 1930, ruled that the members of the various boards of elections were to be considered as state officers. This ruling had reference to appointments made under sections 4785-8 of the General Code.[11]

---

8. G. C. sec. 4785-25.
9. G. C. sec. 4785-13.
10. G. C. sec. 4785-13.
11. See George C. Trautwein, ed., *Supplement to Page's Annotated General Code 1926-1935,* note on p. 688.

The clerk of the board is required to keep a record of the proceedings of the board and of all moneys received and expended, and to file and preserve in his office all records of the board. Poll lists and tally sheets are to be preserved for two years, ballots for thirty days. These records are open to the inspection of the public under regulations established by the board.[12]

All records are located in the board of elections' vault.

---

12. G. C. secs. 4785-14, 4785-147.

Minutes

464 . MINUTE BOOK

1891—. 2 volumes. (2; 1 unlabeled)

Minutes of the board of elections, showing date and place of meeting, names of members present, approval of bills and claims, and names of precinct election officials appointed; annual statement of receipts and expenditures, showing receipts itemized, total amounts, expenditures itemized, and total amount. Arranged chronologically by dates of meetings. No index. Handwritten. Average 300 pages. 18 x 12 x 2.

Electors' Records

Registers

465. REGISTER OF ELECTORS

1912-1928. 191 volumes. (dated). Subtitled by names of voting districts. Quadrennial registration list of electors of Tiffin and Fostoria, showing name and address of elector, ward number, precinct letter or number, age, residence last registration, length of residence, occupation, nativity, if naturalized citizen, personal description, elector's signature, registration number, and remarks. Arranged numerically by registration numbers. For index, see entry 466. Handwritten on forms. Average 75 pages. 12 x 18 x .5.

466. ALPHABETICAL LIST OF ELECTORS

1912- 1928. 191 volumes. Subtitled by names of voting districts.

Index to Register of Electors, entry 465, showing name of elector, registry number, age, and residence. Arranged alphabetically by names of electors. Handwritten on forms. Average 75 pages. 14 x 10 x .5.

467. [REGISTRATION CARDS]

1930— .100 file drawers. (labeled by contained numbers and precinct numbers or letters).

File case contains original elector's registration cards, showing name and address of elector, ward number, precinct number or letter, date registered, residence at last registration, place of birth, nativity, personal description, and elector's signature; file drawers contain copies of elector's registration cards. File drawer arranged alphabetically by names of electors; file cases arranged numerically by ward numbers, thereunder by precincts and alphabetically thereunder by names of electors. No index. Handwritten on printed forms. File drawer, 1 x 10 x 24; file cases, 3.5 x 9 x 18.5.

468. APPLICATIONS FOR TRANSFER OF REGISTRATION

1931—. 1 file box.

Original applications by electors for transfer of registration to another precinct, showing name and old address of applicant, ward, and precinct; new address, ward, and precinct, and signature of applicants. Arranged alphabetically by names of applicants. No index. Handwritten on printed forms. 4 x 5.5 x 20.

469. REGISTRATION CARDS [Inactive]

1930—. 1 file box.

Registration cards withdrawn from current files because of death or removal from city, showing name and address of elector, ward; precinct, date registered, residence at last registration, place of birth, nativity, personal description, elector's signature, date withdrawn from current file, and reason for withdrawal. Arranged alphabetically by names of electors. No index. Handwritten on printed forms. 10.5 x 14 x 20.5.

Poll Books (See also entries 141-144)

470. POLL BOOKS AND TALLY SHEETS [General Elections]
1934—. 371 volumes. (dated). Subtitled by names of voting districts.

Precinct poll books and tally sheets general election: poll books, showing date of election, name of town, ward number, precinct letter of number or name of township and precinct number, voter's consecutive number, and name and address of voter; tally of votes received by each, and total votes received by each candidate; summary of ballots cast, showing number of ballots cast, number of unmarked ballots, number of defaced ballots, and names of precinct judges and clerks. Whole books arranged numerically by consecutive voter numbers; tally sheets by names of offices in order of importance. No index. Handwritten on forms. Average 20 pages. 22 x 16 x .25.

471. POLL BOOKS AND TALLY SHEETS [Primary elections]
1934—. 378 volumes. (dated). Subtitle by names of voting districts; also, Republican, Democrat.

Precinct poll books and tally sheets for primary elections; poll books, showing name of political party, date of election, name of town, ward, and precinct or township and precinct, voter's consecutive number, and name and address of voter; tally sheets, showing name of office, names of candidates, tally of votes received by each candidate, and total votes each candidate; summary of ballots cast, showing number of ballots cast, number of unmarked ballots, number of defaced ballots, and names of precinct judges and clerks. Poll books arranged numerically by voter's consecutive numbers; tally sheets, by names of offices in order of importance. No index. Handwritten on forms. Average 20 pages. 22 x 16 x .25.

472. POLL LIST
1934—. 168 volumes. Subtitled by names of voting districts.

Poll list of electors of city of Tiffin voting at general and primary elections, showing year, ward number, precinct letter or number, and name and address of elector. Arranged alphabetically by names of electors. No index. Handwritten on forms. Average 64 pages. 15 x 10 x .5.

473. ABSTRACT OF VOTES

1926—. 13 pigeonholes.

Certified abstracts of votes cast for each candidate and issue at general and primary elections, showing date of election, kind of election, statement of issues, names of offices sought, names of candidates for each office, votes cast for each candidate and each issue in each precinct, and total votes cast for each. Arranged chronologically by dates of elections. No index. Handwritten on printed forms. 10 x 10 x 18.

Absent Voters

474. APPLICATIONS FOR ABSENT VOTERS BALLOTS

1935—. 3 pigeonholes.

Original applications of absent and disabled voters for ballots, showing name and address of voter, sex, ward number, precinct letter or number, application number, date of application, manner of delivery, voting place, date of return, how received, and date of election. Arranged chronologically by dates of applications. No index. Handwritten on printed forms. 11 x 4.5 x 18.

475. REGISTER OF ABSENT VOTER'S BALLOTS

1918— . 2 volumes.

Register of absent voters' ballots, showing name of voter, township or town, ward number, precinct letter or number, application number, number of ballots delivered, date delivered, how delivered, date of return of ballots, and how returned. Arranged chronologically by dates returned. No index. Handwritten on forms. Average 200 pages. 14 x 9 x 1.

Candidates' Records

476. DECLARATION OF CANDIDACY

1925—. 1 file drawer.

Sworn statements of declaration of candidacy, showing name and address of candidate, name of city and county, pledge as member of respective party, office sought, petition to place name on ballot, names and addresses of signers, and dates filed. Arranged chronologically by dates filed. No index. Handwritten on printed forms. 10.5 x 14 x 20.

477. NOMINATING PETITIONS

1937—. 1 bundle.

Original nominating petitions filed by candidates when no primary election was held, showing name and address of candidate, name of office, town or township, ward number, precinct letter, names of signers, notarization, signature of candidate, and date filed. No index. Handwritten on printed forms. 6 x 11 x 17.

478. STATEMENT OF CANDIDATES

1919—. 1 file drawer, 1 pigeonhole.

Original sworn statements by candidates of amount of receipts and expenditures of funds received for election campaign expenses, showing date of statement, name and address of candidate, date of election, what office sought, itemized statement of expenditures, name of payee, amount, for what purpose expended, notarization, signature of candidate, and date filed. Arranged chronologically by dates filed. No index. Handwritten on printed forms. File drawer, 10.5 x 14 x 20.5; pigeonhole, 11 x 4.5 x 18.

479. STATEMENT OF CANDIDATES HAVING NO EXPENDITURES

1933—. 1 pigeonhole.

Original sworn statements by candidates having no election campaign contribution or expenditures, showing name and address of candidate, name of office sought, ward number, precinct letter or number, notarization, signature of candidate, and date filed. Arranged chronologically by dates filed. No index. Handwritten on printed forms. 11 x 4.5 x 18.

Appointments

(See also entry 483)

480. APPOINTMENT RECORD

1937—. 1 volume.

Record of appointments of precinct election judges and clerks, showing date of appointment, date of election, town, ward, precinct or township and precinct, name and title of appointee, political party, and by whom recommended. Arranged chronologically by dates of appointments. No index. Handwritten on forms. 325 pages. 11.5 x 9 x 1.5.

Financial Records

481. CASH BOOK

1916—. 1 volume.

Record of receipts and expenditures of funds: receipts, showing date of receipt, amount, and source; expenditures, showing date of expenditure, amount, for what, and what fund debited. Arranged chronologically by dates of entries. No index. Handwritten on forms. 200 pages. 11.5 x 11 x 1.

482. VOUCHERS

1934—. 2 volumes. (labeled by contained voucher numbers).

Stubs of vouchers issued for payment of bills and claims, showing date, voucher number, name of payee, amount, for what, and what fund debited. Arranged numerically by voucher numbers. No index. Handwritten on printed forms. Average 100 pages. 10.5 x 12.5 x 1.

483. APPOINTMENTS AND PAYROLLS

1891-1902 . 2 volumes.

Record of appointments and payroll for each voting precinct, showing name of presiding judge, names of judges and clerks, political party affiliation, date of appointment, amount of wage, and date paid. Arranged chronologically by dates of appointments. No index. Handwritten on forms. Average 300 pages. 16 x 11.5 x 1.5.

For other records of appointments, see entry 480.

484. RECEIPTS FOR FEES

1928—. 2 volumes.

Stubs of receipts for declaration of candidacy and filing fees, showing receipt number, name of candidate, name of office sought, date of election, date fee was paid, and amount of fee. Arranged chronologically by dates of entries. No index. Handwritten on printed forms. Average 100 pages. 10.5 x 13 x .5.

The county board of education, a modern administrative and supervisory agency developed during the last two decades, supplanted the smaller educational units, which, established during the early period of Ohio history, became inefficient and unable to meet the modern requirements as demanded by rural communities.

During the earlier period of Ohio history, educational administration, because of the newness of the state, the sparseness of the population, and the undeveloped means of transportation was, by necessity, local in character. For fourteen years after the accession of Ohio to statehood, though the constitution stated that means of education should be encouraged by the general assembly, no legislation was enacted for public schools.[1] It was not until 1817 that the legislature authorized six or more people to form associations to build school houses and to be incorporated for educational purposes.[2]

The first permanent law for the organization of schools in Ohio was passed in 1831. Under the provisions of this act, the electors of the township were authorized to vote on the proposition of dividing the townships into school districts. If the proposal carried, there were to be elected three school commissioners, who, in turn, were authorized to select a clerk and a collector who should act as a treasurer. They were instructed also, to levy taxes for the support of schools and to hire teachers.[3]

As education began to advance in the early years of the nineteenth century, some kind of state control was needed. Accordingly, in 1837, the office of state superintendent of schools was established.[4] A year later an act was passed making the county auditor also the county superintendent of schools; and in each township the clerk became superintendent of the smaller unit. The county superintendent was made responsible to the state superintendent in all educational affairs. In the same year each incorporated city, town, or borough not regulated by a charter was made a separate school district. The voters in each division were authorized to elect three directors.[5] The effectiveness of this organization, however, was destroyed in 1840, when the legislature abolished the office of state superintendent and the secretary of state took over his functions of tabulating and transmitting school statistics.[6]

---

1. *Ohio Const. 1802,* Art. VIII; secs. 3, 25, 27.
2. *Laws of Ohio,* XV, 107.
3. *Ibid.,* XIX, 52.
4. *Ibid.,* XXXV, 82.
5. *Ibid.,* XXXVI, 21.
6. *Ibid.,* XXXVIII, 130.

Seven years later, twenty-five counties inclusive of Seneca were allowed to have county superintendents,[7] and in 1848 the provision of the previous act were extended to Seneca and all other counties in the state.[8]

Although marked changes were made in the curricula of the schools, the history of education in Ohio from 1850 to the early part of the twentieth century was largely one of gradual transference of power from districts to townships, and from townships to county in the interest of a better system of education. It was not, however, until within the last three decades that the county became a unit for educational administration.[9]

Although the county superintendent was known as early as 1838, the first permanent law for the establishment of a county board of education was enacted in 1914. Under this act the school districts were classified, and provision was made for a county school district, exclusive of the territory embraced in any city or village having a population of three thousand or more desiring exemption. The county district was to be under the supervision of five board members elected by the presidents of the village and rural school boards. The members were to hold office for one, two, three, four, and five years respectively, and each year thereafter the members were to be selected to serve for a five-year term.[10]

The county board of education was authorized to change school district lines; afford transportation for children living more than two miles from a schoolhouse; appoint a county superintendent; and certify annually to the county auditor the number of teachers and superintendents employed, their salaries, and the amount apportioned to each school district for the payment of the salaries of the county and district superintendents. The county superintendent, acting as secretary of the board, was required to keep a book provided for the purpose a full record of the proceedings of the board properly indexed. Each motion, together with the name of the person making it and the vote thereon, was to be entered on the record.[11]

---

7. *Ibid.,* XLV, 32.
8. *Ibid.,* XLVI, 86.
9. *Ibid.,* LXX, 195, 242; XCVII, 354.
10. *Ibid.,* CIV, 133.
11. *Ibid.,* CIV, 133; CVIII, 704.

The county was divided into administrative divisions containing one or more villages or rural school districts. Each district was to be under the supervision of a district superintendent, who was required to visit the schools in his charge, direct and assist teachers in the performance of their duties, and classify and control promotion of pupils. Moreover, he was required to report annually to the county superintendent on matters under his charge, and assemble teachers for the purpose of conferring on curricular matters, discipline, and school management.[12]

Significant changes were made by an act of 1921, under which the board members became elective by popular votes. They were authorized to appoint one or more assistant county superintendents for a term of three years. Seneca county, however, has no assistant. The board was authorized to publish, with the advice and consent of the county superintendent, a minimum course of study to serve as a guide to local board members. The same act abolished the office of district superintendent.[13]

The county organization has placed the rural schools on a plane of equality with the city schools. The consolidation of the smaller units has eliminated the small, ill-equipped schools, and provides, under one roof, facilities and instruction suited to the needs of the rural children under the supervision of educational specialists.

All records are located in the office of the county superintendent of schools, 70 East Market Street, Tiffin, Ohio.

---

12. *Laws of* Ohio, CIV, 133-145.
13. G. C. secs. 4728-1, 4729; *Laws of Ohio,* CIX, 242.

Minutes and Reports

485. RECORD OF MINUTES

1914—. 2 volumes.

Minutes of the board of education, showing date and place of meeting, names of members present, resolutions and motions introduced and considered, yay and nay votes, and approval of bills and claims filed; record of transfer of territory from one school district to another, showing names of districts, description of territory, names of property owners involved, and reason for transfer. Arranged chronologically by dates of meetings. No index. Handwritten. Average 375 pages. 11.5 x 8.5 x 2.

For separate record of transfers, see entry 497.

486. FINANCIAL REPORTS

1930—. 6 envelopes.

Copies of annual financial reports from superintendent of schools to state department of education, showing year of report, receipts itemized, date credited, amount, from what source, what fund credited, total receipts each fund, and grand total; expenditures classified by funds, showing name of fund, date of expenditure, name of payee, amount, for what, total each fund, and grand total; credit or debit balance each fund, total credit or debit balance, and date filed. Arranged chronologically by years. No index. Handwritten and typed on printed forms. 12 x 9 x .25.

487. STATISTICAL REPORTS

1934—. 3 envelopes.

Copies of annual statistical reports from superintendent of schools to state department of education, showing year of report, name of school district, total taxable property value, total school taxes levied, itemized statement of income from other sources, total receipts, expenditures classified under amount teachers' salaries, amount for supervision, fuel, janitor salary, bond principal and interest, transportation, incidentals, total expenditures, total outstanding indebtedness, number of school buildings, number of rooms, number of teachers employed, number of principals, number of elementary pupils, boys and girls, number of high school pupils, boys and girls, number of elementary school graduates, number of high school graduates, number of weeks school in session, average daily attendance, boys and girls, total average, number of school bus routes, number of pupils transported to and from school, and grand total each item for county. Arranged chronologically by years. No index. Handwritten and typed. 12 x 9 x .25.

Teachers' Records

488. APPLICATIONS

1926—. 1 file box.

Original applications filed for teaching positions, showing application number, name and address of applicant, age, sex, place of birth, number of months experience, kind of certificate, name of school preferred, names and addresses of references, and date filed. Arranged chronologically by dates filed. No index. Handwritten and typed on printed forms. 9 x 5 x 19.

489. RECORD [Teachers Examinations]

1889-1913 ,1923-1929. 4 volumes. (4 -6 ; 1 unlabeled).

Record of examination of applicants for teaching certificates, showing date and place of examination, names of examiners, names and addresses of applicants, age, sex, branches examined in, grades, teaching experience, average grade, type of certificate issued (if passing grade received), Arranged chronologically by dates of examinations and alphabetically thereunder by names of applicants. No index. Handwritten on forms. Average 200 pages. 17 x 14 x 1.5.

490. TEACHERS' CERTIFICATES [Stubs]

1922-1935. 7 volumes. Discontinued; law repealed.

Stubs of teachers certificates issued on examination to successful applicants, showing certificate number, name of teacher, grades received on examination, average grade, kind of certificate, and date issued. Arranged numerically by certificate numbers. No index. Handwritten on printed forms. Average 100 pages. 8.5 x 10 x .5.

Pupils' Records

491. ATTENDANCE RECORDS

1935—. 2 bundles.

Original monthly attendance reports of each pupil from teachers, showing year, month, name of school, grade, name of pupil, age, days present, days absent, times tardy, average attendance for month, date filed, and name and address of teacher. Arranged chronologically by months and alphabetically thereunder by names of pupils. No index. Handwritten on forms. 8.5 x 14 x 3.

492. ATTENDANCE PERCENTAGE

1927—. 1 envelope.

Record of attendance percentages, showing year, name of township or special district, name of school, name of teacher, grade, daily enrollment of boys and girls, total, average daily attendance boys and girls, total, totals for each school, total for each township or special district, totals for county, and date filed. Arranged chronologically by dates filed. No index. Handwritten on printed forms. 9 x 12 x 1.

493. CARD INDEX, PUPILS

1930—. 3 bundles, 1 file drawer, 1 file box.

Card record of pupils enrolled in elementary schools, showing name of school, name of township, name of pupil, age, birth date, birthplace, sex, grade, record of immunization and vaccinations, and name and address of parent or guardian. Arranged alphabetically by names of townships, alphabetically thereunder by names of schools and thereunder by names of pupils. No index. Handwritten on printed forms. Bundles, 1930-1936, 4.5 x 6 x 8; file box, 1937, 5 x 7.5 x 8; file drawer, 1938—, 5 x 7.5 x 18.5.

494. RECORD OF GRADUATES

1915—. 1 volume.

Record of graduates from elementary schools, showing name and address of pupil, age, sex, date of graduation, name of township, and name of school district. Arranged chronologically by dates of graduation. No index. Handwritten on forms. 200 pages. 11 x 8 x 1.

Financial Records

495. BILLS

1927—, 10 envelopes. (dated).

Original bills and claims filed by creditors, showing bill number, date of bill, name and address of creditor, item, quantity, unit price, total price, total of bill, date filed, date approved, and voucher number. Arranged chronologically by dates approved, no index. Handwritten and typed. 5.5 x 9.5 x 1.

496. SCHOOL TREASURER'S ACCOUNTS

1914-1916. 1 volume.

Treasurer's record of credits and debits school funds. Credits, showing name of fund, date of credit, amount, from what source; debits, showing date of expenditure, name of payee, amount, for what, warrant number, and monthly credit or debit balance. Arranged by names of funds and chronologically thereunder by dates of credits and debits. No index. Handwritten on forms. 200 pages. 14 x 9 x 1.5.

Transfers
(See also entry 485)

497. TRANSFERS
1914— . 27 folders.
Record of transfer of territory from one district to another consisting of owners petition for transfer, remonstrance petitions against transfer, notice of hearing on petition, resolution of board of education approving or rejecting petition for transfer, showing date of various papers filed, names of school districts affected, description of territory to be transferred with boundaries defined, name and addresses of petitioners, and reason for transfer. All papers of each transfer file together in folder showing name of school districts. Arranged chronologically by dates of filing. No index. Handwritten and typed. 11 x 14.

The general health district, or county health department, is one of the recent developments in county health administration. An act of the legislature in 1919 provided that townships and municipalities in each county, exclusive of any city with 25,000 population, should constitute a general health district; cities with 25,000 or more population a municipal health district; and municipalities of not less than 10,000 nor more than 25,000 population and maintaining a board of health meeting the qualifications of the legislative act, were authorized after examination by the state health department to continue operation as separate health districts.[1]

An amendment in December 1919 made each city a health district; the townships and villages in each county were combined into a general health district; and a city and general health district might combine for administrative purposes.[2] The mayor of each municipality not constituting a city health district, and the chairman of the trustees of each township, are authorized to meet at the seat of justice and by selecting a chairman and a secretary organize a district advisory council which selects and appoints a district board of health composed of five members, one of whom must be a physician, who serves without compensation.[3]

Within thirty days after their appointment the members of the district board of health–the county board of health–organized by appointing one of their members president and another president pro tempore. The board is authorized to appoint as district health commissioner a licensed physician who servers as secretary to the board. This official is designated deputy state registrar of vital statistics and is required to report monthly to the state registrar of vital statistics.[4]

On recommendations of the district health commissioner the board appoints a full-time public health nurse, a clerk, and such additional public health nurses, physicians, and others as may be necessary for the proper conduct of its work. The board studies the prevalence of disease, especially communicable diseases, provide treatment for venereal diseases, and is authorized to make any and all regulations it deems necessary for the prevention or restriction of disease, and the prevention, abolition, or suppression of nuisances.

---

1. *Laws of Ohio,* CVIII, pt. i, 238.
2. *Ibid.,* CVIII, pt. ii, 1085.
3. *Ibid.,* CVIII, pt. ii, 1085.
4. G. C. sec. 1261-32; *Laws of Ohio,* CVIII, pt. i, 238-242.

It provides for inspection of public charitable, benevolent, correctional, and penal institutions; and may provide inspection of dairies, stores, restaurants, hotels, and other places where food is manufactured, handled, stored, sold, or offered for sale. The board is authorized to carry on necessary laboratory tests by established a laboratory or by contracting with existing laboratories. All state institutions supported in whole or in part by public funds must furnish such laboratory service to a county board of health under the terms agreed upon.[5]

The health department is financed by public taxation. The district board of health annually estimates in itemized form the amount needed for the fiscal year, and these estimates are certified to the county auditor and submitted by him to the county budget commissioners who may reduce any item but cannot increase any item or the aggregate of all items. The total amount fixed by the budget commissioners is apportioned by the county health department on the basis of taxable valuations in the townships and municipalities composing the district.[6]

All records are located and board of health office.

---

5. *Laws of Ohio,* CVIII, pt. ii, 1088, 1089.
6. *Ibid.,* CVIII, ii, 1091.

Minutes and Reports

498. RECORD OF MINUTES

1920— .4 volumes . (1-4).

Minutes of county (or district) health board, showing date and place of meeting, and names and members present; records of complaints concerning sanitary conditions filed by residents, showing name of complaint, nature of complaint, and action taken on complaint; record of reports are contagious diseases, showing name and address of patient, name of attending physician, name of disease, date reported, date quarantined, and dates released from quarantine; record of bills and claims filed and approved for payment, showing date of bill, name of creditor, amount, for what, date approved, and voucher number; and all other routine matters pertaining to the department. Arranged chronologically by dates of meetings. No index. Typed. Average 130 pages. 12 x 9 x 1.

499. MINUTES OF ADVISORY COUNCIL
1920—. 1 volume.

Minutes of district advisory council, showing date and place of meeting, names of members present, record of appointments, giving name of appointee and position or capacity, and resolutions of approval of administration of department. Arranged chronologically by dates of meetings. No index. Typed. 150 pages. 12 x 9 x 1.

500. REPORTS
1920—. 19 envelopes.

Copies of monthly and annual reports from county health commissioner to state board of health, showing period of report, number cases of contagious diseases each type, total, number cases of communicable diseases each type, total, number births, number deaths classified as the cause, total all causes, number school children vaccinated, number antitoxin administrations, number of restaurants, dairies, and retail food establishments inspected, number visits to indigent patients, number visits made by county visiting nurse, other miscellaneous items, and date filed. Arranged chronologically by dates filed. No index. Handwritten on printed forms. 10 x 12 x .5.

501. RECORD OF EXAMINATIONS
1926— .1 file drawer.

Report of periodic examination of school pupils by visiting nurse, showing name of township, name of school, name of pupil, age, birth date, sex, color, weight, height, notation of any defects, name and address of parents or guardian, date of examination, and name of health commissioner and visiting nurse. Arranged alphabetically by names of townships, alphabetically thereunder by names of schools, and alphabetically thereunder by names of pupils. No index. Handwritten on printed forms. 11.5 x 14 x 2.

Vital Statistics

(See also entries 260-2 62 , 510)

502. BIRTH RECORD
1908—. 12 volumes . (labeled by district numbers).

Copies of birth certificates, showing certificate number, primary district number 1920—, name of child, date of birth, place of birth, sex, color, name and age of father, maiden name and age of mother, father's occupation, residence of parents, name of attending physician, and date filed. Arranged chronologically by dates filed. For index, see entry 503. Typed on printed forms. Average 250 pages. 14.5 x 10.5 x 1.5.

503. BIRTH RECORD INDEX

1908—. 1 volume.

Index to birth record, entry 502, showing name of child, date of birth, certificate number, and volume and page number of record. Arranged alphabetically by the names of children. Typed on forms. 150 pages. 14 x 9 x 1.

504. DEATH RECORD

1908—. 14 volumes. (labeled by district numbers).

Copies of death certificates, showing certificate number, primary district number 1920—, name of deceased, late residence, date of death, place of death, age, birth date, color, occupation, cause of death, name of physician signing certificate, place of internment, name of undertaker, and date filed. Arranged chronologically by dates filed. For index, see entry 505. Typed on printed forms. Average 200 pages. 14.5 x 10.5 x 1.

505. DEATH RECORD INDEX

1908—. 1 volume.

Index to Death Record, entry 504, showing name of deceased, date of death, certificate number, and volume and page number of record. Arranged alphabetically by names of decedents. Typed on forms. 150 pages. 14 x 9 x 1.

506. REPORTS, CONTAGIOUS DISEASES

1920—. 2 volumes.

Record of reports of contagious diseases, filed by physicians, showing date of report, date of first visit, name and address of patient, age, sex, color, diagnosis, date quarantine posted, termination of case, date quarantine released, and name of attending physician. Arranged chronologically by dates of reports. No index. Typed on forms. Average 250 pages. 14.5 x 9.5 x 1.

507. VENEREAL DISEASES

1920—. 1 volume.

Record of reports of venereal diseases filed by physicians, showing name and address of patient, date reported, age, sex, color, diagnosis, termination of case, and name of physician reporting case. Arranged chronologically by dates reported. No index. Typed on forms. 150 pages. 14.5 x 9.5 x 1.

Financial Records
(See also entry 510)

508. LEDGER
1920—. 1 volume. (1).
Record of credits and debits: credits, showing name of fund, date credited, amount, and source of credit; debits, showing name of fund, date debited, name of payee, amount, and for what; semiannual balance or deficit each bond, and total credit or debit balance. Arranged chronologically by dates of credits and debits. No index. Handwritten on forms. 250 pages. 11 x 14 x 1.5.

509. ACCOUNT BOOK
1921—. 1 volume.
Record of accounts with physicians for services in quarantining homes and vaccinating and immunizing school pupils, showing name of physician, date of account, amount, for what service, and date paid. Arranged chronologically by dates of accounts. No index. Handwritten on forms. 100 pages. 14 x 9 x 1.

Miscellaneous
(See also entries 502, 508)

510. MISCELLANEOUS
1933—. 1 file drawer.
Miscellaneous records consisting of copies of annual budget requests to budget commission, showing date of request, expenditures for past year, itemized by funds, totals, estimated amount required for current year itemized by funds, and total estimates; list of births for 1936, showing name of child, date of birth, sex, color, name of father, maiden name of mother, and residence of parents; record of treatments afforded crippled children, showing name of child, age, nature of deformity, and improvement in case; record of laboratory services, showing nature of service, and date. Arranged alphabetically by subjects and chronologically thereunder by dates of records. No index. Handwritten and typed. 11.5 x 14 x 26.

In 1908 the county commissioners were authorized to use county funds, levy taxes, or sell bonds for the construction and maintenance of a county tuberculosis hospital. The infirmary directors were given the duty of providing care, treatment, and maintenance for the patients at such hospitals and the expenses incurred were to be paid as were other expenditures for county infirmary purposes. In the event the county commissioners did not provide a county tuberculosis hospital they were authorized to contract with a municipal tuberculosis hospital in the county or with the tuberculosis hospital of any county for the care of its patients. Upon presentation of the facts by the state board of health, the probate judge was authorized to order for removal of a tuberculus person from the infirmary to a place of treatment.[1]

The district hospitals for pulmonary tuberculosis were established under authority of an act of the legislature in 1909 which allowed the commissioners of not less than two nor more than five counties to form themselves into a joint board and to appoint a board of trustees, of one member from each county represented. A later act in 1921 authorized the county commissioners to act as a board of trustees.[2]

In 1913 it had become increasingly evident to the legislature that the tuberculus patients were not receiving the proper care and in many instances were left in the county infirmary to the jeopardy of the general health. It was therefore ordered that such patients should be transferred to a hospital or other institution in the state for treatment and maintained there at the expense of the county of legal residence, or if not a resident of the state at the expense of the county maintaining the infirmary from which removal was made.[3]

If a person suffering from tuberculosis is found in the infirmary of a county not maintaining a tuberculosis hospital or participating in a joint hospital, the state board of health may order his removal to a municipal, county, or district hospital for tuberculosis. The state board of health has general supervision of county and district hospitals for tuberculosis and shall prescribe and may enforce rules and regulations.[4]

---

1. *Laws of Ohio,* XCIX, 62, 63, 121.
2. *Ibid.,* C, 86-88; CVIII, pt. i, 253; CIX, 212.
3. *Ibid.,* CIII, 492.
4. *Ibid.,* CVII, 495-499.

The remodeling was completed at a cost of $18,888.82. Space was provided in the main building for nontubercular inmates requiring hospitalization. They remodeled structure provided segregation and special care for tubercular patients.[5] The hospital is located two and a half miles south of Tiffin, Ohio, on State Route 100.

---

5. Commissioners' journal, XXXVI, 355, 419, 488.

511. CASE CARDS

1936—. 2 file boxes. 1 subtitled Active Cases; 1, Inactive Cases. Record of each tubercular patient in hospital, showing name and address, case number, marital status, date admitted, date discharged or date of death, age, date of birth, religion, and diagnosis. Arranged alphabetically by names of patients. No index. Handwritten on forms. 3.5 x 5 x 3. Superintendent's office, Hospital, County Home grounds, Tiffin, Ohio.

512. RECORD OF INDIVIDUAL PATIENTS

1936—. 50 folders (labeled by names of patients and case numbers). Complete case history of each patient admitted to hospital, showing clerical charts, county nurses' record sheets, certificate of indigency charged stating the facts warranting admission of applicant for relief indicated. One for each patient admitted, except a few cared for prior to the time the complete records were kept; front cover of folder, showing name of patient and case number, date of admission, name and address of person or physician by whom referred, condition of patient on admission, name of attending physician, name of admitting officer, preliminary diagnosis, final diagnosis, condition on discharge, and signature of nurse. No obvious arrangement. No index. Handwritten and handwritten on printed forms. 12 x 9. Superintendent's office, Hospital, County Home grounds, Tiffin, Ohio.

513. PATIENTS' RECORD

1936—. 1 notebook.

General census record of hospital, showing name of patient, case number, date admitted, date discharge, released to another hospital, or date of death. Beginning at back page is a statistical record for each month, 1937—, listing names of patients in hospital at the beginning of month, those admitted during month with date admitted, those discharged during month with date of discharge, and those who died during month with date and hour of death. Arranged alphabetically by names of patients. No index. Handwritten on forms. 100 pages. 10 x 8 x .5. Superintendent's office, Hospital, County Home grounds, Tiffin, Ohio.

By the provisions of the legislative act of 1816, the county commissioners were authorized to build a "poor house," and to appoint annually seven persons to constitute a board of directors. This board, a corporate body, was authorized to make such rules and regulations as were necessary for the management of the institution, and to appoint a superintendent. This officer was directed to receive only persons who had the required order from the township trustees. He was directed to keep a book listing the name and age of every person received, together with the date of admission.[1] The board of directors, or a committee of that board, was required to visit the "poor house" monthly to examine the condition of the institution and to make a report on such matters as the food, clothing, and treatment of the inmates. Moreover, they were required to inspect the books and accounts of the superintendent. The board was required to report annually to the county commissioners the "state of the institution" with a full and correct account of all their proceedings, contracts, and disbursements; and the expense of establishing and supporting the institution were to be paid on the order of the county commissioners out of the money in the treasury not otherwise appropriated.[2]

By the legislative act of 1831, the membership of the board was reduced to three. This board, like its predecessor, was authorized to appoint a superintendent. It was his duty, upon the order of the board, to discharge from the poorhouse any person who had been admitted because of illness when he had sufficiently recovered.[3] Moreover, the directors were authorized to remove paupers to their legal place of residence.[4] Besides this, any pauper rejected by the board of directors could be turned over to the township overseers to be cared for by contracting with the lowest bidders.[5] In 1842 the board was made elective for a three-year term.[6]

In 1850 the name county poorhouse was changed to that of county infirmary.[7] Fifteen years later, in 1865, the board of infirmary directors, consisting of three resident electors, was to be elected by the voters of the county for a three-year term.

---

1. *Laws of Ohio,* XIV, 447.
2. *Ibid.,* XIV, 499.
3. *Ibid.,* XXIX, 316.
4. *Ibid.,* XXIX, 316.
5. *Ibid.,* XXIX, 321-322.
6. *Ibid.,* XL, 35.
7. *Ibid.,* XLVIII, 62.

The board was still authorized to appoint a superintendent, and was still required to make inspection visits, and report their findings to the county commissioners.[8]

Although reports have been required in previous years, it was not until the decade of the 1870s that the legislature enacted laws looking forward to some business-like management of this ancient institution. Accordingly, in 1872, an act was passed which required each infirmary director, as well as the superintendent, to give bond conditioned for the faithful performance of their duties of his office.[9] Under this act the directors were required to report semi-annually to the county commissioners the condition of the infirmary, the number of inmates, and such other information as the county commissioners believed proper. Furthermore, the board of directors was required to file a full account "of all moneys received and paid out, together with a vouchers . . . from whence received, to whom and for what paid out" with the county commissioners, who, after examining it, entered the report in the minutes of their proceedings. This report, as well as the vouchers, was to be filed in the auditor's office, and was to be "safely preserved" by that office.[10]

The county infirmary served also as a place for the confinement of children, the mentally ill, and person afflicted with epilepsy. Although the state assumed responsibility for the mentally ill in the early years of the nineteenth century, it was not until 1898 that it was made unlawful to confine adult insane and epileptics in the county home.[11] Previously, in 1884, the legislature prohibited the housing of children in the county infirmary who were eligible to the county children's home or to some other charitable institution unless separated from adults.[12] However, exceptions were made in the case of insane, idiotic, and epileptic children.[13] The latter provision is still effective in Ohio.[14]

By an act of May 31, 1911, effective January 1, 1913, the board of infirmary directors was abolished and the powers formally exercised by this body were transferred to the county commissioners and the infirmary superintendent[15] The superintendent was required to keep a record of the inmates, as prescribed by statute, and to report annually to the county commissioners.

---

8. *Ibid.,* LXII, 24-25.
9. *Laws of Ohio,* LXIX, 120-121.
10. *Ibid.,* LXIX, 121-122.
11. *Ibid.,* XCIII, 274.
12. *Ibid.,* LXXXI, 92.
13. *Ibid.,* CIII, 890.
14. G. C. sec. 3091.
15. *Laws of Ohio,* CII, 433.

This report, the acceptance of which was evidenced by entry in the commissioners' journal was filed with the county auditor and by him preserved.[16] In 1919 the name county infirmary was changed to that of county home.[17]

Under the General Code county commissioners are still authorized to make provisions for the establishment and maintenance, of the county home, appoint a superintendent, and make regular inspection visits. The superintendent is appointed from a list of names of persons eligible under civil service regulations.[18] The superintendent is authorized to appoint a matron and other employees.[19] Moreover, since 1882, they have been authorized to appoint an infirmary physician, who, like the superintendent, is required by statute to report to the county commissioners. This report, made quarterly, includes such information as the nature and extent of medical services rendered, to whom, and the character of the disease treated.[20]

Although there is some relation between the old age pension system and the county home the newer form of aid is merely supplementary to the institution. As always the county home cares for those whose condition is such that they cannot be satisfactorily cared for except in an institution.[21] Since the inauguration of aid for the aged there has been a slight reduction in the population of the county homes throughout the state.[22] An act of 1937 provides that whenever the buildings of a county home become unsuitable for habitation, or its inmates are too few for economic operation, or for any other reason made of record, the county commissioners may close it and make other provisions for the care of the inmates and others who may become charges of the county by reason of indigency.[23]

The Seneca County board of county commissioners took up the question of establishing an infirmary as early as June 7, 1841, but it was not until March 18, 1854 that a decision was reached as to a site for the home.[24] The institution is located on State Route 100, two and a half miles south of Tiffin, Ohio. Its 251.96 acres represent three purchases of farmland.[25]

---

16. G. C. sec. 2535. See entry 9.
17. *Laws of Ohio,* CVIII, 68.
18. Ohio Attorney General, *Opinions,* III, 2021.
19. G. C. sec. 2522.
20. G. C. sec. 2546; *Laws of Ohio,* LXXXIII, 233; LXXIX, 90; CII, 436; CVIII, pt. i, 269.
21. *The reorganization a county government in Ohio* . . . 132, 135.
22. Ohio Auditor of State, *Comparative Statistics, Counties of Ohio, passim.*
23. *Laws of Ohio,* CVXII, 313.
24. Warner, Beers and Co. *Op. cit.,* 259.
25. Deed Record, XXVIII, 26, 215; XXIX, 62.

For a time the original farm buildings were used. The first new building erected is the main building of an ever growing group of useful structures. All are brick except the barns, chicken houses, and hog houses. An extensive remodeling program was undertaken in 1935 as a WPA project. The program included additions, remodeling, redecorating, and general renovation. Included in the project were fireproofing, heating, plumbing, electrical work, waterproofing, and painting. The Seneca County Home, at present, has a capacity of 90 inmates. There are now domiciled within its comfortable quarters a total of 84 persons who call it their home.

All records are located in the superintendent's office, county home, State Route 100, Tiffin, Ohio, unless otherwise specified.

Minutes and Reports

514. JOURNAL

1900-1912 .1 volume. Discontinued; board of infirmary directors abolished. Minutes of board of infirmary directors consisting of resolutions, motions, orders, and approvals of appointments relative to administration of infirmary affairs, showing date and place of meeting, names of members present, title and text of resolutions, motions, etc., record of yay and nay votes, names of appointees, to what position, and appointments made by superintendent. Chronological by dates of meetings. Indexed alphabetically by subjects or names of principals. Handwritten. 600 pages. 16 x 11 x 3. C. C., Auditor's vault.

For subsequent journal of county home, see entry 3.

515. DAILY MOVEMENT OF POPULATION

1933—, 6 volumes. Prior records missing.

Daily record of movement of population, showing day of month, number of males and females on hand at beginning of day, number received during day, number discharge during day with totals in each group; also average and total for months; each page is one month's record and at bottom of page is shown the number continuously present during month, number of deaths during month and number of persons received who were former inmates; the record also shows number of males, females, and total in each classification. One page in back of book has summary of the year by months, showing daily average of inmates, number received during each month and number discharge during each month; also number of deaths each month with name of deceased and date of death. Arranged chronologically by months and days. No index. Handwritten on forms. Average 12 pages. 14 x 9 x .25.

516. REPORTS OF SUPERINTENDENT TO STATE DIVISION OF CHARITIES

1913-1914, 1917—. 1 file box.

Copies of superintendent's annual reports to the state division of charities, department of public welfare, showing date of report, all expenditures and receipts, expenses for new equipment and structures, improvements, general statistics covering inmates, analysts of inmates as to age, physical and mental condition, nativity and color, a statement of amount expended for outside relief or care of indigence outside of home; includes inventory giving total number of acres, acres of improved land, estimated value of land, buildings, furniture, livestock, and machinery. Arranged chronologically by years. No index. Typed on printed forms. 10 x 4.5 x 13.5.

For Commissioners copies, see entry 9.

Case Records

517. RECORD OF INMATES

1856—. 3 volumes. (1-3).

Register of indigents admitted to county home, showing, 1856-1881, brief case history of inmate, name, from what township admitted, names, relationship and addresses of relatives, cause of indigency, previous occupation and habits, age, sex, color, physical and mental condition, nativity, date admitted, and date discharged or died; register of admissions, 1881—, showing date of admission, name, age, birth date, birthplace, sex, color, nativity, from what town or township admitted, physical and mental condition, and date of discharge or death. 1856-1881, arranged chronologically by dates of entries; 1881—, arranged alphabetically by names of inmates. 1856-1881, indexed alphabetically by names of inmates; 1881—, no index. Handwritten on forms. Average 575 pages. 18 x 13 x 3.

518. CERTIFICATE OF INDIGENCY

1900—. 1 file box.

Original certificates of indigency filed by township trustees certifying that named persons are eligible to provide and care for themselves and are making application for admission to county home, showing date of certificate, name of township, name of indigent, age, sex, color, names of relatives, how long resided in township, place of residence before locating in county, date of last relief provided, cause of indigency, care required if any, and signature of township trustees. Arranged chronologically by dates of certificates. No index. Handwritten on printed forms. 5 x 4.5 x 9.

519. TOWNSHIP CLERK BOARD OF EDUCATION [Poor Relief Record]
1913-1920. 1 volume.
Record of relief provided outside county home from county home fund, showing name and address, township, date investigated, number in family, ages, nature of relief provided, amount, by whom investigated, date investigated, date relief provided. Arranged chronologically by dates relief provided. Indexed alphabetically by names of clients. Handwritten on forms. 150 pages. 14 x 9 x 1. County courthouse Auditor's vault.

520. MEDICAL AND NARCOTIC RECORD
May 5, 1937—. 1 volume. Prior records missing.
A day by day record of narcotics administered to inmates, showing date, amount in grains, kind of narcotic given, name of patient, and name of physician prescribing narcotic. Arranged chronologically by dates narcotic given. No index. Handwritten. 200 pages. 4.25 x 12 x .5.

Financial Records

521. LEDGER
1912-19 36. 1 volume.
Superintendent's record of income of inmates from outside sources, showing date of entry, name of inmate, from what source or from whom received, amount, and for what purpose used. Arranged alphabetically by names of inmates and chronologically thereunder by dates of entries. No index. Handwritten on forms. 152 pages. 14 x 9 x 1. County courthouse Auditor's vault.

522. DAY BOOK

1886-1921. 4 volumes.

Superintendent's record of supplies and materials purchased, showing date purchased, item, unit price, from whom purchased, and total cost. Arranged chronologically by dates purchased. No index. Handwritten on forms. Average 275 pages. 14 x 9 x 1.5. County courthouse Auditor's vault.

523. CASH BOOK

1886-1912. 6 volumes.

Superintendent's record of farm crops, produce, and livestock produced, showing date of entry, item, number of bushels or pounds or number of heads of livestock, amount of each consumed at institution, value, amount of each sold, cash credit, total credit for year, number of meals served each year, and average monthly registration. Arranged chronologically by dates of entries. No index. Handwritten on forms. Average 275 pages. 14 x 9 x 1.5. Auditor's vault.

Inventories

524. INVENTORY OF COUNTY INFIRMARY

1904-1923. 2 volumes.

Record of annual inventory of county infirmary equipment and furnishings, showing date equipment and livestock received, total value of equipment and livestock, from whom purchased, description of property, purchase price, number of acres, value of farm lands, value of buildings, and total value of farm lands and buildings. Arranged chronologically by dates of entries. No index. Handwritten. Average 150 pages. 5.5 x 11.5 x .5. Auditor's vault.

The board of county visitors, an agency for the examination and inspection of county institutions supported wholly or on part by county municipal taxation, was created by an act of the general assembly in 1882. Under this act, the judge of the court of common pleas was authorized to appoint five persons, three of whom were to be women, who were to visit periodically such county institutions as the county infirmary, county jail, municipal prisons, and children's home, and file annually a report of their proceedings and recommendations for changes with the clerk of courts, and to forward a copy to the state board of charities. The members, appointed for an indefinite period, were to serve without compensation.[1]

By the act of 1892 the personnel of the board was increased to six persons, three of whom were to be women, and not more than three to have the same political affiliation. Furthermore the act made it the duty of the probate judge, whenever proceedings were instituted in his court to commit a child under sixteen years of age to the boys' industrial home or to the girls' industrial home, to have noticed given to the board of such proceedings; and it made the duty of the board of visitors to attend the meetings of the court, as a body or as a committee, to protect the interest of the child.[2]

While the provisions of the act of 1892 were redefined by the acts of 1898 and 1900, these acts did not, in the main, affect the duties of the board.[3] The latter act, however, made the board a continuous body with two members serving for one year, two members serving for two years, and two members serving for three years. In addition to this, the board was allowed a minimum expense schedule for the services.[4] Six years later the board was authorized to recommend to the county commissioners measures for the more economic administration of county institutions. Their report, together with their recommendations, was to be filed each year with the judge of probate court and with the prosecuting attorney. The power of appointment of members of the board of county visitors was given to the judge of probate court.[5]

---

1. *Laws of Ohio,* LXXIX, 107.
2. *Ibid.,* LXXXIX, 161.
3. *Ibid.,* XCIII, 57; XCIV, 70.
4. *Ibid.,* XCIV, 70.
5. *Ibid.,* XCVIII, 28.

By provisions of an act of 1913 the juvenile judge, like the probate judge under the act of 1892, was authorized to notify the visitors when any proceedings were instituted in his court for the commitment of any child to a state institution for correction.[6] The practice of annually filing reports of the board with the probate judge, prosecuting attorney, and states board of charities has been continued.[7]

The board of county visitors keep no separate records; for record of appointments, 1891-1912, see entry 174, 1913—, see entry 223; for reports, see entry 223.

---

6. *Ibid.,* CIII, 173-174, 888.
7. G. C. sec. 2876.

The soldiers' relief commission was established by an act of the legislature passed on May 19, 1886, entitled "an act to provide for the relief of indigent Union soldiers, sailors, and marines, and the indigent wives, widows and minor children of indigent or deceased Union soldiers, sailors, and marines." Under provisions of this act the commissioners of each county were authorized to levy a specified tax for the purpose of creating a fund for the relief of such beneficiaries; and the judge of the court of common pleas was authorized to appoint three county residents, at least two of whom were honestly discharged Union soldiers, to serve for a term of three years as members of the commission, which was organized by the selection of a chairman and a secretary and was known as the soldiers' relief commission.[1]

An amendment passed on March 4, 1887, provided that councilman of city wards, as well as the board of trustees of the townships, certify to the soldiers' relief commission the names of those requiring and entitled to aid under the act.[2]

By the act of the legislature, passed on April 28, 1890 the soldiers' relief commission was required to appoint annually a committee of three in each township and a committee of three in each ward in any city in the county, whose duty it was to receive all applications for aid and to certify them to the soldiers' relief commission.[3]

Section 2930 and 2933-4 of the General Code was amended, March 6, 1917, to provide for the appointment to each county commission of one member who is the wife, widow, son, or daughter of an honorably discharged soldier, sailor, or marine of the Civil War or of the Spanish-American War, the other two members to be honestly discharged soldiers, sailors, or marines of the United States; and for the appointment to each township and ward committee of a wife or widow of a soldier, sailor, or marine of the United States.[4] Two years later, in 1919, the provisions of the act were extended to include indigent veterans of the World War and indigent parents, wives, widows, or minor children of such veterans.[5]

---

1. *Laws of Ohio,* LXXXIII, 232.
2. *Ibid.,* LXXXIV, 100.
3. *Ibid.,* LXXXVII, 352.
4. *Ibid.,* CVII, 27.
5. *Ibid.,* CVIII, 633.

Sections 2930 and 2934 of the General Code were amended on April 6, 1929 to provide for the appointment by the court of common pleas in each county of a soldiers' relief commission, to consist of three members, one to be the wife, widow, son or daughter of an honorably discharged soldier, sailor, or marine of the Civil War, of the Spanish-American War, or of the World War, the other two members to be honorably discharged soldiers, sailors, or marines of the United States, one of whom should, if possible, be a member of the Spanish-American War Veterans, the other a member of the American Legion.[6]

All records are located in soldiers' relief commission office, 102 ½ South Washington Street, Tiffin, Ohio.

---

6. *Laws of Ohio,* CXIII, 466.

525. MINUTES

1914- 1929, 1936—. 2 volumes.

Minutes of soldiers' relief commission and record of applications for relief and grants recommended, showing date and place of meeting, names of members presents, resolutions and motions introduced and acted on relative to rules of procedure in handling applications and investigations on applications and other routine proceedings relative to administering relief to veterans or the dependents, showing date of application received, name and address of applicant, age, war service, or if dependent relationship to deceased veteran, action on application, amount of grant recommended, or if continued reason for continuance. Arranged chronologically by dates of meetings. No index. 1914-1929 handwritten; 1936—, typed. Average 300 pages. 16 x 11 x 1.5.

For auditor's record, see entry 368.

526. [POSTING CARDS]

1935—. 2 file boxes.

Card record of relief grants to indigent veterans or dependents of deceased veterans, showing date of application, application number, name and address of veteran or dependent, veteran of what war, date of grant, amount of grant, date of revision of grant, reason for revision of grant, and date payment due. Arranged alphabetically by names of clients. No index. Handwritten on printed forms. 6 x 8.25 x 18.

527. CASE HISTORIES

1920—. 3 file drawers.

Case histories of indigent veterans or their dependents applying for relief consisting of applications, reports of investigation on application, recommendations of commission, showing application number, date of application, name and address of applicant, and, if veteran, age, color, birthplace, length of residence in county, occupation, marital status, name and ages of dependents, date of last employment, physical condition, veteran of what war, date of enlistment, place of enlistment, rank, company, regiment, brigade, corps or vessel, date of discharge, place of discharge, discharge certificate number, service record; if dependent of deceased veteran, name and address of applicant, name of deceased veteran, relationship to deceased veteran, number in family, veteran of what war, date of enlistment, place of enlistment, rank, number of company, regiment, brigade, corps or name of vessel, date of discharge, discharge certificate number, property statement, income if any, signature of applicant, and date filed; verification of application statements and amount of relief recommended or if case continued, reason for continuance, date grant effective, record of revision of grant, amount of revision, reason for revision, date case closed, and reason for closing. All papers of each case filed together in a folder showing name of applicant and application number. Arranged alphabetically by names of applicants. No index. Handwritten and handwritten on printed forms. 11.5 x 13.5 x 26.

In 1884 the legislature made provision for soldiers' burial committees in each county, to consist of three persons in each township appointed by the county commissioners, which were directed to defray the expense incurred in the interment of any honorably discharged Union soldier, sailor, or marine who died in poverty. These committees, serving at the pleasure of the appointing power, were required to report to the county commissioners the name, rank, and command of the decedent, which report was transcribed by the county commissioners in a book kept for that purpose.[1] The original act, amended in 1891, extended the provisions of the act to include the internment of the wives or widows of Union soldiers.[2] In 1893 the act was again amended to provide for the internment of mothers of Union soldiers, sailors, and marines, and army nurses.[3] In 1908 the personnel of each committee was reduced to two.[4]

Under the present law which became effective in 1921 the county commissioners are authorized to appoint two suitable persons in each township and ward in the county, who are directed to contact with the undertaker selected by the family or friends of the deceased, and to direct the burial in a respectable manner of the body of any honorably discharged soldier, sailor, or marine having at any time served in the army or navy of the United States, or the mother, wife, or widow of any soldier, sailor, or marine, or that of any war nurse who served at any time in the army of the United States who died in poverty.[5]

The burial committees are instructed to enforce all laws relative to the burial of indigent veterans, investigate the financial status of the decedent's family, and report its findings to the county commissioners, together with the name, rank, and command to which the deceased belonged, date of death, place of burial, occupation while living, and an itemized statement of the cost of burial.[6]

---

1. *Ibid.,* LXXXI, 146-147.
2. *Ibid.,*LXXXVIII, 330-331.
3. *Ibid.,*XC, 177.
4. *Ibid.,*XCIX, 99.
5. G. C. sec. 2950; *Laws of Ohio,* CVIII, 34; CIX, 211.
6. *Laws of Ohio,* XCIX, 100.

Upon receiving this report of the burial committee, the county commissioners transcribe the information in a book kept for that purpose, and certify the expense to the county auditor who draws his warrant for payment to the person or person specified by the county commissioners.[7]

The amount contributed by the county for the burial of an indigent veteran set by the legislature at $35 in1884 was increased to $75 in1908, and to $100 in 1921.[8] Since 1908 each member of a burial committee has been allowed one dollar for each service performed.[9]

These agencies keep no records of their proceedings; for record of appointments and actions taken relative to the burial of indigent soldiers, sailors, or dependence of ex-service men, see entry 1; for reports, see entry 5.

---

7. *Ibid.,* XCIX, 101.
8. *Ibid.,* LXXXI, 146, 147; XCIX, 99; CIX, 212; G. C. sec. 2951.
9. *Laws of Ohio,* XCIX, 99; G. C. sec. 2951.

Provision for the relief of the indigent was made in 1805, but it was not until 1898 that the legislature provided separate relief for the indigent blind. The act authorized the township trustees to certify to the county commissioners an amount not to exceed $100 per person per annum for such relief, the certification to be made a record listing the name of the beneficiary and the amount required, and directed the county commissioners to levy on the township to the amount certified. This amount was to be paid into the county treasury and thence to the township treasurer to be used for blind relief.[1]

Six years later, in 1904, certification authority was transferred from the township trustees to the probate judge, who was required to register the name and address of the beneficiaries and to issue to each a certificate giving his name, address, and the amount to be drawn. Persons eligible for relief were blind males over twenty-one and blind females over eighteen years of age, without property or means of support. Not less than two county citizens, one a physician selected by the court, were required to testify that the applicant has been a resident of the state for five years and the resident of the county for one year immediately proceeding the filing of an application for relief as a condition for granting aid.[2]

The act of 1904 was declared unconstitutional for the reason that it required spending for a private purpose public funds raised by taxation.[3] Hence, in 1908, an act was passed authorizing the county commissioners to levy a stipulated tax to create a fund for relief of the needy blind, the maximum benefits not to exceed $150 per person per annum to be paid quarterly; and authorizing the probate judge to appoint a blind relief commission consisting of three members to serve for a three-year term. The commission was directed to meet annually in the office of the county commissioners to examine applications recorded in order of their receipt in a book furnished by the county commissioners. This record was required to be kept open for public inspection.[4]

The blind relief commission was abolished by the legislature in 1913 and its powers and duties were transferred to the county commissioners.[5]

---

1. *Laws of Ohio,* XCIII, 270.
2. *Ibid.,* XCVII, 392-394.
3. *Auditor of Lucas County* v. *The State, Ohio State Reports,* LXXV, 114-137.
4. *Laws of Ohio,* XCIX, 56-58.
5. See pp. 3, 4.

528. APPLICATIONS

1908-1911. 1 volume. (1).

Register of applications and grants for blind relief, showing date of application, application number, name and address of applicant, age, sex, color, marital status, date of medical examination, date of physician's report on examination, date application approved, amount of quarterly grant, date effective, date grant revised or discontinued, amount of revision, reason for revision, and reason for discontinuance. Arranged alphabetically by names of applicants. No index. Handwritten on forms. 190 pages. 17 x 14.5 x 1. Auditor's vault.

For subsequent records, see entry 40.

529. RECORD OF PAYMENTS

1908-1913. 1 volume. Discontinued; commission abolished.

Record of quarterly payments for blind relief, showing case number, name and address of client, date of payment, what quarter, amount, and voucher number. Arranged alphabetically by names of clients and chronologically thereunder by dates of payments. No index. Handwritten on forms. 200 pages. 17 x 12 x 1. Auditor's vault.

For auditor's records, see entry 372.

Old age pensions, although well known in Europe at the end of the nineteenth and beginning of the twentieth century and in a few American States during the same period, were not provided for in Ohio until recently.[1] In 1933 an "Old Age Pension" law, purposed by initiative petition, was voted upon at the general election of that year, providing for the granting of aid to the aged in Ohio under certain conditions. The law was adopted by a majority of electors voting thereon.[2] The act, as amended in 1936, provides, among other things, that a person sixty-five years of age or upward (unless confined in any penal or corrective institution or the state hospital) who is a citizen of the United States, who has resided in Ohio not less than five years during the nine prior to making application for aid, and who has resided for one year in the county wherein application for aid is made is eligible to receive a pension, providing his income from all and every source does not exceed $480 per year.[3] Moreover, the applicant must be unable to support himself, and have no husband, wife, child, or other person who is legally responsible for his support, and found by the division of aid for the aged able to support him. In addition to this, the net value of all real and personal property of the unmarried applicant, less all encumbrances and liens, must not exceed $3,000; if the applicant is married the net value of the property of husband and wife shall not exceed $4,000. It may be required that such property, as a condition precedent to payment of aid, be transferred to the division of aid for the aged in trust. This provision does not, however, prohibit the applicant or his wife from occupying such property during their lifetime.[4] An amendment to the act in 1937 eliminated the transfer of property as a possible condition precedent to granting aid, leaving the transfer optional. The amended act further states that any property, either real or personal, which has heretofore been conveyed to the division in trust could be reconveyed to the grantor by the division.[5]

---

1. Arthur Lyon Cross, *A Shorter History of England and Greater Britain* (New York, 1925), 746-747; J. Salwyn Schapiro, *Modern and Contemporary European History 1815-1928* (New York 1931), 275, 347, 396, 790.
2. *Laws of Ohio,* CXV, pt. ii, 431-439.
3. *Ibid.,* CXVI, pt. ii, 86-88, 216-221; CXVIII, 739-740.
4. *Ibid.,* CXV, pt. ii, 431-439.
5. G. C. sec. 1359-6.

For the purpose of administering the old age pension law there was created in 1933 in the state department of public welfare a division of aid for the aged. The chief of the division of the aid for the aged, appointed by the director of public welfare with the approval of the governor, is authorized to appoint all necessary assistance, clerks, stenographers, and other employees and fix their salaries, subject to the approval of the director of public welfare.[6]

In each county the commissioners constitute a board for administering the act. However, if the commissioners by a majority vote declined to serve in such capacity, the chief of the division of aid for the aged was authorized, with the consent of the director of public welfare, to appoint a board consisting of three or five members, who, like the county commissioners, served without compensation. The local boards were required to keep such records and make such reports as the division may prescribe, and were also authorized to employ, subject to the approval of the division, such investigators, clerks and other employees as are necessary for the performance of their duties.[7]

In 1937 the chief of the division was directed to appoint an advisory board in each county consisting of five citizens of such county. The members of the board, appointed for two years, are required to take an oath of office before entering upon their duties. The board succeeded to the duties formally performed by the county commissioners.[8]

Applications for relief were made annually to the local board but an act of the legislature in 1937, reorganizing the division of aid for the aged, omitted the provision for annual reapplication.[9] Each application is thoroughly investigated. In its investigations the local board is not bound by common law or statutory rules of evidence, but is authorized to make inquiries in such a matter as seems "best calculated to conform to substantial justice." For the purpose of its investigations, each county board has the power to compel the attendance and testimony of witnesses. Decisions of the local boards may be appealed to the division.[10]

---

6. *Laws of Ohio,* CXV, pt. ii, 431-439.
7. *Ibid.,* CXV, pt. ii, 431-439.
8. G. C. sec. 1359-12.
9. G. C. sec. 1359-14.
10. *Laws of Ohio,* CXV, pt. ii, 431-439.

After the applicants have been investigated by the local boards, "certificates of aid" are granted to persons entitled to relief in conformity with the provision of the law. Each certificate, bearing the applicant's name and the pension allowed, as well as the records pertaining to the investigation, is forwarded to the division, which may approve, modify, or reject the certificate and findings of the board.[11]

Under the provisions of this act the state became the general guardian of public and private welfare. The pension system relieves the increasing burdens placed upon county homes, which, even under the most favorable conditions, are poor substitutes for homes. In February 1934 the general assembly made its first appropriation for old age pensions covering the last half of the calendar year 1934.[12] The total cost to the state and federal government for old age pensions in the administration of the old age pension system in Ohio from 1934 to 1938 has been $99,509,315.43. The cost to the state of Ohio for the year 1938 exclusive of federal grants was $17,887,439.62.[13]

All records are located in the board of aid for the aged office, 112½ East Market Street, Tiffin, Ohio.

---

11. *Ibid.,* CXV, pt. ii, 435.
12. *Ibid.,* CXV, pt. ii, 186.
13. Ohio Auditor of State, *Annual Report, 1934*, p. 244; *ibid., 1935,* p. 269; *ibid.,* 1936, p. 202; *ibid.,* 1937, pp. 133, 131, *ibid.,* 1938, pp. 7, 36, 58, 144.

530. REGISTER OF APPLICATIONS RECEIVED

1937—. 1 volume.

Register of applications for old age pensions, showing application number, date of application, name and address of applicant, status of case, progress on application in county office, and final action by state office. Arranged alphabetically by names of applicants. No index. Handwritten on forms. 125 pages. 8 x 12 x 1.

531. PROGRESS BOOK

1934—. 1 volume.

Record of progress on each application, showing date of application, application number, name and address of applicant, age, birth date, birthplace, sex, color, citizenship, any means of support by relatives, financial factors, date investigation completed, date referred to county board, action of board, and date forwarded to state office, and action of state board. Arranged numerically by application numbers. No index. Typed on printed forms. 142 pages. 10.5 x 14.5 x 1.

532. CASE RECORDS [Pending Cases]
1934—. 1 file drawer.

Original papers filed consisting of applications, verifications of birth, residence, citizenship, marital, and financial status, showing application number, date and place of birth, citizenship, marital status, living arrangement, income and other aid, budget, names and addresses of children, value and description of real and personal property, amount of life insurance, war service, condition of health, names and addresses of references, and sources of various verifications. When application is approved by state department the records are transferred to file Case Records [Active], entry 537; records of cases when death occurs before grant is awarded remains in this file. Arranged the alphabetically by names of applicants. No index. Typed on printed forms. 11 x 14.5 x 26.

533. CASE CARDS [Pending Cases]
1934—. 1 file drawer.

Card records of pending cases, showing name and address of applicant, application number, date of application, date approved by county board, and date forwarded to state office; if death of applicant occurs shows date of death. Arranged alphabetically by names of applicants. No index. Handwritten and typed on printed forms. 4 x 6 x 17.

534. CASE RECORD [Rejected Cases]
1934—. 1 file drawer.

Original papers filed in rejected cases, showing same information as Case Records [Pending Cases], entry 532; also shows, date of investigation, date of rejection, and reason for rejection. Arranged alphabetically by names of applicants. No index. Typed on printed forms. 11 x 14.5 x 26.

535. CASE CARDS [Withdrawals and Denials]
1934—. 1 file drawer.

Card record of cases in which the application was withdrawn or application rejected by the county board or state department, showing name and address of applicant, application number, date and reason for withdrawal or rejection. Arranged alphabetically by names of applicants. No index. Handwritten and typed on printed forms. 4 x 6 x 17.

536. CERTIFICATE REGISTER

1934—. 1 volume.

Register of certificates of grants of aid, showing name of client, certificate number, application number, date of issue, amount of grant, and date effective. Arranged numerically by certificate numbers. No index. Handwritten on forms. 100 pages. 8 x 12 x .5.

537. CASE RECORDS [Active]

1934—. 12 file drawers.

Original papers in active aid for the aged cases, showing same information as Case Records [Pending Cases], entry 532, date approved by the county board and forwarded to state department, date approved by state department and certificate of award issued, amount of monthly award, and date effective. All papers of each case filed together in a folder showing case number (application number). Arranged numerically by case numbers. For index, see entry 538. Handwritten and typed on printed forms. 11 x 14.5 x 26.

538. INDEX OF CASES

1934—. 1 file drawer.

Index to Case Records [Active], entry 537, showing name and address of client, application number, case number (certificate number), date grant effective, amount of monthly grant, and notation of increases or decreases in amount of grant. Arranged alphabetically by names the clients. Handwritten and typed on printed forms. 4 x 6 x 17.

539. CASE RECORDS [County Home Cases]

1934—. 1 file cabinet.

Case records of county home inmates receiving aid for the aged, showing same information as Case Records [Pending Cases], entry 532, amount of award, and certificate number. Arranged alphabetically by names of clients. No index. Typed on printed forms. 11 x 14.5 x 26.

540. CASE RECORDS [Deceased Recipients]
1934—. 1 file drawer.

Case records of deceased recipients, showing same information as Case Records [Pending Cases] entry 532, certificate number, amount of grant, and date of death. Arrange the alphabetically by names that clients. No index. Typed on printed forms. 11 x 14.5 x 26.

541. CASE CARDS [Deceased Applicants and Recipients]
1934—. 1 file drawer.

Card record of applications for aid for the aged in which death occurred before completion of investigation of applicant and awarding aid or after payments were begun, showing name and address of applicant or recipient, application number, marital status, date of application, and date of death. Arranged alphabetically by names of applicants. No index. Typed on printed forms. 4 x 6 x 17.

542. [QUARTERLY VISIT FILE]
1934—. 2 file drawers.

Record of quarterly visits made on clients, showing name and address of client, name of township or town, date visited, application number, case number (certificate number), notations of living conditions, and health of client. Arranged alphabetically by names of towns and chronologically thereunder by dates of visits. No index. Handwritten on printed forms. 4 x 6 x 17.

The office of county surveyor, another English institution transplanted to America during the colonial period, became an important office in frontier Ohio for land titles and boundary lines were often in dispute. The office is purely a creature of statute, there being no constitutional provision for its establishment.

The first act of the general assembly pertaining to the surveyor was passed during the first legislative session of 1803. Under this act the court of common pleas was authorized to appoint a person well qualified to act as a county surveyor. He received his commission from the governor, was required to give bond conditioned for the faithful performance of the duties of his office, and was directed to survey all lands which were sold or were to be sold for taxes, and was authorized to appoint chairmen or markers whose function it was to establish corners. The surveys made by the surveyor or his deputies were the only ones to be accepted as legal evidence in any court of law or equity. For remuneration, the surveyor was permitted to retain all fees collected by him in the operation of his office.[1]

Although it made no fundamental change in the duties of the surveyor, the act of 1816 fixed his term of office at five years; authorized him to appoint deputies, and made him responsible for their official acts; and made him liable to removal by the court for negligence or incompetency, and liable to suit by persons believing themselves damaged by his negligence or that of his deputies.[2] A year later, in 1817, provision was made for the appointment of a successor in the event the office became vacant because of death, resignation, or removal.[3]

The act of 1831 consolidated the previous acts, redefined the duties of the surveyor, increased the amount of his bond, and authorized him, when directed by the county commissioners, to procure for the surveyor general's office a "certified plat, together with the field notes of corners, and bearings trees to each section, quarter section, lot, or original survey in his county, and cause the same to be preserved in a book by him provided for that purpose; which shall be deposited in the county auditor's office, for the use of the landholders in the county." It provided further, that the surveyor shall keep "a fair and accurate record of all official surveys made by himself or by his deputies," in a suitable book to be kept by him for that purpose, and that he should number his surveyors progressively. More significant, however, was the fact that the office was made elected for a three-year term by the act of 1831.

---

1. *Laws of Ohio,* I, 90-93.
2. *Ibid.,* XIV, 424-431.
3. *Ibid.,* XV, 64.

The term remained at three years until 1906 when it was reduced to two-year period; and by the act of 1927, effective with the term of the surveyor elected in 1928, the term was increased to four years.[4]

During the years of the development of the office other duties have been delegated to the surveyor. In 1842 he was given the duty of ascertaining and reporting trespassing on public lands.[5] Later, in 1854, he was given the same powers as the justices of the peace to take acknowledgments of and certify deeds, mortgages, powers of attorney, and other instruments affecting real estate, and to administer oaths, and to take and certify affidavits.[6] In 1867 he was given authority, when directed by the county commissioners, to transcribe any and all dilapidated maps, records of plats, and field notes of surveys of other counties.[7] , in 1881, he was authorized to procure from any office in the state a certified plat together with the field notes of corners, quarter sections, lots, or original surveys and place them in a book provided for that purpose. Certified copies from his book were to be taken as *prima facie* evidence.[8]

With the increase in modern means of transportation, there developed a growing need for more efficient methods of road construction and maintenance. Accordingly, in 1906, the surveyor was directed to act, whenever the services of an engineer were required, in the capacity of an engineer with respect to roads, turnpike, bridges, or ditches, except in cities of the first grade.[9] He was directed by statute to perform all duties in his county which would be done by a civil engineer or surveyor, to prepare all plans, specifications, and estimates of cost, and to submit forms for contracts for the construction and repair of all bridges, culverts, roads, draws, ditches, and other public improvements (except buildings) over which the county commissioners had authority. At the same time, he was made responsible for the inspection of all public improvements, and was directed to keep a complete list of all estimates and bids received for such work, as well as of contracts awarded for improvements.[10]

---

4. *Laws of Ohio,* XXIX, 399; XCVIII, 245-247; CXII, 179.
5. *Ibid.,* XL, 57.
6. *Ibid.,* LII, 70.
7. *Ibid.,* LXIV, 216-217; LXXVIII, 285.
8. *Ibid.,* XXIX, 399; LXXVIII, 285.
9. *Ibid.,* XCVIII, 245-247.
10. *Ibid.,* XCVIII, 245-247.

Similarly, another measure enacted in 1919 increased the duties of the surveyor regarding road construction road maintenance. Under this act the surveyor was authorized to designate one of his deputies as maintenance engineer. This engineer, under the direction of the surveyor, was to have charge of all "road maintenance and road work" in his county. Furthermore when authorized by the county commissioners, the surveyor was to appoint a maintenance supervisor or supervisors to have charge of the maintenance of improved highways within a district or districts established by the commissioners for the surveyor, and containing not less than ten miles of improved county roads.[11] In 1923 the surveyor was delegated to assist the county planning commission whenever such commission was established.[12]

Thus, the general responsibility of planning and directing county road construction is vested, by statute, in the county surveyor. Because of this increased responsibility placed on this office there has been an attempt to raise the general qualifications of those seeking the election to it. Accordingly, in 1935, an act was passed changing the title of the office to that of "county engineer," and eligibility to the office was restricted to "*a registered professional engineer and registered surveyor licensed to practice in the state of Ohio.* "[13] This act was amended in 1936 to permit the incumbent to continue in office upon re-election, regardless of the lack of these qualifications.[14]

All records are located in the engineers main office unless otherwise specified.

---

11. *Laws of Ohio,* CVIII, 497.
12. *Ibid.,* CX, 312.
13. *Ibid.,* CXVI, 283.
14. *Ibid.,* CXVI, pt. ii, 152.

Surveys, Plats, and Maps
(See also entries 73, 75-77, 79-83, 320-322)

543. SURVEYOR'S RECORD
1820-1942. 1 volume.

Certified copies of original government surveys and field notes of territory comprising Seneca County, including copies of contracts with various surveyors, and instructions from Edward Tiffin, Surveyor-General of the United States. Surveys showing boundary lines of the reservation set aside for the Indians, boundary lines of townships, and land tracts, streams, swamps, roads, fords, names of owners of land tracts, and area of tracts; field notes, showing date of survey, names of surveyor and chainman, description and location of survey landmarks, bearing of boundary lines, distance between landmarks, range, township and section numbers, and for whom surveyed. These early surveys were made by John A. Fulton, James T. Worthington, Sylvanius Bourne, and Brice Kellog. Surveys and notes and were transcribed from the originals on file in the state auditor's office, by Charles J. Peters, Seneca County Surveyor, in 1896. No obvious arrangement. No index. Field notes, handwritten; survey and plats, hand drawn, black on white. 640 pages. 16 x 11 x 3.5. Engineer's main office.

544. ORIGINAL FIELD NOTES
1820, 1832. 1 volume.

Copies of original field notes and hand drawn sketches of original surveys of territory now within the boundaries of Seneca County. Sketches of surveys on left hand page, showing survey number, name of survey, boundary lines of tract, township lines, section lines, trails, roads, streams, fords, landmarks, distance between angles and landmarks (stated as poles, chains, and links) and area, name of survey and chainmen, and date surveyed; surveyors field notes on right hand page, showing description of landmarks (kind of trees, diameter, or of corner post or stone), bearing a boundary lines, distance between landmarks, area, and certified statement by county surveyor that the sketch and field notes are a true copy of the original on file in the state auditor's office. Transcribed an 1896 by Charles J. Peters, County Surveyor. No obvious arrangement. No index. Handwritten and hand drawn. 69 pages. 16 x 16 x 1.

545. PLAT RECORD

1854—. 3 volumes. (1-3).

Copies of surveys of townships, farm and tracts, town plats and additions, showing survey number, name of plat or survey, boundary lines (if township, section lines), roads, streams, railroads, distance between landmarks or angles, names of owners of farm tracts, area, and swamp areas; streets, alleys, lot lines, lot numbers, out-lot area, and names of out-lot owners; description of survey, showing location of tract by range, township, and section numbers, quarter section, description of landmarks, corner post or cornerstone, bearing of boundary lines and other survey data, names of surveyor and chainmen, for whom surveyed, date of survey, and date recorded. Prepared by county surveyors department, arranged chronologically by dates recorded. For index, see entry 546. Handwritten and hand drawn. Black on white. Scales vary. Average 200 pages.20 x 15 x 1.5.

546. SURVEY RECORD INDEX

1854—. 1 volume. (1).

Index to Plat Record, entry 545, showing name of owner of tract surveyed or name of plat, range, township, and section numbers, description and location of survey, area, date of survey, name of surveyor, and volume and page numbers of records. Arrange the alphabetically by names of owners or plats. Handwritten on forms. 460 pages. 18 x 13 x 2.5.

547. FIELD NOTES

1897—. 357 volumes. (dated).

Surveyor's field notes on surveys of land tract and plats, road and drainage ditch routes, showing survey number, name and location of survey or construction project, for tracts and plats bearing of boundary lines, distance between angles, landmarks and corner post, area, for whom surveyed, and date of survey; field notes for roads and ditches showing station symbols, elevations, curves, cubic yards cuts, cubic yards fills, cubic yards ditch evacuation, other survey data, name and location of proposed construction, date of survey, and name of surveyor. Arranged chronologically by dates of surveys. No index. Handwritten. Average 150 pages. 8.5 x 5 x 1. 84 volumes, 1897-1901, engineer's vault; 273 volumes, 1902—, Engineer's drafting room.

548. [MAPS SENECA COUNTY]

n. d. 1 wall map.

Political map of Seneca County, showing boundary lines of county, townships incorporated cities, towns and villages, farm tracts, range and section lines, names of townships, cities, towns and villages, and of owners of farm tracts, farm areas, roads, railroads, streams, watercourses (drainage ditches), and road numbers. Prepared by county engineering department. Scale, 1 inch equals 1 mile. Blueprint. 35 x 42.

549. MAP, TIFFIN AND SUBURBS

1936. 1 wall map.

Plat map of the city of Tiffin and suburbs, showing corporation lines, ward lines, suburban plats, streets, alleys, lot lines, lots numbers, in-lot dimensions, out-lot areas, names of owners of out-lots, location of public buildings and parks, railroads, streams, sewer mains, names of suburbs, streets, allies, lot lines, lot numbers, and lot dimensions. Prepared by city of Tiffin, engineering department. Blueprint. Scale, 1 inch equals 300 feet. 33 x 38.

550. HIGHWAY MAP

n. d. 1 wall Map.

Map of Seneca County, showing county and township boundary lines, names of townships, locations and names of cities, towns and villages, roads, road numbers, improved roads under construction; also schedule on margin showing number of miles of various type of hard surfaced, gravel and dirt roads in each township. Corrected to date. Prepared by engineering department. Blueprint. Scale, 1 inch equals 1 1/2 miles. 45 x 48.

551. [DRAINAGE MAP]

n. d. 1 wall map.

Political map of Seneca County, showing county and township boundary lines, range and section lines, drainage system, open and closed (sewer) ditches designated, drainage basin or watershed served by each ditch, names of ditches, names of townships, roads, railroads, and natural streams. Corrected to date. Prepared by county engineering department. Blueprint. Scale, 2 inches equals 1 mile. 66 x 66.

Roads

552. JOURNAL– ROAD REPAIR
1931—. 2 volumes.

Record of cost of repairing or resurfacing improved roads, showing name of township, name or number of road, road section number, type of surface, type of repair, number of linear feet or square yards, specifications for and estimate of cost of repair or resurfacing, and date completed; if proposal submitted to bidders, show names of bidders, amounts of bid, name of contractor, amount, date, and terms of contract, and date completed; also total cost. Arranged alphabetically by names of townships and chronologically thereunder by dates of completion. No index. Handwritten on forms. Average 400 pages. 16 x 11 x 2. Engineer's private office.

553. ROAD SECTION RECORD
1919—. 1 volume.

Identification record of improved roads, showing road number, name of road, classification, type of surface, place of beginning, place of ending, names of townships and towns traversed, length of road in each subdivision, total length, year improved, year resurfaced, condition, and date of inspection. Arranged numerically by road numbers and chronologically thereunder by inspection. No index. Handwritten on forms. 180 pages. 15 x 19 x 1. Engineer's vault.

554. [TOWNSHIP ROADS]
1925—. 6 carton files (dated).

Engineers records of repairing, grading, and resurfacing township roads consisting of copies of bills or materials, engineer's reports to county commissioners of estimates; specifications for repair, and engineer's report to county commissioners on inspections of township bridges and culverts and recommendations for repairs; bills, showing name of township, date of bill, bill number, invoice number, name of creditor, item, quantity, unit price, total bill, and date approved; reports, showing name of township, name and/or number of road, type of road, detailed specifications for repair and estimate of cost, and date report filed; inspections, showing bridge or culvert number, name of water course, detailed statement of condition of bridge or culvert, recommendations for needed repairs, and date filed. Arranged chronologically by dates filed. No index. Bills, hand written on forms; reports, typed. 10 x 8 x 16. Engineer's vault.

555. [CONSTRUCTION AND REPAIR RECORDS]

1930—. 6 file drawers. (labeled by contained letters of alphabet).

Engineer's records of construction and repair of improved roads consisting of pay-roll sheets, specifications, estimates, bills for materials, and correspondence: pay-roll sheets show name of/or number of road, name of township, pay-roll period, name of employee, day and date, number of hours, classification, rate per hour, amount due, and total pay roll; specifications show name and/ or number of road, name of township, road, section number, detailed specifications for construction for repair and estimate of cost; bills, show bill number, invoice number, date of bill, name of creditor, item, quantity, unit price, total price, total bill, and date approved; original incoming and copies of outgoing correspondence relative to construction or repair of improved roads, showing dates, from or to whom, subject, text correspondence, and date filed. All papers for each road file together in a separate folder showing name/or number of road, name of township, construction or repair, and date project approved. 1930-1933, Arranged alphabetically by names of townships; 1934—, by names of roads. No index. Pay rolls and bills, handwritten on forms; specifications and estimates, handwritten on printed forms; correspondence, typed. 12 x 14 x 26.

556. [BLUEPRINTS AND TRACINGS]

1914—. 21 pigeonholes. Subtitled by names of townships.

Blueprints and tracings of surveys for highway improvements, showing proposal number, survey number, date of survey, name of road, name of township, road section number, elevation, cuts, fills, cross section of curve construction, and other pertinent survey data. Prepared by county engineering department. Arranged alphabetically by names of townships. No index. Blueprints and black and white tracings. Scales vary. 12 x 12 x 18. Engineer's vault.

Ditches

557. DITCH RECORDS

1913—. 3 file drawers. Subtitle by names are ditches.

Original orders to make surveys of proposed drainage ditch routes and submit estimates of cost of construction, blueprints and sketches of surveys, and schedules of assessments, showing name of principal petitioners, name of township, name of ditch, date of order, date of survey, grade and other survey data, sketch of drainage basin, boundary lines of farm tracts, names of owners, number of acres, detailed estimate of cost of construction, total amount assessed on benefitted lands for owner's share of cost, name of owner, amount assessed, number of acres, and range, township and section numbers. All papers of each ditch filed together in a folder. Arranged alphabetically by names of ditches. No index. Handwritten on printed forms. Blueprints and hand drawn sketches. Scales vary. 12 x 14 x 26.

558. ESTIMATE RECORD
1903—. 3 volumes. (1-3).
Copies of engineer's estimate of cost of construction of drainage ditches and actual cost, showing name of ditch, location of ditch, detailed estimate of cost, date estimate to filed, date construction started, itemized statement of cost of construction, and date completed. Arranged chronologically by dates estimates filed. Indexed alphabetically by names of ditches. Handwritten on printed forms. Average 300 pages. 12 x 11 x 1.5. Engineer's private office.

Bridges and Culverts

559. BRIDGE LOCATION AND NUMBERS
1919—. 1 volume.
Township maps, showing name of township, boundary lines, section lines, roads, road numbers, streams and watercourses, railroads, bridge locations, bridge numbers, and date map prepared. Margin legend indicating type of bridge. Arranged alphabetically by names of townships. No index. Hand drawn, black and white. Scales vary. 16 pages. 16 x 16 x .5.

560. BRIDGE RECORDS
1913—. 3 file drawers. (dated).
Copies of proposals for construction of bridges, blueprints and drawings, specifications and estimates, showing date proposal advertised, name of paper, location of bridge (township, road name and/or number, name of stream), detailed specifications for construction of substructure and of superstructure, detailed estimate of cost of construction, blueprint and detailed drawing of construction, showing length of spans, length overall, width, size of ironwork, grade of approaches, cross sections of substructure and truss work. All papers of each bridge filed together and a folder showing name, number and location of bridge, and date of proposal. Arranged chronologically by dates of proposals. No index. Handwritten on printed forms. Blueprints, hand drawn black and white sketches. 12 x 14 x 26.

561. BRIDGE AND CULVERT RECORD

1919—. 1 volume.

Identification and inspection record of bridges and culverts, showing name of township, bridge or culvert number, name of stream, type of structure, date constructed, length of spans, number of spans, size of opening (culvert), width of roadway, type of piers and abutments, condition, and date of inspection. Arranged alphabetically by names of townships and chronologically thereunder by dates of inspections. No index. Handwritten on forms. 200 pages. 14 x 19 x 1. Engineer's vault.

562. CONTRACT RECORD

1905-1915. 4 volumes. (1-4).

Engineer's record of contracts let for construction and repair of improved roads and bridges consisting of copies of specifications for construction or repair, estimates of cost of construction or repair, record of bids received, contracts, contractor's bonds, showing proposal number, name and location of improvement, date specifications and estimates filed and approved, detailed specifications of materials to be used and type and method of construction, detailed estimate of cost of materials, of labor, total estimated cost, dates legal notice of proposal for construction published, dates bids received, names and addresses of bidders, amount bid, contract number, date contract let, name of contractor, contract price, terms of contract, amount of contractor's bond, names of sureties or bonding company, and record of payments to contractor on account, showing date of payment, amount, percent of contract price, and percent of work completed. Arranged chronologically by dates of contracts. Indexed alphabetically by names of roads or bridges. Handwritten on printed forms. Average 385 pages. 16 x 11 x 2.

Financial Records

563. LEDGER

1927—. 1 volume.

Surveyor's ledger of record of maintenance, salary and wage, office expense, new equipment, repair and emergency funds, showing name of fund, year, date of credit, amount, source of credit, date of debit, amount, item, and monthly credit balance. Arranged under tabs by names of funds, and chronologically thereunder by dates of credits and debits. No index. Handwritten on forms. 300 pages. (Loose- leaf binder). 11 x 11 x 1.5.

564. GASOLINE TAX RECORD

1929-1932. 1 volume.

Record of amount of excise tax receipts for retail sale of gasoline credited to various townships, showing name of township, date of distribution to township, amount, amount credited to maintenance fund, and amount to new construction fund. Arranged alphabetically by names of townships and chronologically thereunder by dates of distribution. No index. Handwritten on forms. 350 pages. (Loose- leaf binder). 16 x 11 x 1.5. Engineer's private office.

565. [COST, COLD PATCHING]

1925—. 20 carton files (dated).

Copies of bills for cold patch road repair materials (stone, tar) for county roads, showing bill number, invoice number, name and address of creditor, item, quantity, unit price, total price, date delivered, and date approved; also weekly labor time books, showing name of laborer, day and date, number of hours, rates per hour, total wage per week, and name of foreman. No obvious arrangement. No index. Handwritten on forms. 12 x 8 x 16. Engineer's vault.

566. [COST, SURFACE TREATING]

1925—. 20 carton files (dated).

Copies of bills for surface treatment of county roads (stone, oil, asphalt), showing bill number, invoice number, name and address of creditor, item, quantity, unit price, total price, date delivered, date approved; also weekly labor time books, showing name of laborer, day and date, number of hours, rate per hour, total wages for week, and name of foreman. No obvious arrangement. No index. Handwritten on forms. 12 x 8 x 16. Engineer's vault.

567. TIME CARDS

1923—. 1 file drawer.

Engineering department employees time cards, showing name and address of employee, classification or position, rate per hour, date, number of hours worked, total hours and amount due. Arranged chronologically by names of employees, and chronologically thereunder by years. No index. Handwritten on forms. 6.5 x 17 x 26.

568. TIME CARDS, RODMEN AND INSPECTORS

1937—. 1 file box,

Time records of surveyor's rodmen and job inspectors, showing name and address of employee, classification, wage rate, date, number of hours, and total due. Arranged alphabetically by names of employees and chronologically thereunder by years. No index. Handwritten on forms. 5.5 x 7.5 x 12.

569. TIME BOOK

1904-1905. 1 volume.

Record of time worked by surveyor's rodmen, showing date of entry, name of project, location, name of rodman, number of hours, and name of surveyor. Arranged chronologically by dates of entries. No index. Handwritten on forms. 170 pages. 9 x 6 x 1.

570. INSPECTOR'S MEMORANDUM BOOKS

1916-1933. 51 volumes. (dated).

Job inspector's records, showing date of entry, name and location of project, notes of progress of work, of materials on hand, of materials needed, names of laborers on project, number of hours worked per day. Arranged chronologically by dates of entries. No index. Handwritten. Average 100 pages. 7 x 5 x .5. Engineer's vault.

571. FORTNIGHTLY TIME BOOKS

1916-1933. 24 volumes. (dated).

Job foreman's semimonthly record of time worked on construction and repair of county projects, showing name and location of project, dates of beginning and ending of pay period, name of worker, dates, hours worked, rate per hour, total, total number of hours, and total amount due. Arranged chronologically by pay period and alphabetically thereunder by names of workers. No index. Handwritten on forms. Average 100 pages. 8 x 5.5 x .5. Engineer's vault.

572. MISCELLANEOUS RECORDS

1909-1923, 1937—. 16 file drawers. (dated).

Miscellaneous records consisting of copies of survey reports on roads and ditches petitioned for and not allowed; specifications and estimates for proposed construction of bridges and culverts (construction postponed); All showing name of proposed road or ditch, date of survey, preliminary survey data, fragmentary sketches of proposed route (no scale), name of surveyor; also name and location of proposed new bridge or culvert, details specifications of materials, type and method of construction, itemized estimate of cost of materials and labor, total cost, date filed, and name of surveyor; 1909-1923, miscellaneous correspondence received relative to road and bridge construction or repair, showing date of correspondence, subject, text of correspondence, name and address of writer; 1937—, Also includes copies of requests for annual budget appropriation; monthly reports to commissioners on equipment upkeep; invoice list of materials used, original daily reports from road maintenance department, showing date of budget request, expenditures past year, estimated requirements for current year itemized by funds, and total estimates amount required, date of report; month covered, items, amount of expenditures, total for month, date of invoice, items, quantity, unit price, and total amount; reports showing date of report, district number, type of work performed, amount of material used, number men employed, and number hours worked. Arranged chronologically by dates of reports, filings, or requests. No index. Handwritten on printed forms. 12 x 14 x 26. Engineer's private office.

In order to encourage forestry, provide for converting into forest reserves lands acquired for that purpose, and provide for the conservation of the natural resources of the state, including streams, lakes, submerged and swamped lands, provisions were made in 1911 in 1915 for the creation of park districts to be supervised by a board of park commissioners.[1]

An act passed in 1917 repealed the former legislation. Under the provisions of the latter act park districts may include all or a part only of the territory within the county and the boundaries thereof so as not to divide any existing township or municipality within such county. After application has been made and the necessary hearing has been heard by the probate court as provided by law pertaining to the creation of the district, and upon the creation thereof, the probate judge shall appoint three commissioners to take office forthwith and served progressively for one, two, and three years respectively and thereafter for a three-year term. Before entering upon the performance of his duties, each commissioner is required to take an oath of office, and give bond in the sum of five thousand dollars for the faithful performance of his duties. The commissioners served without compensation, but are allowed their actual and necessary expenses incurred in the performance of the duties.[2]

The board of park commissioners is authorized to acquire by gift or devise, by purchase, or by appropriation lands either within or without the district for the creation of parks, parkways, forest reservations and other reservations, and develop, improve, protect, and promote the use of the same in such manner as a board may deem conductive to the general welfare. In furtherance of the use and enjoyment of the lands controlled by the board, it may accept, with the approval of the probate court, donations of money or other property, and use and administer the same as stipulated by the donor, or as provided in the trust agreement.

Where there is a museum of natural history maintained by a private non-project corporation or association in any county within which a park district is in whole or in part located, the board may contract with such private corporation or association for term not exceeding three years for such services and assistance as may be rendered.[3]

---

1. *Laws of Ohio,* CII, 459; CVI, 137.
2. *Ibid.,* CVII, 65.
3. *Ibid.,* CXIII, 659.

Furthermore, the board in order to borrow money in anticipation of the tax collection, was empowered to levy taxes for improvements upon all taxable property within the district not to exceed one-tenth of one mill upon each dollar of accessed value of the property in the district in any one year, subject however, to the combine maximum levy for all purposes otherwise provided by law. The board may also, by agreement with the council or other public authority in control of parks or park lands within any municipality in the district, assume control of all or a portion thereof and in such event, the lands may be developed, improved and protected, as in case of other lands acquired by the board. If the board of park commissioners shall find that any lands it has acquired are not necessary for the purpose for which they were acquired, it is authorized to sell and dispense of them upon such terms and conditions as it deems advisable or may lease or permit the use of the lands for purposes not inconsistent with the purpose for which they were acquired.[4]

A supplemental act of 1939 gave the board power to issue negotiable notes and bonds for the purpose of acquiring and improving lands. The board of parks commissioners is a body politic and corporate, capable of suing and being sued. It may employ a secretary and other necessary employees, and is required to keep an accurate and permanent record of all of its proceedings; compile and publish reports and information relating to the district and to the proceedings and functions of the board.[5]

The Seneca County Park Board developed from the Seneca County Natural Resources Council which was composed of the Farm Bureau, Izaak Walton League, granges, garden clubs, and other similar organizations. On October 19, 1936, the council took steps toward the establishment of a park board and a county museum.

On November 4, 1937, application was filed in probate court by the trustees of Eden, Adams, and Bloom Townships for the creation of a park district in Seneca County for the purpose of encouraging conservation of natural resources and wild life and providing places of recreation. A hearing was held December 30, 1937, and on January 4, 1938, the park district was established. Three park commissioners were appointed on January 6, 1938, to serve three, two, and one-year terms.[6]

---

4. *Ibid.,* CVII, 65; CVIII, pt. ii, 1097.
5. *Ibid.,* CXVIII, 566; CVII, 65; CXIII, 659.
6. Civil Docket, IX, 385; Journal [Probate Court] XLV, 21.

On June 5, 1939, the resignation of the park commissioners were filled in probate court due to disagreement as to surety bonds required by appointees, the resignations were accepted; the amount of bond was settled and three new members were appointed.[7]

---

7. Journal [Probate Court], XLV, 412.

573. [MINUTES OF MEETINGS]

1936—. 1 volume.

Minutes of park commission, showing date and place of meeting, names of members present, recommendations and memorandum offered by civic organizations and committees, and resolutions and motions relative to proposed action of the board. Arranged chronologically by dates of meetings. No index. Typed. 100 pages. 14 x 9 x 1. Located at the residence of R. H. Molineaux, Secretary, County Park Board, 65 Washington Avenue, Tiffin, Ohio.

BOARD OF DIRECTORS OF THE CONSERVANCY DISTRICT

The legislature at its 1914 session, following the disastrous floods of the previous year, made provision for the establishment of conservancy districts in Ohio for the purpose of preventing floods and protecting cities, villages, farms, and highways from inundation. This act, authorized by the constitution amended in 1912,[1] was upheld by the courts as a valid exercise of the police power of the state.[2] Conservancy districts, according to the act, may be established not only to prevent floods but to regulate streams, reclaim overflowed lands, provide irrigation, regulate the flow of streams, or divert watercourses.

The court of common pleas of any county in the state or any judge in vacation is authorized, after a petition signed either by five hundred freeholders or by a majority of freeholders has been filed with the clerk of courts, to establish a conservancy district which might be entirely within, or partly within and partly without the county where the court is located. The court, after conducting hearings on the petition as to the purpose of the district, may declare the district organized and give it a corporate name. The clerk of courts, within thirty days after the district has been declared a corporation by the court, transmits to the secretary of state, and to the county recorder in each county having lands in the district, copies of the findings and the decree of the court incorporating the district which, according to statute, is considered a political subdivision.

Within thirty days after the decree of incorporation the court is authorized to appoint three persons, at least two of whom are freeholders in the district, to serve as a board of directors of the district to serve three, five, and seven years respectfully. After the expiration of their terms the tenure of office is five years. The board of directors, after taking an office that they "will not be interested directly or indirectly in any contract let by the district," organize by selecting one of their members as president and some person, not a member of the board, as secretary. The board is authorized to employ a chief engineer who may be an individual, copartnership, or corporation; an attorney; and such other engineers and attorneys as may be necessary for carrying on the work. The board may provide for their compensation, which, with all other necessary expenditures, shall be taken as a part of the cost of improvement. While the chief engineer prepares plans and specifications of work, all contracts which exceed $1,000 or let by competitive bidding.

---

1. *Ohio Const. 1851,* Art. II, sec. 36.

The board, or its agents, is authorized to enter upon lands within or without the conservancy district for the purpose of making surveys. They are authorized to exercise the right of eminent domain; condemn property, after appraisal, for the use of the district; make regulations to protect their work by prescribing the method of building roads, bridges or fences; to remove bridges, cemeteries, or other structures impending their work; and to co-operate with the federal government, with persons, railways, corporations, the state government of Ohio or other states, for assistance in drainage, conservancy, or other improvements.

To finance such improvements the board is authorized to levy upon the property of the district a tax not to exceed three-tenths of a mill on the assessed valuation. This tax is certified to the county auditor, and to the various treasurers of the counties within the district and is used to pay the expenses of organization, surveys, and plans. The commission is authorized further to borrow money at a rate not to exceed six percent per annum and levy assessments for a bond fund.[3]

The board is required to "keep in a well-bound book a record of all its proceedings, minutes of all meetings, certificates, contracts, bonds given by employees and all corporate acts, which shall be open to the inspection of the owners of property in the district, as well as to all other interested parties." The secretary, who may serve as treasurer, is designated as the "custodian of the records of the district and its corporate seal."[4]

Seneca County is in the Scioto-Sandusky Conservancy District,[5] which embraces seventeen counties and has headquarters in Columbus where the records are located. These records are listed in the *Inventory of the County Archives of Ohio, No. 25, Franklin County.*

---

2. *County of Miami* v. *Dayton, Ohio State Reports,* XCII, 223-224, 236.
3. *Laws of Ohio,* CIV, 13-64.
4. *Ibid.,* CIV, 18.
5. Pending court action serves as an injunction to prevent operation of conservancy projects in Seneca County at the present time.

By act of the legislature passed February 20, 1861, the county agricultural societies were required to report annually to the state board of agriculture, and to send a delegate to meet with the state board at Columbus once each year.[1] In 1883 the legislature provided for the organization of district or county agricultural societies. The act making this provision stipulated that when thirty or more persons, residents of any county or district embracing two counties, organized themselves into an agricultural society, under the rules and regulations of the state board of agriculture, the county might aid such society with a grant not to exceed $400 per year.[2] By act of April 21, 1896, provision was made for representation in a county society of thirty or more residents of any county or district embracing two or more counties.[3] In 1900 the legislature extended the amount of county aid to $800 per year.[4] Later, on May 6, 1902, the legislature passed an act authorizing thirty or more residents of a county or of a district embracing one or more counties, to organize themselves into an agricultural society.[5]

On April 17, 1919, the legislature provided for the organization of county and independent agricultural societies, the payment of class premiums; defined the duties of persons competing for premiums; prescribed the publication of treasurers' accounts and the list of awards by societies; designated conditions of memberships in a county agricultural society; authorized the society to elect a board of directors consisting of eight members, and prescribed their term of office and the manner of their election. The act further stipulated how such societies might obtain state aid, and authorize the county commissioners to insure all buildings belonging to agricultural societies.[6]

The legislature in 1921 passed an act stipulating that the total amount of county aid to county agricultural societies should equal one hundred percent of the amount paid by the society in regular class premiums but not exceed $800.[7]

---

1. *Laws of Ohio,* LVIII, 22.
2. *Ibid.,* LXXX, 142.
3. *Ibid.,* XCII, 205.
4. *Ibid.,* XCIV, 395.
5. *Ibid.,* XCV, 403.
6. *Ibid.,* CVIII, 381-385.
7. *Ibid.,* CIX, 240.

By act of March 27, 1925, the county commissioners were authorized to purchase or to lease for a term of not less than twenty years, real estate whereon to hold fairs under the management of county agricultural societies, and to erect thereon suitable buildings.[8] On March 10, 1927, the legislature authorized the county commissioners to appropriate annually on the request of the agricultural society a sum not less than $1,500 nor more than $2,000 from the general fund for the purpose of "encouraging agricultural fairs."[9]

The most recent legislation affecting agricultural societies was that of March 19, 1935. This act provides that where no duly organized county agricultural society existed, and when no fair was held by a duly organized county agricultural society which has held an annual exposition for three years previous to January 1, 1933, the county commissioner should, on the request of an independent society, appropriate annually from the general fund a sum not more than $2,000 nor less than $500 for the encouragement of independent agricultural fairs.[10]

The Seneca County Agricultural Society was organized in 1842, as evidenced in the report of the treasurer of the State Board of Agriculture in 1851, and in a letter written by Samuel Waggoner, the corresponding secretary in 1845 to the *Ohio Cultivator.*[11]

All records are located at the residence of the secretary of the society, C. B. Baker, Rural Route 4, Tiffin, Ohio.

---

8. *Ibid.,* CXI, 238.
9. *Ibid.,* CXII, 84.
10. *Ibid.,* CXVI, 47.
11. Ohio Department of Agriculture, *Summary of the Activities of the Ohio Department of Agriculture . . . for 1936. A Report and History of the County and Independent Fairs Held in Ohio in 1936 . . . ,* p. 38.

574. MINUTE BOOK

1902—. 1 volume.

Minutes of the board of directors including appointment of various committees, reports from committees, setting dates for holding annual county fairs, appointment of judges of exhibits displayed at fairs, appointment of department superintendents, and schedule of premiums offered for best exhibits, showing date and place of meetings, names of directors and officials present, names of committees, names of appointees to committees, committee reports, showing date of report, itemized statements relative to committees' activities, dates for holding county fair each year, names of exhibit judges, names of superintendent of various departments, first, second and third premium awards each class of exhibit; also includes itemized statement of receipts, showing date received, amount, source of receipts, to what fund credited, and expenditures showing date paid, name of payee, amount, for what, what fund debited, and check or warrant number; also shows names of members of associations and names of officers and directors. Arranged chronologically by dates of meetings. No index. Handwritten. 300 pages. 16 x 11 x 1.5.

575. REPORTS
1933—. 2 volumes.
Copies of annual reports by secretary to state department of agriculture, showing year of report, date of holding county fair, and names of officers and directors of society; statement of cash receipts, showing amount, from what source, total receipts, balance at beginning of year, and total credits; expenditures classified (wages, rent, advertising, printing, premiums, purses racing events, sundries), total expenditures, and balance; number of exhibits each department and each class, number horse racing events, number of entries each event, amount of purse, second, and third place each event, total attendance at fair, and names of officers and directors elected for ensuing year. Arranged chronologically by years. No index. Handwritten on printed forms. Average 150 pages. 14 x 9 x 1.

576. ACCOUNT BOOK
1926—. 4 volumes.
Record of cash receipts and expenditures: receipts, showing date received, name of payer, amount, for what (race event fee, exhibit entry fee, stall rent, concession, general admission, grandstand emission, per capita tax, county tax levy, rent, interest on deposits or donations), and total for year; expenditures, showing date paid, name of payee, amount, check or warrant number, for what, and what fund debited. Arranged chronologically by dates of receipts and expenditures. No index. Handwritten on forms. Average 80 pages. 14 x 12 x .5.

577. DAY BOOK

1937—. 1 volume.

Record of daily cash receipts and expenditures county fair; receipts, showing day and date, amount received, what source, and total for day; expenditures, showing amount paid out, name of payee, for what, and total for day. Arranged chronologically by daily entries. No index. Handwritten on forms. 400 pages. 12 x 8 x 2.

578. ECONOMIC INDEX [Exhibits]

1937—. 1 volume.

Index record of exhibitors and exhibits at county fair, showing department number and name, exhibit number, name of exhibitor, kind of exhibit, class, entry fee, rating given by judges, amount of premium, date premium paid, and check or warrant number. Arranged numerically by department numbers and alphabetically thereunder by names of exhibitors. Handwritten on forms. 80 pages. 16 x 11 x .5.

579. JUDGES BOOKS

1937—. 12 volumes. (dated).

Judges record of exhibits judged, showing name and number of department, entry number, class, premiums awarded (first, second, or third), name of exhibitor, amount of premium, name of judge and date. Arranged by departments. No index. Handwritten on forms. Average 32 pages. 11 x 7 x .25.

580. PREMIUM STATEMENTS

1937—. 4 volumes. (dated).

Record of premiums awarded on exhibits at county fair, showing year, date of exhibit, exhibit number, department, class, premium classification, and amount of premium. Arranged alphabetically by names of exhibitors. No index. Handwritten on forms. Average 100 pages. 8 x 11 x .5.

581. SUMMARY BOOK [Races]

1937—. 2 volumes.

Summary of harness races held at annual county fairs, showing date of race, class, amount of purse, position drawn, name of horse, color, sex, name and address of owner, name of driver, position at finish of race, time of race, and names of judges and timers. Arranged chronologically by dates of races. No index. Handwritten on forms. Average 22 pages. 11 x 17 x .25.

In 1914 the federal government passed an act providing for co-operative agricultural extension service between the state agricultural colleges and the United States Department of Agriculture. The purpose of the extension service was to give instructions and practical demonstrations in agriculture and home economics to persons not attending college, and to give such information through field demonstrations, publications, and other means. The funds for such work were to be supplied in part by the federal government and part by the state.[1]

A year following the federal legislation, the Ohio legislature accepted the provision of the act by providing that when twenty or more residents of a county organized themselves into a "farmers' institute society for the purpose of teaching better methods of farming, stock raising, fruit culture and business connected with agriculture," accepted a constitution and bylaws conforming to the rules and regulations prescribed by the trustees of Ohio State University, and elected proper officers, the institute could be a corporate body. The Ohio State University was required to furnish speakers for their annual meeting. At the close of the session the trustees were authorized to publish the lectures in pamphlet or book form.

Besides maintaining an institute, the society was authorized to maintain a county experiment farm. Furthermore, the county commissioners were authorized to select a county agent subject to the approval of the dean of college of agriculture of the Ohio State University. It is the duty of the agent to inspect and study the agricultural conditions in his county, distribute agricultural literature, co-operate with United States Department of Agriculture and the college of agriculture of the Ohio State University. In the event the commissioners failed to make such an appointment, the electorate could require them to do so on a referendum vote.[2]

In 1919 the original legislation was amended so as to authorize the employment of a home demonstration agent. An act of 1929, which is still effective, empowered the trustees of the Ohio State University to employ boys' and girls' club agents as well as agricultural and home demonstration agents. The county extension agent was given the additional duty of carrying the teachings of the college of agriculture of the Ohio State University and agriculture and home economics to the residents of his county through personal visits, bulletins, and practical demonstrations.

---

1. *United States Statutes at Large,* XXXVIII, pt. i, 372-374.
2. *Laws of Ohio,* CVI, 356-259.

Furthermore, it was his duty to render educational service not only in relation to agricultural production, but also in relation to economic problems including marketing, distribution, and the utilization of farm products.[3]

The initial legislation contained a clause which required the county commissioners to appropriate annually $1,000 dollars if they wished to obtain services of an agricultural agent. This amount was to be matched by the state. Under the present system the commissioners are empowered to levy a tax and to appropriate money from the proceeds thereof or from the general fund of the county an amount not to exceed $3,000 for each agent to be paid into the state treasury to the credit of the agricultural extension fund. Amounts in excess must have the unanimous consent of the commissioners.[4]

The Seneca County commissioners by a resolution passed in March 1918 provided for the cooperation with the agricultural extension department of the Ohio State University, in farm extension work. The first extension agent was appointed in 1918.[5]

All records are located in the agricultural extension agents' office, room 222, Federal Building, South Washington Street, Tiffin, Ohio.

---

3. *Ibid.,* CVIII, 364; CXIII, 82-83.
4. *Laws of Ohio,* CXIII, 82-83.
5. Commissioners' Journal, XXVII, 144.

Extension and Conservation Records

582. DAILY ACTIVITIES RECORD

1933—. 9 folders.

Record of daily office activities including daily sheets, showing date, all office and telephone calls and subject, circulars sent out and subject, information given out for news articles and subject, the number of personal letters sent out, bulletins distributed and subject, all assistance received from specialist, from Ohio State University, local leaders or committees and others: all meetings attended and home visits made by county agent and home demonstration agent. Arranged chronologically by dates of entries. No index. Handwritten. 8.5 x 11.

583. LISTING SHEETS
1933-1935. 5 volumes.

Record of farmers operating under the provision of the agricultural adjustment administration wheat and corn-hog programs showing name of farm operator, township, year, name of farm owner, number of acres tillable land, number of acres allotted to wheat growing, number of acres not sown in wheat, number of acres allotted to corn growing, number of acres not planted in corn, number of head of hogs to be produced for market, amount of remuneration to farm operator and owner for uncultivated acres, and limited hog production. Arranged alphabetically by names of townships; alphabetically thereunder by names of farmers and chronologically thereunder by years. No index. Handwritten on printed forms. Average 75 pages. 24 x 30 x .5.

584. MASTER SHEETS
1933—. 4 volumes.

Record of agricultural conservation under the supervision of county agent, showing year, name of township, name of farm owner or operator, number of acres of tillable land, type of soil, outline of program to be followed, progress of program, and result of program. Arranged chronologically by names of farm operators. No index. Handwritten on printed forms. Average 75 pages. 24 x 36 x .5.

4-H Club Records

585. ENROLLMENT CARDS
1937—. 1 file box.

Enrollment cards 4-H club members, showing name and address of member, name of township, name of club, age, birth, sex, grade in school, name of school attended, name of parent or guardian, and date of enrollment. Arranged alphabetically by names of clubs and alphabetically thereunder by names of members. No index. Handwritten on printed forms. 6.5 x 8 x 16.

586. REPORTS
1937—. 1 file box.

Reports from secretaries 4-H clubs, showing name of club, name and address of secretary, date of report, date of meeting, number of members, boys, girls, number members present at meeting, number visitors present, subjects discussed, name of club advisor, and name of club president. Arranged alphabetically by names of clubs and chronologically thereunder by dates of reports. No index. Handwritten on printed forms. 6.5 x 8 x 16.

587. [4-H CLUB MISCELLANEOUS]
1937—. 1 file drawer.
Reports from 4-H club advisors, showing date of report, name of club, name of advisor, period of report, number of meetings held, average attendance, and [text missing].

Financial Records

588. SALARY RECORD
1933—. 4 volumes.
Record of accounts with employees of the agency, showing name of employee, position, number of days worked, wage rate, total die, and pay period dates. Arranged alphabetically by names of employees and chronologically thereunder by pay period dates. No index. Handwritten on forms. Average 284 pages. 9 x 6 x 1.5.

589. OFFICIAL RECEIPTS
1933-1936. 4 volumes. Discontinued.
Receipts from farm owners for checks covering the wheat program, 1933-1936, corn-hog program, 1934-1935, Agricultural Adjustment Administration program, showing date of receipt, receipt number, name of payee, name of township, contract number, amount, and signature of payee. Arranged alphabetically by names of townships and thereunder by names of payees (farm owners), No index. Handwritten on printed forms. Average 300 pages. 11.5 x 15 x 1.5.

590. MONTHLY AND ANNUAL REPORTS
1928—. 1 file drawer.
Copies of county agents' monthly and annual reports to state agricultural Department and Ohio State University Agricultural Extension Department, showing period of report, name of agent, time spent in office, time spent in field (demonstration work), number of meetings attended (extension and demonstration work), number of home demonstration clubs operating, number organized during period of this report, number of 4-H clubs active, number organized during period of this report, number 4-H club members enrolled, boys, girls, total number, number of farms visited for first-time, number of local leaders home demonstration and

economics, number 4-H club advisors, and date filed. Arranged chronologically by dates filed. No index. Handwritten on printed forms. 11.5 x 13.5 x 26.

Correspondence

591. GENERAL CORRESPONDENCE
1933—. 10 file drawers.

General correspondence from and to agricultural agents, pertaining to extension work and informative material on various subjects including entomology, horticultural, livestock, farm management, and forestry, showing date, from or to whom and subject matter. Arranged alphabetically by subjects and chronologically thereunder by dates. No index. Typed. 11.5 x 13.5 x 26.

592. CORRESPONDENCE Home Demonstration Work
1937—. 1 file drawer.

Correspondence from and to the county agent pertaining to work of the home demonstration department, showing from or to whom, date, subject. Arranged chronologically by dates of correspondence. No index. Typed. 11.5 x 13.5 x 26.

Archival Materials and Published Documents

Acts of the General Assembly, 1803-1941 (119 volumes, published annually by state authority).

Baldwin, William Edward, ed., *Throckmorton's Ohio Code Annotated* (certified ed., Banks-Baldwin Co. Cleveland, 1936).

Carter, Clarence Edwin, ed. and comp., *The Territorial Papers of the United States* (8 volumes, U. S. Government Printing Office, Washington, 1934, in progress).

Chase, Salmon P., comp., *The Statutes of Ohio and of the Northwestern Territory . . . 1788-1833* . . . (3 volumes, Corey and Fairbank, Cincinnati, 1833-1835).

Civil Docket, 1852—, 10 volumes, entry 218.

Commissioners' Journal, 1824—, 37 volumes, entry 1.

Constitution of Ohio, 1802.

Constitution of Ohio, 1851.

Curwen. Maskell E., comp., *Public Statutes at Large of the State of Ohio* . . .(3 volumes, published by the author, Cincinnati, 1853-1854),

Deed Record, 1821—, 234 volumes, entry 43.

Hammond, Charles, William Lawrence, Edwin M. Stanton, and others, eds., *Reports of Cases Argued and Determined in the Supreme Court of Ohio in Bank* . . . (20 volumes, Robert Clark and Co., Cincinnati, 1821-1852),

Journal [Court of Common Pleas], 1834—, 56 volumes, entry 174.

Journal [Probate Court], 1852—, 46 volumes, entry 223.

Laning Jay F. Comp. *Revised Statutes and Recodified Laws of the State of Ohio* . . . (2d ed., 3 volumes, The Laning Co., Norwalk, Ohio, 1905).

Law Record, 1825—, 139 volumes, entry 178.

Laws of the Territory of the United States Northwest of the River Ohio (3 volumes, published by authority, Philadelphia and Cincinnati, 1792-1796).

"The Legislature of the Northwest Territory, 1795," *Ohio State Archaeological and Historical Quarterly,* XXX (1921). 13-53.

McCook, G. W., E. O. Randall, J. W. Henney, and others, eds., *Reports of Cases Argued and Determined in the Supreme Court of Ohio* (new series, 137 volumes, various publishers, Columbus, New York, and Cincinnati, 1853-1941).

Ohio Attorney General, *Opinions,* 1914-1939 (published annually by state authority).

Ohio Auditor of State, *Annual Report,* 1836-1939 (published by state authority), Printed prior to 1836 and the Senate and House Journals.

Ohio Auditor of State, *Comparative Statistics, Counties of Ohio,* 1906-1938 (published annually by state authority).

Ohio Department of Agriculture, *Annual Report,* 1846-1936 (68 volumes, published by state authority).

Ohio Secretary of State, *Annual Report* (published by state authority, 1836-1940). Some volumes titled: *Ohio Statistics.*

Ohio Secretary of State, *Ohio Fifteenth Federal Census, 1930* (published by state authority, 1931).

Ohio Tax Commission, *Annual Report,* 1910-1938 (published by state authority).

Order Book [Supreme Court of Ohio], 18 volumes. Titled: Journal, 1903—, 18 volumes.

Pease, Theodore Calvin, comp., *The Laws of the Northwest Territory 1788-1800* (Illinois State Historical Library, *Law Series,* Springfield, 1925, I).

Sayler, J. R., comp., *The Statutes of the State of Ohio* . . . (4 volumes, Robert Clark and Co., Cincinnati, 1876).

Shepherd, Vinton R., ed., *The Ohio NISI PRIUS REPORTS* (new series, 32 volumes, Ohio Law Reporter Co., Columbus and Cincinnati, 1904-1934).

Smith J. V. Rep., *Official Reports of the Debates and Proceedings of the Ohio State Convention . . . Held at Columbus Commencing May 6, 1850, and at Cincinnati, Commencing December 2, 1850* (Scott and Bascom, Columbus, 1851).

Trautwein, George C., *Supplement to Page's Annotated General Code 1926-1935* (W. H. Anderson and Co., Cincinnati, 1935).

U. S. Bureau of the Census, *Fifteenth Census of the United States, 1930, Agriculture* (4 volumes, U. S. Government Printing Office, Washington, 1931-1932).

U. S. Bureau of the Census, *Fifteenth Census of the United States, 1929, Manufacturers* (3 volumes, U. S. Government Printing Office, 1933).

U. S. Bureau of the Census, *Fifteenth Census of the United States, 1930, Population* (6 volumes, U. S. Government Printing Office, Washington, 1931-1933).

U. S. Bureau of the Census, *Fifteenth Census of the United States, 1930, Unemployment* (2 volumes, U. S. Government Printing Office, Washington, 1931-1932).

U. S. Bureau of the Census, *Religious Bodies: 1926* (2 volumes, U. S. Government Printing Office, Washington, 1929-1930).

U. S. Bureau of the Census, *Twelfth Census of the United States, 1900, Population* (2 volumes, U. S. Census Office, Washington, 1901-1902).

United States Statutes at Large, 1789-1941 (54 volumes, U. S. Government Printing Office, Washington, 1848-1941).

Diaries and Memoirs

Burnet [Jacob], *Notes on the Early Settlement of the North-Western Territory* (Derby, Bradley and Co., Cincinnati, 1847).

Darlington, William M., ed., *An Account of the Remarkable Occurrences in the Life and Travels of Col. James Smith . . .* (Robert Clarke and Co., Cincinnati, 1870).

General Histories and Reference Works

Adams, George Burton, *Constitutional History of England* (Henry Holt and Company, New York, 1921).

Ayer, N. W. and Sons, publishers, *Directory of Newspapers and Periodicals* (Philadelphia, 1937).

Channing, Edward, *A History of the United States* (6 volumes, Macmillan Co., New York, 1905-1925).

Cross, Arthur Lyon, *A Shorter History of England and Greater Britain* (Mcamillan company, New York, 1925).

Gwynne, A. E., *A Practical Treatise on the Law of Sheriff and Coroner with Forms and References to the Statutes of Ohio, Indiana, and Kentucky* (H. W. Derby and Co., Cincinnati, 1849).

Karraker, Cyrus Harreld, *The Seventeenth-Century Sheriff: A Comparative Study of the Sheriff in England and the Chesapeake Colonies, 1607-1687* (University of North Carolina Press, Chapel Hill, 1930).

Pollock, Sir Frederick, and Frederic William Maitland. *The History of English Law Before the Time of Edward I* (2 volumes, Cambridge University Press, Cambridge England, and Little, Brown and Co., Boston, Massachusetts, 1895).

Schapiro, J. Salwyn, *Modern and Contemporary European History 1815-1928* (Houghton Mifflin Co., New York, 1931).

Sutherland, Edwin H., *Principles of Criminology* (J. B. Lippincott and Co., Chicago, 1934).

Van Waters, Miriam, *Youth in Conflict* (Republic Publishing Company, New York, 1925).

Willoughby W. F., *Principles of Judicial Administration* (The Brookings Institution, Washington, 1929).

The World Almanac (New York World Telegram, New York, 1937).

Regional and Local Histories, Treatises, and Monographs

Amer, Francis J., *The Development of the Judicial System in Ohio from 1787* to *1932* (*Institute of Law Bulletin No. 8,* Johns Hopkins Press, Baltimore, 1932).

Baughman, A. J., *History of Seneca County Ohio: A Narrative Account of its Historical Progress, Its People, and Its Principal Interest* (2 volumes, Lewis Publishing Co., Chicago and New York, 1911).

Bond, Beverley W., Jr., *The Civilization of the Old Northwest: A Study of Political, Social, and Economic Development, 1788-1912* (Macmillan Co., New York, 1934).

Butterfield, Consul W., *History of Seneca County* (D. Campbell and Sons, Sandusky, 1848).

Daughters of the American Revolution, Ohio–Dolly Todd Madison Chapter, comps., and pubs, *Ohio Early State and Local History* (Tiffin, 1915).

Dildone, Frank, *From Wilderness to City* (n. pub., n. p., n. d).

Estrich, Willis A., ed., in chief, *Ohio Jurisprudence* (43 volumes, The Lawyers Co-operative Publishing Company, Rochester, New York, 1928-1938).

Fess Simeon, D., ed., *Ohio Reference Library* (4 volumes, The Lewis Publishing Company, Chicago and New York, 1937).

Heiges, R. E., *The Office of Sheriff in the Rural Counties of Ohio* (published by the author, Findlay, 1933).

Howe, Henry, comp., *Historical Collections of Ohio* (published by state authority, Norwalk, 1896).

Kennedy, Aileen Elizabeth, *The Ohio Poor Law and Its Administration* (Sophonisba P. Breckinridge ed., Social Service Monographs, No. 22, University of Chicago Press, Chicago, 1934).

Kilbourne, John, comp., *The Ohio Gazetteer or Topographical Directory* (10th ed., published by the editor, Columbus, 1831).

Knapp, H. S. *History of the Maumee Valley* (Blade Mammoth Printing and Publishing House, Toledo, 1872).

McCarty, Dwight G., *The Territorial Governors of the Old Northwest: A Study in Territorial Administration* (The State Historical Society of Iowa, Iowa City, 1910).

Mills, William G., *Archaeological Atlas of Ohio* (Ohio Archaeological and Historical Society, Columbus, 1914).

Moley, Raymond, "The Sheriff and the Coroner," in the Missouri Association for Criminal Justice, *The Missouri Criminal Survey,* pt. ii, (Macmillan Co., New York, 1926).

Ohio Study of Local School Units, *A Study of the Public Schools of Seneca County, with Recommendations for Their Future Organization* (Ohio State Department of Education, Columbus, 1937).

Peters, William E., *Ohio Lands and Their Subdivision* (Second edition, W. E. Peters, Athens, Ohio, 1918).

Rawson, Abel, *Address Before the Seneca County Pioneer Association* (Star Printing House, Tiffin, 1869),

Report of the Geological Survey of Ohio (Second series, 6 volumes, published by state authority, 1873-1893).

The Reorganization of County Government in Ohio: Report of the Governor's Commission on County Government (n. pub., n. p., submitted to the governor, December 1934).

Roseboom, Eugene Holloway, and Francis Phelps Weisenbarger, *A History of Ohio* (Prentice-Hall, Inc., New York, 1934).

Stewart, D. J., comp., *Combination Atlas Map of Seneca County, Ohio* (Binder's title: *New Historical Atlas of Seneca County, Ohio,* published by the compiler, Philadelphia, 1874).

Van Tassel, Charles S. ed., *Story of the Maumee Valley, Toledo, and the Sandusky Region* (2 volumes, S. J. Clark Publishing Company, Chicago, 1929).

Warner, Beers and Co., comp., *History of Seneca County, Ohio* (Warner, Beers and Company, Chicago, 1886).

Winter, Nevin O., ed., *A History of Northwest Ohio* (3 volumes, The Lewis Publishing Company, Chicago and New York, 1917).

Articles in Periodicals

Atkinson R. C., "County Home Rule Developments in Ohio," *National Municipal Review,* XXIII (1934), 235.

—, "Ohio– County Charter Elections," *National Municipal Review,* XXIV (1935), 702-703.

—, "Ohio–Optional County Legislation," *National Municipal Review,* XXIV (1935), 228.

Downes, Randolph Chandler, "Evolution of Ohio County Boundaries," *Ohio State Archaeological and Historical Quarterly,* XXXVI (1927), 340-447.

Dykstra, C. A., "Cleveland's Effort for City-County Consolidation," *National Municipal Review,* VIII (1919), 551-556.

Gates, Charles M., "The Administration of State Archives," *The Pacific Northwest Quarterly,* XXIX (January, 1938), No. 1; also in *The American Archivist,* I (July 1938), 130-141.

Graham A. A., "The Military Post, Forts and Battlefields Within the State of Ohio," *Ohio State Archaeological and Historical Quarterly,* III (1895), 300-311.

Kaplan, H. Eloit, "A Personal Program for County Service," *National Review,* XXV (1936), 596-600.

King, I. F., "Introduction of Methodism in Ohio," *Ohio State Archaeological and Historical Quarterly,* X (1902), 165-219.

Miller, Edward A., "The History of Educational Legislation in Ohio," *Ohio State Archaeological and Historical Quarterly,* XXVII (1919), 1-271.

Morris, William A., "The Office of Sheriff in the Anglo-Saxon Period." *English Historical Review,* XXXI (1916), 20-40.

Stone, Donald C., "The Police Attack Crime," *National Municipal Review,* XXIV (1935), 39-41.

Newspapers

Ohio State Journal, 1840, 1933.

ROSTER OF COUNTY OFFICIALS 1824- 1941

Commissioners*

William Clark (Part of year) 1824
Jesse Olmstead (Part of year) 1824
Benjamin Whitmore 1824-1826
Doctor Dunn 1824-1826
(Resigned in May)
Thomas Boyd 1824-1832
(Resigned in February)
James Gordon 1826
(Appointed in June)
James Gordon 1826-1827
Timothy P. Roberts 1826-1832
Case Brown 1827-1833
David Risdon 1832
(Appointed in March)
John Keller 1832-1833
John Crum 1833-1834
Marcus Y. Graff 1833-1834
(Resigned in April)
John Seitz 1833-1839
Nicholas Goetschier 1834
(Appointed in May)
Benjamin Whitmore 1834-1838
Lorenzo Abbott 1834-1840
John Terry 1838-1844
Andrew Moore 1839-1842
George Stoner 1840-1843
Joseph McClellan 1842-1848
Morris P. Skinner 1843-1849
Jacob Decker 1844-1847
(Resigned in March)
Benjamin Tomb 1847
(Appointed in April)
Jacob Decker 1847-1850
Samuel Saul 1848-1854
Barney Zimmerman 1849-1852
David Burns 1850-1856
Calvin Clark 1852-1855
Isaac Stillwell 1854-1857
James E. Boyd 1855-1858
Enoch Trumbo 1856-1859
Henry Opt 1857-1863
Robert Byrne 1858-1863
(Resigned in April)
Michael Beard 1859-1862
Peter Ebersole 1862-1868
Samuel Grelle 1863
(Appointed in April)
Samuel Grelle 1863-1867
Thomas W. Watson 1863-1869
Heron B. Rakestraw 1867-1873
Joseph E. Magers 1868-1874
Stephen M. Ogden 1869-1872
Stephen M. Osgood 1872-1875
Robert McClellan 1873-1879
Solomon Gamber 1874-1880
Nathaniel G. Hayward 1875-1878
William F. Histe 1878-1884
James H. Fry 1879-1882
(Died in July)
Edward Childs 1880-1886
Truman H. Bagby 1882
(Appointed in July)
D. P. Lynch 1882-1885
Truman H. Bagby 1884-1890
Levi Haines 1885-1888
Henry F. Hedden 1886-1891
Nicholas Burtcher 1888-1895
Frank Shannon 1890-1893
Truman Zeis 1892-1896
John A. Bain 1894-1897
James H. Knapp 1896-1898
Christian Trott 1897
Julius Kiessling 1897-1902
John P. Warnement 1897-1903
Henry Eissler 1898-1901
(Died in February)

Commissioners* (continued)

Burton W. Finch (Appointed in February)	1901	W. A. Jordon	1919-1925
Herbert G. Ogden	1907-1907	William C. Roller	1919-1922
Frank J. Fry	1902-1913	F. W. Dudrow	1919-1929
J. M. Schatzel	1903-1906	Charles L. Park	1923-1927
Nicholas Wall	1906-1911	M. R. Hooper (Died in May)	1925-19325
Charles D. Holtz	1907-1909	Samuel A. Dreitzler	1927*1935
John W. Cook	1909-1913	F. L. Myers	1929-1933
Christian Miller	1911-1915	Edward V. Burke (Appointed in May)	1932-1933
David Auble	1913-1915	J. V. Weiker	1933-1937
Charles Aldrich	1913-1919	Anson B. Hoover	1933-1937
George F. Weaver	1915-1919	Clarence B. Baker	1935—
Charles Nepper (Died in September)	1915-1918	Harry L. Stultz	1937—
W. A. Jordon (Appointed in September)	1918-1919	Bloom L. Myers	1937—

*The board of county commissioners with three members, each serving a three-year term was established in 1804 (2 O. L. 150). In 1906 the term of office was changed to two years (98 O. L. 271); in 1920 it was increased to four years, and so remains (108 O. L. pt. ii, 1300).

Compiled from: Commissioners' Journals, 1824—. Dates given are dates of assuming duties of office and retiring from office.

Recorders**

David Smith (Part of year)	1824	William DeWitt (Died in January)	1872-1874
Beal McGaffey	1824-1828	Thomas J. Kintz (Appointed in January)	1874-1875
Abel Rawson	1829-1839	Thomas J. Kintz	1875-1881
William H. Kessler (Office declared vacant)	1839-1846	John H. Bennehoff	1882-1887
Samuel G. Breslin (Appointed in August)	1846	George F. Wentz	1888-1893
Robert M. C. Martin	1846-1853	Thomas H. Drohen	1894-1900
William Kline	1853–1859	Louis Wagner	1900-1903
Albert Brilharz	1860-1865	Harry Taggart	1903-1909
James T. Martin	1866-1871	L. J. Wingart	1909-1913

Recorders** (continued)

Louis Wagner (Died in May)	1913-1917	N. A. Seibenaller	1917-1921
		J. D. McConnell	1921-1925
Francis E. Wagner (Appointed in May)	1917	Estelle V. George	1925-1935
		Harry Taggart	1935—

**From 1803 to 1828 recorders were appointed by the associate judges of the court of common pleas for a term of seven years (1 O. L. 136). In 1829 the office became elective for a three-year term, reduced to two years in 1905, and increased to four years in 1936 (27 O. L. 65; *Ohio Const. 1851,* Art. XVII, sec. 2; 116 O. L. pt. ii, 184).

Compiled from: Deed Record, 1821—.

Clerk of Courts ***

Neil McGaffey (Resigned in September)	1824-1829	Charles A. Gribble (Resigned in June)	1895-1897
Joseph Howard (Resigned in March)	1829-1834	Irvn N. Rex (Appointed in June)	1897
Luther A. Hall	1834-1840	Irvin N. Rex	1897-1903
Charles F. Dresbach	1840-1846	Francis R. Mann	1904-1908
Henry Ebbert	1846-1852	George N. Young	1909-1915
Philip Spielman	1852-1857	Ernest A. Wetzel	1916-1919
George S. Christlip	1858-1863	John Dreitzler	1920-1923
William M. Dildine	1864-1869	W. E. Lautermilch	1923-1929
Jacob C. Millhime	1870-1875	Roy W. Chatfield	1929-1933
Jeremiah Rex	1876-1881	Arthur S. Myers	1934-1941
James V. Magers	1882-1888	Grottan B. Deats	1941—
Lewis Ulrich	1889-1894		

***Called prothonotary under the laws of the Northwest Territory and appointed by the governor. Under the constitution of 1802 the clerk was appointed by the judges for a seven-year term (Art. III, sec. 9). Under the constitution of 1851 the office was made elective for a three-year term (Art. IV, sec. 16). In 1905 by constitutional amendment the term was changed to two years and in 1936 to four years (96 O. L. 641; 116 O. L. pt. ii, 184).

ROSTER OF COUNTY OFFICIALS 1824- 1941

Judges of the Court of Common Pleas*

President judges under the Constitution of 1802 for District II which included Seneca County

Ebenezer Lane	1824-1831	Ozias Bowen	1838-1852
David Higgins	1831-1838		

Associate judges for the district which included Seneca County under the constitution of 1802

William Cornell (Resigned in March)	1824-1832	Henry C. Brish (Resigned in March)	1839-1843
Jacques Hulbert	1824-1831	Henry Ebert (Resigned)	1845-1848
Matthew Clark (Resigned in April)	1824-1831	William Toll	1845-1852
Seldin Graves (Resigned in April)	1831-1838	John Zimmerman (Deceased)	1848-1850
Agreen Ingraham	1831-1839	Thomas Lloyd (Resigned in April)	1850-1851
Benjamin Pittenger	1832-1838	Henry C. Brish	1851-1852
Lowell Robinson	1838-1845		
Andrew Lugenbeel	1838-1852		

Judges under the Constitution of 1851 for the districts which included Seneca County

Lawrence Hall	1852-1856	Thomas Beer	1878
William Lawrence	1857	John McCauley	188-1883
M. C. Whitley	1857	Luther M. Strong	1883
George E. Seney	1858-1862	George F. Pendleton	1884-1888
Josiah S. Plants	1862	John H. Ridgely	1888-1893
M. C. Whitley	1862-1866	J. W. Schaufellberger	1893-1902
Chester R. Mott	1867	Frank Taylor	1899
James Pillars	1868	William Duncan	1902-194
James Mackenzie	1868-1869	Frank Taylor	1903
James Pillars	1870-1878	Charles C. Lemert	1903
Chester R. Mott	1871	George E. Schroth	1904-1908
Abner M. Jackson	1872-1873	William F. Duncan	1909-1910
Thomas Beer	1875	Frank A. Baldwin	1909-1910
Selwin N. Owen	1877	W. P. Henderson	1909-1914
Henry H. Dodge	1878-1888	William F. Duncan	1914

Judges of the Court of Common Pleas** (continued)

Resident judges under the constitutional amendment of 1912

James H. Platt (Died in July)	1915-1933	Ralph Sugrue (Unexpired term of James H. Platt)	1933-1939
John T., Carver (Acting judge April term)	1924	Ralph Sugrue	1939—

**Under the Constitution of 1802 the president and associate judges were appointed for seven-year terms by joint ballot of both houses of the general assembly (*Ohio Const. 1802*, Art. III, sec. 8). Under the Constitution of 1851 the office was made elective for five-year terms and required the incumbent to be a resident of the district in which elected (*Ohio Const. 1851* Art. IV, sec. 12). An amendment in 1912 changed the term to six years, required the election of at least one judge in each county, who must be a resident of the county in which elected (Art. IV, sec. 12, as amended September 3, 1912).

Compiled from: Law Record, 1825, and [Common Pleas] Journal, 1852—.

Judges of the Probate Court*

William Lang	1852-1855	J. C. Rickenbaugh (Appointed in June)	1887
John K. Hord (Resigned in November)	1855-1857	John C. Royer	1887-1894
Truman H. Bagby (Appointed in November)	1857-1858	Alexander Kiskadden	1894-1897
		Winfield Scott Wagner	1897-1903
Truman H. Bagby	1858-1864	Hal William Michael	1903-1909
William Johnson	1864-1873	George M. Hoke	1909-1918
Upton F. Cramer	1873-1879	Clyde C. Porter (Resigned in September)	1918-1929
Jacob F. Bunn	1879-1885		
Harrison Noble (Resigned in January)	1885-1887	Herbert Abbot (Appointed in October)	1929-1930
		V. A. Bennehoff	1930—

*The probate court, established under the laws of the Northwest Territory in 1788, consisted of a probate judge and two judges of the court of common pleas (Pease, *op. cit.*,9). Under the Constitution of 1802 it lost its identity completely in the court of common pleas. It emerged with its present functions in 1852, with a single judge serving a three year term, under the Constitution of 1851 (Art. V, secs. 7, 8). On September 3, 1912, the term was changed to four years (Art. IV, sec. 7, as amended in 1912). Compiled from [Probate Court] Journal and Commissioners' Journal.

1824- 1941

Prosecuting Attorney*

Rudolphus Dickinson (Resigned in March)	1824-1826	George M. Bachman (Appointed in January)	1873
Abel Rawson	1826-1833	George M. Bachman	1874-1877
Sidney Smith	1834-1835	Guilford B. Keppel	1878-1881
Selah Chapin, Jr.	1836-1837	Perry M. Adams	1882-1887
John J. Steiner (Resigned in May)	1838-1841	William H. Dore	1888-1890
		George E. Schroth, Sr.	1891-1896
Sidney Smith (Appointed in May)	1841	Milton Saylor	1897-1902
		James M. Platt	1903-1908
Joel W. Wilson	1842-1845	Harry P. Black	1909-1910
William Lang	1846-1849	James H. Platt	1911-1912
William P. Noble	1850-1851	Russell M.Kuepper	1913-1916
W. N. Johnson	1852-1855	Calvin D. Spitler	1917-1920
Luther A. Hall	1856-1857	John L. Lott	1921-1922
Robert L. Griffith	1858-1861	Walter K. Keppel	1923-1926
Alfred Landon	1852-1865	George E. Schroth, Jr.	1927-1930
John McCauley	1866-1869	Paul A. Flynn	1931-1936
Frank Baker (Resigned in January)	1870-1873	Robert C. Carpenter	1937—

*At first appointed by the supreme court and later (1805) by the court of common pleas, alaw passed January 23, 1833, made the office of prosecuting attorney elective for a term of two years (31 O. L. 13). In 1881 the term was increased to three years, in 1906 reduced to two, and in 1936 increased to four (78 O. L. 260; 98 O. L. 271; 116 O. L. pt ii, 184.

Compiled from: Law Record and Commissioners' Journal.

1824- 1941

Coroners*

Leverett Bradley 1824
Christopher Stone 1824-1828
William Toll 1828-1832
George Flack 1832-1834
Eli Norris 1834-1836
Levi Kellar 1836-1838
Henry McCartney 1838-1840
Daniel Brown 1840-1842
George H. Shaw 1842-1846
Samuel Herrin 1846-1850
George Ransbury 1850-1854
Samuel Herrin 1854-1858
James W. Lawhead 1859-1860
Paul Bollinger 1861-1864
Jonas M. Hasberger 1865-1866
James Paine 1867-1868
Sylvester B. Clark 1869-1872
James Van Fleet 1872
(Elected October but failed to qualify)
Charles Mutchler 1873
(Appointed in January)
George W. Wilton 1873-1876
William Smith 1877-1884
Edward Lepper 1885-1915
(Died in April)
Burton R. Miller 1915-1916
(Appointed in May)
J. D. McConnell 1916-1920
V. T. Carr 1921-1923
(Resigned in January)
Frank Dildine 1923
(Appointed in January - resigned in January)
Isaac P. Rule 1923-1926
(Appointed in January)
Perry T. Perin 1927-1941
W. H. Benner 1941—

*Established in 1788, the county coroner was appointed for a two-year term by the territorial governor (Pease, *op. cit.,* 24, 25). The Ohio Constitution of 1802 (Art. VI sec. 1) made the office elective without changing the term, which remained at two years until 1936, when it was increased to four years (116 O. L. pt. ii, 184).

Compiled from: Law Record, 1825-1852, and Commissioners' Journal, 1852—.

ROSTER OF COUNTY OFFICIALS 1824- 1941

Sheriffs*

Agreen Ingraham	1824-1828
William Patterson	1828-1830
David Bishop	1830-1834
Joel Stone	1834-1838
Levi Kellar	1838-1842
Uriah Coonrod	1842-1846
Eden Lease	1846-1850
Stephen M. Ogden	1850-1854
Ephriam C. Wells	1855-1856
Jesse Weirick	1857-1860
Levi Weirick	1861-1862
Edward Childs	1863-1866
Peter P. Myers	1867-1870
John Werley	1871-1874
George D. Acker	1875-1878
Lloyd N. Lease	1879-1882
Thomas F. Whalen	1883-1886
George Homan (Resigned in August)	1887-1890
John L. Huff (Appointed in August)	1890
Alonzo Burman	1891-1894
Joseph Van Nest	1895-1896
W. Morris Shaffer	1897-1900
Albert J. Henzy	1901-1902
Henry Brohl	1903-1904
Charles Nepper	1905-198
Philip H. Reif	1908-1912
George E. Bare (Died in November)	1913
Charles H. Bare (Appointed in November)	1913-1914
Charles H. Bare	1915-1916
Charles J. Mutchler	1917-1920
Joseph W. Parks	1921-1924
A.B. Grossman	1925-1928
George A. Burkett	1929-1932
Verne F. Deats	1933-1940
George B. Steinmetz	1941—

*Under the territorial government the sheriff was appointed by the governor from the time the office was created in 1792 (Pease, *op. cit.,* 8). Under the first constitution the office was made elective for a two-year term (*Ohio Const. 1802*, Art, VI, sec. 1) and was not changed until 1936, when the tern was increased to four years (116 O. L. pt. ii, 184).

Compiled from: Law Record, 1825-1852, and [Common Pleas] Journal, 1852—.

1824- 1941

Auditors*

David White	1824-1832
David E. Owen	1832-1836
Levi Davis	1836-1841
Gabine J. Keen	1841-1845
Frederick W. Green	1845-1851
Richard Williams (Died in September)	1851-1852
John J. Steiner (Appointed in September)	1852-1853
John J. Steiner	1853-1855
James M. Stevens	1855-1859
E. G. Bowe	1859–1861
Isaac Kagy	1861-1867
John F. Heilman	1867-1869
Walter F. Burns (Died in April)	1869-1870
G. A. Allen (Appointed in April)	1870-1871
G. A. Allen (Office declared vacant)	1871-1872
Isaac Kagy (Appointed in June)	1872-1873
Levi B. Kagy	1873-1877
Victor J. Zahn (Resigned in October)	1877-1881
Frances E. Stoner (Appointed in October)	1881-1883
Frances E. Stoner (Died in August)	1883-1885
James A. Norton (Appointed in August)	1885-1886
James A. Norton	1886-1892
William H. Schlosser	1892-1898
Lee Nighswander	1898-1904
Romanus R. Bour	1904-1909
John R. Lennartz	1909-1913
James E. Hershberger	1913-1917
Jacob H. Morcher	1917-1923
Arthur B. Powell	1923-1931
F. W. Grill	1931-1939
John C. Harriman	1939—

*Office established by legislative act, February 18, 1820 (18 O., L, 70). At first appointive, it was made elective annually by an act of February 2, 1821, the person elected taking office March 1 each year (19 O. L. 16). In 1831 the term was set at two years, in 1877 at three years, in 1906 at two years, and in 1919 at four years (29 O. L. 280; 74 O. L., 381; 98 O. L. 271; 108 O. L. pt. ii, 1294).

Compiled from Commissioners' Journals.

1824- 1941

Treasurers*

Milton McNeal	1824-1827	Benjamin F. Myers	1886-1890
Agreen Ingraham	1827	Charles A. Goetz	1890-1894
Jacob Plane	1828-1834	Henry Mansfield	1894-1898
John Goodin	1834-1840	James D. McDonel	1898-1902
Joshua Seney	1840-1844	Charles Ash	1902-1906
Richard Williams	1844-1848	Wm. Morris Shaffer	1906-1910
George Krupp	18481852	William D. Heckert	1910-1914
Thomas Hemming	1852-1856	Arthur B. Powell	1914-1918
George H. Hemming (Resigned in July)	1856-1858	Forrest R. Miller (Failed to qualify)	1918
Lewis E. Holtz (Appointed in July)	1858	William M. Shaffer (Appointed in September)	1918-1919
Samuel Herrin	1858-1862	Frank A. Maberry	1919-1923
Silas W. Shaw	1862-1866	John H. Thompson	1923-1927
J. H. Zahn	1866-1868	Amandus B. Grossman	1927-1931
David Huss	1868-1870	Ray W. Harding	1931-1935
William Lang	1870-1874	Edgar Burdell Straub (Resigned in December)	1935-1936
Francis Wagner	1874-1878	Louis P. Schaffer (Appointed in January)	1937
John W. Barrick	1878-1882	Harry R. Read	1937—
John Heabler (Died in June)	1882-1885		
Isaac Kagy (Appointed in June)	1885-1886		

*Omitted from the Constitution of 1802, the office of treasurer was created by legislative act in 1803 (1 O. L. 98). Appointive, by the associate judges in 1803 and, annually, by the county commissioners frolm 1804 to 1827, when the office became elective for two-year terms (1 O. L. 98; 2 O. L. 154; 25 O. L. 25-32). The constitution of 1851 provided that no person should hold the office for more than four years of any six. (Art. X, sec. 3). In accordance the constitution of 1851 and an act of the general assembly in 1859 term remained at two years (56 O. L. 105). In 1936 it was increased to four years, as at present (116 O. L. pt. ii, 184).

Infirmary Directors*

Andrew Lugenbeel 1856-1865
John Kerr 1856-1858
(Resigned in August)
Daniel Brown 1856-1859
Jonas Hampshire 1858-1861
(Vice John Kerr)
Thomas Swander 1859-1861
George S. Christlip 1861-1865
Barney Zimmerman 1861-1868
(Resigned in January)
Harrison Noble 1866-1871
Eden Lease 1866-1871
Uriah P. Conrad 1868-1873
(Vice Barney Zimmerman)
Jesse Weirick 1872
(Died in December)
Peter Heafling 1872-1877
George W. Bachman 1873
(Appointed in January)
Charles Mutchler 1874-1876
John Britt 1874-1880
Lewis Spitler 1877-1882
George Hepler 1878-1882
(Resigned in May)
George B. Acker 1882
(Appointed in May)
Joseph E. Magers 1881-1883
James Saunders 1883-1888
William H. Kline 1883-1888
Daniel Metager 1884-1889
John Rehinbolt 1889-1894
William King 1889-1894
John Roller 1890-1895
Emanuel Fisher 1895
(Died in May)
Elmer Fisher 1895
(Appointed in May)
John L. Arnold 1895-1897
George R. Huss 1895-1897
James H. Bowser 1896-1899
(Office declared vacant in September)
John Y. Gahris 1898-1903
John Kripp 1898-1903
Frank P. Sherman 1899
(Appointed in September)
Frank P. Sherman 1900-1904
James T. Williams 1904-1906
Lewis Hufford 1904-1906
Daniel B. Crissel 1905-1907
David H. Good 1907-1909
Jacob Staib 1907-1909
Samuel Dreitzler 1908-1913
John R. Jewett 1910-1913
David Auble 1910-1913

*This office was authorized by a legislative act in 1816, providing for the appointment by the commissioners of seven directors, to have charge of the poorhouse (later county infirmary) and choose its superintendent (14 O. L. 447-448). By an act of 1831, the membership of the board was reduced to three, and in 1842 the members were made elective for terms of three years I29 O. L. 317; 40 O. L. 35). The board was abolished by law in 1913, and its powers and duties were transferred to the board of county commissioners and the infirmary superintendent (102 O. L. 433).

1824- 1941

Surveyors*

David Risdon
George W. Gist
(Resigned in November)
James Durbin
(Appointed in November)
Jonas Harshbarger
Thomas Hemming
C. Dewitt
Marcus Schuyler
(Appointed in December)
George Hamming
Thomas Burnsides
Dennis Molloy
Patrick H. Ryan
Dennis Molloy
Samuel Nighswander
George McGormley
Charles J. Peters
W. B. Dildine
(Elected but died prior to taking office)
Charles J. Peters
(Appointed in September)
Charles J. Peters
John W. Price
(Resigned in September)
William O. Bulger
(Appointed in September)
Charles J. Peters
Henry B. Puffenberger
Charles J. Peters
James L. Oberlander
Charles E. Hutchinson
Harold J. Hakes
James B. Puffenberger
(Died in January)

*From 1803 to 1831 the surveyor was appointed by the court of common pleas and commissioned by the governor (1 O. L. 90-93. From 1831-1906 he was elected for a three-year term, from 1906-1928 for a two-year term, and since 1928 for a four-year term (29 O. L. 399; 98 O. L. 245-247; 112 O. L. 179).

Engineers**

Chalmer Mohr (Appointed in January)	1935-1936
Chalmer Mohr	1937-1941
Gerald W. Fling	1941—

**An act of 1935 changed the title of surveyor to engineer (116 O. L. 283).

All addresses are Tiffin, Ohio, unless otherwise noted.

Auditor
109 South Washington Street
Suite 2206
https://senecacountyauditoroh.gov/

Board of Elections
71 South Washington Street
Suite 1101
https://www.boe.ohio.gov/seneca/

Clerk of Courts
103 East Market Street
https://senecacountyclerk.org/

Commissioners
111 Madison Street
https://www.countyoffice.org/seneca-county-commissioner-tiffin-oh-b11/

Common Pleas
103 East Market Street
https://senecaohcourts.gov/

Coroner
81 Ashwood Road
https://www.countyoffice.org/seneca-county-medical-examiner-coroner-tiffin-oh-398

Dog Warden
3140 South State Route 100
https://senecacountydogwarden.wordpress.com/

Engineer
3300 South TR 151
https://sencoeng.com/

Health Department
92 East Perry Street
https://senecahealthdept.org

Probate/Juvenile Court
103 East Market Street
https://www.senecajpcourt.com/

Prosecutor
79 South Washington Street
https://www.senecapros.org/

Recorder
109 South Washington Street
Suite 2104
https://www.countyoffice.org/seneca-county-recorder-of-deeds-tiffin-oh-2bf/

Seneca Parks
3362 South TR 151
https://www.senecacountyparks.com/

Sheriff
3040 South State Route 100
https://senecacountyso.org/

Treasurer
109 South Washington Street
Suite 2105
https://senecacountytreasurer.org/

Non-governmental websites

FamilySearch
https://www.familysearch.org/search/catalog

FamilySearch is a free website with digitized records. Records located for Seneca County include: Auditor, Clerk of Courts, Common Pleas, Coroner County Home, Probate Court, Recorder, and Supreme Court.

Bowling Green State University
Jerome Library, 5th Floor
Center for Archival Collections
https://maurice.bgsu.edu/search/X?SEARCH=seneca+county&searchscope=1

BGSU's Archival Collections encompass the nineteen northwestern Ohio counties. From the above link, select Seneca County for a listing of over 100 entries regarding the county; from newspaper articles, to family histories, cemetery inscriptions, and court records. Contact the university for specific court records for Seneca County.

Tiffin-Seneca Public Library
77 Jefferson Street
https://www.tiffinsenecalibrary.org/genealogy
Email: infoservices@tiffinsenecalibrary.org

The library offers online databases for genealogical websites, a Seneca County digital library (Ohio Memory), as well as a link to information found at the library. The library houses atlases, plat maps, and deeds; military information such as military rosters, the Soldiers' Relief Commission and Military Discharges, and others. Cemetery and church information is extensive including 30 churches whose records on are microfilm. Also at the library are school records, census and city directories; newspapers and obituaries, plus a variety of special collections.

Abstracts of voters, 473
Accounts, *see* Financial records
Adjustment of taxes, *see* Taxes
Administration of estates, *see* Estates
Adoptions, minors, 223, 224
Agreements
See also Contracts
indentures, 38
leases, 50, 53
partnerships, 91, 93, 100, 145, 146
Agricultural extension agent
Entries (records)
correspondence, 591, 592
extension and conservation, 582, 584
financial, 588-590
4-H clubs, 585-587
Agricultural society
entries (records), 1, 574-581
Aid for the aged, board of
entries (records) 530-542
Aid to the blind, *see* Blind cases
Aid to dependent children, *see* Minors
Aliases, fugitives, 307
Aliens, 149, 174, 184-186, 258, 259
Animals
dogs
licenses, 8, 389, 390
unlicensed, 8, 311, 314
livestock
appraisements, 402
brands, 313
claims for damages, 1, 8, 26, 362, 402
county home,9, 516, 524
reports on, 159
Antitoxin, reports on, 500
Appearance dockets
circuit court, 200
court of appeals, 209
Appearance docket (continued)
court of common pleas, 162, 164
juvenile court, 278
Applications
absence of voters, 474
administrators of estates, 220, 223, 232, 234, 251
admit wills to probate, 230
aliens or citizenship papers, 259
board of park commissioners, 296, 297
county Commissioners, 410
of electors or transfer, 468
executors of estates, 220, 223
for licenses
beverage dealers, 397
cosmetic dealers, 397
for dogs, 389
vendors, 397
in lunacy cases, 255, 257
mothers pensions, 285, 287, 288, 290
for relief
for the aged, 530-532
blind cases, 40, 42, 528
emergency cases, 30
soldiers, 527
school teachers, 488
Appraisements
estates, 102, 220, 221, 223, 232, 233, 241, 242, 244, 251, 252, 352
personal property, 90, 402
real estate, 301, 303, 321 325-327
Appropriation of funds
for relief, 1, 33, 34, 367, 370, 373, 402
to sheriff's office, 195
Army, United States, 101
Articles of incorporation, 92, 100
Assessors
for county, 402

Assessors (continued)
- reports, 160

Assignees of estates, 223, 239
Assignment commissioners, 129
Assignments, 217, 223, 224
Auctioneers licenses, 174
Auditor, county
- certificates of funds and treasury, 13
- entries (records)
  - Bonds, 412-415
  - financial, 358-288
  - licenses and permits, 389-398
  - miscellaneous, 416-418
  - plats and maps, 320-322
  - property transfers, 316-319
  - reports and statements, 399-411
  - settlements, 353-347
  - tax records, 323-352
  - weights and measures, 419

Auditor, state, 345, 349

Bailiffs, 129
Ballots, 143, 144, 470, 471,472, 475
Banks
- deposits, 373, 277
- protest, 103, 104

Bar dockets
- circuit court, 203
- court of appeals, 203, 211
- court of common pleas, 170
- district court, 196

Bids
- coal dealers, 29
- public improvements, 10, 12, 16, 19, 22, 29, 552, 562

Bills
- against county, 206
- board of education, 485, 495
- Board of health, 498
- county officials, 1, 3, 4, 29, 359-362, 365, 387, 388
- of exceptions, 117
- of particulars, 178, 182, 191, 193
- relief of, 361
- of sale, 100, 125, 128

Births, *see* vital statistics
Blind cases, 38, 156, 207, 280, 1, 29, 40-42, 372, 373, 402, 528, 529
Board of aid for the aged, 361, 530-542
Board of county commissioners, *see* Commissioners, county
Board of county visitors, 174, 223, 280
Board of education, *see* Education, board of
Board of elections, *see* Elections, board of
Board of equalization, *see* Revision, board of
Board of health, 498-510
Board of public assistance, 290
Board of review, *see* Revision, board of
Board of revision, *see* Revision, board of
Board of school examiners, 407, 409
Bonds
- administrators of estates, 220, 223, 232, 234, 236, 237, 244
- approved by county commissioners, 1, 378, 412, 413, 415, 453, 455, 463
- assignees of estates, 223, 239
- clerk a board of education, 414

Bonds (continued)
contractors for public improvements, 1A-1C, 10, 12, 15, 16, 19, 21, 562
court attendance, 174
custodian of, 232
deputies to county officials, 174, 417
executors of estates, 220, 223, 233, 236, 237
guardianships, 221, 223, 235, 238, 244
injunctions, 239
notices of, 252
officials, 1, 286, 412, 413, 453
park commissioners, 296
petitioners, 1, 1A, 1B, 10, 12, 15, 16
for public improvements, 1, 378, 415, 455, 463
trustees for the sinking fund, 35, 246, 378, or 63
Bounties, soldiers, 1
Brokers licenses, 140
Bridges, 5, 1C, 19, 21, 23, 554, 559-562, 572
Budget commissioners
budgets, 456, 457, 572
Budgets
budget commissioners, 29, 456, 457, 572
county commissioners, 275, 382, 456, 457
taxes, 323
Burials, soldiers, 1, 5

Calendars, 217
Candidates for elections, 143, 144, 470, 471, 473, 476-479
Case records
blind cases, 42
Case records (continued)
board of aid for the aged, 532, 534, 537, 539, 540
county home, 517
sheriffs, 257, 306
soldiers relief commission, 527
tuberculosis hospital, 511, 512
Cashbook
board of elections, 481
clerk of courts, 150
county home, 523
juvenile court, 174, 286
probate court, 270
sheriffs, 308
treasurers, 444
Cemeteries, deeds to, 46
Chancery cases, 180
Chattel mortgages, *see* Mortgages
Chattels, *see* Personal property
Children, *see* Minors
Churches, 92
Cigarette dealers licenses, 396
Cigarette tax stamps, 34, 434
Circuit court
entries (records), 200-208
Cities
list of electors, 465, 472
maps, 79-82, 549, 550
plats, 76, 77
taxes, 402
Citizens Building Association, 58
Citizenship, *see* Naturalization
Civic societies, 92
Claims
auditors, 352, 359, 362, 365, 402
board of elections, 464, 482
board of health, 498
county commissioners, 1, 3, 4, 8, 10, 26, 27
estates, 241, 243, 251, 252, 254, 352

Claims (continued)
livestock, 1, 8, 26, 362, 402
Clerk of courts
entries (records)
Commissions and licenses, 131-140
dockets, 106-110
elections, 141-144
Financial reports, 150-156
general court, 111-117
jury and witness, 118-124
miscellaneous, 157-161
motor vehicles, 125-130
partnerships, 145, 146
reports, 147-149
fees, 200, 209, 364
Clubs, 4-H, 585-587, 590
Coal dealers bids, 29
Commission, state tax, 402
Commissioners, blind relief
applications, 400-42
entries (records), 528, 529
reports, 373
Commissioners, budget, 29, 456, 458, 572
Commissioners, county
bills, 1, 3, 4, 29, 359, 360
bonds approved by, 1, 378, 412, 413, 415, 453, 455, 463
budgets, 275, 456, 457
Entries (Records)
Aid to blind, 40-42
financial, 26-28
improvements, 10-25
minutes, 1-4
miscellaneous, 29
relief administration, 30-39
reports, 5-9
orders to sheriff's, 315
Commissioners, jury, 291, 292
Commissioners, park board, 223
Commissions issued by governor, 131-133
Common pleas court, *see*
Court of common pleas
Contractors
bonds, 1, 1A-1C, 10, 12, 15, 16, 19, 21, 562
liens, 62, 63
Contracts
public improvements, 1, 1A-1C, 10, 12, 15, 16, 19, 20, 21, 25, 543, 562
recorders, 100
Coroners, county
bonds, 412
entries (records), 296, 297
reports, 147-149, 276, 295-297
Corporations
appropriations, 356
partnerships, 91, 93, 100, 145, 146
stocks, 91
taxes, 67, 353, 354
Cosmetic dealers licenses, 397
Cosmetics, tax stamps, 438
Cost
aid to dependent children, 288, 290
circuit court cases, 208
coroners cases, 147, 148, 297
county home, 9, 25, 522
court of appeals cases, 216
court of common pleas cases, 29, 182
district court cases, 199
estates, 102, 254, 352
juvenile court cases, 280, 284, 286
magistrates court cases, 108, 164
probate court cases, 219, 225, 244, 251, 252, 254, 352

Cost (continued)
- public improvements, 14-16, 22, 24, 410, 416 552, 554, 557, 558, 560, 562, 565, 566, 572
- soldiers burial, 5
- supreme court cases, 193

County home
- appointments, 4, 514
- entries (records)
  - case records, 517-520
  - financial, 521-523
  - inventories, 524
  - minutes, 514-516
- journals, 3, 4
- registrations, 9, 515, 517

Court of appeals
- entries (record), 209-216

Court of common pleas
- entries (record)
  - court proceedings, 174-183
  - dockets, 162-163
  - naturalization, 184-186
  - Reports, 187
- orders, 302

Court dockets
- circuit court, 202
- court of common pleas, 166
- district court, 194
- supreme court, 188

Courthouse
- floor plans, 29

Court orders, *see* Writs

Court reporters, 157

Criminal cases
- court of common pleas, 168-171, 174, 178, 182
- magistrates courts, 111, 403
- probate court, 219, 222, 223, 227
- prosecuting attorneys, 187-189
- supreme court, 189, 191, 193

Culverts, 1, 19-21, 554, 561, 572

Dairies, inspection of 500

Dance hall permits, 269

Deaths, 260, 262-504

Deeds
- cemeteries, 46
- real property, 43, or 6, 49, 105, 318

Demurres
- circuit court, 204, 206, 208
- court of appeals, 212, 216
- court of common pleas, 171, 178, 182
- district court, 197, 198
- supreme court, 191, 193

Department of public welfare, 9, 516

Deputies
- to county officials, 157, 174, 382, 417

District court
- entries (record), 194-199
- journal entries, 102, 197

Ditches
- construction of, 1B, 15, 16, 18, 557, 558
- maps, 551
- surveys, 547, 557, 572

Division of aid for the aged, 361, 530-542

Divorce cases
- clerk of courts, 149, 156

Dockets
- circuit court, 200, 202, 203
- clerk of courts, 106, 108-110, 120, 122
- court of appeals, 209, 211
- court of common pleas, 162, 164-168, 170-172
- district court, 194-196
- jury, 118-120
- juvenile court, 278

Dockets (continued)
probate court, 218-221
sheriffs, 298
supreme court, 188
Dogs, *see* Animals
Dog warden
appointments, one
reports, 8
Dow tax law, 337

Education, county board of, *see also* Schools
entries (records)
Financial records, 495, 496
minutes and reports, 485-487
pupils records, 491-494
teachers records, 488-490
Transfers, 497
request for appropriation of funds, 356, 456, 457
Education, state department, 402, 486, 487
Elections
ballots, 143, 144, or 70, 471, 474, 475
Board of
entries (records)
Appointments, 480
candidates, 476-479
electors, 465-475
financial, 481-484
minutes, 464
general, 143
mayors, 141, 142
pay rolls, 183
poll list, 143, 144, 470, 471
primary, 144
Elections (continued)
surveyors, 286
tally sheets, 143, 144, 470, 471
votes, 36, 143, 144, 471, 473
Electors lists, 124, 291, 292, 465, 467, 468, 472
Embalmers licenses, 134
Emergency relief *see* Relief
Engineer, county
entries (records)
Financial, 563-571
improvements, 552-562
miscellaneous, 572
surveys, plats, maps, 543-551
Enrollments, *see* Registrations
Epilepsy cases, 223
Estates
administrators of, 220, 223, 232, 234, 236, 237, 244-246, 251, 331
appointments of fiduciaries, 220, 223, 232-234, 236, 251
appraisements, 102, 220, 221, 223, 232, 233, 241, 242, 244, 251, 252, 352
appraisers for, 220, 241, 244, 251, 252, 352
claims, 241, 243, 251, 253, 254, 352
cost, 102, 254, 352
estimates, 83, 102, 232-234, 254
executors of, 26, 154, 220, 223, 233, 236, 237, 246, 251, 254, 331
Hedges, Josiah, 83, 102.
inheritance taxes, 223, 253, 351, 352, 355, 432

Estates (continued)
- inventories, 102, 223, 241, 251, 252, 254, 352
- letters of fiduciary, 232-234, 251
- maps, 83
- notices, 232-234, -240, 243, 244, 246, 251, 252
- orders, 220, 221, 223, 232-235, 241, 244, 251, 252, 352
- petitions, 220, 223, 231, 244, 251
- property not subject to tax, 254
- sales, 102, 223, 244, 251, 352
- settlements, 245, 246, 251, 331
- taxes, 1, 223, 253, 254, 331, 351, 352, 432
- wills, 102, 228, 230, 234

Estimates
- estates, 83, 102, 232,,-234, 254
- public improvements, 14-16, 19, 22, 327, 410, 416, 554, 557, 558, 562, 572

Examiners
- schools, 407, 409
- state medical, 268
- of treasury, 277
- weights and measures, 419

Execution, writs of, 106, 108, 112, 113, 115, 298

Executors of estates, *see* Estates

Exhibits, county fairs, 574, 575, 578, 579

Fairs, county, 574-576, 578-581

Federal relief cases, 38, 39, 370, 373, 402

Federal tax liens, 69

Feeble-minded cases, 223, 256

Fees, *see also* Salaries
- appraisers, 362
- clerk of courts, 129, 150, 162, 164, 209, 364
- coroners, 296

Fees (continued)
- elections, 484
- foreign sheriffs, 150, 271
- justice of the peace, 364
- for licenses, 8, 135, 137, 395-398
- mayors, 364
- police courts, 364
- recorders, 97-99
- school examiners, 407
- sheriff's, 150, 162, 164, 165, 200, 209, 255, 257, 271, 286, 299, 309-311
- treasurers, 364, 366
- witnesses, 120-123, 150, 153, 222, 271, 376

Ferry licenses, 174

Financial records
- agricultural extension agent, 588-590
- agricultural society, 574-577
- aid for the blind, 372, 373
- board of education, 323, 495, 496
- board of elections, 464, 478
- board of health, 508, 509
- budget Commissioners, 456-458
- clerk of courts, 150-156
- county auditor, 7, 358-388, 399-411
- county Commissioners, 26-28
- county engineers, 563-571
- county home, 9, 28, 379, 521-523
- county recorder, 97-99
- county sheriff, 1, 308-311
- county treasurers, 1, 400, 444-452
- estates, 102, 245, 246, 251, 331
- foreign counties, 267
- justices of the peace, 409

Financial records (continued)
probate court, 270-273
township officials, 406, 409
Fingerprinting, prisoners, 198, 306, 307
Fishing licenses, 137, 138
Foods, inspection of, 500
Foreclosures, property, 109, 301-303
Foreign counties, 267, 379
Foreign writs, 299
Fostoria, city of
list of electors, 465
maps, 82
tax assessments, 402
4-H clubs, 585-587, 590
Franchise, public utilities, 22
Fraternal organizations, 92
Fugitives, 307

Gas leases, 50
Gasoline tax, 564
Gerhart, Reverend E. V., 13
Governor of Ohio
commissions issued by, 131-133
Grand jury
electors, 291, 292
reports, 174, 187
term of, 118, 119, 1 2 3
testimonies, 291
Guardianships
accounts, 241, 242, 244, 245, 248-258
applications, 221, 223, 235, 252
appointments, 221, 223, 235, 252
appraisements, 241, 242, 244
bonds, 221, 223, 235, 238, 244
claims, 241
dockets, 221
4-H club members, 585
inventories, 241
letters of authority, 235, 252

Guardianships (continued)
of minors, 265, 266
sales of property, 244
Guards, Ohio National, 161

Health, county board of
entries (records)
financial records, 508, 509
minutes and reports, 498-501
miscellaneous, 510
vital statistics, 502-507
Health, state board, 500
Hedges, Josiah, 83, 102
Heirs of estates, 220, 223, 231, 232, 234, 253
Highways, *see* Roads
Horse racing events, 575, 581
Hospitals, 511-513
Hunting licenses, 135, 136

Indians, 322, 543
Indictments, 118, 178, 182, 187, 295
Infirmary, *see* County home
Inheritance taxes, *see* Taxes
Injunctions, probate court, 224
Inquest, 147-149, 255, 257, 295-297
Insanity cases, 223, 224, 255, 257
Insurance agents certificates, 95
Insurance companies certificates, 95, 96

Jails
fugitives from, 307
matrons, 361
prisoners, 1, 29, 304-307, 315
register, 304
reports, 29
sketch of, 29
Josiah Hedges estate, 83, 102

Journals
- auditors, 364, 365
- circuit court, 204
- commissioners, 1, 3, 4
- county home, 3, 4, 514
- court of appeals, 212
- court of common pleas, 174
- district court, 197
- juvenile court, 279
- probate court, 223
- supreme court, 189
- trustees of the sinking fund, 463

Judgments
- against merchants, 114
- clerk of courts cases, 106, 108-110, 112-115, 149
- court of common pleas, 165, 172, 176, 177
- district court, 195, 198

Jury commissioners
- entries (records), 291, 292

Justices of the peace
- commissions, 132
- fees, 364

Juvenile court
- entries (records)
  - aid to dependent children, 287-2 90
  - court proceedings, 278-282
  - dependents, 283-285
  - financial, 286

Kennel licenses, 390

Land, *see* Real property

Leases, 50, 53

Ledgers
- auditors, 358, 367, 379
- county home, 521
- engineers, 563

Ledgers (continued)
- treasurers, 445

Letters of fiduciary, 232-234, 251

Levies, *see* Taxes

Licenses
- auctioneers, 174
- beer, 398
- beverage dealers, 397
- brokers, 140
- cigarette dealers, 396
- cosmetic dealers, 397
- dogs, 8, 389, 390
- embalmers, 134
- fees, 8, 135, 137, 290, 395-398
- ferry, 174
- fishing, 137, 138
- hunting, 135, 136
- insurance agents, 95
- insurance companies, 95, 96
- limited practitioners, 268
- malt, 398
- marriages, 263
- ministers, 174, 267
- nurses, 268
- optometrist, 139
- peddlers, 395
- real estate brokers, 140
- real estate salesman, 140
- surgeons, 268
- tavern, 174
- vendors, 391-395
- wort, 398

Liens
- bonds, 71, 72
- contractors, 62, 63
- dockets, 108
- federal tax, 69
- judgments to operate as, 110
- motor vehicles, 70, 129
- partition cases, 302
- sheriff's sales, 303

Liens (continued)
stallion keepers, 65
tax, 66-69
Limited practitioners, 268
Liquor dealers licenses, 337,343, 426
Livestock, *see* Animals
Lunacy cases, 223, 255,257

Malt licenses, 398
Malt tax, 364, 436
Maps, 79-83, 320, 322, 548-551, 556, 559
Marines, United States, 101
Marriages, *see* Vital statistics
Matrons for jails, 361
Mayors, 141, 142, 364
Measures, 419
Mechanics liens, 61, 64, 105
Medical certificates, 255-257
Medical state board of examiners, 268
Ministers, 174, 267
Minors
See also Juvenile court
adoptions, 175, 223, 224
aid to dependent children, 175, 176, 283-285, 287, 288, 290, 361, 369-371, 402
health records, 288
housing and private homes, 284
lunacy cases, 255-257
marriages, 265, 266
Mortgages, 49, 54, 57-60, 85, 86, 105, 302, 303
Mothers pensions, 278, 279, 285, 287, 288, 269-371
Motor vehicles
accidents, 312
Motor vehicles (continued)
certificates of titles, 129
liens, 70, 129
tax on, 357
Muster roll, Ohio National Guard 161

Narcotics, 520
National Guards of Ohio, 161
Naturalization of aliens, 149, 174, 184-186, 258, 259
Notaries public, 131
Notices
estates, 232-234, 240, 243, -244, 246, 251, 252
juvenile court cases, 280
relative to fugitives, 307
sales, 90, 109, 298, 301, 302, 361
stray livestock, 158
tax, 68, 361
Nurses
army, 5
county visiting, 500, 501
licenses, 268

Ohio commission for the blind, 42
Ohio National Guard, 161
Oil leases, 50
Old age pensions, 530-542
Optometrist licenses, 139

Park board commissioners, 573
Parks, 81, 549
Paroles of prisoners, 1
Partition cases, 84, 109, 300-302
Partnerships, 91, 93, 100, 145, 146
Pay-in-orders, 383-385, 452
Pay rolls
aid to dependent children, 290
auditors, 380, 381
board of electors, 483

Pay rolls (continued)
- county employees, 29
- engineers, 404, 555
- public employees retirement system, 380, 381
- state highway department, 410

Peddlers licenses, 395
Pensions
- blind relief cases, 40-42, 372, 373, 528, 529
- board of aid for the aged, 530-542
- mothers, 278, 279, 285, 287, 288, 369-371

Permits
- buildings, 416
- dance halls, 269

Personal property
- taxes
  - appraisements, 90, 402
  - county home, 516, 524
  - mortgages, 85, 86
  - sales, 90, 113, 125, 128, 223
  - stocks, 91
  - transfers, 85, 86

Petitioners bonds, 1, 1B, 10, 12, 15, 16
Petit jury
- electors for, 124, 291, 292
- verdicts, 118, 120, 121

Photographs of fugitives, 307
Physicals
- licenses, 268
- reports, 42, 373, 498, 506
- salaries, 1

Plans, courthouse, 22
Plats, 73, 75-77, 91, 320, 321, 545, 547
Police court fees, 364
Poll books, 143, 144, 470-472
Poor house, *see* County home
Population
- county home, 515

Postmortems, 297
Power of attorney, 94, 105, 158, 274
Practitioners licenses, 268
Premiums, fairs, 574, 578-580
Primary elections, 144
Prisoners
- custody of, 315
- fugitives, 307
- identifications, 306, 307
- paroles, 1
- registrations, 304

Probate court, entries (records)
- calendars and dockets, 217-222
- court proceedings, 223-227
- estates and guardianships, 232-252
- financial records, 270-273
- inheritance taxes, 253, 254
- juvenile court records, 278-279
- licenses and permits, 267-269
- miscellaneous, 274-277
- naturalization, 258, 259
- records of incompetence, 255-257
- vital statistics, 260-266
- wills and determination of heirship, 228-231

Probation officers, 286
Prosecuting attorneys
- entries (records), 293-295

Public utilities, 22, 67, 68
Pupils, *see* Students

Railroads
- maps, 549, 551
- policemen, 133

Rates, tax, *see* Taxes
Real estate, *see* Real property
Real estate brokers licenses, 140

Real estate salesmen licenses, 140
Real property
appraisements, 9, 301, 303, 321, 325-327
claims, 10
county home, 265, 516
deeds, 43, 46, 49, 105, 318
liens *see* Liens
mortgages, 54, 57-60
pledged as security for bonds, 71, 72
sales, 109, 113, 244, 298, 300, 303, 318, 348
titles, 319, 375
transfers, 43-60, 105, 316, 317, 332, 485, 497
wills, 48
Recorder, county entries (records)
corporations and partnerships, 91-93
financial records, 97-99
grants of authority, 94-96
miscellaneous, 100-105
personal property transfers, 85-90
real property transfers, 43-84
Registrations
county home, 515, 517
4-H clubs, 585, 590
leases, 53
schools, 353, 493
trade-marks, 110, 161
Relief
appropriations, 1, 33, 34, 367, 370, 402
bills, 361
blind cases, 1, 29, 40-42, 52, 372, 373, 402, 528, 529
board of aid for the aged, 282, 283, 530-542
Relief (continued)
dependent children, 283-285, 287-290, 361, 369-371
emergency cases, 30-39, 516, 519
soldiers, 1, 174, 368, 525-527
state division of charities, 9, 290, 361
tax receipts, 402
township committees for, 1
Request for funds
budget commissioners, 456, 457, 572
township trustees, 356, 456, 457
Restaurants, inspection of, 500
Revision, county board of
adjustments, 1
appraisements, 327
complaints, 328
entries (records), 459-462
Revision, state board, 402
Roads
bids, 562
blueprints, 556
bonds issued for improvements, 455
construction of, 1A, 10, 12-14, 21, 24, 554, 555, 562, 572
costs, 404, 410, 552, 554, 555, 562
maps, 550, 559
surveys, 543-545, 547, 572
viewers reports, 1B, 10, 12, 15, 16

Sales
estates, 102, 223, 244, 251, 352
partition cases, 109, 300-302
personal property, 43, 94, 110, 125, 128, 223

Sales (continued)
- real property, 100, 109, 113, 244, 298, 300, 303, 319, 348
- sheriff's, 109, 298-313
- tax stamps, 364, 433-438

Sanatoriums *see* Tuberculosis hospital
Savings and loan companies, 57
Scales
- inspection of, 419
- petition for erection of, 29

Schools, *see also* Education, board of
- accounts, 323, 407, 496
- enumeration records, 418
- examiners, 407
- levies, 364
- medical, 268
- nurses, 501
- registrations, 353, 493
- relief issued to, 288
- reports, 353, 402, 405, 407, 408, 411, 487, 491
- statistics, 353, 487, 493
- taxes, 354, 355
- teachers, 402, 487, 490
- treasurers, 354, 406, 408, 414

Sealer of weights and measures, 419
Sheriff, county
- bills, 1, 29
- bonds, 4, 12
- deputies, 157
- entries (records)
  - court orders and sales, 298-303
  - financial records, 308-311
  - miscellaneous, 312-315
  - prisoners and futurities, 304-307

Sheriff, county (continued)
  - fees, 150, 162, 164, 165, 200, 209, 255, 257, 271, 268, 299, 309-311
- reports, 231
- returns on writs, 109, 112, 113, 174, 180, 182, 189, 191, 193, 197-199, 204, 206, 208, 212, 216, 224, 225, 227, 231, 244, 251, 252, 255-257, 280, 298, 299, 305
- sales, 109, 298-303, 361

Sinking fund trustees, 463
Social Security Act, 42
Societies, incorporation of, 92
Soldiers
- burial committees, 1, 5
- discharges, 101
- licenses to peddle, 395
- relief to, 1, 5, 174, 368, 525-527

Soldiers burial committees, 1, 5
Soldiers relief commission, 525, 527
Specifications, 1A-1C, 10, 12-16, 19, 22, 23, 25, 554, 555, 560, 562, 572
Stallion keepers liens, 65
Stamp tax, 264, 433-438
Statements
- auditor, financial, 7
- candidates for elections, 476
- ownerships, personal property, 125, 128

State school examiner, 407, 409
State tax commission, 67, 68, 402
Students school records, 353, 487, 491-494, 500
Subcontractors liens, 62, 63
Summonses
- circuit court, 206
- district court, 198
- probate court, 231, 257

Summonses (continued)
supreme court, 191
Superintendent of county home, 4, 514-524
Supreme court
entries (records), 188-193
Surgeons licenses, 268
Surveyors *see* Engineers
surveys, 13, 19, 73, 75-77, 322, 543-545, 547, 557, 572

Tally sheets, 249, 143, 144, 470, 471
Tavern licenses, 174
Tax collectors, 1
Taxes *see also* Revision, board of
adjustments, 1, 340-342, 402, 459-562
appraisements, 325-327, 334
appropriations, 355, 357, 367, 402
auditors, 323-357
budgets, 323
cigarette dealers, 355, 425, 441
collections, 231, 329, 330, 354, 355, 364, 402, 422, 429, 439-444
complaints, 328, 462
corporations, 67, 353, 354
delinquent
certificates of, 3 4 5, 346, 428, 429
collections, 355, 422, 440
forfeited lands, 349
liens, 66-69
lists, 420
penalties for, 230, 67-69, 337, 344-350, 355, 420, 423, 425-431

Taxes (continued)
personal property, 322, 350 420, 423-427, 430, 431, 440
real property, 332, 344-346, 348, 349, 402, 420-422, 427-429, 440
duplicates
auditors, 332, 335-337, 340, 341
treasurers, 420-422, 425, 426, 431
excise, 30, 34, 67, 68, 402, 434-438, 564
exemptions, 254, 334
fairs, 576
franchise, 67, 68
gasoline, 564
income, 1
inheritance, 223, 253, 351, 352, 355, 432
levies, 1, 323, 354, 355, 364, 378, 487
liquor dealers, 337, 343, 426
lists, 338, 339, 423, 424
malt, 364
notices, 68, 361
orders to remit, 342
personal property, 330-332, 338, -339, 350, 355, 357, 420, 423, 424, 430, 442, 462
public improvements, 10, 12, 13, 15, 16, 18
public utilities, 67, 68
rates, 324, 330, 338, 339, 424
reports, 402
returns, 330, 352
schools, 354
settlements, 331, 353-355
treasurers records, 420-443

Tax stamps, 364, 433-4 38
Teachers institute, 407
Teachers, schools, 402, 487, 488, 490
Testimonies, 180, 293
Tiffin, city of, 29, 81, 549
Tiffin Savings and Loan Association, 57
Time books, engineers, 569, 571
Titles
personal property, 129
real property, 319, 375
transfers of, 46-48, 375
Towns, 91, 550
Townships
clerks, 408
levies, 323, 364
maps, 320, 550, 559
plats, 75, 320
relief commission, 1
request, 356, 456, 457
trustees, 323, 356, 409, 454, 456, 457
Trade-marks, 161
Traders records, 93
Transfers
of funds to foreign counties, 29
titles to property, 43, 46-50, 53, 54, 57-72, 85, 86, 105, 316-318, 332, 375, 497
Treasurers to board of education, 406, 408, 414
Treasurers county,
auditors deposits with, 13, 364
entries (records)
bonds, 453-455
financial records, 444-452
tax records, 420-443
inspection of, 1, 277
Treasurers, schools, 354, 406, 408, 414
Trustees of estates, 223, 236, 237, 239, 245
Trustees of the sinking fund
bonds, 378
entries (records), 463
Trustees of township, 323, 356, 409, 454, 456, 457
Tuberculosis hospital, 4, 511-513

United States
army (navy), 101
citizenships, 149, 174, 184-186, 258, 259

Vaccinations, school pupils, 500
Vendors licenses, 391-395
Verdicts
grand jury, 295
petit jury, 118, 120, 121
Veterans *see* Soldiers
Villages
incorporation of 91
maps, 550
Visitors, board of county, 174, 223, 280
Vital statistics
births, 260, 261, 502
deaths, 260, 262, 504
marriages, 263, 265, 266
reports on diseases, 506, 507
Volunteers, war, 1
Voters, absent, 474, 475
Votes
appraisers, 29
elections, 143, 144, 470, 471, 473
municipal corporations, 91
Vouchers
auditors, 360
board of elections, 482
relief, 5, 33-35, 37, 42, 373, 386

Warrants
auditors, 365, 366, 373, 386-388, 450, 451
court of common pleas, 305
probate court, 255-257
Weights, 419
Welfare department, 9, 516
Wills, 48, 102, 228, 230, 234
Wine tax stamps, 435
Witnesses
to accidents, 312
coroners cases, 147, 148, 297
court cases, 175, 120, 122, 123, 170, 178, 222, 224
fees, 120, 122, 123, 150, 153, 222, 271, 376
Works Progress Administration, 38, 39
Wort licenses, 398
Wort tax stamps, 436
Writs
circuit court, 204, 206, 208
clerk of courts, 106, 108, 109, 112, 113, 115, 116
court of appeals, 212, 216
court of common pleas, 174, 178, 180, 189, 191, 193, 212, 214, 216
district court, 198, 199
juvenile court, 280
probate court, 219, 224, 225, 227, 231, 244, 251, 252, 255-257
sheriff's, 298, 299, 305
supreme court, 189, 191, 193

Heritage Books by Jana Sloan Broglin:

Additions and Corrections to the W.P.A. Inventory of Adams County, Ohio: West Union

Additions and Corrections to the W.P.A. Inventory of Allen County, Ohio: Lima

Additions and Corrections to the W.P.A. Inventory of Ashland County, Ohio: Ashland

Additions and Corrections to the W.P.A. Inventory of Athens County, Ohio: Athens

Additions and Corrections to the W.P.A. Inventory of Belmont County, Ohio: St. Clairsville

Additions and Corrections to the W.P.A. Inventory of Cuyahoga County, Ohio: Cleveland

Additions and Corrections to the W.P.A. Inventory of Fulton County, Ohio: Wauseon

Additions and Corrections to the W.P.A. Inventory of Geauga County, Ohio: Chardon

Additions and Corrections to the W.P.A. Inventory of Hancock County, Ohio: Findlay

Additions and Corrections to the W.P.A. Inventory of Lake County, Ohio: Painesville

Additions and Corrections to the W.P.A. Inventory of Lorain County, Ohio: Elyria

Additions and Corrections to the W.P.A. Inventory of Lucas County, Ohio: Toledo

Additions and Corrections to the W.P.A. Inventory of Medina County, Ohio: Medina

Additions and Corrections to the W.P.A. Inventory of Muskingum County, Ohio: Zanesville

Additions and Corrections to the W.P.A. Inventory of Seneca County, Ohio: Tiffin

Additions and Corrections to the W.P.A. Inventory of Wayne County, Ohio: Wooster

Hookers, Crooks and Kooks, Part I: Hookers

Hookers, Crooks and Kooks, Part II: Crooks and Kooks

Lucas County, Ohio, Index to Deaths, 1867–1908

Mason County, Kentucky Wills and Estates, 1791–1832, Second Edition

www.ingramcontent.com/pod-product-compliance
Lightning Source LLC
Chambersburg PA
CBHW060133280326
41932CB00012B/1500